AF848698

REGIONAL ECONOMIC GROWTH, SMEs AND THE WIDER EUROPE

This book makes an important and interesting contribution to the wider debate on European regional development. It looks beyond the confines of the EU proper and combines interesting and relevant case studies from a broader pan-European perspective. Also, the approaches adopted are informed by a variety of theoretical positions.

By addressing the changing roles of SMEs in different regions of Eastern Europe, readers will gain insights into the different dimensions of SME development and the link between SMEs and regional growth.

The book will appeal to academics researching European development and teaching courses in Economics, Social Policy, Urban Studies, Regional Development and Economic Geography, students in various faculties and departments with a regional perspective, economic and regional planners and researchers, and policy makers at national and regional levels.

Regional Economic Growth, SMEs and the Wider Europe

Edited by

BERNARD FINGLETON
University of Cambridge, UK

AYDA ERAYDIN
Middle East Technical University, Turkey

RAFFAELE PACI
University of Cagliari, Italy

Routledge
Taylor & Francis Group
LONDON AND NEW YORK

First published 2003 by Ashgate Publishing

Reissued 2018 by Routledge
2 Park Square, Milton Park, Abingdon, Oxon OX14 4RN
711 Third Avenue, New York, NY 10017, USA

Routledge is an imprint of the Taylor & Francis Group, an informa business

Copyright © Bernard Fingleton, Ayda Eraydın and Raffaele Paci 2003

Bernard Fingleton, Ayda Eraydın and Raffaele Paci have asserted their right under the Copyright, Designs and Patents Act, 1988, to be identified as editors of this work.

All rights reserved. No part of this book may be reprinted or reproduced or utilised in any form or by any electronic, mechanical, or other means, now known or hereafter invented, including photocopying and recording, or in any information storage or retrieval system, without permission in writing from the publishers.

Notice:
Product or corporate names may be trademarks or registered trademarks, and are used only for identification and explanation without intent to infringe.

Publisher's Note
The publisher has gone to great lengths to ensure the quality of this reprint but points out that some imperfections in the original copies may be apparent.

Disclaimer
The publisher has made every effort to trace copyright holders and welcomes correspondence from those they have been unable to contact.

A Library of Congress record exists under LC control number: 2003041917

ISBN 13: 978-1-138-71452-6 (hbk)
ISBN 13: 978-1-315-19786-9 (ebk)

Contents

List of Figures *vii*
List of Tables *ix*
List of Contributors *xiv*

1 Introduction: SMEs and Regional Growth 1
Bernard Fingleton, Ayda Eraydın and Raffaele Paci

PART I: REGIONAL GROWTH AT THE EUROPEAN SCALE

2 Non-Orthodox Approaches to European Regional Growth Modeling: A Review 13
Bernard Fingleton

3 Growth and Convergence Across Economies: The Experience of the European Regions 49
Enrique López-Bazo

4 Disparities in Economic Growth and Unemployment Across the European Regions: A Sectoral Perspective 75
Raffaele Paci, Francesco Pigliaru and Maurizio Pugno

5 Dynamics and Agents of Regional Growth: The Performance of SME Clusters in Europe 103
Ayda Eraydın

PART II: SMEs AND REGIONAL DEVELOPMENT AT THE NATIONAL SCALE

6 Accounting and Modelling SMEs in the Regional Economy 129
Bjarne Madsen and Chris Jensen-Butler

7 Norwegian Regional Development and the Role of SMEs 149
Steinar Johansen

8 Regional Development and SMEs in Ireland 161
Edgar Morgenroth and Eoin O'Malley

9 Small and Medium-Sized Business as a Regional Development Factor in Lithuania 192
Vytautas Snieška, Regina Virvilaitė, Jūratė Banytė, Vaida Kvainauskaitė and Asta Savanevičienė

10 The Role of SMEs in the Regional Development of the Czech Republic 209
Vaclav Beran and Jana Frková

PART III: CASE STUDIES ON SMEs AND REGIONAL DEVELOPMENT

11 The Changing Role of SMEs in the Regional Growth Process: The Case of Denizli 229
Bilge Armatlı Köroğlu and Burak Beyhan

12 Small Entrepreneurs in Međimurje: Between Tradition and Challenges of New Forms of Cooperation 246
Drago Čengić

13 Small and Medium Enterprises and Their Role in the Innovative Environment of the Bratislava Region 270
Jana Gašparíková, Milan Buček and Štefan Rehák

14 Spatial Industrial Dynamics in the Uddevalla Local Labour Market Region: An Application of the Lead-Lag Model 289
Charlie Karlsson and Martin Andersson

Index *313*

List of Figures

Figure 2.1	The path of two regions moving to steady state under neoclassical assumptions.	17
Figure 2.2	The path of two regions with endogenous technical progress.	23
Figure 2.3	Convergence in output and productivity growth for two regions (Dixon and Thirlwall model).	28
Figure 2.4	Output and productivity growth with one divergent and one convergent region.	29
Figure 2.5	Divergent output and productivity levels for two regions.	30
Figure 2.6	The distribution of manufacturing labor productivity in 1975 (quantiles).	35
Figure 2.7	The distribution of manufacturing labor productivity in 1995 (quantiles).	36
Figure 2.8	Simulated dynamics of 178 EU regions with shocks.	39
Figure 2.9	The mean manufacturing labor productivity gap (quantiles).	40
Figure 2.10	The variance of the manufacturing labour productivity gap (quantiles).	41
Figure 3.1	Estimated density functions for simulated distributions.	56
Figure 3.2	Estimated stochastic kernel for simulated distributions.	57
Figure 3.3	Estimated density functions for GDP per capita in the EU regions.	61
Figure 3.4	Estimated density functions for GDP per worker in the EU regions.	62
Figure 3.5	Estimated stochastic kernel for GDP per capita in the EU regions. 5-yearly transitions from 1975 to 1996.	63
Figure 3.6	Estimated stochastic kernel for GDP per worker in the EU regions. 5-yearly transitions from 1975 to 1996.	63
Figure 3.7	Actual and virtual distributions for GDP per capita, 1980 (left) and 1996 (right).	67
Figure 3.8	Actual and virtual distributions for GDP per worker, 1980 (left) and 1996 (right).	69
Figure 4.1	Dispersion among the Northern and Southern European regions.	79
Figure 4.2	Initial labor share in agriculture (QA75) and its variation 1975-97 (QAD).	83
Figure 4.3	Variation 1975-97 of labor share in agriculture (QAD) and growth rate of aggregate labor productivity (% annual average, YG).	83
Figure 4.4	Variation 1975-97 of labor shares in agriculture (QAD) and manufacture (QMD).	86

Figure 4.5	Variation 1975-97 of labor share in manufacture (QMD) and growth rate of aggregate labor productivity (% annual average, YG).	86
Figure 4.6	Variation 1975-97 of the labor share in agriculture (QAD) and of the overall employment rate (ERD).	88
Figure 4.7	Clusters of the European regions.	91
Figure 5.1	The share of SMEs and regional growth.	110
Figure 5.2	The share of SMEs and innovativeness.	111
Figure 6.1	Simplified version of LINE. The cost price circuit.	137
Figure 6.2	Simplified version of LINE. The real circuit.	138
Figure 8.1	The Irish planning regions.	165
Figure 8.2	The evolution of indices of regional gross value added per capita as measured against the national average from 1981 to 1998 (State=100).	166
Figure 9.1	Distribution of the gross domestic product (GDP) in the regions of Lithuania during the period 1996-2000, by percentage.	200
Figure 9.2	Distribution of the gross domestic product (GDP) per capita in the regions of Lithuania during the period 1996-2000, by percentage.	201
Figure 9.3	Number of SMEs per 1000 of citizens in the regions of Lithuania during the period of 1999-2000, by percentage.	202
Figure 9.4	The established and liquidated SMEs in the regions of Lithuania in the year 2000, by percentage.	204
Figure 9.5	The distribution of SME exports per person in Lithuanian regions in 1999-2000, by percentage.	205
Figure 9.6	The distribution of SME imports per person in Lithuanian regions in 1999-2000, by percentage.	205
Figure 10.1	Regions NUTS III in the Czech Republic and their names.	211
Figure 10.2	Real growth of GDP in transition period of CR.	221
Figure 10.3	Scheme of Dynamic Development model of regional growth (main elements).	223
Figure 11.1	Number of establishments in manufacturing by the provinces in Turkey and districts of Denizli with strong tradition in textile industry, 1999.	232
Figure 12.1	The geographical position of Međimurje county in Croatia.	251
Figure 13.1	The share of SMEs in industrial production (1999).	274
Figure 13.2	Trends in Gross Expenditures on R&D relative to GDP.	279
Figure 13.3	Priorities for the government in the next five years.	285
Figure 13.4	Priorities for the economic policy of the government in the next five years.	289

List of Tables

Table 2.1	Estimates of equation 23.	37
Table 3.1	Estimates of the rate of convergence for the EU regions.	60
Table 4.1	European regions growth process. Final cluster centers for the included variables.	92
Table 5.1	Definition of the variables used in regression analysis.	113
Table 5.2	OLS analysis: Per capita GDP growth 1986-96.	118
Table 6.1	A one-region SAM for a closed economy.	133
Table 6.2	An interregional SAM with 2 regions and a foreign sector.	140
Table 6.3	Characteristics of Danish firms (1999).	145
Table 6.4	Turnover by numbers of employees by sector 1999 (million Dkr; 1 Euro = 7.42 DKK).	145
Table 6.5	Export in relation to turnover by sector 1999 (%).	146
Table 6.6	Gross profits in relation to turnover by sector 1999 (%).	146
Table 6.7	Gross investment per employee (DKK 1000, 1 Euro = 7.42 DKK) 1999.	147
Table 7.1	Employment by sector and type of region 1998. Index: national share = 100.	153
Table 7.1a	Principles for dividing the country into regions.	159
Table 7.2a	Number of municipalities and inhabitants in five types of regions 1998.	160
Table 8.1	Average annual growth rates of Total Regional Gross Value Added (GVA) for the period 1991-99 and sectoral decomposition.	166
Table 8.2	Relative GVA growth rates and sectoral contributions to total GVA growth.	167
Table 8.3	Annual average percentage change in manufacturing employment, Ireland, EU and OECD, 1980-88 and 1988-96.	168
Table 8.4	Average annual percentage change in volume of manufacturing production, Ireland, EU and OECD, 1985-87 and 1987-95.	169
Table 8.5	Average annual percentage employment change in indigenous manufacturing, by size class.	170
Table 8.6	Average annual percentage change in total manufacturing employment, by size class, 1973-99.	171
Table 8.7	Average annual percentage change in total manufacturing employment, with annual reclassification by size class.	173
Table 8.8	Average annual percentage change in Irish indigenous manufacturing employment, by size class.	175

Table 8.9	Average annual percentage change in Irish indigenous manufacturing employment, with annual reclassification by size class.	176
Table 8.10	Average annual percentage change in foreign-owned manufacturing employment, by size class.	177
Table 8.11	Average annual percentage change in foreign-owned manufacturing employment, with annual reclassification by size class.	178
Table 8.12	Annual average percentage change in gross output (current values) and employment, by size class, total manufacturing, 1991-99.	179
Table 8.13	Manufacturing employment change by region, SMEs and large establishments, 1973-79.	181
Table 8.14	Manufacturing employment change by region, SMEs and large establishments, 1979-87.	182
Table 8.15	Manufacturing employment change by region, SMEs and large establishments, 1987-93.	183
Table 8.16	Manufacturing employment change by region, SMEs and large establishments, 1993-99.	185
Table 8.17	Percentage distribution of employment in foreign-owned manufacturing, by region, 1973-99.	187
Table 9.1	Differences by regions in evaluations of the importance of different forms of business support for the acceleration of SMB development.	206
Table 10.1	GDP in the Czech Republic by NUTS III, data 1999.	212
Table 10.2	Regional comparisons in 2000.	214
Table 10.3	Structure and economic power of businesses in industry (1999).	216
Table 10.4	The comparison of small and large enterprises according to performance indicators.	217
Table 10.5	Comparison of sectors.	218
Table 10.6	The shares of SMEs in total production and value added.	218
Table 10.7	Value added share on production (%) - time series 1995 to 2000.	219
Table 10.8	Value added share in investment (%) 1995-2000.	220
Table 11.1	The number of establishments and employees in the textile sector of Denizli compared with the total of all sectors according to the size of the establishments.	237
Table 11.2	The share of establishments and employees in the textile sector of Denizli and average firm sizes.	238
Table 11.3	The growth rates of firms and employment in manufacturing and textile industry.	239
Table 12.1	Total revenues and employment by economic activity in Međimurje county, 2000.	250
Table 12.2	Distribution of employees according to the size of enterprises in Međimurje county in 2000.	251
Table 12.3	Sample structure of enterprises by institutional type of entrepreneurship and activity (%).	252

Table 12.4	Number of employees (owners included) (in %).	252
Table 12.5	Perception of reasons for entrepreneurship development in Međimurje (in %).	254
Table 12.6	Perception of fundamental values assessed by a scale from 1 to 5 (%).	255
Table 12.7	Present ownership structure of craft businesses/enterprises (%).	256
Table 12.8	Respondent age structure (in %).	257
Table 12.9	Respondents according to a school completed (in %).	258
Table 12.10	Perception of business operation during the past three years (in %).	258
Table 12.11	Perception of key business indicators in the coming year (in %).	259
Table 12.12	Perception of barriers to enterprise growth in Slovenia and Međimurje (Croatia).	262
Table 12.13	Primary markets for produce/services (in %).	263
Table 12.14	Main forms of cooperation with foreign partners (in %).	264
Table 13.1	Share of per capita GDP of the EU (in SKK).	274
Table 13.2	The distribution of firms by regions 1998.	275
Table 13.3	Regional differences in human potential.	276
Table 13.4	Number of R&D organizations by sector.	276
Table 13.5	Frequency of interactions with the following institutions in the innovation process.	280
Table 13.6	Conditions underpinning innovative development of firms/questionnaire.	282
Table 13.7	Analysis of knowledge transfer.	285
Table 14.1	An analysis scheme based upon a classification of industries given their regional specialization in the SLLM Region in 1990 and their employment growth and decline in the rest of the country during the period 1990-99.	294
Table 14.2	Regression results for the relationship between the number of private sector industries represented and population in local labour market regions in Sweden (logarithmic values).	296
Table 14.3	Private sector industries in the ULLM Region in 1999 (1990) classified according to regional specialization in the SLLM Region in 1990 and employment growth and decline in the rest of Sweden 1990-99.	297
Table 14.4	Share of private sector industries in the different industry groups represented in the ULLM Region in 1999 (%).	297
Table 14.5	Regression results for the relationship between total employment in private sector industries and population in local labour market regions in Sweden (logarithmic values).	298
Table 14.6	The total employment in private sector industries in the ULLM Region in the year 1999 distributed over the cells of the model of analysis. The figures for Sweden as a whole are given in parentheses (%).	299

Table 14.7 Specialization in the ULLM Region in the year 1999 (1990) in the different private sector groups measured by the location quotient (%). 299

Table 14.8 Relative changes in employment in the different industry groups in the ULLM Region during the period 1990-99. The figures for Sweden as a whole are given in parentheses (%). 300

Table 14.9 The competitive share component of the employment change in the different industry groups in the ULLM Region during the period 1990-99. 301

Table 14.10 Regression results for the relationship between total number of plants in private sector industries and population in local labour market regions in Sweden (logarithmic values). 301

Table 14.11 Average plant size in the different industrial aggregates in the ULLM Region in 1999. (Average plant size for Sweden as a whole is given within parentheses.) 302

Table 14.12 Relative changes in the number of plants in the different industry groups in the ULLM Region during the period 1990-99. The figures for Sweden as a whole are given in parentheses (%). 303

Table 14.13 The competitive share component of the change in the number of plants in the different industry groups in the ULLM Region during the period 1990-99. 303

Table 14.14 Regression results for the relationship between the number of employees with a long university education and the number of employees in private sector industries in local labour market regions in Sweden (logarithmic values). 304

Table 14.15 Regression results for the relationship between the number of employees with any type and any length of post senior high school education and the number of employees in private sector industries in local labour market regions in Sweden (logarithmic values). 305

Table 14.16 Share of the employees with a long university education (three years or more, including a Ph.D. training) in the different industrial aggregates in the ULLM Region in 1999. The figures for Sweden as a whole are given in parentheses (%). 305

Table 14.17 Educational intensity in the different industrial aggregates in the ULLM Region in 1999 measured in terms of employees with a long (three years or more) university education (Sweden as a whole = 100). 306

Table 14.18 Share of the employees with any kind and any length of post senior high school education (including a Ph.D. training) in the different industrial aggregates in the ULLM Region in 1999. The figures for Sweden as a whole are given in parentheses (%). 306

Table 14.19 Educational intensity in the different industrial aggregates in the ULLM Region in 1999 measured in terms of employees with all types of post senior high school education (Sweden as a whole = 100). 307
Table 14.1a The total employment in private sector industries in the ULLM Region in the year 1999 (1990) distributed over the cells of the model of analysis (%). 309
Table 14.2a Employment in the different private sector groups in the ULLM Region in the year 1999 (1990). 310
Table 14.3a Absolute changes in employment in the different industry groups in the ULLM Region during the period 1990-99. 310
Table 14.4a Average plant size in the different industrial aggregates in the ULLM Region in 1999 (1990). 310
Table 14.5a Number of plants in the different industrial aggregates in the ULLM Region in 1999 (1990). 311
Table 14.6a Absolute changes in the number of plants in the different industry groups in the ULLM Region during the period 1990-99. 311

List of Contributors

Martin Andersson, PhD Candidate in Economics, Jönköping International Business School, Jönköping University, Sweden.

Jūratė Banytė, Associate Professor, Marketing Department of Economics and Management Faculty, Kaunas University of Technology, Kaunas, Lithuania.

Vaclav Beran, Associate Professor, Department of Economics and Management, Technical University in Prague, Czech Republic.

Burak Beyhan, Research Assistant, Department of Urban and Regional Planning, Middle East Technical University, Ankara, Turkey.

Milan Buček, Professor, Department of Regional Development and Geography, University of Economics in Bratislava, Slovak Republic.

Drago Čengić, Principal Reseacher, Institute for Social Research Ivo Pilar, Zagreb University, Zagreb, Croatia.

Ayda Eraydın, Professor, Department of Urban and Regional Planning, Middle East Technical University, Ankara, Turkey.

Bernard Fingleton, Chairman of the Centre for Urban and Regional Studies, Cambridge University, Cambridge, United Kingdom.

Jana Frková, Senior Lecturer, Department of Economics and Management, Technical University in Prague, Czech Republic.

Jana Gašparíková, Senior Researcher, Institute for Forecasting, Slovak Academy of Sciences, Bratislava, Slovak Republic.

Chris Jensen-Butler, Professor and Departmental Chairman, Department of Economics, University of St Andrews, Scotland, UK.

Steinar Johansen, Project Manager, Ministry of Local Government and Regional Development, Oslo, Norway.

Charlie Karlsson, Professor, Economics of Technological Change, Jönköping International Business School, Jönköping University, Sweden.

Bilge Armatlı Köroğlu, Research Assistant, Department of City and Regional Planning, Gazi University, Ankara, Turkey.

Vaida Kvainauskaitė, Lecturer, International Economics and Trade Department of Economics and Management Faculty, Kaunas University of Technology, Kaunas, Lithuania.

Enrique López-Bazo, Lecturer in Applied Economics and Co-ordinator of the AQR research group at the University of Barcelona, Barcelona, Spain.

Bjarne Madsen, Director of Research in the Institute of Local Government Studies (AKF), Copenhagen, Denmark.

Edgar Morgenroth, Research Officer, Economic and Social Research Institute (ESRI), Dublin, Ireland.

Eoin O'Malley, Senior Research Officer at the Economic and Social Research Institute (ESRI), Dublin, Ireland.

Raffaele Paci, Professor of Applied Economics, University of Cagliari and Director of CRENoS (Centre for North South Economic Research), Italy.

Francesco Pigliaru, Professor of Economics, University of Cagliari, Cagliari, Italy.

Maurizio Pugno, Professor of Economics, University of Trento, Trento, Italy.

Štefan Rehák, Junior Teaching and Research Associate, Department of Regional Development and Geography, University of Economics in Bratislava, Slovak Republic.

Asta Savanevičienė, Associate Professor, Management Department of Economics and Management Faculty of Kaunas University of Technology, Kaunas, Lithuania.

Vytautas Snieška, Professor and Head of International Economics and Trade Department of Economics and Management Faculty, Kaunas University of Technology, Kaunas, Lithuania.

Regina Virvilaitė, Professor, Head of Marketing, Department of Economics and Management Faculty, Kaunas University of Technology, Kaunas, Lithuania.

Chapter 1

Introduction: SMEs and Regional Growth

Bernard Fingleton, Ayda Eraydın and Raffaele Paci

The purpose of this book is to explore, by combining interesting and relevant case studies, the different processes underlying regional economic growth and the contribution of SMEs to development. The contribution of SMEs is acknowledged to have underpinned regional policies in many countries in the last two decades, but there is only limited appraisal of the impact. In this book we examine economic development with SMEs in mind, since a key question for all the authors is what instruments can be used to best stimulate the development of lagging regions. What is important in this book is the relative economic growth of regions, the nature of the dynamics and the type of convergence, if any, that might in the long run occur, and what role SMEs might play in this process. The book is written by authors who, on the whole, would considered themselves to live, either physically, emotionally or culturally, on the margins of Europe, or as we like to call it within 'the wider Europe'. The wider Europe is a place where peripherality is a big issue; it is where an adverse location delivers relatively poor access to markets and suppliers, and where small size and remoteness from the corridors of power limit access to the agenda setting debate about the continent's governance. The problems posed by a relatively remote location and exclusion from the social and economic mainstream of the continent therefore loom large in the consciousness of the contributing authors, whether they come from Sardinia, Norway, Slovakia, Ireland or Turkey. This commonality of experience, of being on the outside and looking towards the centre, with relatively limited control over our economic prospects, is what provides a unity of purpose and perception which is a thread running through the book. In spite of our diversity in terms of theoretical stance, preferred methodological tools, or interpretation of the dominant forces controlling the economic landscape we inhabit, there is an underlying harmony among the contributors which elevates to a high status questions of policy and process related to the relative economic development of the regions, from which all else flows.

After the crisis in traditional regional policy in the 1970s, there have been several attempts to theorize the dynamics of territorial and regional development and to define new policies accordingly. Local potential based on small and medium enterprises (SME) and industrial clusters were at the core of the regional development literature in the 1980s. This interest continued in the decade that followed via soft institutional theories with increasing emphasis on learning and innovation. Concurrently, economists were interested in explaining contemporary issues by modifying the traditional theories of economic growth. Both of these two theoretical perspectives, however, have recently been criticized because of their limited contribution to regional policy issues. The evidence shows that while the inequality between countries has decreased, only the most dynamic regions have profited from integration. This situation leads a crucial question, whether the peripheral regions will ever be able to catch up with the core regions in Europe.

This is why there is need for a critical evaluation of growth at the European regional level as well as evaluation of the regional policies and their outcomes at national and regional levels. By examining regional policies focused on SMEs in different national and cultural settings, including the prospective EU-accession countries, it will be possible to assess how the currently in vogue model based on endogenous growth and SMEs can be reformulated in such a way that the peripheral regions become part of the learning economy. By addressing the changing roles of SMEs in different regions of Eastern Europe, it is hoped that this book will help us to understand the different dimensions of SME development and to unravel the complex relationship between SMEs and regional growth.

The contributions in this volume are written by researchers who have explored the regional growth concept in some detail, with some emphasis on SMEs at a range of scales (EU, national and regional). The varied background and experiences of the contributors means that together they have been able to collaborate to produce a book which provides deep insights about the role of SMEs in regional development. They came together initially as part of a European Concerted Research Action designated as COST Action A17 and entitled *Small and Medium Enterprises, Economic Development, and Regional Convergence in Europe*. This book is one outcome of this work, which is edited by members of the Management Committee of the Action. We would like to thank the European Commission for their support of the work of the COST Action and all colleagues who have been involved in its success, particularly the Chairman Professor Jordi Suriñach. Without their encouragement and critical insights as various Chapters were presented at meetings in Brussels, Vanersborg, Ankara, Oslo, Barcelona and Cambridge, this work would not have been possible.

The Volume comprises three main sections. The first section is devoted to more theoretical issues, which clearly identifies the different theoretical discourses on regional growth as well as illustrating some significant empirical findings concerning the growth dynamics of the European regions. In the second section of the Volume the experience of certain countries with regards to regional development strategies and the role of attributed to SMEs in this process are presented. The third part of the book presents the case studies that discuss the contribution of SMEs on the growth potential of different regions.

Chapter 2 (Fingleton) presents a wide-ranging theoretical overview that provides a context for subsequent Chapters. The intention is to highlight, explain and evaluate various approaches that have been used to gain insight into the prospects for Europe's regions. The Chapter therefore discusses in varying levels of detail mainstream neoclassical growth theory, endogenous growth theory, new economic geography or geographical economics, systems models of cumulative causation, stochastic equilibrium and the work of mathematical geographers using complex systems analysis, commenting on their theoretical assumptions and empirical coherence with regard to the real world. The consensus view is that, almost irrespective of the theoretical stance, there is unlikely to be smooth convergence to a single equilibrium level of GDP per inhabitant across the EU's regions. The future seems to be one in which regions will be differentiated in terms of relative output per worker or inhabitant, and possibly polarized between core and periphery, unless there is policy intervention across Europe on an unprecedented scale. To highlight this, the Chapter gives some empirical analysis and simulated outcomes for EU regions, which show that significant regional disparities are likely to remain a feature of the geo-economics of Europe into the foreseeable future.

Chapter 3 (López-Bazo) concentrates mainly on the mainstream theories related to economic convergence as the background to the empirical analysis, which again concerns the ensemble of EU regions. However, the analytical approach adopted differs from the standard neoclassical growth model analysis, which provides only a limited view of regional growth dynamics. The main data analysis method used, namely the stochastic kernel, provides insights regarding the entire distribution of GDP per capita by region and its evolution, showing that the EU's regions are converging to a steady state which is still somewhat dispersed and which is not collapsing to a single point as is predicted by the simplest neoclassical growth theory. Moreover, rather than a smooth progression to steady-state, we see intra-distribution dynamics as regions transit between income states with different probabilities. Overall, the picture obtained, is therefore not unlike that produced by the simulations described in Chapter 1. The Chapter concludes that geographical location and proximity to markets are of prime importance in explaining interregional disparities, and that industrial structure also plays a part, although much remains unknown.

Chapter 4 (Paci, Pigliaru and Pugno) starts a process of disaggregation that continues as we move towards the core of the book, by examining the relationship between economic growth and unemployment from a sectoral perspective, and by arguing that a better understanding of convergence is possible by means of a multi-sectoral perspective. The analysis divides the economy into agriculture, industry and services, which provides a unified framework, and it is the differences between these sectors in terms of their capacity to employ labour and induce output and productivity growth, that lies at the core of the analysis in the Chapter. Regional differences in these components are seen as important for convergence, and there is a role for economic policy targeted at the sectoral mix within a region. The Chapter provides evidence suggesting that out-migration from agriculture is strongly associated with convergence in aggregate productivity, and that the magnitude of the impact of agricultural out-migration on aggregate growth depends significantly on which sector absorbs the migrating workers.

Chapter 5 (Eraydın) provides a bridge between the foregoing emphasis on regional economic growth and the subsequent focus in Part II on the role of SMEs in regional development, drawing together the diverse literatures on regional growth theory and SMEs, and highlighting the limitations of the former and the reasons why the latter have become prominent as a potential instrument in policy circles. The Chapter adds to the diversity of the theory reviewed in this book by referring to territorial models of growth, and specifically to the literature described under the headings of innovative milieux, industrial districts, new industrial spaces and learning regions. The point is made that while these approaches rightfully emphasize localized externalities and increasing returns mechanisms, they are also somewhat obscure and it is difficult to get a clear or precise view of what they actually imply for the dynamics, growth and change. The Chapter also emphasize clusters and the production advantages they evidently provide by virtue of enhanced access to knowledge, but again the emphasis on case studies in much of this literature makes it difficult to scientifically evaluate the relative contribution of different factors. The empirical analysis in the Chapter seeks to provide an objective comparative evaluation of relative effects of factors hypothesized to be important for growth, such as innovativeness, externalities associated with clustering, human capital and human resources. With regard to the impact of SME clusters on growth, the Chapter shows that in spite of scepticism about the sustainability of growth in SME, most of the regions with higher shares of SMEs have performed quite well, although the relation is not strong. The chapter concludes by calling for refinement in both data and in analytical techniques.

The second part of the book concentrates on the role of SMEs in regional development in various countries including EU members Denmark and Ireland and Lithuania and Czech Republic which are accession countries. It also includes Norway, which has a special position with respect to the European Union.

The Chapters in this section of the book indicate an upsurge of interest in regional development together with the changing context and tools for regional development. There are different national trends that are related to the varied economic backgrounds of the countries studied. However, all of them have a common feature, the search for new ways to deal with the increasing divergence that is seen among their regions. In Norway there is a change from strong redistributive policies, the so-called Scandinavian Model, towards a more liberal view. This is manifest in the loss of some of the public-funded schemes of regional development that characterized the earlier period, although the low population density regions remain on the agenda. In Ireland, on the other hand, there is a renewed interest in regional policies. The National Development Plan for the period 2000-06 places a greater emphasis on regional development and the Irish government is currently drawing up a national spatial strategy.

The two accession countries, the Czech Republic and Lithuania, are faced with the problem of defining their regional policies as they move into a period of rapid economic transition. The Czech experience is one of continuous efforts to handle economic and industrial restructuring while at the same time giving close attention to their impact on different regions. In Lithuania the interest in regional policies, which were overlooked for a long time due to the emphasis on national economic development, is rather new.

What is also evident from all Chapters is that SMEs are defined as major agents of development, especially for initiating growth in less developed regions. Obviously the role and weight of SMEs in the national and regional economies vary extensively and this situation reflects itself in the various definitions of SMEs used in the various Chapters. In Norway a large company is defined as one which has more than 100 employees, a small company employs less than 20 and a micro company less than 5, whereas in Ireland and the Czech Republic more than 250 employees identifies large companies whereas those with 10 to 250 are denoted as SMEs. In Lithuania enterprises with less than 9 employees are classed as small, those with 10 to 49 are medium sized while it takes only 50 or more for a firm to be considered large. Obviously, this situation increases the difficulty of making comparisons between countries regarding the importance of SMEs for regional growth.

Chapter 6 (Madsen and Jensen-Butler) concentrates on an accounting framework for modelling SMEs in a regional economy and emphasizes the need to define the contribution of SMEs at different scales in a country where they constitute an important part of the economy. In this chapter therefore they introduce a SAM (social accounting matrix) in order to capture economic activity in the form of SME's and their interaction with the rest of the production system, including forward and backward interaction, both intra- and interregional, as well as interaction between production and intermediate and final demand. The paper makes a significant new contribution in that it includes discussion of how positive externalities deriving from the interaction between the SMEs and the regional system can be identified. The analysis begins with a pure linear and 'simple' description of the regional economy and the interaction between firms. By gradually including interaction (for example externalities) and non-linearities (increasing returns to scale in production etc.) a more realistic and full picture of the role in SME's in the regional economy is given. Unfortunately, the SAM framework described theoretically in this chapter has not yet been made operational.

Chapter 7 (Johansen) is an interesting contribution that reminds us that even in resource-rich countries, regional problems may still be very important, although they may also be substantially different from the regional development problems faced by many less prosperous countries. The Chapter places emphasis on the difference between regional development and regional growth in Norway. Being a rich country where most of the wealth comes from oil, for a long time redistributive policies and a flow of resources in support of local government were important instruments used to overcome unwanted over-centralization and depopulation of the peripheries. Recently, however, under the pressure of EEA and EU regulations, there has been a change to regional development policies that emphasize endogeneous processes of sustainable regional growth. According to

Johansen, these new trends may cause new regional problems and if this happens then endogenous factors and small medium size enterprises will become more important to regional economic development.

Chapter 8 (Morgenroth and O'Malley) reflects the renewed interest in regional development in Ireland in the wake of the exceptional national growth performance of recent years. This has been accompanied by increasing divergence between the Irish regions, and in this context the Chapter discusses the contribution of different types of enterprise, particularly SMEs, in regional and national economic performance. The Chapter presents interesting features of the Irish experience. Firstly, as O'Malley and Morgenroth emphasize, somewhat in contrast to many countries, the analysis of economic growth in Ireland necessarily involves foreign owned multinational enterprises (MNEs) due to their weight in the economy (more than 9 per cent of manufacturing employment and 76 per cent of manufacturing gross output). The findings indicate that in the period from the 1960s to the 1980s, foreign MNEs and large enterprises, tended to locate in the least industrialized regions, which contributed to convergence between the regions. This situation changed in the 1990s, when foreign owned firms began to go increasingly to the more highly developed regions, with consequences for convergence since these firms were important determinants of the relative growth performance of different regions. In contrast the Irish indigenous manufacturing sector showed little growth and actually declined from the mid-1960s to the late 1980s, although then this weak performance was reversed even though its growth still lagged behind that of the MNE sector. Small enterprises are observed to have been more active in generating employment during the 1973-87 period in the indigenous manufacturing sectors. Interestingly the growth of SMEs and decline of larger firms during the 1970s and 1980s was seen a problem that needed to be rectified, given the objective to build companies with competitive power in international markets. In fact the figures show that after 1987 while the contribution of SMEs to employment is limited, the larger enterprises become the major source of new employment opportunities.

Secondly, O'Malley and Morgenroth examine patterns of growth by size class at the regional level in four different periods. According to their findings, the relationship between regional growth and the weight of SMEs in each region is rather mixed. During the 1973-79 period, at the national level employment in large firms declined in contrast to the increase in SMEs, so that SMEs made an important contribution to regional growth. The next period, 1979-87, also shows a relation between relatively good growth and the relative importance of SMEs in each region. However the general trend in the third period (1987-93) is completely different since in this period the large firms made a greater contribution to regional growth. In the most recent period covering the years 1993-99, which is an era of exceptional growth in the national economy, there is little indication of a relationship between regional growth and size of firms. In the light of this evidence, the authors maintain that they have not found compelling evidence that

SMEs have generally had an especially important role in regional growth in Ireland.

In many Eastern European countries the concept of regional development is relatively novel, although in the past they sometimes experienced command economy style of territorial planning which is strongly associated with the influence of the former Soviet Union. Chapter 9 outlines the attempts at economic development and its consequences for the regions of Lithuania. The chapter gives special emphasis to small and medium size business, which is believed to be crucial for the economic development of the country. In the Chapter Snieška, Virvilaitė, Banytė, Kvainauskaitė and Savanevičienė argue that increasing regional divergence in Lithuania can only be controlled by attracting SMEs and creating growth poles in different regions. They add, however, that their research shows that rather unfavourable social and economic conditions hinder the effective growth and development of SMEs in the peripheral regions, thus limiting their role in Lithuania's economic development. However they also show that SMEs make quite an important contribution to the generation of new jobs, since regions with higher numbers of SMEs per capita exhibit relatively lower rates of unemployment.

Chapter 10 (Beran and Frková) is dedicated to economic transition, industrial restructuring and the search for the new regional policies in the Czech Republic. The change in the political system at the end of 1980s was marked by the need to define new economic and regional policies. These involved SMEs which became one of the major instruments of industrial restructuring and a means of solving problems of structurally deficient and lagging regions within the country. One of the reasons why SMEs are seen as so efficacious, according to Vaclav and Frkova is their low investment requirement, which is only half that of large enterprises. However that is not the only reason why they emphasize their importance for regional development. In addition, they highlight the significance of SMEs as a factor promoting social cohesion, in enhancing the supply of certain services, and in facilitating the adaptation to changing conditions and innovative activities. However, they also note that in order to fully realize these benefits, there is still a need to get rid of obstacles in the path of further SME development in the Czech Republic.

The papers presented in Part 2 have shown how SMEs affect the aggregate growth of the whole country, in Part 3 we have assembled four case studies which allow us to gain some useful insight into the various factors which play a key role in the performances of SMEs and consequently in the local growth processes of the wider Europe. The contributions deal with candidate countries (Turkey, Croatia, Slovakia) as well as a member country (Sweden). A positive feature of this part of the volume is that the methodological approaches are quite different, ranging from the core-periphery model to the industrial district methodology, and from the local innovation system approach to sociological analysis.

The first case study, discussed in Chapter 11, is strictly related to the Part 2 Chapters although it takes a more specific perspective since it examines the role played by SMEs in the development process of a specific area. Bilge Armatlı Köroğlu and Burak Beyhan present a well documented investigation of the long run development of Denizli, a province of the Aegean region which in recent decades has experienced remarkable economic development based on the textile industry. Using as their theoretical background the industrial district model, the authors show how the development of the region has followed a continuous process of adapting to new market conditions in which SMEs have played a crucial role. With a basis in a strong tradition of artisan fabric production, the driving force behind rapid growth and rapid capital accumulation in Denizli was the homogeneous identity of the population; this was the foundation upon which local cooperation among SMEs was built. Cooperation was based on both formal and on informal relations, such as friendship and residence in the same town. Following these earlier developmental stages, the next stage of development shows the integration of the industrial district with the global production network. However the export boom attracted new firms and population from all regions of the country, and this resulted in a decline in cooperative relationships. At the same time the emergence of leading firms producing for the international markets gave new impetuous to the development of the area. The valuable lesson from this Chapter is the importance of the two-way link between changes in market conditions and social transformation in the local area.

These themes constitute the core interest of Chapter 12 where Drago Čengić presents a sociological analysis, based on interviews with owners and managers of 230 SMEs, of the role of small entrepreneurs in the development of the Međimurje county, a region situated in north-eastern Croatia. Within a book mainly devoted to economic analysis, this Chapter suggests a very fruitful approach to the relationship between SMEs and local economic growth involving a deep analysis of historical, social and cultural factors. The Chapter helps to provide answers to problems which are of a more general concern: the internal or external nature of local development; the propensity to establish entrepreneurial networks; the forms of cooperation between SMEs and large companies at the local level and abroad; and the role of state regulation of entrepreneurs. As regards the nature of local development the results are somehow discordant. On one hand social capital seems to have been partly imported into Međimurje by generations of workers employed abroad who, having returned, often established their own small shops and crafts. At the same time the survey does not show any direct impact on the development of local businesses in Međimurje of trans-border cooperation. Moreover, no significant entrepreneurial networking has been perceived, probably due to factors such as weak competition and the presence of monopoly in the domestic market, the perception of networking as being both a time-consuming and organizationally very demanding activity, and the lack of trust among business partners which generates scepticism towards new forms of industrial organization.

Chapter 13 concentrates on the relationship between SMEs, universities and research institutes in the Bratislava regions. The main aim of Jana Gašparíková, Milan Buček and Štefan Rehák's work is to assess how economic policy helps to develop innovation networks and human potential in the area. It presents the preliminary results of a survey carried out on 35 SMEs (in the electro-technical, chemical and machinery industries) and 20 research institutes, looking at their potential for cooperation and collaboration and at the nature of technology and knowledge transfer. The Bratislava region proves to be a very interesting case study for analysing the effects of innovation policy in a transition economy, given the location in the area of a growing number of SMEs strongly associated with innovative activities. Moreover this area benefits from a well developed university infrastructure, public research centres and also a well educated workforce. The results show that in spite of the fact that Bratislava enjoys a favourable situation in terms of industrial structure and research facilities it does not make full use of these opportunities. The survey shows that firms tend to concentrate on internal problems due to the insufficient level of knowledge transfer from the research institutes. This situation prompts the authors to call for new legislation aimed at promoting effective cooperation between research institutes and SMEs, through the establishment of research branch companies and regional innovation centres.

The last Chapter in the volume is a methodological contribution where the leader-follower model is applied to the analysis of the industrial development in a specific area, the Uddevalla region located north of Gothenburg in Western Sweden. Charlie Karlsson and Martin Andersson present an interesting methodological approach which offers precise guidelines about how to analyse the composition and development of the industrial structure in a specific region. The idea behind this spatial industrial dynamics model is that in each country it is possible to identify a limited number of leading urban regions where economic activities are continuously created, imitated and developed. Over time those activities tend to diffuse to other peripheral locations due to forces like product life cycles, changes in the organization of production, and increased demand in non leading regions. Given these hierarchical patterns of functional urban regions the lead-lag model is used by the authors to assess the development process of an individual region taking into account some basic features of its industrial structure, namely the number of plants and their employment and growth rate, the level of industry diversification, and educational intensity. This valuable approach also allows one to describe more precisely the direction of future development in different regions and to designate appropriate policy measures. For instance it allows one to assess which industries in the follower region are expected to gain new jobs and therefore the number of workers in each different profession or trade that are required to bring about the structural change process.

PART I:
REGIONAL GROWTH AT THE EUROPEAN SCALE

Chapter 2

Non-Orthodox Approaches to European Regional Growth Modeling: A Review

Bernard Fingleton

Introduction

The comparative economic development of Europe's regions has long been a focus of attention, with many analysts monitoring the progress of the EU's regions for evidence that increased economic integration has boosted growth and GDP per capita in lagging regions. The expectation that we should see regional convergence as an accompaniment to macro-economic convergence is derived from a particular world-view involving specific, often rather implicit, assumptions about the underlying causes of regional development and growth. This is generally centered around an orthodox view based on neoclassical economic theory, which has for a long time been the dominant paradigm in policy and legislative circles. However, more recently this has been challenged, both by the empirical facts that have not supported the concept of rapid and complete regional convergence as a reality even though there has been a considerable degree of macro-economic convergence at the national level, and by the development of new theory that sees widening regional disparities as a possible outcome of the lowering of trade barriers. While the conceptual basis for such an eventuality has long been in the literature, it has taken the advent of the new theory, so-called geographical economics or new economic geography, as represented in the book by Fujita, Krugman and Venables (1999), to place it at center stage. This theory provides a formal analysis of what might happen when we lower trade costs in the presence of increasing returns and imperfect competition, and a key element of this theory is that extreme geographical disparities emerge as an equilibrium outcome of a formal general equilibrium model.

While it is an attractive and elegant theory, this in itself is not sufficient to provide the scientific credibility necessary for it is to be taken seriously as an explanation of real world processes and mechanisms[1]. We therefore in this Chapter attempt to examine a range of approaches to thinking about the evolution of Europe's economic space, probing their ability to combine theoretical coherence with empirical consistency. These include mainstream neoclassical analysis in the form of the neoclassical growth model, endogenous growth theory, systems models of cumulative causation, stochastic equilibrium and the work of mathematical geographers using complex systems analysis. This diverse group has as a unifying feature a basis in mathematical modeling, and this means that they potentially have something precise and quantifiable to say about the long-term future of Europe's regional economies.

These various approaches are characterized by different degrees of conformity to the dominant model of mainstream economics, the neoclassical orthodoxy. Neoclassical growth theory (Solow, 1956; Swan, 1956) provides the basic pattern, with an emphasis, when adapted to the multi-economy situation, on diminishing returns and therefore the catching-up of faster growing initially poorer regions, albeit in the form of conditional convergence to different equilibrium levels of development. Geographical economics has some orthodox characteristics but also a major difference, increasing rather than diminishing returns. Diminishing returns are seen to be inconsistent with the presence in the real world of economic agglomeration and with the reality of persistent and accumulating differences between levels of development in different regions. As Krugman (1998) puts it, 'it is impossible even to discuss the important phenomena sensibly without assigning a key role to increasing returns', a belief which incidentally has long been 'almost an article of faith' among regional economists (Fingleton and McCombie, 1998). However, with an emphasis on micro-behavioral foundations, with emergent structure based on assumptions of individual utility and profit maximizing behavior subject to constraints in the context of the Dixit-Stiglitz (1977) theory of monopolistic competition, new economic geography is closer to the contemporary economics mainstream than other approaches which give little or no emphasis to the micro-level.

There are differences in emphasis regarding how best to show what is true, and this in essence involves a contrast between induction and deduction. Approaches grounded in the development of econometric models and the estimation of real-world effects, which is my preferred mode of analysis, naturally emphasize realism and therefore a model with some initial basis in theory has to be confronted by, and possibly modified until it is consistent with, data, even though the resulting model may turn out to be somewhat messy. Otherwise, if significant factors are omitted, the resulting estimates will tend to be biased. For instance in the face of the reality of diverse external economies, such as technological externalities involving spillover effects across regional boundaries, it may be necessary to add variables to a model in order to provide a closer match to data and produce unbiased estimates of the direction, magnitude and significance of the principal effects. An alternative approach is to opt for theoretical purity and assume away effects that interfere with the logical coherence of the model. The prime example of this is of course new economic geography, which captures pecuniary externalities but, in its pure and original form, ignores technological externalities. The benefits of simplifying assumptions are seen as paramount, enabling clarity and logical consistency. This approach is not designed for a confrontation with data, but it tells a story about the real world by creating a simplified version and showing what is 'going on' by illustrating 'what would go on' were it not for the complexities of reality.

There are fundamental differences in the role attributed to the constraints imposed by supply and demand conditions. In the neoclassical tradition, the supply of factors of production is what determines output growth, but in less orthodox approaches, typically post-Keynesian analysis, demand is fundamental in eliciting growth and the supply of factors of production. Here the role of demand is apparent in the importance attributed to the growth of regional exports as a stimulus to output and productivity growth, which by virtue of circular causation enhances regional competitiveness and hence export growth. This school, which emphasizes increasing returns and the divergent tendency of regional economies, provided an important precursor to the emphasis given to circular and cumulative causation in new economic geography.

The dynamics associated with different approaches are contrasting. Dynamics may involve convergence to a deterministic steady state, irrespective of the starting conditions, or at the other extreme dis-equilibrium or chaos may considered be a more natural state of affairs for the long-run. In between, a stochastic rather than deterministic equilibrium may be an outcome, or there may be abrupt changes from one equilibrium to another beyond critical points, as typifies new economic geography theory.

In the following sections, I review these various approaches commencing with the most orthodox from an economics perspective and ending with the least, placing emphasis on what is in my view the most reasonable and useful from the perspective of applied regional economic analysis. This provides a background to the various case studies and theoretical stances adopted in other Chapters.

Neoclassical Analysis

At its most simple, neoclassical growth theory (Solow, 1956; Swan, 1956) assumes that regions tend to the same equilibrium growth path for capital and hence output per worker. From the perspective of European regional analysis, this is not very realistic, since in order to achieve this unlikely outcome, one has to assume that the capital share, rate of technical progress, the savings rate, depreciation rate, and the population growth rate are constants across regions. As we shall suggest below, an injection of realism can be introduced by instead assuming, at least, that population and hence workforce growth rates[2] vary according to region. Consider for instance, two regions that behave exactly as envisaged under Solow-Swan theory, and are identical apart from the rate of growth of population. The consequence is that the one with the faster population growth rate will tend to a lower level of capital per capita in equilibrium. It will more quickly reach an upper limit of capital per person at which all savings are used up offsetting the effects of depreciation and population growth. Some less restricted extensions (Barro, 1991; Barro and Sala-i-Martin, 1995; Mankiw, Romer and Weil, 1992) of the basic theory typically involve a reduced form estimated by fitting regression models to cross-sections of regions or countries. This provides an easy-to-estimate[3] empirical model that allows regional differences in steady state by the introduction of covariates representing the effects of institutional differences, differences in levels of political stability, different tax policies, subsidies etc. However, there remains a considerable degree of scepticism among many regional economists for fundamental reasons, not least the assumption of constant returns.

The dynamics of the neoclassical economy result in a stable steady state where per capita capital stock gives output that generates saving and investment sufficient to maintain the per capita capital stock. Above the stable point, saving will be higher because output is higher, but because the marginal product of capital is diminishing, whereas depreciation is linear in capital, the savings schedule lies below the depreciation schedule and this position is unsustainable. Likewise, below the equilibrium point, the savings schedule is above the depreciation schedule and the economy is therefore not stationary but moves towards the equilibrium point since capital stock increases at a rate that depends on the distance between the two, falling monotonically towards zero at the unique stable steady state. At this point capital stock, consumption and output grow at the same rate as population and the supply of labor, hence in the absence of technical progress per capita values are constant. Extending the basic single economy theory to a number of regional economies each with different equilibrium levels, regional differences in the initial capital/labor ratio causes growth to vary region by region as each moves towards its own steady state from its different starting position.

To show the neoclassical approach in slightly more technical detail, we adapt the account provided by Jones (1997). Assume two hypothetical regions, with different fundamental characteristics and different disequilibrium starting positions. The dynamics given in Figure 2.1 show how for region 1, convergence of GDP per worker is from above, with the initial position above the equilibrium path. In contrast, region 2 starts from below its equilibrium path. Also, region 2's per worker growth is faster than region 1's, even though it is converging to a lower steady state level of GDP per worker. In order to trace these dynamics, it is necessary to know the level of GDP per worker of each region given by the model at each time point.

The level of GDP is equal to

$$Y_t = K_t^{\alpha} (A_t H_t)^{1-\alpha} \qquad \textbf{(1)}$$

in which K_t denotes the level of capital at time t, A_t is labor augmenting total factor productivity, and H_t is skilled labor. The coefficient α is capital's share in income; augmented labor's share is equal to $1-\alpha$ indicating diminishing returns to both inputs. It is common practice to assume that technology (A) evolves with an exogenously determined growth rate equal to *g*, and we assume that skilled labor is a function of raw labor (*L*), number of years schooling (*c*) and the rate of return to a year of schooling (ϕ). Raw labor grows at a rate (*n*) equal to the population growth rate. The level of capital at time t is determined by the level of investment at t-1 and the depreciation rate *d* applied to K_{t-1}. The level of investment I_t equals the level of GDP multiplied by the investment or savings rate *s*.

$$\begin{aligned} A_t &= A_{t-1} \exp(g) \\ H_t &= L_t \exp(\phi c\ ) \\ L_t &= L_{t-1} \exp(n) \\ K_t &= I_{t-1} + (1-d) K_{t-1} \\ I_t &= s Y_t \end{aligned} \qquad \textbf{(2)}$$

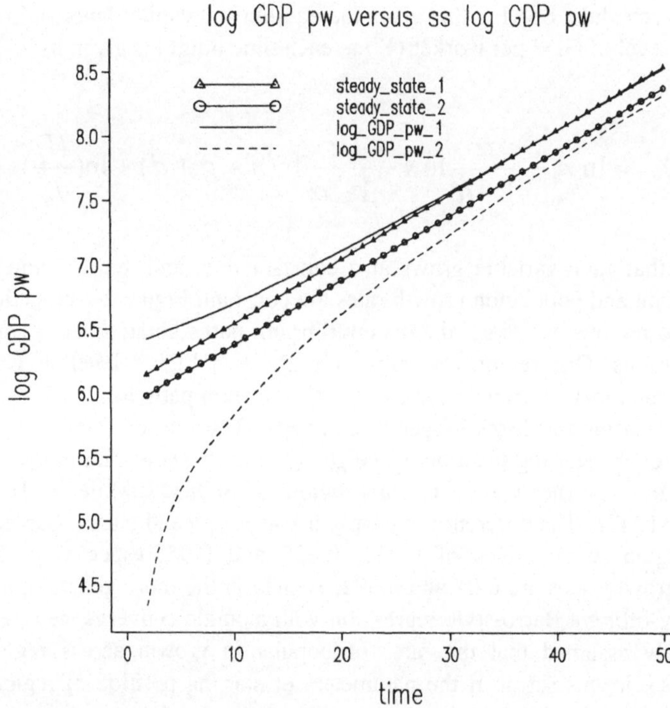

Figure 2.1 The path of two regions moving to steady state under neoclassical assumptions.

Apart from the impact of initial conditions, the different paths for Y in each region are determined by different assumptions about $c, \alpha, \phi, d, i, g,$ and n in the two regions. However, because of lack of data in the regional context we are unlikely to possess regionally differentiated savings or investment rates, or know the differential rate (if any) of return on schooling, or capital's share in income in the two regions, or anything about regionally varying depreciation rates. Technology here is a public good and thus the rate of growth is assumed to be equal in both regions.

With regard to the equilibrium or balanced growth paths to which each region is converging, the key expression is

$$\dot{k}_t = sy_t - (n + d)k_t \tag{3}$$

in which the lower cases indicate variables normalized by the size of the labor force, sy_t is the (nonlinear) savings schedule and $(n + d)k_t$ is the (linear) depreciation schedule. Solving this gives the equilibrium capital-labor ratio k^*. The equilibrium level of GDP per worker (Y^*) at each time point t is given by

$$\ln Y_t^* = \ln A_t + \frac{\alpha}{1-\alpha}\ln s - \frac{\alpha}{1-\alpha}\ln(n + g + d) + \ln(\frac{H_t}{L_t}) \tag{4}$$

Assume that each variable grows at a constant rate, and the investment rate, years schooling and population growth rates are constant. Figure 2.1 plots the paths to which two regions converge, the dis-equilibrium paths being given by arbitrary starting positions. One region converges rapidly to a higher level of GDP per worker than the other, starting out above the equilibrium path. Region 2 starts well below, grows faster and takes longer to converge. The rate of convergence[4] β is independent of the starting position, since $\beta = (1\text{-}\alpha)(n + d + g)$, and the parameters in this simulation are such that for the first region, $\beta = 0.08337$, while for the second region, $\beta = 0.05136$. The difference is simply because α, d and g are assumed equal for each region, with values of 0.333, 0.025 and 0.05 respectively, but the population growth rates are 0.05 and 0.002. Hence, in the more general context of n regions, by fitting a Barro-style regression with a single convergence rate β, it is also implicitly assumed that the rates of population growth across regions are constant. Also, in this set up if the parameters or starting position of region 1 are changed so that its path changes, this has no effect on region 2's path, even if regions are close neighbors.

A modification of the neoclassical model is given by Fingleton and McCombie (1998, 1999), who relax the assumption that β is constant and also allow for spatial effects. The starting point of this study is the equation

$$p_t \approx -\beta(\ln P_{t-1} - \ln \widetilde{P}_{t-1}) + g \tag{5}$$

in which p_t is the rate of growth of manufacturing productivity, P_{t-1} is the level of manufacturing productivity at time t-1 and ~ above P_{t-1} denotes the steady state level of productivity. This simply states the neoclassical maxim that as the difference between the actual and steady state levels falls to zero, growth equals the exogenously determined rate of growth of technology. Integrating and rearranging this equation gives

$$\ln P_t = (1 - \exp(-\beta T)) \ln \widetilde{P}_0 + gT + (\exp(-\beta T)) \ln P_0 \tag{6}$$

where T is the length of time between time 0 and time t. Simplifying and adding errors υ gives the familiar catch-up equation

$$\ln P_t = b_0 + b_1 \ln P_0 + \upsilon \tag{7}$$

so that

$$\hat{\beta} = -(\ln \hat{b}_1)/T \tag{8}$$

Relaxing the restriction that β is a constant is achieved by recognizing that in reality the growth rate n is not constant. In reality labor grows at different rates in different regions, and this then leads to the alternative specification that

$$\begin{aligned} &\ln P_t = b_0 + b_1[\ln P_0 \exp(-(1-\alpha)nT)] + b_2[\exp(-(1-\alpha)nT)] + \upsilon \\ &b_1 = \exp(-\beta' T) \\ &b_2 = -\exp(-\beta' T) \ln \widetilde{P}_0 \\ &\beta' = (1-\alpha)(g+d) \end{aligned} \tag{9}$$

Given this, it is now possible to estimate the convergence rate for each region i, which is

$$\hat{\beta}_i = -\ln \hat{b}_1 / T + (1-\alpha)n_i \qquad \textbf{(10)}$$

Secondly, the model allows for spatial effects since it is invariably the case that given regional data, a model that simply assumes that υ is distributed as N(0, σ^2) is not appropriate, showing up as spatially autocorrelated residuals. The reason for this could be the existence of effects due to omitted variables which are themselves spatially autocorrelated. This type of misspecification can be difficult to handle since, as we have seen from the work of Barro and Sala-i-Martin (1995) and Levine and Renelt (1992), there are many omitted variables that we may wish to consider but which are unavailable. This is certainly the case when working with data at the NUTS 2 regional system of the EU. In this case we chose the second best option of modeling the error autocorrelation that we assume represents the net effect of omitted regressors. This is done by means of the specification

$$\begin{aligned} \upsilon &= \rho W \upsilon + \xi \\ \xi &\sim N(0, \sigma^2) \end{aligned} \qquad \textbf{(11)}$$

in which $W\upsilon$ is the matrix product of square matrix W and the error vector υ. In this paper, the definition of W is

$$\begin{aligned} W_{ij}^{\bullet} &= \frac{1}{d_{ij}^2} \qquad if \qquad d_{ij} < 250km \\ W_{ij}^{\bullet} &= 0 \qquad if \qquad i = j \\ W_{ij} &= \frac{W_{ij}^{\bullet}}{\sum_j W_{ij}^{\bullet}} \end{aligned} \qquad \textbf{(12)}$$

which implies that each cell of υ is a weighted average of υ in other regions with weight diminishing with distance between regions[5]. This thus endeavors to pick up the spatial autocorrelation that is typically observed in residuals under the simpler model. Estimation is then via maximum likelihood with the form of the likelihood function governed by the assumed distribution of ξ.

Endogenous Growth Theory

Endogenous growth theory attempts to remedy some limitations of the neoclassical model, while retaining some important conceptual links. In particular, two major limiting assumptions from the perspective of regional development are addressed, namely diminishing returns and the assumption that productivity growth is ultimately determined by an exogenously determined rate of technical progress. The development of endogenous growth theory was stimulated by early insights by Arrow (1962) that technical progress could be endogenous, resulting from 'learning by doing', and these insights led to the modern endogenous growth theory initiated by the work of Romer (1986) and Lucas (1988). In Romer (1986), knowledge spill over compensates for private diminishing returns to investment in knowledge creation so that the stock of knowledge capital in the economy as a whole is raised. Lucas (1988) envisages a spill over mechanism involving educational improvements by individuals motivated by the prospect of higher wages.

We see this spill over notion at its simplest in the so-called AK model, which is a natural development from the neo-classical model in that it retains the assumption of diminishing private returns to capital, but also assumes constant social returns, hence

$$Q = A\left(\frac{K}{E}\right)^{\phi} K^{\alpha} E^{\beta} \qquad \textbf{(13)}$$

in which Q is the level of output, A is technology, K is capital, E is labor and the constant social returns to capital are given by $\phi + \alpha = 1$ and diminishing private returns by $\alpha + \beta = 1$. In this model spill over offsets the diminishing returns and causes output to increase proportional to capital. The line of reasoning captured by the AK model sees further elaboration in the work of Romer (1987, 1990, 1994) and others. An important implication for regional analysis of these models is the link between the scale of the economy and growth, and the divergence in incomes per worker across regions or countries.

Within the context of the European regions, the work of Cheshire and Carbonaro (1995) has a basis in the Romer (1990) model. Their analysis embodies increasing returns to human capital as a result of spill over which occurs due to the non-rival and partially non-excludable component of knowledge generation. They model the rate of growth of non-rival knowledge as a function of the total human capital that is employed in research multiplied by the stock of knowledge, taking care to allow for the differential concentration of human capital among regions. This is made operational by means of a proxy variable, namely the number of research and development establishments (in top companies) per unit of population, and this is raised to various powers in order to capture various degrees of increasing returns.

To show the impact of endogenous technical progress in a little more detail, we follow the approach typical of Romer (1990), Grossman and Helpman (1991, 1994) and Aghion and Howitt (1992), and assume that the level of resources devoted to research and development increases the rate of growth of productivity. Assume again that there are only two regions, and that the model structure is as in the neoclassical set up, except that the rate of growth of technology is endogenous, and depends on the number of workers (L_A) involved in the creation of knowledge rather than directly in production (L_Y), where $L = L_A + L_Y$. Hence the technical progress rate is

$$\frac{\dot{A}}{A} = \kappa L_A \qquad \textbf{(14)}$$

$$A_t = A_{t-1} + A_{t-1}\kappa L_A$$

The effect of endogenising technical progress in this way is shown by Figure 2.2, which plots log GDP per worker for the two regions (which are identical, with the same initial values and exogenous coefficients, to those of Figure 2.1). The fact that the growth of workers is faster in region 1 means that the number of workers involved in knowledge creation becomes larger and therefore the rate of technical progress is faster. The outcome is not convergence to equilibrium paths so that the ratio of the levels of GDP per worker is constant over time, but instead the ratio increases with time. The increasing scale of the region with the larger workforce boosts the rate of growth of technology and therefore the growth of GDP per worker.

However endogenous growth theory is open to attack because by arguing that an increase in the level of resources devoted to research and development increases the rate of growth of GDP per worker, it is seen to defy the rationale of neoclassical growth theory. Scale effects are unreasonable from this theoretical perspective, since they negate the existence of a balanced growth path. Jones (1995) also suggests that they are unrealistic in the face of empirical evidence. He shows that the increase in the number of knowledge workers has not been matched by a commensurate increase in total factor productivity in the USA. On the other hand, for many the theory still seems to contain too much of a neoclassical, supply-oriented, flavor. While neat models may be the outcome of assumptions about rational, profit maximizing agents developing new technologies, others consider that real behavior is much more complex and is not properly described by conventional micro-theory, and rather than make insecure behavioral assumptions, they would prefer to remain neutral on this issue. Nevertheless, workers within a more heterodox tradition see virtue in the argument that scale effects are important for regional analysis. From the European perspective, with some exceptions, it does seem to be the case that the regions devoting most to research and development do seem to be the wealthiest, and it appears that success breeds success, with rich regions becoming increasingly rich and economic activity concentrating where it already exists.

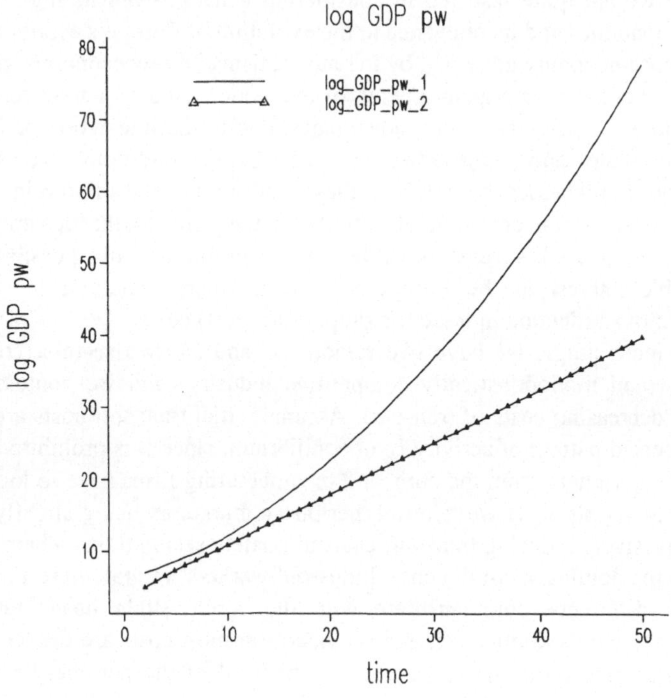

Figure 2.2 The path of two regions with endogenous technical progress.

New Economic Geography

New economic geography lies squarely within the realm of mainstream economics, but in many ways it is also non-orthodox, a sentiment that is shared by Donald R. Davis' comment printed on the loose cover of the book by Fujita, Krugman and Venables (1999), that 'the work is an even more radical departure from orthodoxy than the new trade theory of the 1980s'. For instance, equilibrium exists, although it is somewhat different from the kind of equilibrium associated with the neoclassical growth model reviewed above. Fujita, Krugman and Venables (1999) set out the theory in detail, and useful accounts are also provided by Brakman, Garretsen and van Marrewijk (2001), Schmutzler (1999), and Neary (2001). Although the basic theory does not address the issue of regional growth explicitly, the dynamic evolution towards equilibrium involves differential development paths. Also, recent literature (Martin and Ottaviano, 1999; Baldwin and Forslid, 2000) has focussed on growth using the same theoretical structure as the static model, so we are quite justified in considering it here, given its high impact on regional economics and its relevance to the evolution of Europe's economy.

In a space-economy governed by the mechanisms of new economic geography, large agglomerations emerge as a result of the hidden hand of market forces rather than due to any particular natural advantages, due to the interaction of increasing returns to scale and transportation costs. Once conditions are such that agglomeration processes commence, they tend to be self-reinforcing and the dynamics lead to concentration of activity in the core, to the detriment of the periphery, as one of several possible stable equilibria. This possibility is of considerable interest in the European context, where increased integration is tantamount to a reduction in trade (or simply transport) costs.

At its most simple we have two regions (C and P), two sectors (competitive agriculture and monopolistically competitive industry) and we contemplate the impact of decreasing costs of transport. Assume initial transport costs are high, so that a dispersed pattern of activity is an equilibrium, since it is prohibitively costly to serve the periphery from the core, and manufacturing firms have to locate in the periphery to supply it. If we take the periphery market as being slightly smaller, then progressively reducing transport costs ultimately sets in train a chain of events leading to the dominance of the core. Industrial workers[6] migrate in response to the real wage difference commensurate with the core's slight head start, which reinforces the core's dominance, and provided transport costs are low enough, the stable equilibrium turns out to be one in which all of the periphery's market is served entirely from the core, it has no indigenous industry left. With increasing returns, the advantages of concentrating production, even allowing for the depressing effect of extra competition, dominate the advantages of serving the market locally from within the periphery. Because of a slight asymmetry in agricultural production, the core emerges as the unique equilibrium for manufacturing. Of course, if it were the periphery that had marginally the greater share of demand, then it would ultimately turn out to be the dominant location. So, the outcome is dependent on initial conditions and there are major consequences of minor differences in initial conditions.

Depending on the specific values allotted to the exogenous parameters, equilibrium may be stable or unstable. For instance if it takes only the smallest perturbation at an equilibrium point to set in motion a process of further real wage differences and migration, then the equilibrium is not stable. However if increasing worker share produces negative feedback, so that wages fall and migration is choked off, then the share returns to the stable equilibrium point, and likewise we will be brought back to equilibrium as a result of diminishing worker share and increased wages. The share associated with these stable equilibria depend on the model parameters, sometimes stable equilibrium occurs when 100 per cent of workers are located in one region, sometimes stable equilibria occur at some other share allocation.

An important message of these dynamics for regional development is that once established, stable equilibrium may persist over a range of transport cost parameters, but critical points exist at which there is a sudden shift to a new equilibrium, so we have multiple equilibria and sharp changes in equilibrium solutions as particular values of parameters are passed.

Krugman argued that this scenario was consistent with what occurred in Italy once railroads were introduced in the 19th century, exposing local manufacturing to competition that led to its collapse. A pan-European appraisal was carried out by Amiti (1998), who provides evidence that industries that are more concentrated in a European countries with good market access are also ones that have more scale economies and a larger proportion of intermediate inputs in final production, features that are consistent with the theory. She cites work supporting the home market effect, where a demand increase produces a more than proportional increase in workers and manufacturing production, which is a key characteristic of the Fujita, Venables and Krugman (1999) synthesis. The implications for the future development of the EU are that if trade barriers (transport costs) fall further, we will see increased geographical concentration, even among EU regions with similar endowments. However on the whole we should remain cautious about the predictions of a theory that is based on untested or unreal theoretical assumptions. In essence the theory is primarily an exercise in formal, deductive modeling, in which mathematical tricks are employed to allow a neat, general equilibrium solution rather than because they are necessarily realistic. While the current research agenda involves modification to introduce more realistic assumptions, together with more rigorous empirical analysis than simply appealing to stylized facts and using location quotients or other simplified localization measures (Krugman 1991; Glaeser et al., 1992), on the whole this is likely to be a difficult task[7].

Systems Models and Cumulative Causation

One line of analysis which preceded, and to some extent motivated (Krugman, 1991), the new economic geography literature, evokes cumulative or circular causation by means of a system of equations. This approach is non-orthodox since it avoids explicit micro-economic assumptions of constrained utility or profit maximization at the level of the individual or firm, does not set out the market structure in detail. There are various strands in this literature, often emanating from the models set out by Myrdal (1957) and Kaldor (1970, 1972). In this section attention focuses initially on the mathematical model of cumulative causation developed by Dixon and Thirlwall (1975). The model assumes that growth of output (g_t) in an economy depends on export growth (x_t) and export growth is partly a function of productivity growth (r_t) which itself is induced by the growth of output. The latter relation between productivity and output growth embodies increasing returns which we have mentioned above is considered by many to be the sine qua non of regional economics. Equations (15) give more concrete shape to the model, with t indexing time,

$$\begin{aligned} g_t &= \gamma x_t \\ x_t &= \eta p_{dt} + \delta p_{ft} + \varepsilon z_t \\ p_{dt} &= w_t - r_t + \tau_t \\ r_t &= r_a + \lambda g_t \end{aligned} \tag{15}$$

and in which p_{dt} denotes the rate of growth of domestic (export) prices, p_{ft} is the rate of growth of competitor prices, z_t is the rate of growth of real income in the export markets, w_t is the nominal wage inflation rate, and τ_t is the rate of change of mark-up on labor costs (in fact, despite the lack of explicit representation of market structure, the presence of the mark-up implies imperfect competition). The coefficients which are assumed to be fixed over time are the elasticity of output growth with respect to export growth (γ), the price elasticity of demand for exports (η), the cross-elasticity of demand for exports (δ), the income elasticity of demand for exports (ε), the autonomous rate of productivity growth (r_a) and the so-called Verdoorn coefficient (λ), after Verdoorn (1949). The relationship between productivity growth in the export sector and the rate of growth of output form the kernel of the process which sustains differences in growth rates between regions which result from some initial advantage favoring one region over another. It is possible from these equations to derive an expression for the equilibrium growth rate for a given region, hence

$$g^* = \frac{\gamma[\eta(w - r_a + \tau) + \varepsilon z + \delta p_f]}{1 + \gamma\eta\lambda} \tag{16}$$

equilibrium depends on abs$(\gamma\eta\lambda) < 1$. Otherwise, we see explosive growth which is unrealistic. Similarly, the equilibrium rate of productivity growth is given by

$$r^* = \frac{r_a + \gamma\lambda(\delta p_{ft} + \eta(w + \tau) + \varepsilon z_t)}{1 + \gamma\eta\lambda} \tag{17}$$

The reason for the equilibrium condition is shown by the general solution to a difference equation in g showing the transition dynamics to equilibrium when a single period time lag[8] is introduced to one of the equations. Hence, assume that export growth depends on the previous period's growth of prices and incomes, so that

$$x_t = \eta p_{dt-1} + \delta p_{ft-1} + \varepsilon z_{t-1} \quad \textbf{(18)}$$

this results in a solution to the first order difference equation

$$g_t = A(-\gamma\eta\lambda)^t + \frac{\gamma[\eta(w_{t-1} - r_a + \tau_{t-1}) + \varepsilon z_{t-1} + \delta p_{ft-1}]}{1+\gamma\eta\lambda} \quad \textbf{(19)}$$

in which A represents the initial condition. Clearly, the first term on the right hand side would be increasing in t if the equilibrium condition did not hold, and diminish to zero under the equilibrium condition. In the latter case, the differential growth by region depends then on regional differences in the parameters and variables in the second right hand side term. Further analysis of feasible assumptions regarding these are given in Dixon and Thirlwall (1975) and McCombie and Thirlwall (1994).

The reason why explosive output and output per worker growth is not really the most appropriate vision of the dynamics of this model is that it is not observed as a sustained phenomenon in reality. We expect the controlling parameters and variables to take values that produce equilibrium.

For example, it would be reasonable to expect the price elasticity of demand for exports η to take an absolute value of less than 2 (Dixon and Thirlwall, 1975). We can also reasonably assume that exports[9] are a constant proportion of output so that $\gamma \approx 1$ and estimated values of λ are commonly in the region of 0.5. Assuming values in this range gives the dynamics for output and output per capita growth illustrated in Figure 2.3. In this case, abs$(\gamma\eta\lambda) < 1$ and therefore productivity and output growth tends to an equilibrium. Note that the dynamics for two different regions are plotted, the difference being simply the result of setting the income elasticity of demand for exports (ε) at a slightly higher value for region 1. Different income elasticities would be a result of initial differences in industrial specialization, and under cumulative causation this would tend to be reinforced and lead to the emergence of a center-periphery structure. Note also that, since according to Equations (15) the variables p_{ft}, z_t, w_t, τ_t and r_a are exogenous rather than related to the dynamics of any other region, there is no interaction between regions in this simulation, the fact that region 2 has a faster equilibrium output and productivity growth rate has no effect on region 1. In fact region 2 could have no steady state output growth, and yet under this model there would be no consequence for region 1. This outcome with abs$(\gamma\eta\lambda) > 1$ for region 2 is shown in Figure 2.4, for the first 10 periods. While region 1 traces a path 'identical' to that in Figure 2.3, region 2 growth rates do not tend to a steady state.

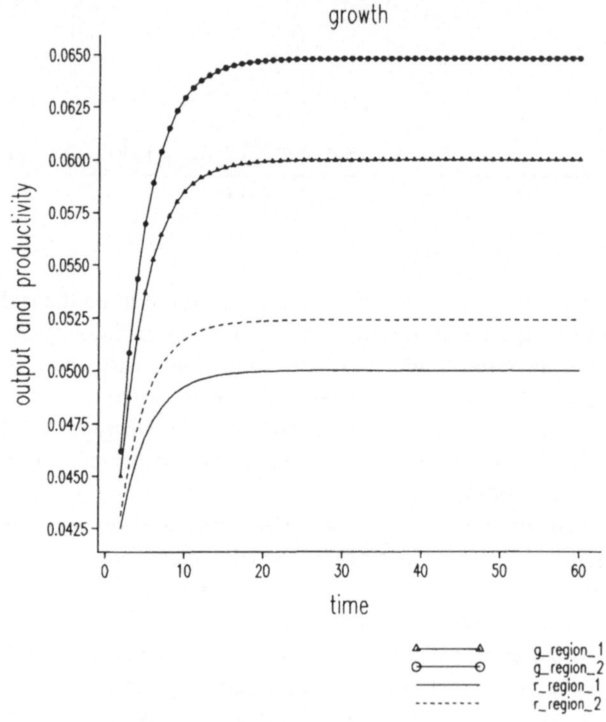

Figure 2.3 Convergence in output and productivity growth for two regions (Dixon and Thirlwall model).

The consequence is that the levels of output and productivity diverge dramatically, as shown by Figure 2.5. Even if both regions do converge to equilibrium growth rates, in the case when they are unequal, output and productivity levels increase inexorably and the gap between the levels widens.

While this may appear to be unrealistic, it is possible to produce models of this genre that result, despite the presence of increasing returns, in convergence to a common steady state growth rate for levels. One example (Fingleton, 2000b) also includes explicit spatial interaction between regions, as a result of the effect of surrounding productivity levels on a region's rate of productivity growth, and this can be shown to cause more rapid convergence to equilibrium levels than would otherwise be the case. The presence of spatial interaction between the regions also produces a more spatially clustered pattern than would otherwise be the case, with neighboring regions tending to similar equilibrium values, and this enhances the reality of the model's outcome.

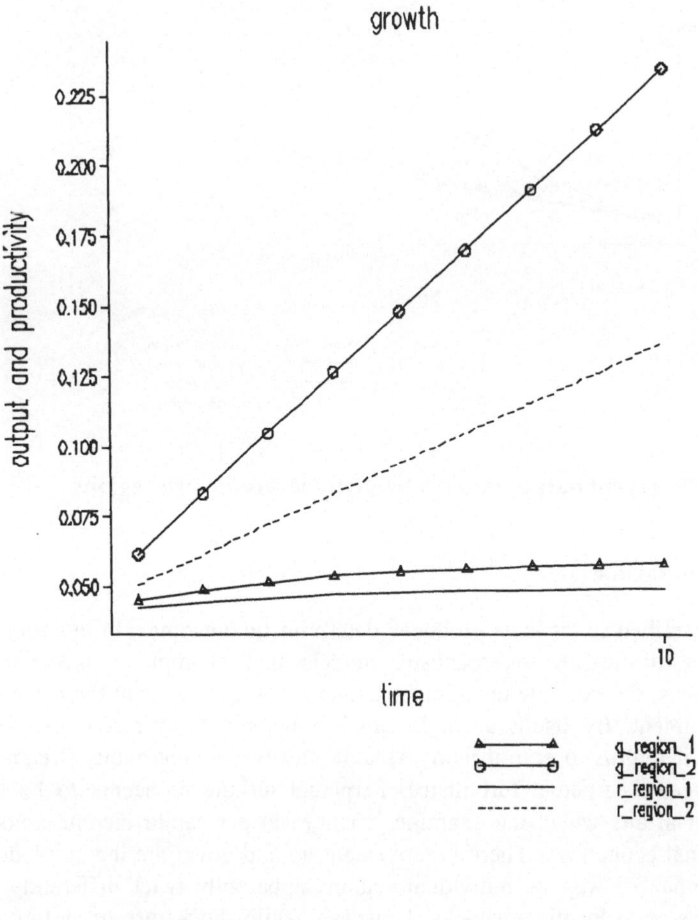

Figure 2.4 Output and productivity growth with one divergent and one convergent region.

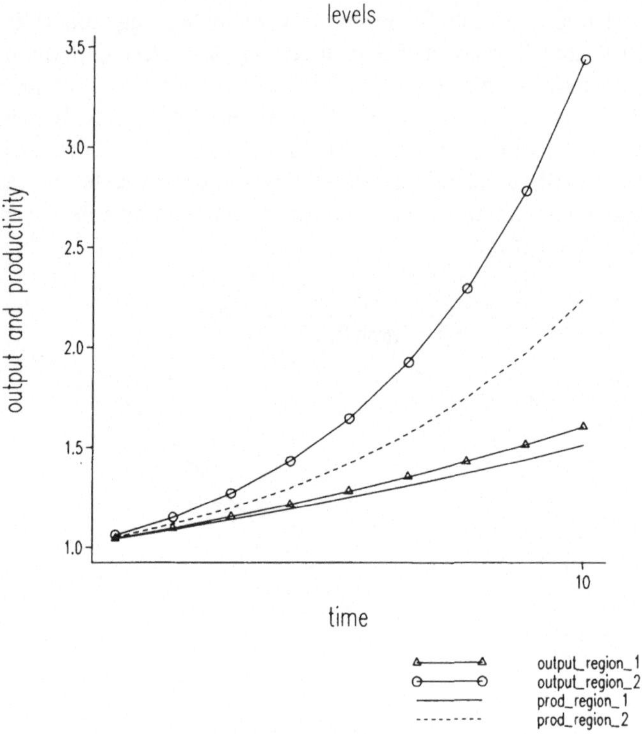

Figure 2.5 Divergent output and productivity levels for two regions.

Stochastic Equilibrium

The models described so far have produced deterministic outcomes. In this section we extend the discussion to stochastic models that attempt to incorporate exogenous shocks, for example unanticipated changes in policy, or in the social or natural environment. By itself, a single shock may only temporarily disturb a system before it returns to equilibrium. Assume however a continuous stream of shocks that creates perpetual turbulence. Perpetual turbulence seems to be the natural state of affairs when one examines changes in per capita income among Europe's regional economies. There is movement up and down the income ladder in a fairly haphazard way as individual regions apparently react differently to common shocks or to localized shocks. However, while shocks are by definition unexplained and unpredictable, there is none the less an underlying order to the income level movements of regions. One approach to capturing the order within chaos that appears when we look at regional income dynamics is via Markov chain models[10]. These have the interesting property that the equilibrium to which the system converges is a stochastic one, consisting of a time-constant probability for each income state[11].

Despite the added realism provided by a stochastic perspective, there are several areas of criticism associated with the Markov chain approach, and these bring us eventually to a mode of analysis that is an attempted response to these limitations. The first is that it is rather inexplicit in terms of theory, and although stochastic turbulence is suggestive of a Poisson-like processes at the micro-level[12], micro-level underpinnings are not explicit or fundamental to the approach. The second area of criticism relates to the problem of 'discretization'. Thirdly, the Markov approach per se tells us little about the dynamics of any particular region, it simply models the dynamics of the system as a whole. The fourth area of criticism is the role played by interregional dependence.

Discretization means the division of a continuous variable such as GDP per capita into discrete income states, such as rich, above average, below average and poor. Bulli (2001) reminds us that improper discretization can 'lead to very misleading results', due to the loss of the Markov property (that the transition probability of moving from state i to state j does not depend on any movements an individual region made prior to its arrival in state i). Bartholomew (1981) also points this out with regard to the amalgamation of states, stating that 'except in very special circumstances the property is destroyed and this might appear to jeopardize the use of Markov models since the arbitrariness in forming the categories is almost certain to ensure that the process in non-Markovian' although 'successful application of the model does not depend on the assumptions being precisely true', since 'what matters is whether the model is an adequate approximation' (Bartholomew, 1981; see also Cheshire and Magrini, 2000). We might therefore simply explore the robustness of the results obtained from various arbitrary discretizations, to see if they make any practical difference to the conclusions drawn. Alternatively, some (for example Quah, 1997; Fingleton and López-Bazo, 2002) have opted to work with the stochastic kernel (which in the continuous equivalent to the Markov transition probability matrix). Modeling the transition probabilities may help transcend the particular discretization (Fingleton, 1997) and more generally the problem of longer time effects could be approached by means of generalized linear models involving higher order dependencies[13].

With regard to the role of interregional dependence, the fact that spatial data are almost invariably autocorrelated means that the observations are not independent and therefore the standard tools of inference, why rely on independent observations, are inappropriate. This is highlighted in the work of Fingleton (1997, 1999a, 1999b) and Rey (2001), who suggest some possible avenues when working with regional data. As has been stressed above, the fact that regions interact should be a feature of our model rather than assumed away, and this is particularly difficult to accomplish in the Markov context. With no explicit representation of the role of spatial interaction or externalities in regional dynamics, and only being concerned with a system of regions, there is little knowledge gained about the dynamics of nominated regions. Markov chains *per se* do not provide the analytical cutting edge needed for a deeper understanding of why regional differences occur and persist.

The question of how we might avoid some of these limitations while retaining something that we can call stochastic equilibrium has been addressed in Fingleton (1998, 2002c). The starting point is the relationship between manufacturing productivity growth (p) and manufacturing output growth (q),

$$p = \lambda + b_1 q \tag{20}$$

This we have seen is typically the kernel of models of cumulative causation. Fingleton and McCombie (1998) estimate this relationship using data for the NUTS 2 regions of the EU, and find that, controlling for spillover effects and innovation diffusion, there exists a significant positive relationship indicating the presence of internal and external increasing returns to scale. More recently, Fingleton (2001a, 2001b) has used the same relationship but in the context of urban economic theory (Abdel-Rahman, 1988; Rivera-Batiz, 1988; Quigley, 1998; Abdel-Rahman and Fujita, 1990; Fujita and Thisse, 1996), with competitive industry and monopolistically competitive services as in Dixit-Stiglitz (1977) theory. This suggests that the increasing returns derive from the increased variety of services as the scale of activity increases, and depends on the relevance of services to manufacturing production, and the elasticity of substitution of services.

Given increasing returns, the development of the model proceeds by endogenizing the rate of growth of technology (λ) so that for a given region it depends on the specific values of variables in that region and also, because of spillover, on values in other regions. Within the region, the hypothesis is that the technical progress rate is partly a function of the density of human capital (H) located there, which reflects the industrial structure and its labour force and the intensity of educational attainment and the complexity of social networks. It is assumed that knowledge spread and assimilation within the local economy, in other words technological externalities, will be higher wherever the density and level of human capital is higher. Secondly, the hypothesis is that the initial level of technology within each region also determines subsequent technical progress. If technology is initially at a low level, there are higher benefits from innovation adoption compared with regions initially at a high technological level, so we should see a positive relationship between the initial level of technology gap (compared to the leading region), denoted by G, and technical progress, as low technology regions catch-up by adopting diffusing innovations. This is likely also to include the effects of regional policies aimed at promoting the adoption of new technology, which will be targeted at the lowest technology regions, and become weaker as regions become more technologically advanced.

The above are intra-regional determinants of the technical progress rate. With regard to extra-regional factors, the assumption is that knowledge spills over from 'neighbouring' regions. This seems a reasonable proposition given that the estimates described below are based on 178 NUTS 2 regions of the EU, which exhaustively partition the major part of the EU territory. NUT2 regions tend to be administrative entities not functional urban regions, and are open to the influence of economic activity in surrounding regions. However, the spatial extent of spillover is assumed to be limited by information transmission mechanisms. Assume that knowledge is embodied within workers and its transmission is via workers switching jobs within local labour market areas, learning new skills and passing them out to the workforce in general mediated by social networks as a technological externality[14]. The limiting factor here is commuting distance, although one cannot exclude an effect due to worker migration. The second mechanism is disembodied knowledge moving directly between firms due to demonstration effects of the efficacy of new knowledge. The inherent weightlessness of information[15] means that for some information there will be a global spread with no impediment due to distance, in other words zero distance decay, and this we have attempted to model via G. However, we also recognize that for other types of information, distance between originator and receiver will be an obstacle which will localize its transmission. For instance if firms collaborate with other firms in a local production chain, demonstration effects will tend be along narrow fairly localized channels rather than being broadcast globally. Likewise, competition between firms producing in the same local economy will also create localised knowledge transfers as knowledge of a particular type is demonstrated to enhance productivity. The literature on endogenous growth theory reminds us that initial adopters of innovations seeking to gain competitive advantage will find it difficult to fully internalize the benefits of investment in new knowledge, despite patenting laws and confidentiality clauses in employment contracts to restrict leakages. The benefits will spillover to other firms in the local economy within and across region boundaries who do not have to bear the same research and development costs and equivalent risks associated with incorrect technology choices.

In practice, while distance is seen as a factor, there is unlikely to be a sharp cut-off to information flow but a gradual decline as increasing remoteness reduces its relevance, volume and impact. Within an increasingly integrated economy such as the EU, all regions interact and the quantity of information flow per unit of time is likely to depend both on the distance separating, and the sizes of, the regional economies. Large isolated regions are more likely to communicate more frequently and with a greater volume of information flow than small isolated ones, for example London and Athens will have more interaction than one would anticipate from their distance apart. This is a theory which can be embodies in a W matrix (we introduced this idea initially in the neoclassical analysis above). The details of how this is done are discussed below, here we simply state that the net outcome of specific assumptions about the determinants of spatial interaction between regions, as embodied within the W matrix, is the vector of values, one per region, given by the matrix product Wp. The definition of W ensures that vector Wp comprises weighted averages of the rate of productivity growth p for the 'surrounding' regions.

Collecting the different effects together gives us the technical progress sub-model

$$\lambda = b_0 + vH + \eta G + \rho Wp + \xi \quad \textbf{(21)}$$

To summarize, equation (21) assumes the technical progress rate is determined by the human capital and technology gap variables H and G which represent intra-regional conditions, plus an autonomous rate of technical progress b_0 and other unknown intra-regional effects which we represents as random shocks $\xi \sim N(0, \sigma^2 I)$. In addition it depends on productivity growth Wp in 'surrounding' regions, so that if productivity growth in neighboring regions is high, this will act as a stimulus to technical progress and hence productivity growth locally. It follows that

$$p = b_0 + vH + \eta G + \rho Wp + b_1 q + \xi \quad \textbf{(22)}$$

We thus have a model with dependent variable p and endogenous right hand side variable Wp, with productivity growth in a region is partly determined by, and partly determines, productivity growth in 'neighboring' regions. This has implications for estimation, and in this case maximum likelihood or two stage least squares are appropriate for consistent estimation.

In the empirical analysis (see Fingleton 2001b) reported here, the productivity gap is defined as $G = 1 - (P_0/P^*_0)$, where P_0 is the region's level of (manufacturing) productivity per (manufacturing) worker in the base year and P^*_0 is the highest level of productivity per worker at time 0. In practice, in the absence of adequate or reliable human capital data, we assume that human capital will be a function of a region's degree of peripherality within the EU (denoted by L) and whether or not a region is urban or rural (denoted by D). Regarding these assumptions, as a broad generalization within the EU, it is evident that peripheral regions tend to have lower educational attainment rates and a non-industrial legacy implying lower level of human capital appropriate to manufacturing. Peripherality is measured simply by using the great circle distance[16] of each regional center from Luxembourg. In addition, the assumption is that urban agglomerations possess larger human capital stocks and educational attainment rates than rural regions, a rough approximation which nevertheless is supported by the limited data available for EU regions. Higher density of human capital is assumed to accelerate the transmission of knowledge within urban areas, boosting innovation creation and adoption and hence technical progress and manufacturing productivity growth. The dummy variable D takes values 1 and 0 according to whether the population density is above 500 inhabitants per square km[17].

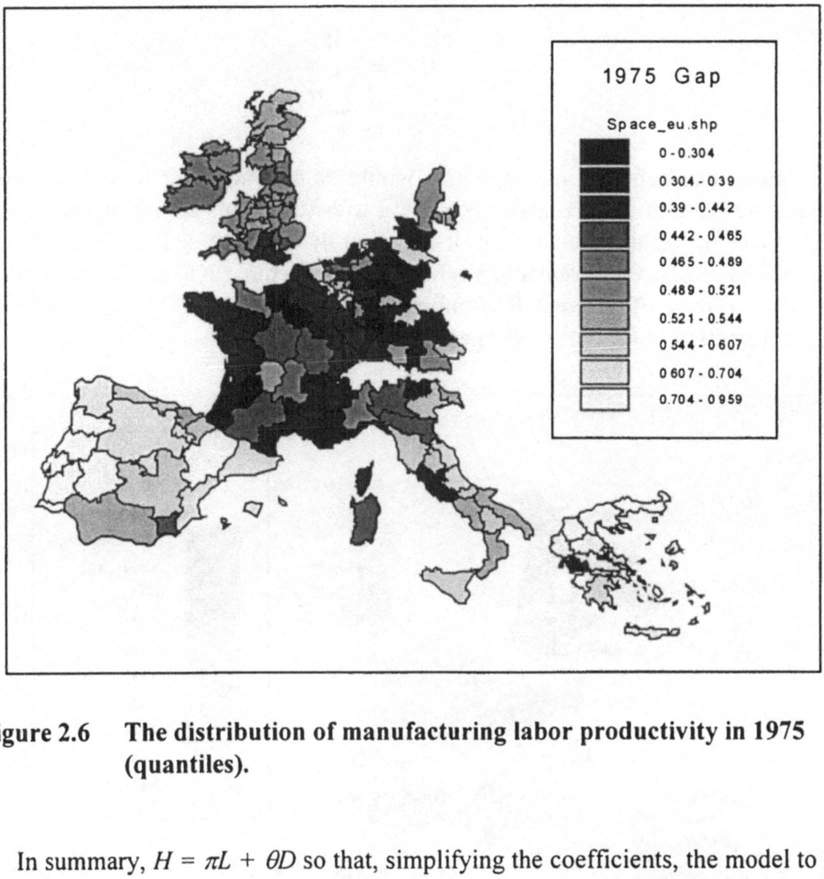

Figure 2.6 The distribution of manufacturing labor productivity in 1975 (quantiles).

In summary, $H = \pi L + \theta D$ so that, simplifying the coefficients, the model to be estimated is

$$p = \rho Wp + b_0 + b_1 q + b_2 G + b_3 L + b_4 D + \xi \qquad \textbf{(23)}$$

The W matrix embodies our theory about how regions interact, namely that region i's productivity growth is affected by p in all regions, with the effect diminishing with distance between typical regions i and j holding size constant, and increasing with size (denoted by respective star-of-period[18] output levels Q_i and Q_j) holding distance constant. Also, we standardize W^* to produce W by dividing by row totals, so that the matrix product Wp is the vector weighted averages[19] of 'surrounding' regions. In other words,

$$W^*_{ij} = \frac{Q_i^{\chi} Q_j^{\upsilon}}{d_{ij}^{\gamma}}$$
$$W_{ij} = \frac{W^*_{ij}}{\sum_j W^*_{ij}} \quad \textbf{(24)}$$

Rather than being estimated, which would be technically somewhat complex, values are allotted to χ, υ and γ according to assumptions regarding the relative importance of distance versus size. It turns out that a value of 2 for each of these parameters produces reasonable results (see Fingleton (2001a) for an analysis based on a range of different *W* assumptions, and Anselin (1988) for a discussion of the formation of alternative *W* specifications).

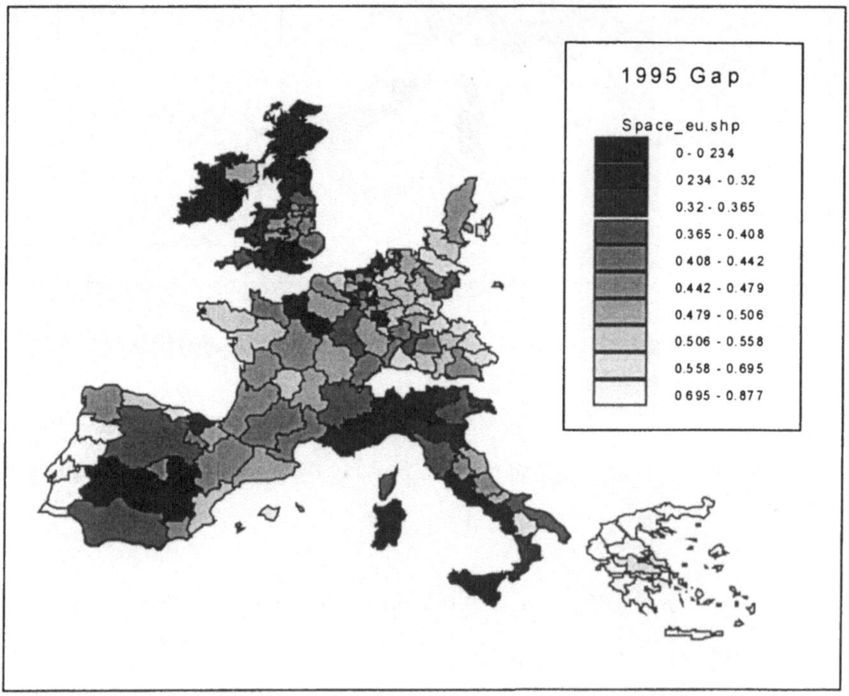

Figure 2.7 The distribution of manufacturing labor productivity in 1995 (quantiles).

The data used to fit the model are annual average manufacturing productivity and output growth for 178 NUTS regions of the EU over a period of 20 years (1975-1995) provided by Cambridge Econometrics. This relative distribution of productivity levels (in the form of the quantiles for the variable *G*) at the start and end of the study period are given in Figures 2.6 and 2.7. Table 2.1 summarizes the final maximum likelihood[20] estimates that emerged as the outcome of a process of model comparison and diagnostic analysis. The model fits reasonably well given that we are analyzing cross-sectional data, with the R^2 analogue equal to 0.4947 and the squared correlation between observed and fitted values equal to 0.5447. There is no evidence of residual autocorrelation, but we assume groupwise heteroscedasticity, so that $\xi \sim N(0,\sigma_i^2 I)$ where the subscript i indicates whether or not the region is in the periphery or core[21].

Table 2.1 Estimates of equation 23.

coefficient	Estimate	S.D.	z-value	Probability
ρ	0.650123	0.128873	5.044684	<0.000001
b_0	-0.019942	0.00419611	-4.752487	0.000002
b_1	0.444352	0.0614415	7.232119	<0.000001
b_2	0.06645	0.00767723	8.655467	<0.000001
b_3	-1.4311E-05	2.48029E-06	-5.769887	<0.000001
b_4	0.00929659	0.00279149	3.330328	0.000867
GROUP VARIANCES				
σ^2_1	0.000205032	2.80647E-05	7.305692	<0.000001
σ^2_2	0.000101419	1.70634E-05	5.943683	<0.000001
HETEROSC.				
TEST	DF	VALUE	PROB	
Lik.Ratio	1	8.820509	0.002979	

Table 2.1 shows that each of the variables is statistically significant and appropriately signed, and that the estimated values are as anticipated, for instance the estimated b_1 linking manufacturing productivity and manufacturing output complies with the presence of increasing returns. The estimated ρ shows the existence of a significant endogenous interaction between productivity growth rates in different regions, suggestive of externalities operating across regional boundaries. Also, peripherality significantly reduces productivity growth and urban regions see significantly faster productivity growth, which we interpret as a boost emanating from the greater human capital of core, urban regions. Also, regions with an initially large technology gap experienced faster productivity growth, an effect attributed to the diffusion of innovations. The significant residual heterogeneity, with peripheral regions' productivity growth significantly more

variable than core regions', is perhaps indicative of the spatial and economic 'disconnectedness' of some of the peripheral economies.

The estimated model provides the empirical basis for stochastic equilibrium (Fingleton, 2000a). To show this, it is convenient to work in matrix algebra, so that

$$p = Xb + \rho Wp + \xi \tag{25}$$

with *Xb* denote the matrix product of the n by k matrix *X* and the k by one vector *b*. Matrix *X* comprises a column of ones, and columns corresponding to the values of q, G, L and D across n regions, *b* contains the coefficients $b_0\, b_1\, b_2\, b_3\, b_4$. We add the counter t to represent the iteration number, and rearrange the matrix equation so that one round of the iterative sequence, commencing with a random draw from the vector ξ, is as follows

$$\begin{aligned}
&\xi_t \sim N(0, \sigma_t^2 I) \\
&p_t = (I - \rho W)^{-1}(X_t b + \xi_t) \\
&P_{t+1} = P_t \exp(p_t) \\
&P^*_{t+1} = P^*_t \exp(p^*_t) \\
&G_{t+1} = 1 - \frac{P_{t+1}}{P^*_{t+1}} \\
&X_{t+1,v} = G_{t+1}
\end{aligned} \tag{26}$$

In order to run the iteration, we take the variables and estimates given in Table 2.1, with the exception of *q* which is assumed[22] to be equal to the EU mean for the 1975-1995 period. It seems unreasonable to assume that the differences between regions will be maintained in equilibrium, since in equilibrium productivity growth will be constant and that will induce constant output growth. The results of iterating from t = 1 to t = 100 are illustrated in Figure 2.8, which is the result of a single simulation. It is noticeable in this that the paths traced by the individual economies are not independent. Simultaneous reactions occur when the leadership changes, since then the fastest growing region replaces a slower growing region as productivity leader, and the other regions show a commensurate fall, showing up as peaks and valleys. These can also occur if there is no leadership change, if a large shock favors the leader's growth at the expense of the other regions, or causes a comparatively large slowdown. Moreover, because regions in disequilibrium interact spatially, we evidently have turbulence cycles of faster and slower growth as the net outcome of shocks simultaneously transmitted across regions. Rerunning the simulation using different random number streams produces the same phenomena, although the peaks and valleys are in different positions.

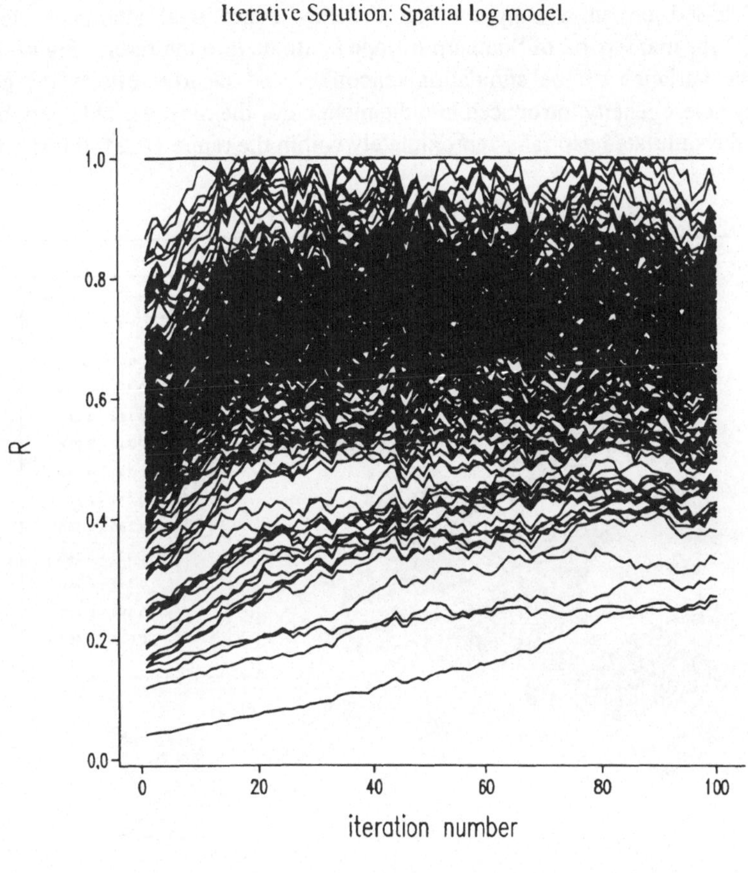

Figure 2.8 Simulated dynamics of 178 EU regions with shocks.

Figure 2.8 is a single realization that depends on the sequence of random numbers that the computer happened to generate. Clearly there are (at least in theory) infinitely many different realizations, and in order to illustrate an 'average' realization, we obtain the mean *G* for each region, having repeated the process used to create Figure 2.8 100 times, using a different random number sequence on each occasion. The result of this is a simulated EU mean[23] gap equal to 0.2801, with region-specific means distributed as in Figure 2.9. compared with historical EU means for 1975 and 1995 of 0.494 and 0.453 respectively. Figure 2.9 shows that the catching up experienced by some of the regions of Southern Europe over the period 1975-95 (see Figures 2.6 and 2.7) is not maintained in the long run. In Italy for instance, the simulation holds the gap in the vicinity of 0.4, which for many regions is no improvement on the 1995 position. This is however simply one scenario based on an assumption that the low educational attainment levels recorded[24] for many parts of Southern Europe continue into the future. Figure 2.10 shows the variance of the simulation outcomes, and clearly reflects the core-periphery heterogeneity introduced into the model. For the most variable peripheral regions, the simulated gap falls approximately within the range +/- $2 * \sqrt{0.003} \approx 0.1$.

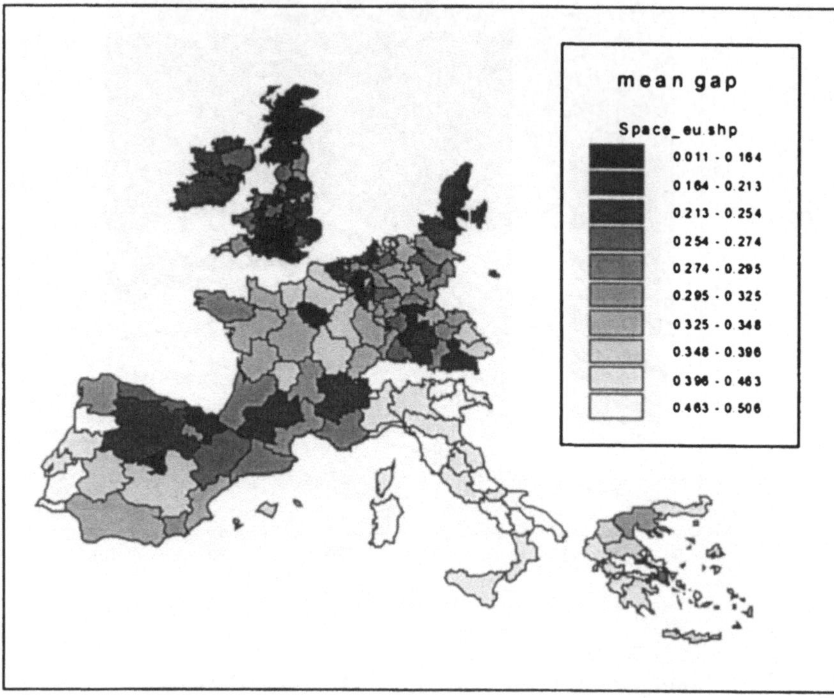

Figure 2.9 The mean manufacturing labor productivity gap (quantiles).

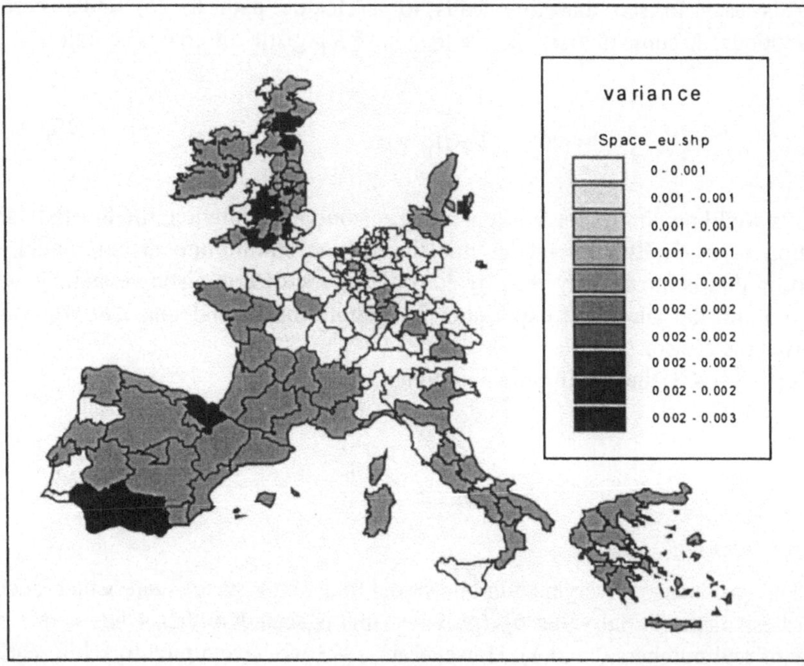

Figure 2.10 The variance of the manufacturing labour productivity gap (quantiles).

Complex Systems, Chaos and Mathematical Geographers

Outcomes like Figure 2.8 can be generated by a different mechanism, with parameter instability the driver rather than random shocks. The interest in this alternative source of chaos-like paths derives from empirical evidence[25] for across-time (and space) parameter instability, a topic that has been of interest to mathematical geographers using complex systems analysis to understand regional dynamics. For simplicity, let us consider our model of the previous section and examine how a lack of convergence may arise from allowing just one parameter to vary. The crucial parameter in the model is b_2, since it is the positive sign on this coefficient which causes regions with a lower level of technology gap (G) to experience faster productivity growth, and this is the fundamental cause of convergence to equilibrium in the model. Let us now assume that b_2 evolves through time such that

$$b_{2t} = \alpha b_{2t-1} - \beta b_{2t-1}^2 \qquad (27)$$

It is easy to see that this leads to a chaotic path for b_2 under certain assumptions. Assume that $\alpha = \beta$, we then have a logistic difference equation

$$b_{2t} = \alpha b_{2t-1}(1 - b_{2t-1}) \qquad \alpha \geq 0 \tag{28}$$

It is well known that for $0 \leq \alpha < 1$ there is only one solution, the locally stable solution $b_{2*} = 0$. But this means that there is no equilibrium in our model, an assertion that is most easily seen by considering the deterministic version (ie with $\xi_t = 0$) and the analytical expression for equilibrium (Fingleton, 2001b), which involves the divisor b_2.

For $1 < \alpha < 3$, the equilibrium solution is

$$b_{2*} = \frac{\alpha - 1}{\alpha} \tag{29}$$

This produces convergence in our model to a single steady-state which occurs regardless of the initial value b_{20} (provided this is scaled so that it lies within the range of real numbers 0 and 1). However at $\alpha = 3$ we have a pitchfork bifurcation and with $3 < \alpha < 3.449$ there exists a stable two-cycle solution which depend on α. The outcome for the regions is convergence at different alternating rates. A steady. state emerges in which each region cycles between two different growth rates and two different level of technology gaps, with the two-cycle solutions unique to each region. For $\alpha \geq 3.44949$ stable three and higher period cycles appear, but these break down for $\alpha \geq 3.5699456$ (the Feigenbaum point), when a deterministic chaos emerges, up to $\alpha = 4$, which marks the end of chaos. The outcome, typically, is paths indistinguishable from those of Figure 2.8. It appears that deterministic chaos is almost indistinguishable from stochastic equilibrium, although chaotic dynamics possess a hidden determinism. It is worth observing also that, depending on the value of α, a chaotic sequence can become quiescent and then suddenly switch to oscillatory behaviour, so chaos may be consistent with apparent stability. Within the context we have set for the possibility of chaos, as applying to a crucial parameter of our model, the consequence is not total chaos, but rather 'organized chaos'. A chaotic sequence for b_2 none the less means that, since each solution is positive, convergence will continue to occur, albeit in an unsmooth and unpredictable way. Paradoxically, it is when the b_2 sequence is non-chaotic and $b_{2*}=0$ that equilibrium is destroyed.

In the general context, modeling that involves developments in the mathematics of dynamic systems, chaos and complexity theory and the evolution of nonlinear systems opens a 'Pandora's box' of possibilities, in which 'other possible worlds' can be explored by simulation and experimentation. There are important methodological and conceptual implications for economic analysis, regional economics and regional science, and for geographical analysis, which are discussed by writers such as Arthur (1994), Beker (1999), Batten (2001), Marino (1999), Plummer (1999), Plummer and Sheppard (2001) and Wilson (2000). A general feature of the introduction of complexity and chaotic systems is that outcomes are often path dependent and involve the unpredictable evolution of systems far from equilibrium. Initial conditions are important, the outcome is highly sensitive to the choice of starting value. So, while the chaotic sequence is deterministic and hence in theory predictable, in practice it is quite unpredictable because what occurs depends fundamentally on the initial conditions, and we never know these precisely.

Summary

The analysis of regional and international variation in the growth and steady-state levels of GDP per capita or productivity has been strongly influenced by neoclassical orthodoxy in the form of the neoclassical growth model and the Barro-style regression model, which is the reduced form behind countless estimates of convergence to a common or differentiated steady state (conditional convergence). Conditional convergence appears to be somewhat more realistic than convergence to a common steady state even within the context of the European regions, but nevertheless it is evidently based on somewhat questionable underlying assumptions, notably diminishing returns, exogenously determined constant technical progress, and the existence of a stable steady state to which regions are converging, and this rather unreal theoretical foundation has encouraged regional economists to develop alternative, more realistic, approaches. Within the spectrum of alternative, non-orthodox theory, new economic geography emerges as an interesting development which, though closely tied to mainstream economic theory, is sufficiently different, accommodating increasing returns, (pecuniary) externalities, and multiple equilibria, to be considered un-orthodox, or perhaps not quite yet the current orthodoxy. The presence of multiple equilibria introduces the possibility that enhanced economic integration could cause a shift to a stable equilibrium in which the core of Europe is completely dominant, and thus helps cast further doubt on more conventional neoclassical analysis with the built-in presumption that poorer regions will tend to catch-up the richer regions and a more equal distribution of activity will naturally ensue. However, from an applied perspective it is still seen as a rather restricted theory in need of extension to be of real value for the scientific analysis of regional systems, particularly when the main focus of analysis is the estimation and simulation of possible scenarios for real, as opposed to artificial, systems of regions. Other approaches emphasize continuous change rather than assume that what we see are simply transition dynamics as economies shift from one equilibrium to another. Technological externalities are also given a prominent role in non-orthodox modelling as an influential force helping to preserve and deepen inter-regional disparity. In addition, in this chapter we have also placed some emphasis on systems model which seem somewhat in danger of written out of the story in the flurry of enthusiasm that surrounds new economic geography, but which still provides valuable insights. Of course all models are flawed, and we cannot know the future, and it therefore seems that the best strategy is to adopt an eclectic, multi-faceted stance that is open to new theoretical and empirical insights, and which maintains a probabilistic framework for any predictions that flow from our theory.

Notes

1 See Martin (1999) for a wide-ranging critique, or Neary (2001) for an economist's view of the technical limitations.

2 We might also wish to assume that savings and technical progress rates vary across regions.

3 In the literature it is a standard procedure to model GDP per worker (y) across regions or countries via the reduced form equation $(1/T)\log_e(y_t) = \alpha - (1/T)e^{-\beta T}\log_e(y_{t-T}) + u_t$, or this equation augmented by covariates to allow for differentiated steady states, estimated by iterative nonlinear least squares (NLS). The outcome is an estimate of the convergence rate β which is independent of length of time period T; and this method provides the standard error of β directly. However, it is also the case that the equation is intrinsically linear so it can be estimated by conventional OLS and the estimated β and its standard error can be recovered from the OLS estimates (see Fingleton, 1999a).

4 From the Taylor series expansion around the steady state, the growth of y at time t is approximately $-\beta$ times ($\ln y_{t-1} - \ln y_{t-1}^*$) plus the exogenous rate of technical progress (equal to the growth of y^*). So the rate of convergence β quantifies how the difference between y and y^* affects the growth of y and thus the y level in its path to convergence.

5 There are numerous other definitions that are possible, although the results obtained are often reasonably robust to minor variations in the specification of W, for instance different exponents, or a related functional form such as a negative exponential rather than power function.

6 An alternative mechanism is via inter-industry linkages, which 'provide another channel for agglomeration and lead to an analysis that is almost identical to that of labour mobility' (Neary, 2001).

7 The model turns out to be a set of nonlinear simultaneous equations with non-monotonic outcomes, which is hardly a recipe for ease of estimation.

8 The one chosen does not matter, the results generalise to a lag attached to the other equations.

9 Here we are discussing regional exports, so that there is no constraint on growth because of its possible effect on the balance of payments and exchange rates, it is assumed that the regions are in effect part of a single currency area.

10 Quah (1993) introduced the application of finite state space Markov processes to the study of economic dynamics.

11 A useful property of the Markov model is that it permits estimation of the time the system takes to evolve to the (stochastic) steady-state, thus facilitating comparison (Fingleton, 1999a) with the estimated time to convergence based on Barro-style regression analysis. We see that for the regions of the EU, the estimated time to (conditional) convergence is approximately 400 years in either case.

12 As embodied in the endogenous growth models of Grossman and Helpman (1994) and Aghion and Howitt (1992).

13 Fingleton (1984) and Upton and Fingleton (1989) discuss loyalty effects in different contexts.

14 The assumption here is that these are not mediated by the labour market (ie not pecuniary externalities as a result of unrealised investment in training being captured by new employers), but are outside the market.

15 As emphasised by Quah (2000).

16 Pinelli et al. (1998) consider a more sophisticated measure that distinguishes between peripheral regions that have different levels of accessibility, but the simpler measure used also here is just as successful in accounting for productivity variations.

17 A measure suggested as appropriate to Pinelli et al. (1998) by the European Commission.

18 Over the estimation period, W is assumed to be constant. However it might be argued that in the long run it is a function of time since $Q_{t+1} = Q_t exp(q_t)$. However in simulations, we typically assume constant q which has the effect that W is constant.

19 An advantage of standardisation is that it simplifies estimation and interpretation, since maximum likelihood entails that $\rho < 1/i^{max} = 1$ where i^{max} denotes the largest eigenvalue of W.

20 To accommodate the endogenous variable p.

21 Core regions are within 500km of Luxembourg.

22 The effects of relaxing this assumption are explored in a deterministic setting in Fingleton (2001b).

23 Equal to the mean of the region means.

24 In interpreting this, it is important to appreciate that educational attainment measures are potentially inconsistent across countries because of different standards employed.

25 Fingleton (2001a, 2002a,b) estimates models similar to that outlined above and shows that significant differences occur in parameter values through time and across space.

References

Abdel-Rahman, H. (1988), 'Product differentiation, monopolistic competition and city size', Regional Science and Urban Economics, vol. 18, pp. 69-86.

Abdel-Rahman, H. and Fujita, M. (1990), 'Product variety, Marshallian externalities and city size', *Journal of Regional Science*, vol. 30, pp. 165-183.

Aghion, P. and Howitt, P. (1992), 'A model of growth through creative destruction', *Econometrica*, vol. 60, pp. 323-351.

Amiti, M. (1998), 'New trade theories and industrial location in the EU: a survey of evidence', *Oxford Review of Economic Policy*, vol. 14, 45-53.

Anselin, L. (1988), *Spatial Econometrics: Methods and Models*, Kluwer Academic Publishers, Dordrecht.

Arrow, K.J. (1962), 'The economic implications of learning by doing', *Review of Economic Studies*, vol. 29, pp. 155-173.

Arthur, W.B. (1994), *Increasing Returns and Path Dependence in the Economy*, University of Michigan Press, Ann Arbor.

Baldwin, R.E. and Forslid, R. (2000), 'The core-periphery model and endogenous growth: stabilizing and destabilizing integration', *Economica*, vol. 67, pp. 307-324.

Barro, R.J. (1991), 'Economic growth in a cross section of countries', *Quarterly Journal of Economics*, vol. 106, pp. 407-443.

Barro, R.J. and Sala-i-Martin, X. (1995), *Economic Growth*, McGraw Hill Inc., New York.

Bartholomew, D.J. (1981), *Mathematical Models in Social Science*, Wiley, Chichester.

Batten, D.F. (2001), 'Complex landscapes and spatial interaction', *Annals of Regional Science*, vol. 35, pp. 81-111.

Beker, V.A. (1999), 'Non-linear dynamics and chaos in economics', in S.B. Dahiya (ed.), *The Current State of Economic Science Volume 1*, Spellbound Publications, Rhotak, pp. 169-193.

Brakman, S., Garretsen, H. and van Marrewijk, C. (2001), *An introduction to geographical economics*, Cambridge University Press, Cambridge.

Bulli, S. (2001), 'Distribution dynamics and cross-country convergence: a new approach', *Scottish Journal of Political Economy*, vol. 48, pp. 226-243.

Cheshire, P. and Carbonaro, G. (1995), 'Convergence-divergence in regional growth rates: an empty black box?', in H.W. Armstrong and R.W. Vickerman (eds), *Convergence and Divergence among European Regions*, European Research in Regional Science, Pion, London, pp. 89-111.

Cheshire, P. and Magrini, S. (2000), 'Endogenous processes in European regional growth: convergence and policy', *Growth and Change*, vol. 31, pp. 455-479.

Dixit, A. and Stiglitz, J. (1977), 'Monopolistic competition and optimal product diversity', *American Economic Review*, vol. 67, pp. 297-308.

Dixon, R.J. and Thirlwall, A.P. (1975), 'A model of regional growth rate differences on Kaldorian lines', *Oxford Economic Papers*, vol. 27, pp. 201-14.

Fingleton, B. (1984), *Models of Category Counts*, Cambridge University Press, Cambridge.

Fingleton, B. (1997), 'Specification and testing of Markov chain models: an application to convergence in the European Union', *Oxford Bulletin of Economics and Statistics*, vol. 59, pp. 385-403.

Fingleton, B. (1998), 'Regional economic growth and convergence: insights from a spatial econometric perspective', paper presented at *Regional Science Association Conference*, November, Santa Fe, New Mexico.

Fingleton, B. (1999a), 'Estimates of time to economic convergence: an analysis of regions of the European Union', *International Regional Science Review*, vol. 22, pp. 5-35.

Fingleton, B. (1999b), 'Generalised linear models, loglinear models and regional dynamics', in S.B. Dahiya (ed.), *The Current State of Economic Science Volume 1*, Spellbound Publications, Rhotak, pp. 285-307.

Fingleton, B. (2000a), 'Spatial econometrics, economic geography, dynamics and equilibrium: a third way?', *Environment and Planning A*, vol. 32, pp. 1481-1498.

Fingleton, B. (2000b), 'Convergence: international comparisons based on a simultaneous equation model with regional effects', *International Review of Applied Economics*, vol. 14, pp. 285-305.

Fingleton, B. (2001a), 'Theoretical economic geography and spatial econometrics: dynamic perspectives', *Journal of Economic Geography*, vol. 1, pp. 201-225.

Fingleton, B. (2001b), 'Equilibrium and economic growth: Spatial econometric models and simulations', *Journal of Regional Science*, vol. 41, pp. 117-148.

Fingleton, B. (2002a), 'Theoretical economic geography and spatial econometrics: Bridging the gap between theory and reality', in H. Zoller, A. Getis and J. Mur (eds), *Advances in Spatial Econometrics*, McMillan, London, forthcoming.

Fingleton, B. (2002b), 'Space-time contrasts in European manufacturing productivity growth: implications for theory and development', *Proceedings of the International Seminar on Economy and Space*, Faculty of Economics, Federal University of Minas, Gerais, Brazil.

Fingleton, B. (2002c), 'Regional economic growth and convergence: insights from a spatial econometric perspective', in L. Anselin and R. Florax (eds), *New Advances in Spatial Econometrics*, Springer-Verlag, Heidelberg.

Fingleton, B. and López-Bazo, E. (2002), 'Explaining the distribution of manufacturing productivity in the EU regions', in B. Fingleton (ed.), *European Regional Growth*, Springer-Verlag, Heidelberg, forthcoming.

Fingleton, B. and McCombie, J. (1998), 'Increasing returns and economic growth: some evidence for manufacturing from the European Union regions', *Oxford Economic Papers*, vol. 50, pp. 89-105.

Fingleton, B. and McCombie, J. (1999), 'Increasing returns and economic growth: some evidence for manufacturing from the European Union regions: a correction', *Oxford Economic Papers*, vol. 51, pp. 574-575.

Fujita, M. and Thisse, J-F. (1996), 'Economics of agglomeration', *Journal of the Japanese and International Economies*, vol. 10, pp. 339-378.

Fujita, M., Krugman, P. and Venables, A.J. (1999), *The Spatial Economy*, MIT Press, Cambridge and Massachusetts.

Glaeser, E., Kallal, H., Scheinkman, J. and Shleifer, A. (1992), 'Growth in cities', *Journal of Political Economy*, vol. 100, pp. 1126-1152.

Grossman, G.M. and Helpman, E. (1991), *Innovation and Growth in the World Economy*, MIT Press, Cambridge.

Grossman, G.M. and Helpman, E. (1994), 'Endogenous innovation in the theory of growth', *Journal of Economic Perspectives*, vol. 8, pp. 23-44.

Jones, C.I. (1995), 'R&D-based models of Economic growth', *Journal of Political Economy*, vol. 103, pp. 759-784.

Jones, C.I. (1997), 'Convergence revisited', *Journal of Economic Growth*, vol. 2, pp. 131-153.

Kaldor, N. (1970), 'The case for regional policies', *Scottish Journal of Political Economy*, vol. 17, pp. 37-48.

Kaldor, N. (1972), 'The irrelevance of equilibrium economics', *Economic Journal*, vol. 82, pp. 1237-1255.

Krugman, P. (1991), *Geography and Trade*, Leuven University Press and MIT press, Cambridge and Massachusetts.

Krugman, P. (1998), 'What's new about the new economic geography?', *Oxford Review of Economic Policy*, vol. 14, pp. 7-16.

Levine, R. and Renelt, D. (1992), 'A sensitivity analysis of cross-country growth regressions', *American Economic Review*, vol. 82, pp. 942-963.

Lucas, R.E. Jr (1988), 'On the mechanics of development planning', *Journal of Monetary Economics*, vol. 22, no. 1, pp. 3-42.

Mankiw, N.G., Romer, D. and Weil, D.N. (1992), 'A contribution to the empirics of economic growth', *Quarterly Journal of Economics*, vol. 107, pp. 407-437.

Marino, D. (1999), 'Dynamics and complexity in economics', in S.B. Dahiya (ed.), *The Current State of Economic Science Volume 1*, pp. 149-167.

Martin, P. and Ottaviano, G.I.P. (1999), 'Growing locations in a model of endogenous growth', *European Economic Review*, vol. 43, pp. 281-302.

Martin, R. (1999), 'The new 'geographical turn' in economics: some critical reflections', *Cambridge Journal of Economics*, vol. 23, pp. 65-91.

McCombie, J.S.L. and Thirlwall, A.P. (1994), *Economic Growth and the Balance-of-Payments constraint*, McMillan, Basingstoke.

Myrdal, G. (1957), *Economic Theory and Underdeveloped Regions*, Duckworth, London.

Neary, J.P. (2001), 'Of hype and hyperbolas: introducing the new economic geography', *Journal of Economic Literature*, vol. XXXIX, pp. 536-561.

Pinelli, D., Giacometti, R., Lewney, R. and Fingleton, B. (1998), *European Regional Competitiveness Indicators*, Discussion Paper Series 103, Department of Land Economy, Cambridge University, pp. 1-67.

Plummer, P. (1999), 'Capital accumulation, economic restructuring, and nonequilibrium regional growth dynamics', *Geographical Analysis*, vol. 31, pp. 267-287.

Plummer, P. and Sheppard, E. (2001), 'Must emancipatory economic geography be qualitative', *Antipode*, vol. 33, pp. 194-199.

Quah, D. (1993), 'Empirical cross-section dynamics in economic growth', *European Economic Review*, vol. 37, pp. 426-434.

Quah, D. (1997), 'Empirics for growth and distribution; polarization, stratification, and convergence clubs', *Journal of Economic Growth*, vol. 2, pp. 27-59.

Quah, D. (2000), *Technology Dissemination and Economic Growth, Some Lessons for the New Economy*, University of Hong Kong public lecture, 90th Anniversary celebrations.

Quigley, J.M. (1998), 'Urban Diversity and Economic Growth', *Journal of Economic Perspectives*, vol. 12, pp. 127–138.

Rey, S. (2001), 'Spatial empirics for economic growth and convergence', *Geographical Analysis*, vol. 33, pp. 195-214.

Rivera-Batiz, F. (1988), 'Increasing returns, monopolistic competition and agglomeration economies in consumption and production', *Regional Science and Urban Economics*, vol. 18, pp. 125-153.

Romer, P.M. (1986), 'Increasing returns and long-run growth', *Journal of Political Economy*, vol. 94, pp. 1002-1037.

Romer, P.M. (1987), 'Growth based on Increasing Returns due to Specialization', *American Economic Review Papers and Proceedings*, vol. 77, pp. 56-72.

Romer, P.M. (1990), 'Endogenous Technical Change', *Journal of Political Economy*, vol. 98, pp. 71-102 .

Romer, P.M. (1994), 'The origins of endogenous growth', *Journal of Economic Perspectives*, vol. 8, pp. 3-22.

Schmutzler, A. (1999), 'The new economic geography', *Journal of Economic Surveys*, vol. 13, pp. 355-379.

Solow, R.M. (1956), 'A contribution to the theory of economic growth', *Quarterly Journal of Economics*, vol. 70, no. 1, pp. 65-94.

Swan, T.W. (1956), 'Economic growth and capital accumulation', *Economic Record*, vol. 32, pp. 334-361.

Upton, G.J.G. and Fingleton, B. (1989), *Spatial Data Analysis by Example Volume 2*, Wiley, Chichester.

Verdoorn, P.J. (1949), 'Fattori che regolano lo sviluppo della produttivita del lavoro', *L'Industria*, vol. 1, pp. 3-10.

Wilson, A.G. (2000), *Complex Spatial Systems*, Prentice Hall, Harlow.

Chapter 3

Growth and Convergence Across Economies: The Experience of the European Regions

Enrique López-Bazo

Introduction

Economies grow in the long run. Long term data on labor productivity and income per inhabitant in a set of developed and developing economies tend to support this statement (Maddison, 1995), but there is a certain amount of controversy on some related questions in the literature. Particularly relevant is the absence of consensus on whether growth promotes equalization of productivity, income, and thus welfare across economies. If growth is negatively related to the level of income already achieved, then initially poor and rich economies will tend to show similar levels in the future. Otherwise, the rich ones will remain rich and the poor ones will remain poor, and the gap between them might still increase. Particularly in the latter situation, it may be that policies need to be designed to help poor regions to grow faster. But even in this case, doubts have been raised as to the effectiveness of such policies to enhance growth in the less advanced economies.

Among the large amount of theoretical and empirical contributions on economic growth in the recent literature, there are some that have particularly focused on economic convergence. That is the process by which income per capita tends to equalize across economies. In connection with predictions drawn from the theoretical models of growth, empirical settings have been developed to test the convergence hypothesis. However, the analysis of this literature reveals that the strategies designed for the purpose of testing involve differences in the concept of convergence. For instance, convergence in some of the most popular frameworks can only be construed as poor economies cutting the gap with the rich ones under particular conditions.

Regions within a country, or in a set of integrated economies, such as the European Union, are supposed to be more homogeneous than a set of worldwide economies. The technology of production, consumer preferences, institutions, and so on may be thought to be largely similar across regions. In addition, it is sensible to think that the diffusion of ideas and technology is easier across regions than when heterogeneous societies are involved. As a consequence, convergence is supposed to be a more sensible assumption in this case. The deepening in the process of integration over recent decades should have caused, under this scenario, a reduction in the amount of regional disparities in the EU. However, the literature has identified forces that might counteract the tendency towards convergence. In all, the outcome of these theoretical contributions largely relies on model assumptions and the empirical evidence concerning the EU is mixed, although there is some consensus on certain empirical regularities. In any case, a trip around different areas in the EU easily reveals differences nowadays in the structure of production and the level of income.

In this chapter, I first provide a brief review of the predictions made by the most popular models on comparative growth and the evolution of disparities in income per capita between economies. Then I discuss the methods that have been proposed to check for convergence in a set of economies, concluding in favor of those that consider the study of the whole distribution of the variables under analysis, when convergence is defined as the poor catching up with the rich. In the second part of the chapter, I analyze convergence in product per capita and labor productivity, in a wide set of EU regions, over the period 1975-1996. Additionally, I attempt to assess to what extent dispersion and the other characteristics of the regional distribution of the above-mentioned variables have to do with membership of a country and geographical location, and to what extent they are related to agglomeration and the industrial mix.

Growth Models and Convergence

The analysis of the causes of long-run growth has always been among the major topics of economists. Economic growth is supposed to increase the welfare of the population, so academic results in this field have a clear social impact. In the last few decades a lot of research effort has been devoted to the aim of improving the knowledge of the growth process, both from a theoretical and empirical perspective. The results of such efforts have surely influenced the design of policies at various levels, and even the behavior of agents involved in such a process (individuals, firms, governments, institutions…). An important side effect of economic growth has to do with the relative performance of any given economy when compared with that of the other economies, that is to say, with comparative growth. In this regard, part of the research on growth has focused on economic convergence, as well as policies aimed at fighting against aggregate inequality. A good example of that is the interest in the amount of spatial inequality within the European Union, both at the level of countries and at the regional level. Not only can growth theories help explain comparative growth within the EU, but they have probably influenced policymakers when designing policies aimed at fostering convergence.

Using a rough though useful typology, we can divide growth models into two broad and popular categories: neoclassical and endogenous models. The textbook neoclassical model (Solow, 1956; Swan, 1956) assumes decreasing returns to scale in the technology of production, leaving long-run growth as something caused by (exogenous) technical progress. The steady-state level of output per effective labor is then a function of technological parameters and preferences (return to capital, saving rate, level of technology, depreciation rate, population growth…), thus something that cannot be easily influenced by policies. As a side effect of the model, it can be derived that economies with equal production technologies and preferences share a common steady state stock of capital by effective unit of labor, and then a common long run level of output by effective labor. Additionally, as long as all the economies benefit from technical progress, growth in technology, and then long run growth in output per worker, would be equal across economies.

The assumption of decreasing returns to capital accumulation in the neoclassical model has the consequence that, in the transition to the steady state, each economy follows an interesting rule: the higher the distance to the steady state, the faster the growth. This means that for two economies sharing a common steady state, the model predicts that the poorest one will grow faster than the richest. Therefore, as a general outcome, the neoclassical model of growth predicts convergence across economies. Convergence can be qualified as absolute or strong when all the economies converge to the same steady state, and technology flows easily across economies, as then long-run growth of output per worker will be the same for all of them. Conditional convergence, by contrast, is convergence to different steady states, and when there are barriers to the transmission and absorption of technology across economies. In this regard, it should be stressed that trade and factors mobility is a requirement for the convergence mechanisms of decreasing returns and diffusion of technology to produce an effect (Boldrin and Canova, 2001). As long as further integration and decrease in transport costs favor both, one would expect the process of EU construction to be causing convergence under the scenario outlined by the neoclassical model of growth.

The neoclassical model of growth leaves technology growth as something exogenously driven. In essence, that means that long run productivity growth cannot be explained within the model. In the mid eighties, theoretical contributions, built on the earlier ideas of, for instance, Kaldor (1957) and Arrow (1962), started to explain the determinants of growth endogenously (Romer, 1986; Lucas, 1988). In short, long run growth is the outcome of endogenous growth models as they leave aside decreasing returns. Non-decreasing returns make further investments not less profitable than the previous ones, and thus feed the growth process. In such models, the accumulation of several kinds of capital (human, public, social, technological…) favors technological progress, so that private capital and labor get a higher return when combined with those types of capital. Additionally, their effect might be enhanced by the existence of externalities in the process of accumulation. For example, the profits of R&D investments are not limited to the firm that makes the investment, but other firms will also benefit by, for instance, using the products that embody the technology generated by the investment (see, among others, Grossman and Helpman, 1991).

The consequence of the endogenous growth assumptions for comparative growth follows immediately: there is no role for convergence, as economies which already have large stocks of capital (i.e. which are more productive) will experience faster growth. The 'endogenous growth world' is thus characterized by the spatial agglomeration of economic activity. Economically dense areas will have higher agglomeration economies, leading to larger increasing returns and thus faster growth[1]. In this regard, it should be stressed that endogenous models of growth, contributions from the new economic geography, and those from regional economics, lead to similar conclusions: increasing returns and agglomeration economies attract activity towards the advanced economies, worsening the position of the poor ones. Congestion is the force that prevents complete concentration in a single economy, as firms and workers are discouraged by, among other factors, the price of land, real wages and the costs of living, which increase with agglomeration. Spatial inequalities are supposed to persist (non-convergence), and even increase (divergence), under such a framework, although diffusion of technology across economies, and rapid absorption of such technology by the lagging economies, might in some cases reverse this situation ('miracles').

As long as integration reduces transport costs and eases factors mobility, we should predict further concentration of activity in highly agglomerated economies, if the assumptions of the endogenous family of models are correct. Therefore, further integration translates into more spatial inequality[2].

Considering the outcome of the neoclassical model, and that of the endogenous model, policies can be designed either to enforce convergence or to alleviate divergence. If economic growth in the EU is appropriately characterized by neoclassical assumptions, integration may be expected to foster growth in the less developed regions. In such a case, EU policies should contribute to i) equalize the fundamentals of the less advanced regions with those of the more productive ones, and ii) make diffusion and absorption of technology easier and faster. If, on the contrary, growth is governed by non-decreasing technology and net agglomeration forces then integration will not tend to promote the equalization of regional economies. In such a situation, policies should favor local conditions in the less developed regions to ensure that they can break even. That is to say, policies should compensate agglomeration economies in the rich regions, by at least equalizing the returns that private capital gets in the poor regions with those it gets in the rich ones. In this regard, increasing amounts of funds have been allocated by the EU with the aim of balancing out regional economic activity. However, there is a controversy about the real effects of that policy[3]. Although the evidence is mixed, one general conclusion is that there are some particular positive experiences ('miracles'), but there is no generalized positive effect across the recipient regions. This suggests that results might be influenced by local conditions in each region. For example, the profitability of EU funds might be different if the stock of capital in the recipient area has already reached a certain threshold, as suggested by Azariadis and Drazen (1990), and the literature following their contribution. It might also be thought to depend on the entrepreneurship structure in that economy.

The location of large firms and FDI, looking for low congested areas and low relative wages, might well be influenced by such incentives, but the final outcome might also depend on the likelihood of the endogenous generation of a system of dynamic SMEs that, among other things, might exploit the benefits of forward and backward linkages within the region.

Empirical Analysis, Methodologies and Data

β- and σ-convergence

Influenced by the contrasting predictions of growth models, the empirical convergence analysis has become increasingly popular in recent decades. Initial studies of the convergence hypothesis tested, in a rather ad hoc manner, whether the poor economies in a given sample had experienced faster growth than the rich ones (Baumol, 1986; Dolar and Wolff, 1988). But it was in the early nineties that the negative relationship between growth rates and initial product per capita under the neoclassical assumptions was demonstrated (Mankiw et al, 1992; Barro and Sala-i-Martin, 1992). Additionally, it was shown that, under such a scenario, dispersion in the distribution of product per capita in a set of economies should decrease over time. In all, the concepts of β- and σ-convergence became very popular.

Tests of the β-convergence hypothesis have been based on specifications of the following form:

$$g_y = \text{constant} + \lambda \ln Y_0 + X\gamma + \varepsilon \qquad \textbf{(1)}$$

where g_y is the rate of growth of product per capita over a period of dimension T, Y_0 is product per capita at the beginning of the period, $\lambda = (1-e^{-\beta T})/T$ and β is the rate of convergence. X collects observations for the economies in the sample on variables aiming at controlling differences in the steady state and technology across economies (capital accumulation rates, population growth, sectoral composition, socio-political characteristics...), and γ is the compatible vector of coefficients for such variables. Finally, ε is a perturbance that reflects the non-deterministic nature of the growth process, as well as the influence of omitted factors.

In the simplest neoclassical model $\beta=(1-\alpha)(n+g+d)$, where α is the return to capital and (n+g+d) the effective rate of depreciation. Therefore $\alpha<0$ implies $\beta>0$, and then (β-) convergence. Convergence is qualified as absolute when β is estimated as greater than zero, without the need to control for the variables in X. In contrast, conditional convergence is the conclusion when X is required to get that result. Empirical results provide weak evidence for absolute convergence in samples of countries including developed and developing economies. This type of convergence is only observed when tested on more homogeneous samples of, for instance, OECD countries. Nevertheless, when controlling for differences across countries in an assorted number of variables[4], conditional convergence is the usual outcome. Lots of studies have also tested β-convergence using samples of regional economies (Sala-i-Martin, 1996; Armstrong, 1995). In that case, it is more likely to lead to absolute convergence, as regions are more homogeneous economies than countries are. Although there is evidence supporting such an assumption (US states, Japan, Canada, regions within EU member states), the rate of (absolute) convergence has clearly declined since the mid-eighties, and doubts have been raised as to its significance for some samples.

The estimated rate of β-convergence in most cross-section samples is around 2 per cent per year. This is a low rate that is only compatible with a broad definition of capital (that includes, for instance, human capital). Recent studies, however, have estimated higher rates by pooling cross-section and time series, and controlling for fixed economy effects. This means allowing for separate steady states for each economy in the sample[5]. Estimates of the rate of convergence in these cases are much higher (around and above 10 per cent per year). Actually, López-Bazo et al (2001), in a meta-analysis of the Spanish literature, show how controlling for fixed effects makes the most important difference in the estimates of the rate of convergence. However, it should be stressed that this is the most extreme case of conditional convergence, as each economy in the sample is converging to its own steady state. This has clear consequences if we want to draw conclusions from these results concerning the evolution of inequality within the sample of economies. More generally, the problem is one of drawing conclusions concerning the dynamics of the whole distribution of product per capita on the basis of the inference obtained from an average economy in the sample (Quah, 1996a).

The other measure of convergence addresses the evolution of inequality in the distribution of product per capita. σ-convergence implies that a measure of the dispersion within the distribution (the standard deviation of the logarithm of product per capita) tends to decrease over time. This pattern has been observed for homogeneous samples of economies (including sets of regions), although the process stopped in the eighties in almost all cases (Boldrin and Canova, 2001). However, it should be noticed that this measure of convergence neglects some interesting features of the distribution, for instance the convergence of some groups of economies to separate steady states.

Convergence as Distribution Dynamics

As a result of these criticisms of β- and σ-convergence, Quah (1993, 1996a) proposed a methodology for analysing comparative growth, using the information provided by the whole distribution of product per capita. The analysis of the dynamics of the distribution then provides us with evidence that allows us to address questions that are of interest when convergence is defined as the process by which the gap between poor and rich economies tends to diminish. When this is the case, the distribution tends to collapse to a single point, in the long run. Otherwise, it might remain stable or even increase its dispersion. More interestingly, focusing the analysis on the whole distribution permits the detection of convergence clubs: that is, groups of economies converging to separate levels of product per capita. Neither β-convergence nor σ-convergence supply evidence for this phenomenon.

Two features of the distribution of product per capita in a set of economies are of interest. First, the (external) shape of the distribution and the way it evolves over time. The shape of the distribution can be proxied by the estimation of the density function of the distribution. The density function can be estimated non-parametrically by the kernel method. The kernel density estimator replaces the 'boxes' in a histogram by smooth 'bumps' (Silverman, 1986). Smoothing is done by putting less weight on observations that are further removed from the point being evaluated. (A more detailed description is given in the Appendix.)

The external shape of two or more distributions can be compared by means of the estimated density functions. More specifically, the change in the shape of the distribution, over the period under analysis, can be assessed by comparing the density function for product per capita in different years. This point can be illustrated by using some simulated distributions. Let us assume that in period t_0 the distribution of product per capita in a set of economies is given by panel a in Figure 3.1. This is the kernel estimate of the density function for a random sample of 108 observations drawn from a normal distribution, with expected value equal to 100, and standard deviation equal to 20. K-periods ahead, t_0+k, the distribution shows less dispersion; that is, it is more concentrated around the average (Panel b in Figure 3.1). Actually, it belongs to a sample drawn from a normal distribution in which the standard deviation equals 10. The conclusion should be that the distribution is in the process of collapsing around the average, and thus that the economies in the sample are converging. By contrast, divergence would be the conclusion if the latter distribution was more dispersed.

Obviously, the comparison of the estimated variance for both distributions would have produced the same conclusion. But, as has been stated before, there are some other possibilities. For instance, panel c in Figure 3.1 depicts a situation in which the distribution in t_0+k is characterized by two peaks. This means that there are two clusters of economies; one with product per capita well behind the average (in fact the average for that group in the simulation is set at 30 per cent) and another one above the average (its average was set at 120 per cent). This points to the existence of convergence clubs. Traditional measures of dispersion fail to detect such a situation[6].

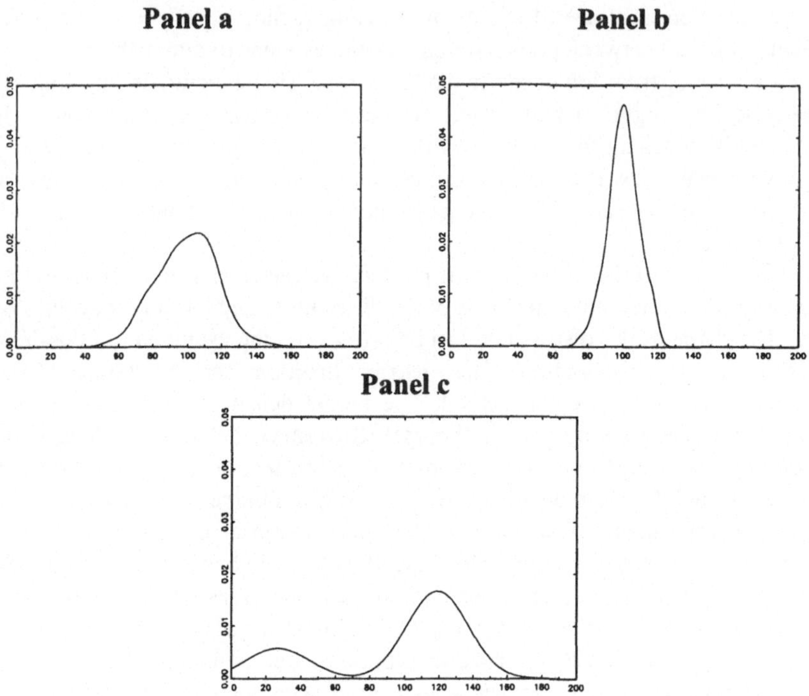

Figure 3.1 Estimated density functions for simulated distributions.

The second important feature has to do with intra-distribution mobility. It is important to recognize that the external shape can remain unaltered, even when there is churning in the distribution. In other words, the shape of the distribution at two points in time might be the same, but the implications would differ if the poor economies remain poor and the rich remain rich, compared with the situation in which a significant degree of churning occurs, so that those who are the poor at the beginning are now the rich, and vice versa. Thus, the focus of intra-distribution dynamics analysis is to reveal how economies transit from any point in the distribution to any other point, which, at its simplest, involves estimating the probability of a poor economy staying poor or becoming rich. In a discrete setting, this means estimating the matrix of probabilities of transitions between different states. Additionally, intra-distribution dynamics can be analyzed, from a continuous perspective, through the estimation of a stochastic kernel (Stokey and Lucas, 1989) for the distribution of income per capita over the period under analysis. This is merely the counterpart of a first-order Markov probability of transitions matrix, where the number of states tends to infinity; that is to say, where the length of the range of income defining each state tends to zero. Thus, the stochastic kernel provides the likelihood of transiting from one place in the range of values of income to the others[7].

Panel a

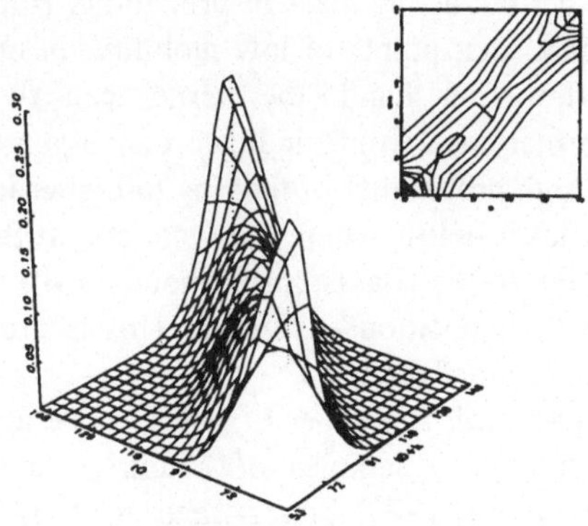

Panel b

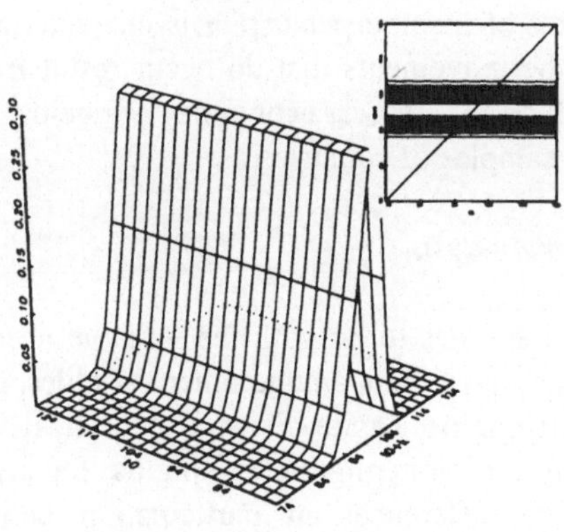

Figure 3.2 Estimated stochastic kernel for simulated distributions.

A more precise description of the estimation of the stochastic kernel can be found in the appendix, but to illustrate the interpretation it may be worthwhile to comment on the results obtained from simulated data. Figure 3.2 collects the graphs that are used to depict the stochastic kernel. The three-dimensional graph, for each value of product per capita at time t_0, shows the probability density k periods ahead, conditional on the density of that value at t_0. That is, it provides the probability of an economy starting at any level of product per capita at t_0 ending up at any of the values after k years. The z-axis in the three-dimensional plot measures the conditional density of each pair of points in the x-y space that defines the values of the variable at t_0 and t_0+k. The lines that run parallel to the t_0+k axis measure the probability of transiting from the corresponding point in the t_0 axis to any other point k periods ahead. The two-dimensional graph in the top right corner is a contour plot of the three-dimensional plot. The lines in this graph connect points at the same height on the three-dimensional plot, that is, points with the same density. Then, panel a in Figure 3.2 reveals that no significant movements occurred over the period, as the mass of probability (the kernel) is allocated along the positive diagonal, that points to low mobility; in other words, there is strong persistence. On the other hand, the kernel can twist clockwise or counter clockwise. The former case would indicate convergence in the distribution, with the poor having a high probability of moving to higher levels, while the rich would tend to move to a level below where they started. At the limit, when the mass of probability is parallel to the t_0-axis, all economies will end up at similar values in t_0+k regardless of their position at time t_0. This is precisely what the stochastic kernel in panel b in Figure 3.2 shows.

Since Quah's proposal, a number of papers have applied this methodology to analyze relative growth in samples of countries and regions (Bianchi, 1997; Fingleton, 1997; Magrini, 1999; López-Bazo et al, 1999; Johnson, 2000; Lamo, 2000). A general conclusion that can be drawn from this diverse set of papers is that the distribution of income per capita is characterized by notable persistence and, if anything, the movements that do occur result from an ongoing process of polarization, in which the poorest economies are being left behind, particularly in the case of a wide samples of countries.

The Variable under Analysis

A final important issue has to do with the variable used to test the hypothesis of convergence. Studies have used, among other variables, product per capita, product per worker, and income per capita. From a theoretical viewpoint, the selection of the precise variable can be negligible as long as, for instance, full employment is assumed. However, differences in participation and employment rates, and deviations between the amount produced and the disposable income of the inhabitants of a given economy, might lead to contrasting conclusions, depending on the variable under analysis. As there are notable differences in participation and unemployment rates across the EU member states and regions, the analysis in the next section will be based on both product per inhabitant and labor productivity (product per worker). In so doing, I will be able to assess whether the process of convergence or divergence is common to both magnitudes or whether, on the contrary, there are differences between them.

The set of regions included in the analysis consists of 108 regions of the 12 first-entry countries in the EU. These data come primarily from the REGIO database, elaborated by EUROSTAT, the Statistical Office of the EU. However, data from different sources, at the member state level, have been used for some regions and years. That data was collected and homogenized in the ESOC-Lab at the London School of Economics. The data set includes 3 NUTS1 regions for Belgium, 21 NUTS2 for France, 11 NUTS1 for Germany, 13 NUTS2 for Greece,

20 NUTS2 for Italy, 4 NUTS1 for The Netherlands, 5 NUTS2 for Portugal, 17 NUTS2 for Spain, and 11 NUTS1 for the UK. Denmark, Ireland and Luxembourg are included as single regions. In all, we have considered a sample of almost contiguous regions for 12 EU member states. The data covers the period from 1975 to 1996, although most of the official REGIO data starts in 1980. For that reason we will provide results for the period that starts in 1975 and for that starting in 1980. Additionally, I will present results for two subperiods. The first covers the period up to 1985 and the second the period from that year to 1996. The idea is to allow for differences in the process of convergence due to different patterns of growth in both subperiods and, basically, to analyze the effect of the deepening on the process of integration which started in the late eighties. Besides, most of the less advanced regions in the sample belong to the member states who joined the EU at the beginning of the second subperiod. Thus, the results could help to determine the net effect of the process of integration on those economies.

Some Evidence for the EU Regions

To start with, I estimate the growth equation given by (1) for the sample of EU regions in the whole period and for both subperiods. I estimate the rate of absolute convergence in GDP per capita, and in GDP per worker, by using a cross section of growth rates over the period and the initial level of the variable. Conditional convergence was estimated by including the shares of sectoral employment in total employment, population density, a measure of market potential (the weighted sum of GDP in the other regions, using the inverse of distance as weights), and the average temperature in each region. By adding these variables, I aim to capture differences in the steady states and temporary shocks that might affect growth rates over the period. Additionally, β-convergence is estimated by using the pool of annual growth rates and 5-yearly growth rates, controlling for unobservable regional fixed effects. That means allowing for separate regional steady states.

The results are summarized in Table 3.1. As for GDP per capita, significant absolute β-convergence is observed, with a rate slightly behind the usual 2 per cent per year from 1975 to 1996, although it decreases to 0.89 per cent when using the period 1980-1996. Significant rates are detected for both subperiods, but the already reported reduction in the speed of convergence is observed. The coefficient in the first subperiod doubles the one in the period starting in the mid-eighties. When growth rates are conditioned to regional differences in the variables described above, the rate of (conditional) convergence increases somewhat in the whole period (going from 1.81 per cent in the absolute convergence case to 2.10 per cent in the conditional one). As expected, allowing for separate steady state by estimating a panel data fixed effects model produces the major change in the estimates of the rate of convergence for the EU regions. It is estimated to be as high as 25.36 per cent (36 per cent) per year for annual (5-yearly) growth rates[8]. However, it needs to be noted that this result should be interpreted as fast convergence of a representative region in the sample to its own steady state. It has nothing to do with the GDP per capita of the less advanced regions in the EU converging to the level of the richest regions. Notable differences are observed when comparing estimates of the rate of convergence for GDP per capita and GDP per worker. In the latter case, estimates of the rate of convergence are higher, pointing to faster convergence across regions in labor productivity than in GDP per capita in the EU. Interestingly, the decrease in the rate of convergence observed in the second subperiod for GDP per capita is not detected in the case of productivity. On the contrary, in this case it goes up to 4 per cent. However convergence to separate steady states seems to be much slower for labor productivity than it is for GDP per capita. This suggests more rapid adjustments of GDP per capita through employment rates and participation decisions when regions are hit by shocks, whereas adjustments that affect productivity require longer periods.

Table 3.1 Estimates of the rate of convergence for the EU regions.

	Cross-section				Panel data	
		Absolute convergence		Conditional convergence[a]	Fixed regional effects	
	1975-96 (1980-96)	1975-85	1985-96	1975-96	annual	5-years
GDP per capita	1.81% (0.89%)	2.52%	1.20%	2.10%	25.36%	36.03%
GDP per worker	2.59% (2.87%)	1.86%	3.94%	3.14%	9.54%	9.72%

[a] The variables included in the regression were the sectoral composition, density, market potential and climate.

Note: Figures refer to the estimated rate of annual convergence. All the estimates were significant at the 1 per cent level.

Focusing the convergence analysis on the whole regional distribution of GDP per capita and per worker in the EU, I will first report estimates of the external shape of the distribution for 1975(80), 1985 and 1996. The density functions were estimated for these variables in deviation from the EU average, and are depicted in Figures 3.3 and Figure 3.4. The mode of the distribution of relative GDP per capita in 1975 and 1980 is around the EU average, although there is a long right tail that corresponds to a few regions with levels well above the average, and, interestingly, an important mass of probability at the left, indicating a large group of regions with GDP per capita above the average. What is interesting is that this separate group of regions seems to vanish over time, as the mass of probability at the left hand side of the distribution is continuously decreasing. This process probably causes the mode of the distribution to derive somewhat to the left of the EU average in 1996. On the other hand, the long right tail persists at the end of the period, and the mass of probability at relative levels between 120 per cent and 140 per cent increases. Overall, the distribution of GDP per capita decreases its dispersion not only in the first subperiod, but particularly in the second one. This is basically due to regions below the average improving their situation, though in parallel, an increasing number of regions is considerably surpassing the EU average at the end of the period.

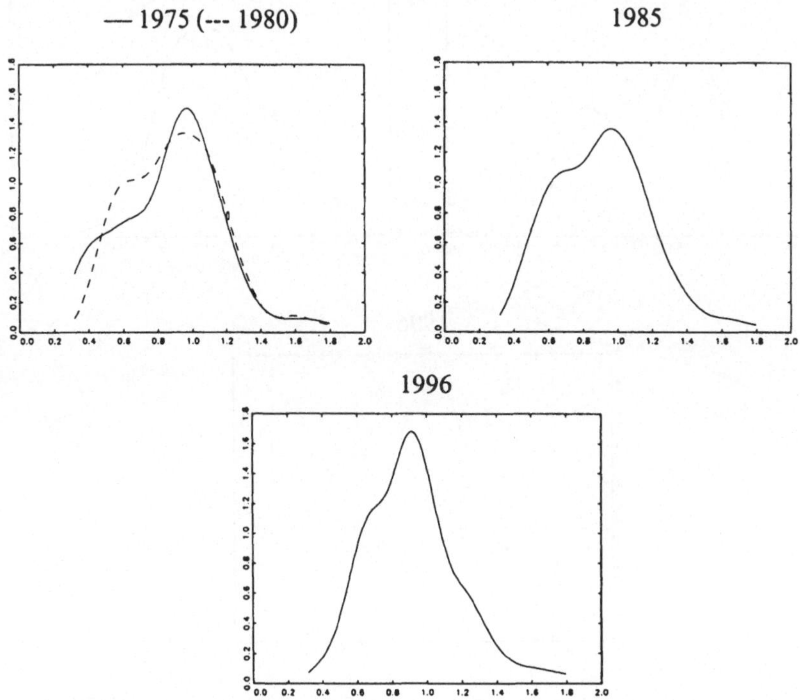

Figure 3.3 Estimated density functions for GDP per capita in the EU regions.

The initial picture for GDP per worker (Figure 3.4) indicates that two clusters of regions characterized the distribution of labor productivity in the mid-seventies and early eighties. There was a first group of regions with a mode around 60 per cent-80 per cent of the EU average, and the other of large relative productivity with a mode at around 120 per cent. The shape of the distribution experienced outstanding changes over the period, as it was already unimodal around the average at 1985, although the mass of probability for low levels of probability was still important. Further concentration is produced in the second subperiod, but two small groups of regions at very low and very high relative productivity levels remain in 1996. Leaving aside those regions, the general conclusion is that there is a continuous process of concentration of the distribution over the period.

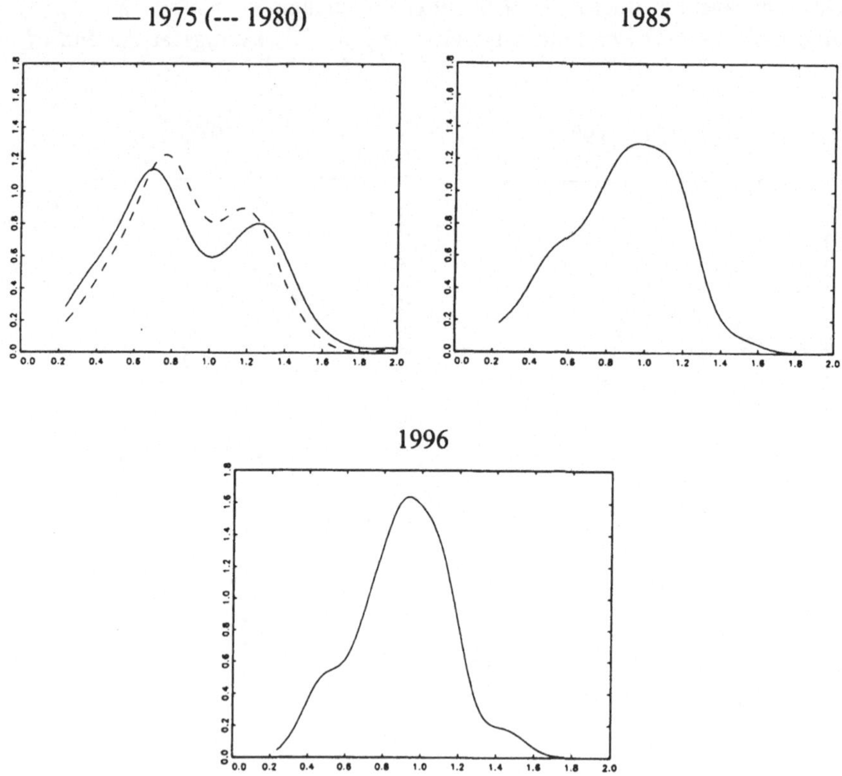

Figure 3.4 Estimated density functions for GDP per worker in the EU regions.

In order to complete the analysis, the stochastic kernels for both variables were computed to measure the movements within the distribution. Stochastic kernels were computed for 5-yearly transitions. Figure 3.5 shows the three-dimensional graph and the corresponding contour plot for the stochastic kernel for GDP per capita. Broadly speaking, the mass of probability is located over the positive diagonal. There is only some clockwise twist at levels below 80 per cent, which corresponds with movements of the less developed regions towards the average. Beside that, there was high persistence in the distribution. Much more churning is observed in the case of labor productivity. Figure 3.6 depicts the estimate of the stochastic kernel for that variable. It can be observed that the kernel shifts up for levels below the average, and down for those above the average. In the latter case, the kernel twists somewhat as well. This means that there were movements in the whole range of the distribution, that caused convergence in the distribution.

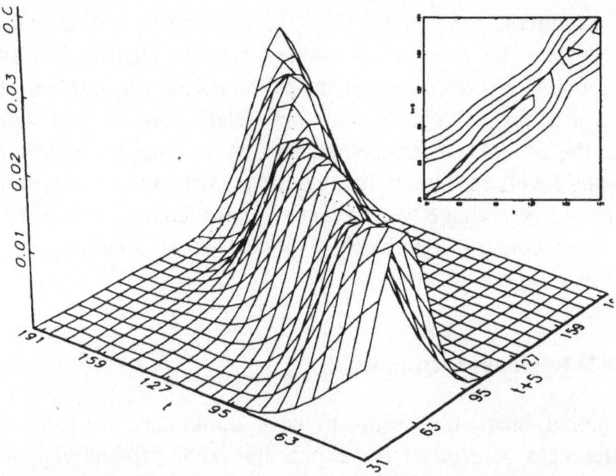

Figure 3.5 Estimated stochastic kernel for GDP per capita in the EU regions. 5-yearly transitions from 1975 to 1996.

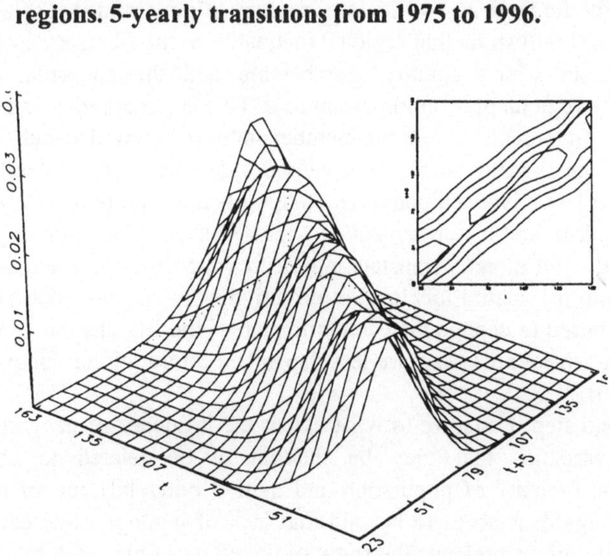

Figure 3.6 Estimated stochastic kernel for GDP per worker in the EU regions. 5-yearly transitions from 1975 to 1996.

To sum up, the distribution of GDP per capita and GDP per worker seems to have been less dispersed in 1996 than it was at the beginning of the period under analysis. Interestingly, this seems to be also the case if we compare the final situation with that in 1985. The process of convergence has probably been more intense in labor productivity than in terms of product per inhabitant. This confirms the results obtained in López-Bazo et al (1999) for a period ending at 1992, and supports the arguments put forward there. In any case, a couple of remarks are in order. First, despite the process of convergence, the distribution still shows an important amount of dispersion at the end of the period for both variables. Second, there remains a group of regions with low relative levels that would not have profited from the process of integration, and, at the opposite extreme, a group of regions showing levels far above the average persists and increases in number. In the next section, I investigate to what extent these features in the distribution can be explained by country membership, geographical location, density, market potential and sectoral composition.

Explaining EU Regional Inequality

Although regional inequality seems to have diminished over the period under analysis, differences in product per capita and labor productivity across the EU were still important in the mid-nineties. The regional distribution of both magnitudes has been shown to be characterized by high persistence, and particularly by the tendency of the poor regions to remain in that relative position. In this section, I will show that regional inequality in the EU is essentially a spatial phenomenon, in which country membership and the particular geographical location of the regions play an important role. This is remarkable, as there has been a process of convergence across the member states in recent decades. However, the convergence across states seems to be caused by the behavior of the most dynamic regions in the less advanced countries, lagging behind the poorest regions in each country (Boldrin and Canova, 2001; Mora, 2002). Thus convergence across countries might not directly translate into decreasing disparities across regions. On the other hand, the spatial localization of activities of the so-called new economy might have started to change the economic map of the EU, insofar as they look for dynamic non-central areas and are less dependent on traditional factors of location (Quah, 1996b).

In a second step, I analyze to what extent the influence of geography is in fact caused by variables that may be thought to be related to economies of agglomeration (density of population and market potential) and of the industrial mix. In this regard, it needs to be said that lack of homogeneous data for a wide sample of EU regions prevents the study of the effect of physical, human and other types of capital in the distribution of income per capita and labor productivity. The results reveal that a large amount of inequality in the regional distribution is related to inequality across countries and geographical areas, but this is only partially due to agglomeration and differences in sectoral composition. In addition, the influence of these factors seems to be decreasing over the period being analyzed. Thus, the effect of the unequal distribution of capital and technology in the EU regions may explain an increasing number of the characteristics of the distribution of productivity and income – see Fingleton and López-Bazo (2002) for some evidence in this regard.

To show the influence of the above-mentioned factors, the actual distribution of GDP per capita and per worker will be compared with some *virtual* distributions. These are the distributions which are obtained when conditioning to (removing the effect of) i) membership of a given state, ii) neighborhood effects, iii) population density, iv) market potential, and v) sectoral composition. If the *virtual* distribution does not differ from the actual one, the conclusion should be that that conditioning factor does not explain the characteristics of the distribution. On the contrary, it contributes to the inequality in the distribution, when dispersion in the virtual distribution is lower than that in the real one. In addition, we can detect if, for instance, the factor is responsible for the mass of probability in the lower levels of income or productivity, if the mass is not present in the *virtual* distribution[9].

We follow the proposal in Overman and Puga (2002) in obtaining the conditional distributions, and compute $Y_C^t = Y_i^t \,/\, Y_G^t$ where subscript C denotes conditional, i refers to the i-th EU region, t refers to the year, and

$$Y_G^t = \sum_{i \in G} Y_i^t \Big/ N_G \qquad \textbf{(2)}$$

is the average of Y in the group of regions G, where N_G is the number of regions in that group. If all the dispersion in the distribution is due to differences across groups of regions, all regions within each group will share the same value for Y, and then Y_C^t will equal 1 for each region. That is, the conditional distribution collapses in 1. In contrast, if the characteristics of the real distribution are independent of the factors used to define the groups, the *virtual* distribution will not differ from the actual one.

As I explained above, I define groups of regions according to country membership and neighborhood. That is, conditional distributions will be computed as ratios of product per capita, and productivity to country average, and average in the set of contiguous regions, respectively[10]. Furthermore, four different groups are defined in the case of variables proxying for agglomeration. For each one of those variables, groups of regions are defined by considering their position in the quartiles of the distribution. That is, the group of low density regions is defined as those regions within the first quartile; the mid-low density group those in the second quartile, and so on. Density is defined as the ratio of population to regional surface, while market potential is computed as

$$\sum_{\substack{j=1 \\ j \neq i}}^{108} \left(GDP_j / d_{ij} \right), \qquad \textbf{(3)}$$

where d_{ij} is the distance between the centroid of regions i and j, computed by using ARC-VIEW from coordinates in the digital map of EU regions produced by EUROSTAT. Finally, regions were grouped into three categories according to their share of employment in agriculture, manufactures and services.

Comparison of the virtual and actual distributions can be done be means of the estimated density functions for both distributions, and by the stochastic kernel mapping the probability of the conditional and unconditional distributions. In the former case, the impact of the conditioning factor on the external shape of the distribution can be analyzed, whereas movements to the different parts of the distribution caused by the factor can be trace out by means of the stochastic kernels. Despite providing complementary information, I am going to report only the effects of the factors on the external shape of the distribution here, in order to save space. Results for the stochastic kernels are available upon request.

Figure 3.7 shows the densities for the real and virtual distributions, for GDP per capita in 1980 (left panel) and 1996 (right panel). It is quite clear that differences across countries explain an important amount of the dispersion in the distribution. The conditional distribution is much more concentrated around the point of no differences (ratio equal to 1). In addition, we can conclude that the position of the less favored regions (the left tail of the distribution) has basically to do with the situation of their country. On the contrary, conditioning out the country effect does not significantly alter the mass of probability at the right of the distribution, that is, the position of the most advanced regions is not just a matter of the country. Conditioning by the income level in the neighboring regions provides us with indirect evidence as to the effect of the geographical location of each region. In other words, in this way we can assess to what extent inequality has to do with the spatial distribution of income. As in the case of the conditioning by country, removing the neighborhood effect causes the distribution to be much more concentrated than the real one. The resulting distribution, in this case, is still more concentrated than the one conditioned by the country membership. Besides, it causes the set of the richest regions to concentrate into separate groups, especially in 1996. This can be read as spatial concentration of the richest regions into separate clusters at the end of the period.

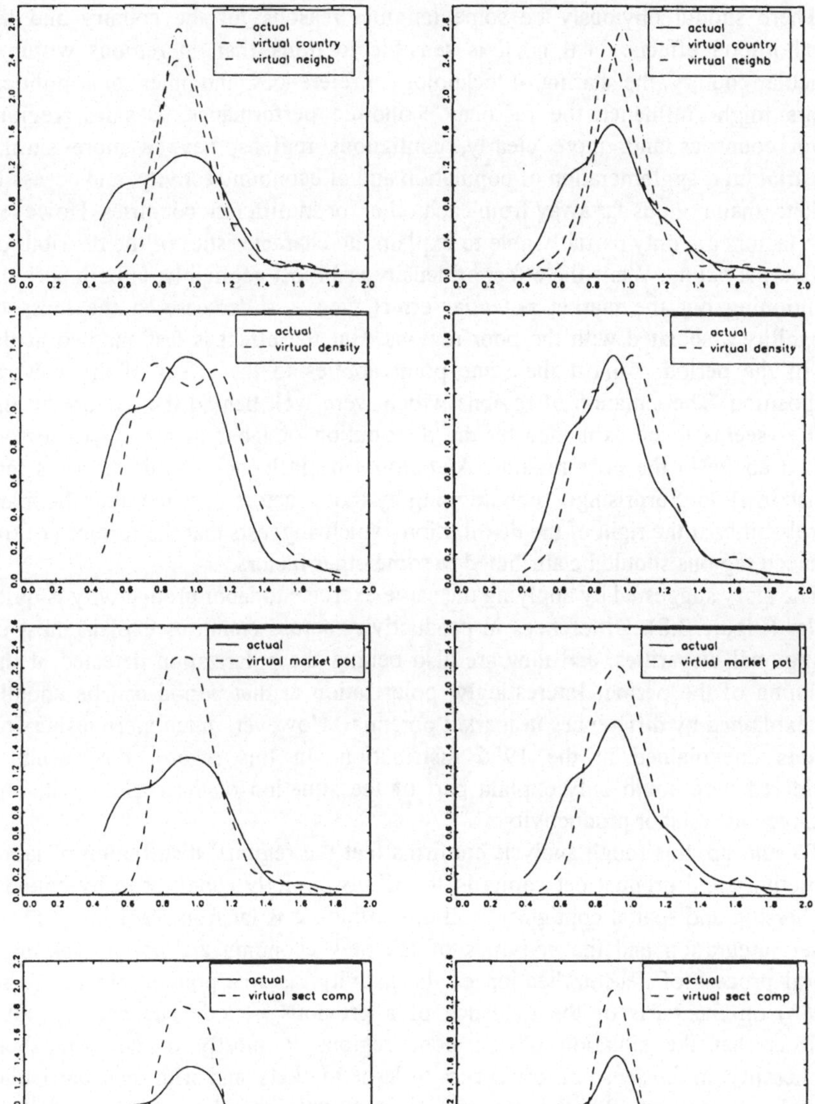

Figure 3.7 Actual and virtual distributions for GDP per capita, 1980 (left) and 1996 (right).

There should obviously be some tangible reasons for the country and the neighborhood effects. That is, it is sensible to think that, in regions within a particular country, the sharing of technology, preferences, and other socio-political factors might influence the regional economic performance. Besides, regions within countries and, more clearly, contiguous regions, have a more similar industrial mix, agglomeration of population and of economic activity, and access to markets, than regions far away from each other, or in different countries. However, these factors are only partially able to explain the characteristics of the distribution of GDP per capita. While the effect of density is almost negligible, in both periods, conditioning out the market potential effect causes a decrease in the mass of probability associated with the poor regions. But the effect is less marked at the end of the period. Almost the same point applies to the effect of the sectoral composition. The situation of regions which were well behind the average in the eighties seems to be explained by the distribution of labor in the macro-sectors defined above in the poor regions. As before, the influence of this effect is less intense in 1996. Surprisingly, conditioning by those factors does not alter the mass of probability at the right of the distribution, which suggests that the fortunes of the advanced regions should be attributed to some other factors.

The story suggested by applying the same exercise to labor productivity is quite similar (Figure 3.8). Differences in productivity across countries explain most of the regional disparities, and they are also behind the polarization detected at the beginning of the period. Interestingly, polarization at that period can be equally well explained by differences in market potential. However, much more dispersion remains unexplained in the 1996 distribution. In this regard, the variables considered here could only explain part of the situation of the regions with the lowest levels of labor productivity.

To sum up, this rough analysis confirms that the regional distribution of labor productivity and product per capita in the EU is strongly conditioned by country membership and spatial contiguity, and this influence is far from vanishing. Thus, further integration and the activities of the new economy are not provoking a general process of decentralization of the activity, as was pointed out by Quah (1996b) on the basis of the evidence of a previous period. The analysis also confirms that the situation of the poor regions is mostly to do with their peripherality, in the sense of low access to large markets, and with their particular sectoral composition. But the argument is not symmetrical, since those factors cannot explain the right tail of the distribution. Further analyses of the effects of different forms of capital, the role of returns to scale and agglomeration economies, technological spillovers, the entrepreneurship structure, and so on, on the whole regional distribution are thus in order.

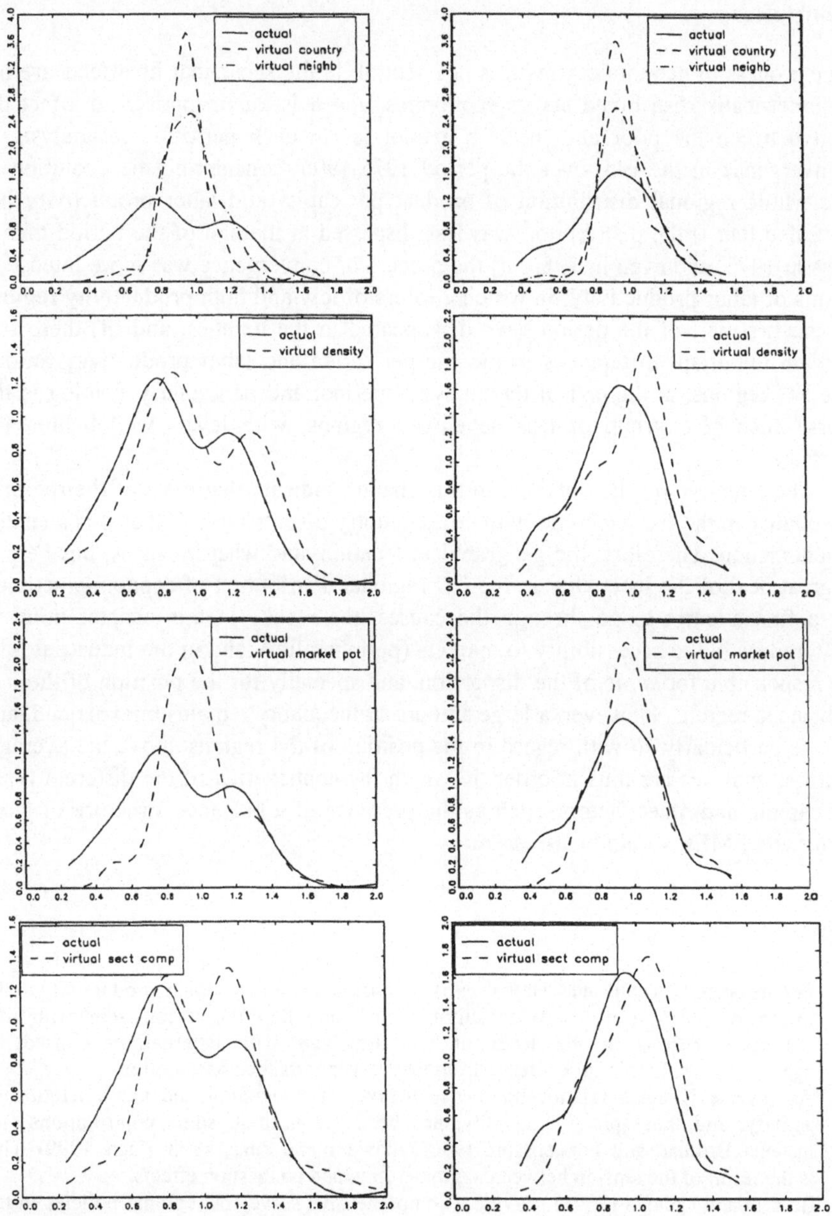

Figure 3.8 Actual and virtual distributions for GDP per worker, 1980 (left) and 1996 (right).

Conclusions

The process of economic growth is not neutral, in the sense that its effects are not symmetrically distributed across economies, and it is thus supposed to affect the gap between the poor and the rich economies in each period. The analysis of convergence in the EU, over the period 1975-1996, considering the evolution of the whole regional distribution of product per capita and labor productivity has revealed that i) the distribution was less dispersed at the end of the period than it was in 1975, and even in 1985, ii) the process of convergence was more intense in terms of labor productivity, in which clusters of low and high productivity regions at the first part of the period have disappeared in the nineties, and iii) there still remain important differences in income per capita and labor productivity among the EU regions, at the end of the analyzed period, and particularly striking is the persistence of a group of less developed regions, with levels well behind the average.

The tentative results obtained in this chapter indicate that most of the regional inequality in the EU has to do with cross-country dispersion, and that it is a spatial phenomenon. Therefore, the geographical location, and what it causes, lies behind a great deal of the inequality in the EU regional distribution of economic activity. In a first attempt to go through the causes, the results in this chapter point to differences in the accessibility to markets (peripherality), and in the industrial mix, as responsible for some of the dispersion, and specially for the position of the less advanced regions. However, a large amount of inequality remains unexplained, and this is particularly so with regard to the position of the regions above the average. Further analyses are thus in order, in which the contribution of the different types of capital, and other factors, such as the presence of a balanced structure of large firms and SMEs, would be assessed.

Notes

1 For instance, Ciccone and Hall (1996) propose a model in which productivity is an increasing function of density of activity. They show how this is consistent with both increasing returns at the level of the firm and with externalities caused by agglomeration. Empirical evidence from the US supports their assumption.

2 An inverse U-shape relationship between level of integration and agglomeration of activity, and thus spatial inequality, has been proposed in some contributions (for instance Brülhart and Torstensson, 1996; Ottaviano and Puga, 1998; Puga, 1999). This is the result of the tension between agglomeration and congestion effects.

3 Boldrin and Canova (2001) provide a comprehensive survey of regional policies in the EU, the types of instruments used, and the arguments in favour and against their effectiveness.

4 Durlauf and Quah (1999) provide a summary of the variables included in such regression and their standard estimated effect.

5 The dynamic nature of the growth equation in (1) causes the ordinary least square estimation of the model that includes fixed individual effects to provide inconsistent estimates (Islam, 1995; Caselli et al, 1996).
6 However, this could be detected by the evolution of a measure of polarisation such as the one proposed by Esteban and Ray (1994).
7 See Durlauf and Quah (1999) for a formal definition and some properties of stochastic kernels in the study of distribution dynamics.
8 As noted before, least squares provide asymptotically biased estimations of the parameters of the growth equation. It has been proved that the bias is positive, so the results reported here probably overestimate the true rate of convergence in the EU regions.
9 The analysis of conditional distributions was proposed in Quah (1997) and recently applied by Overman and Puga (2002) and López-Bazo et al (2002) to the analysis of the regional distribution of unemployment.
10 Observations for those countries which have been considered as regions in our sample were not considered in the computations in this case.

References

Armstrong, H. (1995), 'Convergence among regions of the European Union 1950-1990', *Papers in Regional Science*, vol. 74, pp. 143-152.

Arrow, K. (1962), 'The economic implications of learning by doing', *Review of Economic Studies,* vol. 29, pp. 155-173.

Azariadis, C. and Drazen, A. (1990), 'Threshold externalities in economic development', *Quarterly Journal of Economics*, vol. 105, pp. 501-526.

Barro, R. and Sala-i-Martin, X. (1992), 'Convergence', *Journal of Political Economy*, vol. 100, pp. 223-251.

Baumol, W. (1986), 'Productivity growth, convergence and welfare: what the long run data show', *American Economic Review*, vol. 76, pp. 1072-1085.

Bianchi, M. (1997), 'Testing for convergence: Evidence from non-parametric multimodality tests', *Journal of Applied Econometrics*, vol. 12, pp. 393-409.

Boldrin, M. and Canova, F. (2001), 'Inequality and convergence in Europe's regions: reconsidering European regional policies', *Economic Policy*, vol. 32, pp. 205-245.

Brülhart, M. and Torstensson, J. (1996), 'Regional integration, scale economies and industry location in the European Union', Centre for Economic Policy Research, Discussion Paper: 1435, London.

Caselli, F., Esquivel, G. and Lefort, F. (1996), 'Reopening the convergence debate: A new look at cross-country growth empirics', *Journal of Economic Growth*, vol. 1, pp. 363-89.

Ciccone, A. and Hall, R.E. (1996), 'Productivity and the density of economic activity', *American Economic Review*, vol. 86, pp. 54-70.

Dollar, D. and Wolf, E. (1988), 'Convergence of industry labor productivity among advanced economies, 1963-1982', *Review of Economics and Statistics*, vol. 70, pp. 549-558.

Durlauf, S. and Quah, D. (1999), 'The new empirics of economic growth', in Taylor J., Woodford, M (eds), *Handbook of Macroeconomics*, Elsevier Science, North-Holland, New York and Oxford, pp 235-308.

Esteban, J. and Ray, D. (1994), 'On the measurement of polarization', *Econometrica*, vol. 62, pp. 819-851.

Fingleton, B. (1997), 'Specification and testing of Markov chain models: An application to convergence in the European Union', *Oxford Bulletin of Economics and Statistics*, vol. 59, pp. 385-403.

Fingleton, B. and López-Bazo, E. (2002), 'Explaining the distribution of manufacturing productivity in the EU regions', in B. Fingleton (eds) *European Regional Growth*, Springer Verlag, forthcoming.

Grossman, G. and Helpman, E. (1991), *Innovation and Growth in the Global Economy*, MIT Press, Cambridge, Mass. and London.

Islam, N. (1995), 'Growth empirics: A panel data approach', *Quarterly Journal of Economics*, vol. 110, pp. 1127-70.

Johnson, P.A. (2000), 'A nonparametric analysis of income convergence across the US States', *Economics Letters*, vol. 69, pp. 219-223.

Kaldor, N. (1957), 'A model of economic growth', *Economic Journal*, vol. 67, pp. 591-624.

Lamo, A. (2000), 'On convergence empirics: some evidence for Spanish regions', *Investigaciones Economicas*, vol. 24, pp. 681-707.

López-Bazo, E., del Barrio, T. and Artís, M. (2002), 'The regional distribution of Spanish unemployment, a spatial analysis', *Papers in Regional Science*, vol. 81, pp. 365-389.

López-Bazo, E., Vayá, E., Mora, A. and Suriñach, J. (1999), 'Regional economic dynamics and convergence in the European Union', *The Annals of Regional Science*, vol. 33, pp. 343-370.

López-Bazo, E., Vayá, E. and Moreno, R. (2001), 'Crecimiento y convergencia regional en España: Qué hemos estado midiendo?', [Growth and regional convergence in Spain. What have we been measuring?] in B. Cabrer (eds) *Análisis Regional*, Mundi Prensa, Madrid, pp. 129-140.

Lucas, R. (1988), 'On the mechanics of economic development', *Journal of Monetary Economics*, vol. 22, pp. 3-42.

Maddison, A. (1995), *Monitoring the World Economy 1820-1992*, Organisation for Economic Co-Operation and Development, Paris.

Magrini, S. (1999), 'The evolution of income disparities among the regions of the European Union', *Regional Science and Urban Economics*, vol. 29, pp. 257-81.

Mankiw, N., Romer, D. and Weil, D. (1992), 'A contribution to the empirics of economic growth', *Quarterly Journal of Economics*, vol. 107, pp. 407-437.

Mora, A, (2002), *Sobre convergencia económica. Aspectos teóricos y análisis empírico para las regiones europeas y españolas* [On economic convergence. Theory and empirical analysis for the EU and Spanish regions]. Unpublished PhD Thesis, University of Barcelona.

Ottaviano, G. and Puga, D. (1998), 'Agglomeration in the global economy: A survey of the "New Economic Geography"', *World Economy*, vol. 21, pp. 707-731.

Overman, H.G. and Puga, D. (2002), 'Unemployment clusters across European regions and countries', *Economic Policy*, vol. 34, pp. 117-147.

Puga, D, (1999), 'The rise and fall of regional inequalities', *European Economic Review*, vol. 43, pp. 303-334.

Quah, D. (1993), 'Galton's fallacy and tests of the convergence hypothesis', *Scandinavian Journal of Economics*, vol. 95, pp. 427-443.

Quah, D. (1996a), 'Convergence empirics across economies with (some) capital mobility', *Journal of Economic Growth*, vol. 1, pp. 95-124.

Quah, D. (1996b), 'Regional convergence clusters across Europe', *European Economic Review*, vol. 40, pp. 951-958.

Quah, D, (1997), 'Empirics for growth and distribution: Stratification, polarization, and convergence clubs', *Journal of Economic Growth*, vol. 2, pp. 27-59.
Romer, P. (1986), 'Increasing returns and long-run growth', *Journal of Political Economy*, vol. 94, pp. 1002-1037.
Sala-i-Martin, X. (1996), 'Regional cohesion: evidence and theories of regional growth and convergence', *European Economic Review*, vol. 40, pp. 1325-1352.
Silverman, B.W. (1986), *Density Estimation for Statistics and Data Analysis*, Chapman and Hall, New York.
Solow, R. (1956), 'A contribution to the theory of economic growth', *Quarterly Journal of Economics*, vol. 70, pp. 65-94.
Stokey, N. and Lucas, R. Jr. (1989), *Recursive Methods in Economic Dynamics*, Harvard University Press, Cambridge, Mass. and London.
Swan, T. (1956), 'Economic growth and capital accumulation', *Economic Record*, vol. 32, pp. 334-361.

Appendix

The kernel density estimate of a series X at a point x is estimated by

$$f(x)=\frac{1}{Nh}\sum_{i=1}^{N}\mathrm{K}\left(\frac{x-X_i}{h}\right) \qquad \textbf{(A.1)}$$

where N is the number of observations, h is the bandwidth (or smoothing parameter) and K( ) is a kernel function that integrates to one. The kernel function is a weighting function that determines the shape of the bumps. We have used the Gaussian kernel in our estimates:

$$\frac{1}{\sqrt{2\pi}}\exp\left(-\frac{1}{2}u^2\right) \qquad \textbf{(A.2)}$$

where u is the argument of the kernel function. The bandwidth, h, controls the smoothness of the density estimate; the larger the bandwidth, the smoother the estimate. Bandwidth selection is of crucial importance in density estimation, and various methods have been suggested in the literature. In this paper, we have used the data-based automatic bandwidth suggested by Silverman (1986, equation 3.31):

$$h=0.9N^{-1/5}\min\{s,R/134\} \qquad \textbf{(A.3)}$$

where s is the standard deviation and R the interquartile range of the series.

Intra-distribution dynamics can be analyzed through the estimation of a stochastic kernel (Stokey and Lucas, 1989) for the distribution of income per capita over the period under analysis. This is merely the counterpart of a first order Markov probability of transitions matrix, where the number of states tends to infinity; that is to say, where the length of the range of income defining each state tends to zero. Thus, the stochastic kernel provides the likelihood of transiting from one place in the range of values of income to the others.

Following Johnson (2000), let Y (the ratio of productivity in each economy to the average in the sample) be the variable under analysis, and $f_t(Y=x)$ and $f_{t+k}(Y=x)$ the probability density of Y=x in period t and t+k respectively. Assuming a first-order time-invariant process for the evolution of the distribution of Y, and existence of marginal and conditional density functions for the Y distribution, the relationship between both distributions can be summarized by:

$$f_{t+k}(Y=y)=\int_0^1 g_k(Y=y\,|\,Y=x)f_t(Y=x) \qquad \textbf{(A.4)}$$

where $g_k(Y=y|Y=x)$ is the density of Y=y in period t+k conditional on Y=x, k periods before. Then, $g_k(Y=y|Y=x)$ summarizes information on movements within the distribution over time. It is computed by first estimating the joint density for the distributions at t and t+k by the kernel method and then dividing it by the marginal density of Y at t, obtained by integrating the joint density over Y at t+k.

Chapter 4

Disparities in Economic Growth and Unemployment Across the European Regions: A Sectoral Perspective

Raffaele Paci, Francesco Pigliaru and Maurizio Pugno

Introduction[1]

The recent acceleration of the European integration has been mainly designed so as to produce convergence in the monetary variables, while the disparity in real variables has remained as an open issue, especially the disparities in economic growth and unemployment. Many studies have revealed that the two variables exhibit a great dispersion across the European regions. This fact weakens the whole European Union because it makes external shocks highly asymmetric, and monetary policy more difficult. Moreover, the relationship between economic growth and unemployment is a problem in itself, both from an analytical and interpretative point of view, as well as for policy prescriptions. The bulk of theoretical and empirical literature has dealt with the two phenomena separately, but their correlation is not at all evident, if the cross-section of the European regions is considered. Nevertheless, the policy makers' presumption is invariably that growth absorbs unemployment.

The purpose of this paper is firstly to evaluate the evidence on disparities of economic growth and unemployment across the Western European regions that emerges from the literature, and to highlight the problem of the relationship between the two phenomena. This is pursued in the second section. Secondly, a fairly simple but insightful perspective is obtained by studying and correlating disparities in economic growth and unemployment, focusing on the sectoral subdivision of the economy into agriculture, industry, and services. The three sectors, in fact, are characterized by different capacities to employ labor and to promote growth, and they differ markedly across regions in productivity levels and in their dynamics. The third section will provide an overview of this perspective, which remains partly tentative. We first study the relationship between sectoral dynamics and growth using the traditional subdivision between agriculture and the non-agricultural sector, as Lewis has taught us, as well as the subdivision between industry and services, as Baumol has taught us. In addition to this, we try to cover some of the not much explored grounds of analyzing regional convergence from a three-sector perspective.

In the fourth section the relationship between sectoral dynamics and convergence process is further examined thanks to new empirical evidence. A comprehensive picture, based on a cluster analysis, of the role of structural change, technological capacity and employment rate in the description of different growth patterns is presented. The sectoral perspective makes evident the opportunity to include the governance of the three-sector mix among the objectives of economic policy. A brief discussion of this will appear in the Conclusions.

Disparities in Economic Growth and Unemployment: Evaluation of the Aggregate Evidence

The studies on disparities in the real variables of the European regions concentrate on some specific questions, which can be linked within a simple framework. Let us decompose real per capita income (*Y/P*) into a labor productivity variable (*Y/E*) and an employment or unemployment variable, i.e.:

$$\frac{Y}{P} \equiv \frac{Y}{E}\frac{E}{P} \equiv \frac{Y}{E}\frac{L}{P}(1-u) \qquad \textbf{(1)}$$

where *Y* stands for real income, *P* for population, *E* for employment, *L* for the labor force, and *u* for the unemployment rate, i.e. the unemployment share of the labor force[2]. Five main questions can thus be identified:

(i) whether different regional *Y/P*s have converged toward a same (growing) level over time, which is the question that is investigated most. This question refers to the dynamics of the distribution of new wealth;

(ii) the question of the regional distribution of the unemployment rate (*u*), or of the employment rate (*E/P*), which refers to how much of the labor force is involved in the production of new wealth;

(iii) the question of the convergence of *Y/E*, which refers to the technological capacity to produce new wealth;

(iv) the question of the correlation between *Y/E* and *E,* which includes the apparently obvious view that, at least at the macroeconomic level, a competitive system creates employment;

(v) the question of adjustment of *P* on *E* mainly through migration.

Question (i) does not take account of the other four, rather it is a net outcome of them, since, e.g., convergence in the per capita income can emerge even if the disparity of unemployment rises, although being more than compensated for by the convergence in productivity. Nevertheless, it has been the most studied, and some results have been obtained[3]. On the whole, from the 1950s onwards, convergence in real per capita income among the European regions seems to have taken place, but this fact is also subject to a number of severe limitations. Firstly, the speed of convergence has progressively declined to a very slow rate, passing through the 1980s as a period of crisis. At the current speed the gap among regions would substantially reduce only in several decades. Secondly, the disparity remains very large. In fact, the bottom 10 regions of the European Union exhibit a per capita GDP in the period 1988-97 which is the 26 per cent of that of the 10 top regions[4]. Thirdly, the convergence among the Southern club of regions, inclusive of Portugal, Spain, the South of Italy, and Greece, is more sluggish than that of the Northern club of regions[5]. Fourthly, a contributing factor to the sluggishness in converging towards a common European level seems to be the lack in convergence of the national trends (Canova and Marcet, 1995). Fifthly, spatial contiguity between regions matters in the convergence process (Quah, 1996; Fingleton, 1999; Lopez Bazo *et al.*, 1999; Cuadrado-Roura *et al.*, 2000), so that the emergence of agglomerations may weaken the overall convergence. These results are obtained by means of the analysis of the dispersion, i.e. the σ-convergence, and the analysis of the Solovian β-convergence, as well as the method of the Markovian transition matrices (Quah, 1996).

Question (ii), i.e. that of regional dispersion of the employment (and unemployment) rates has been comparatively little studied, given its importance. The 10 bottom regions exhibit an employment rate in the period 1988-97 which is the 55 per cent of that of the 10 top regions. As is well known unemployment is concentrated in many regions of the Mediterranean countries, and it shows a high persistence over time (European Commission, 2000; Baddeley *et al.*, 1998). After the peak of the mid-1980s, the disparity seems to be reducing, albeit at a very slow speed. Moreover, the regions with high unemployment that are entitled to receive the European Funds of Development, the so-called 'Objective I regions', exhibit a *rising* disparity from the European average (Piacentini and Sulis, 2000).

Also in the case of regional unemployment it has been often called for more flexible wages (Abraham and van Rampuy, 1995; Abraham, 1996; Pench *et al.*, 1999), while migration appears in this case as even a better candidate for adjustment. The argument of the wage flexibility should be taken into consideration, since the Mediterranean countries undoubtedly show many rigidities in the labor market (Koefijk and Kremers, 1996). However, no study has given any idea of how much flexibility is needed to close the unemployment disparity, while very different wages across regions would certainly raise the problem of cohesion in the European Union (Epifani, 1998). The other adjustment mechanism, i.e. migration (our question (v)), has been of little importance in Europe, at least in the most recent decades (Decressin and Fatas, 1995; Bentivogli and Pagano, 1998). More precisely, it seems that interregional migration is particularly low exactly where unemployment disparity is high, i.e. in Italy and in the Southern regions generally (Neven and Gouyette, 1995). Nor do relative wages appear as sound signals for potential migrants regarding the possibility of finding jobs, unless there exists very high unemployment, because wages are mainly set at the national level (Abraham, 1996)[6].

The question of convergence of productivity (question (iii)) could be viewed as less controversial, since technology and capital can be transferred across regions more easily than institutions. The evidence confirms this expectation; however, the speed of regional convergence of productivity remains very slow (Paci, 1997). The 10 bottom regions exhibit labor productivity in the period 1988-97 which is only 32 per cent of that of the 10 top regions.

The questions of the dispersion in the per capita income, in the employment rates and in productivity find a synthetic representation in the three diagrams of Figure 4.1, thus also recalling the decomposition (1). The represented indices are the weighted standard deviation normalized with the group average for the Northern and Southern regions of the EU-15 over the time periods for which data are available. Surprisingly, these indices are neglected by the literature, although they give a more correct picture than the usual unweighted corresponding indices. Moreover, they have better properties, since they provide a guarantee that the European index lies in between the indices of the Northern and the Southern regions, and that the three diagrams are consistent.

A most striking result emerges: that the Southern regions display a far higher disparity in real income, in the employment rate, and in productivity than do the Northern regions, so that those regions can hardly be called a club (see also Tondl, 1998). Secondly, the sluggishness of convergence in all three indices is evident. These results do not emerge, or emerge to a less extent, if unweighted indices are used instead[7].

The last question to briefly discuss pertains to the relationship between productivity and (un)employment (question (iv)). This is extremely important for policy makers, but the literature remains very far from conclusive on this issue. It ranges from the Verdoorn's optimistic view that output growth is positively correlated with both productivity and employment[8], to the pessimistic view by Aghion and Howitt (1994), who rather expect a negative relationship between productivity growth and the employment level. Our data, insofar as they are taken without any sectoral disaggregation, do not add any positive result, but they rather suggest further research. In fact, productivity and (un)employment in the levels exhibit weak correlations[9], while growth in productivity and growth in employment exhibit a negative correlation. Finally, almost no correlation is found between (un)employment and growth in productivity[10]. Therefore, economic growth and unemployment appear as distinct problems, i.e. the solution of one problem does not necessarily appear as also the solution of the other.

Weighted (W) and unweighted (U) coefficient of variation (CV).

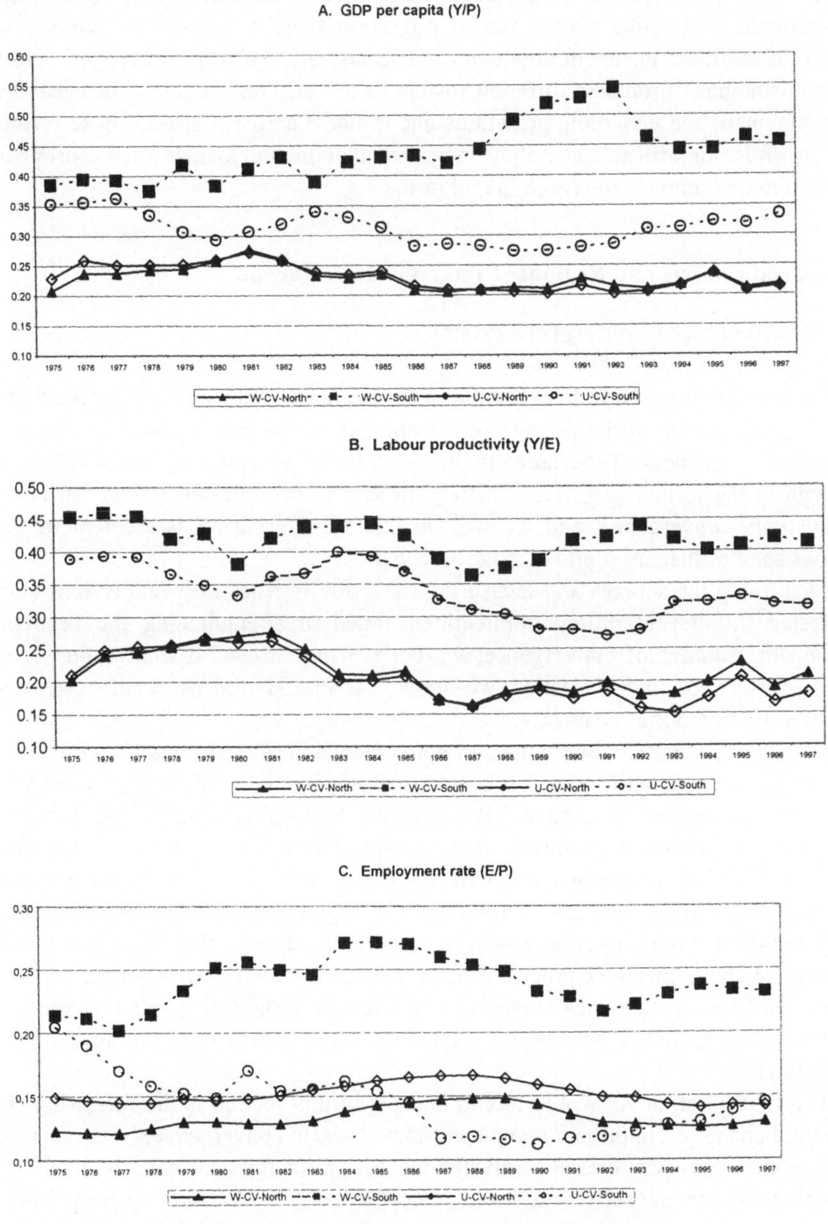

Figure 4.1 Dispersion among the Northern and Southern European regions.

In conclusion, aggregate analysis does not bring us very far. The traditional adjustment mechanisms of rising capital/labor ratios, of transferring technology and capitals, of flexible wages and of migration seem to work insufficiently to reduce disparities in unemployment and economic growth. Moreover, these mechanisms have produced different results in the different regions, thus leaving unemployment and economic growth as uncorrelated across regions. These results are too little for efficacious policy measures that intend to make the European Union a more homogeneous area in real terms.

Structural Change and Regional Convergence in Europe

The Dualism Driven Convergence Process

As we have emphasized in the previous section, convergence in labor productivity is a key component of the process of income per capita convergence. In Europe, the evident weakness of the latter is due – partially, at least – to the insufficient strength of the former (e.g., Paci, 1997). In this section we concentrate on labor productivity convergence, and we will do this by offering an assessment of the various sources that are supposed to drive the process.

Identifying the sources and measuring their role is crucial especially if we are interested in relevant policy implications aimed at strengthening the process. Among the sources of convergence, we believe that structural change has been often overlooked. In this section we show that this is true especially (but not exclusively) in the European case.

Structural change can be a source of convergence in several ways. Even if long-run growth rates are uniform across sectors and regions, sectoral dynamics can still generate convergence as long as (i) the factor-reallocation is growth-enhancing (e.g. labor migration from lower- to higher-productivity sectors), (ii) migration flows of this kind are stronger in poorer regions. Condition (i) clearly implies that sectoral adjustment through inter-sectoral migration is not instantaneous. Interestingly for convergence analysis, conditions determining the speed and strength of the adjustment process can be heterogeneous across regions, so that their identification and measurement can be relevant to the task of interpreting the process at the aggregate level and of obtaining robust policy implications (on this see below).

The first question we would like to address in this section is the following: Is structural change an important component in real-world convergence?

The answer is positive, not only for the European regional data as a whole. Caselli and Coleman (2001) study state convergence in the US starting from 1880. By decomposing overall South-North convergence they find that 'Southern incomes converged to Northern incomes mainly because agricultural wages converged to non-agricultural wages (between industry wage convergence), and because Southern workers left agriculture at a higher speed (labor reallocation)'. More precisely, 'rising relative agricultural wages and agricultural out-migration can explain 81 per cent of the convergence of Southern to Northern per capita service incomes between 1880 and 1950, and 58 per cent of the convergence of Southern to Northern per capita labor incomes between 1940 and 1990' (p. 14). For the US case see also Bernard and Jones (1996a)[11].

Similar results are available for several individual European countries. In particular, the role of sectoral dynamics in the regional convergence process in Italy has been assessed for the period 1970-92 by Paci and Pigliaru (1997), who apply a shift-share methodology to measure the structural change component in the overall observed convergence. The result is striking – once this component is filtered out from the overall growth rates of labor productivity, the within-sector component turns out to be statistically not significant in cross-region growth regressions. In other words, structural change seems to be by far the major component of the (weak) convergence process in Italy. Other papers showing the important role of sectoral dynamics within European countries are, among others, de la Fuente (1996) and de la Fuente and Freire Seren (2000) for the Spanish regions; Siriopoulos and Asteriou (1998) for the Greek regions.

To sum up, not only structural change is relevant for regional convergence analysis in general, in Europe and elsewhere, but we often find a common pattern of sectoral dynamics going hand in hand with aggregate convergence. This pattern is strongly characterized by remarkable shifts of resources out of agriculture. This is so especially in poorer regions, where aggregate productivity is low because of the large size of a relatively backward agricultural sector.

In other words, the pattern of sectoral dynamics typical of a dual economy in its transitional stages seems to be an important factor of convergence. This conjecture is supported by further available evidence on some features of the poorer Southern European regions. Paci and Pigliaru (1999a) show that:

(i) The poorer Southern regions are specialized in agriculture: the average labor share of agriculture is four times higher that in Northern Europe (22 per cent vs 6 per cent in 1980);

(ii) In agriculture does exist a strong negative correlation between sector size and productivity level ($r=-0.7$);

(iii) The North-South productivity gap is higher in agriculture than in the other sectors (2.0 vs 1.2 in industry, 1.1 in services). The coefficient of variation in agriculture is more than double as compared to those of industry and sectors (51, 25 and 23 respectively).

Taken together, these data suggest that poorer Southern European regions are characterized by dualistic features and therefore have a potential for convergence by shifting resources out of a too large agricultural sector.

Two attempts at measuring how much convergence has been achieved by this kind of mechanism are reported in the following. First, Paci and Pigliaru (1999a) measure the sources of convergence across 109 regions in the period 1980-90, using the decomposition methodology proposed in Bernard and Jones (1996a). Sectoral dynamics is characterized by strong flows of out-migration of labor from agriculture towards sectors that are highly heterogeneous across European states and regions (on this more below). In spite of such heterogeneity, out-migration from agriculture is still capable of generating aggregate convergence since, on average, it is stronger in poorer regions and it moves towards higher-productivity sectors. The result is that 76 per cent of the (weak) aggregate labor productivity convergence is due to sectoral dynamics. As for the within effect, productivity growth in agriculture was faster in poorer regions, while the opposite is true for manufacturing.

Second, Paci and Pigliaru (1999b) use an analytical model of the dual economy (Mas-Colell and Razin, 1973) in order to obtain more detailed evidence on what constrains the full functioning of these convergence-enhancing components. In such an economy, the value of marginal productivity in agriculture is lower than in the non-agricultural sector along the transitional path leading to the steady-state. Since wages are determined by marginal values, an automatic incentive exists for out-migration from agriculture. Moreover, since the wage-gap is a decreasing function of the (relative) size of the agricultural sector, the incentive to out-migrate is stronger in the poorer (agricultural) regions. Here fast out-migration is good for aggregate growth because it allows a fast increase of the (high-productivity) non-agricultural sector[12].

Consequently, we should expect lagging agricultural regions to grow faster. Notice that in this context, any obstacle to out-migration is also an obstacle to convergence. We will come back to this important point at the end of the present section.

Paci and Pigliaru (1999b) find that the pattern of convergence characterizing 109 European regions for the period 1980-90 is broadly consistent with most of major predictions of the model.

The new data set used in the present paper yields further supporting evidence. Figure 4.2 shows that, for the European regions, the higher the initial agricultural labor share, the larger the outflow from agriculture (correlation coefficient $r = -0.84$)[13]. This shows the empirical relevance of the theoretical relationship between the initial non-agricultural labor share and its rate of change at the core of the dual model discussed above. Figure 4.3 shows that the larger the outflow from agriculture, the higher the rate of growth of aggregate labor productivity ($r = -0.41$). This suggests that the potential for convergence associated to the dualistic features of the poorer regions has been achieved – partially[14].

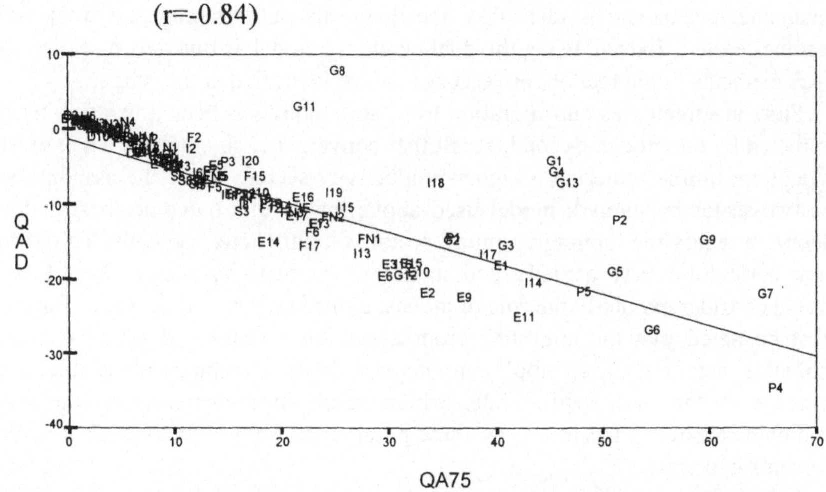

Figure 4.2 Initial labor share in agriculture (QA75) and its variation 1975-97 (QAD).

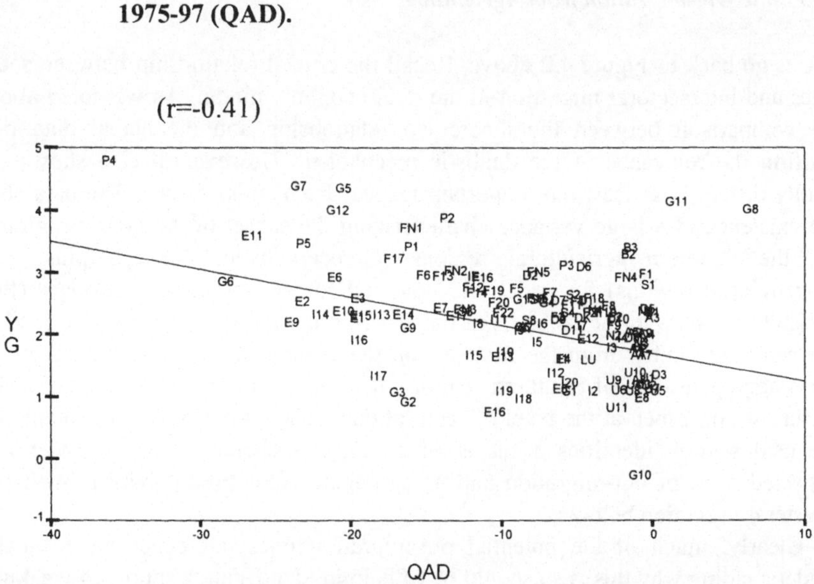

Figure 4.3 Variation 1975-97 of labor share in agriculture (QAD) and growth rate of aggregate labor productivity (% annual average, YG).

However, given the weakness of the overall European regional convergence, the main use of this type of exercise is perhaps that once a relevant convergence-enhancing mechanism is identified, the diagnosis of its strong and weak points becomes easier. Indeed, using the dual-economy model as our starting point, three weak elements in the real of convergence can be identified at this stage.

First, in some cases out-migration from agriculture has been much weaker than predicted by the model. Second, recall that convergence is obtained when existing agriculture implies entering a higher-productivity sector. While the assumption of the two-sector benchmark model used above makes this outcome inescapable in theory, in reality the 'non-agricultural' sector is highly heterogeneous and outflows from agriculture may actually end in a low productivity sector. Therefore we should consider explicitly the role of at least a third sector – i.e. services. Finally, it must be noted that out-migration from agriculture, instead of moving to other economic activities, may imply an increase in the unemployment rate and a decrease in the participation rate, which result in a decrease in the overall employment rate. In the following three paragraphs we will analyze each of these elements in details.

Too Little Out-migration from Agriculture?

Let us go back to Figure 4.2 above. Recall the crucial relationship between sector sizes and intersectoral migration in the dual-economy model. As we noted above, the comparison between the theoretical relationship and the actual data does confirm the relevance of the dualistic mechanism. However, it also shows that reality differs in at least one important respect from (this) theory. The data show the existence of a large variance characterizing the subset of the poorer regions – i.e. the Southern agricultural regions (Greece, Spain, Portugal plus some Mezzogiorno regions) for which the potential for convergence is stronger (their agricultural share in the labor force ranges from around 60 per cent to around 25 per cent). We know from the first section that a large disparity characterizes the main aggregate data of Southern regions. It is interesting to find out that such a feature is confirmed at the level of sectoral data. The cluster analysis contained in the next section identifies a subset of 15 regions characterized by lower than expected rates of out-migration and of aggregate labor productivity growth (see Cluster 4 in section below).

Clearly, much of the potential out-migration does not occur mechanically. Understanding why this is so should be of help in identifying a source of weakness in the process of income per-capita convergence across the European regions. Several testable hypotheses can be advanced at this stage of the analysis, all concerning those regions where out-migration was less than expected by the theory. (a) *Spatial externalities in the non-agricultural sector*: given the existence of important agglomeration economies associated to technology adoption (e.g., Paci and Usai, 2000), the development of a non-agricultural sector in poorer regions might depend crucially on quality of their economic institutions and their adopted policies. (b) *Efficient specialization*: economic integration might assign specialization in agriculture to some of those regions. Under such circumstances, a currently inefficient agriculture might incur important efficiency gains and therefore convergence through the *within-sector* mechanism. (c) *Harmful sectoral policies*: European policy aimed at sustaining the farmer's income might have weakened the incentive to out-migrate and – consequently – overall convergence. Finally, the private cost of migration should also be considered. Migrating from a low- towards a high-productivity sector might require costly individual investment for acquiring sector-specific skills (Caselli and Coleman, 2001). The cost of such investment might vary significantly across regions due to the heterogeneity of educational institutions and the quality of vocational training projects.

The cluster analysis in the next section will yield some evidence concerning especially hypothesis (a). A full assessment of the other hypotheses requires further regional data not yet available at this stage of our research.

Does Out-migration Always Move to the 'Right' Sector(s)?

Let us now turn to the second problem – convergence might have been weak or absent even in some of the regions where out-migration was as strong as expected. As we noticed, in the theoretical two-sector model, migration is necessarily from a low- to a high-productivity sector, with the non-agricultural sector being the growth-enhancing one. However, the non-agricultural sector consists of manufacturing and services, i.e. sectors characterized by large productivity differentials. Analyzing our data by taking account of such a three-sector context, we find that the main relationships between sectoral dynamics and convergence are as follows. First, out-migration from agricultural is faster in regions where the decline of the share of manufacturing is slower. Second, regions where the decline of the share of manufacturing is slower enjoy a faster grow of aggregate labor productivity. These two pieces of evidence are shown in Figures 4.4 and 4.5 respectively. The correlation coefficient in Figure 4.4 is –0.73[15] and in Figure 4.5 is 0.34.

On the contrary, changes in the labor share of both private and public services do not seem to exert a significant influence on aggregate growth ($r = 0.04$ and $r = 0.13$ respectively). Such an absence of correlation also characterizes each individual component of the sector 'private services' in our data set.

If we are looking at the explanation, we could turn to the well-known Baumol model (1967) of unbalanced growth, which would predict a negative effect of growing services on overall productivity growth, even if the service share in real value added were not rising. The basic assumption of the model is that productivity growth is lower in services than in the other sectors, thus defining services as a stagnant sector; the prediction is of a tendency of productivity growth of the economy toward productivity growth of services through expanding service employment. This prediction appears to be supported, at least for 1980-90, by the shift-and-share decomposition of overall productivity growth, since the contribution of services is far larger than the contribution of industry, mainly because of structural change. Moreover, it can be seen that there is convergence of productivity *within* the service sector across regions (Paci and Pigliaru, 1999a)[16].

(r=-0.73)

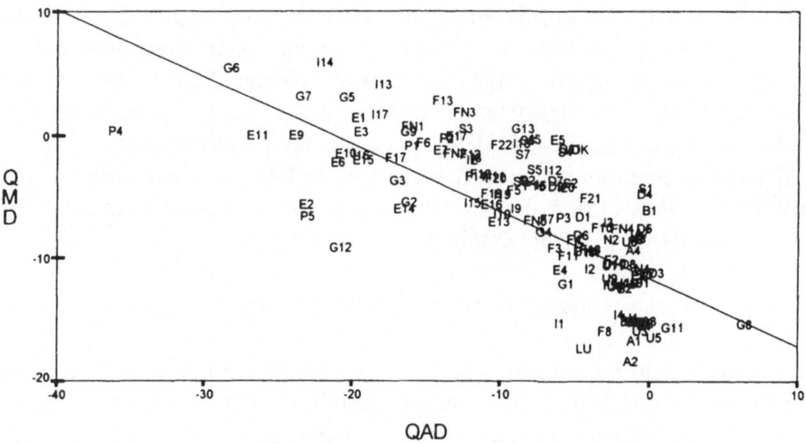

Figure 4.4 Variation 1975-97 of labor shares in agriculture (QAD) and manufacture (QMD).

(r=0.34)

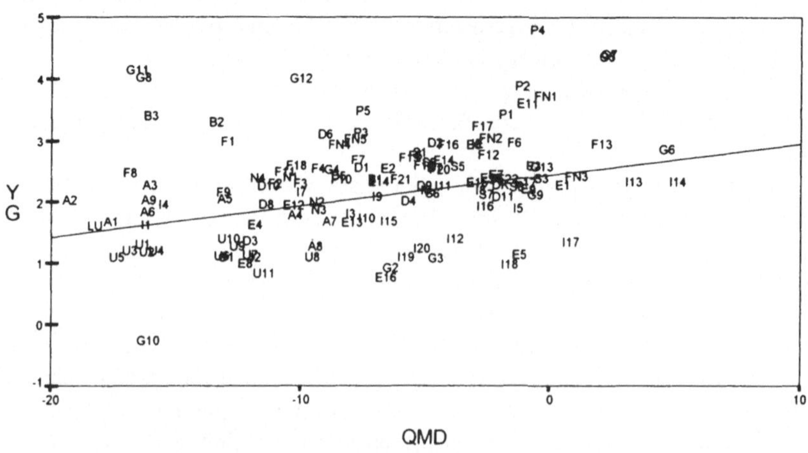

Figure 4.5 Variation 1975-97 of labor share in manufacture (QMD) and growth rate of aggregate labor productivity (% annual average, YG).

A satisfactory test of the hypothesis maintaining that services are harmful to growth, however, would need reliable and disaggregated data, which are not available, at least for the European regions. The basic problem is that of measuring productivity of services in real terms (Storrie, 2000; De Bandt, 1988; Nakamura, 1997). As Solow has noticed, everybody knows that an extraordinary acceleration in productivity has been recently taken place in the activities linked to information technology, and thus also in services, but this does not emerge from national accounts. Hence, Baumol's stagnant sector is more restrictive than the services sector, and a careful selection of service activities would be necessary[17]. Moreover, as far as regional disparity is concerned, the information technology innovations undoubtedly favor accessibility of the peripheral areas, thus favoring convergence in both growth and unemployment (European Commission, 2000).

The original Baumol model considers two final sectors, however some of the literature has recognized that many service activities, like research, counseling, legal services, financial services, etc., are inputs for industries with growth-enhancing effects (Miles, 1993; Windrum and Tomlinson, 1999; Antonelli, 1998; Ochel and Wegner, 1987; Gazier and Thevenot, 2000)[18]. Information technology has magnified these effects. The pessimistic conclusion of the Baumol model for overall productivity growth, therefore, is not at all a certainty. However, this does not necessarily represents good news for the lagging regions, since these growth-enhancing service activities tend to agglomerate geographically, especially in some metropolitan areas.

Although Baumol's model should be applied only with important amendments, it still addresses an inescapable problem: that stagnant activities, now typically represented by performing arts, child and elderly care, will be typified by rising relative prices, thus discouraging demand for them. In particular, many household services find only a limited market externalization, as compared to the US, because of high relative prices (Anxo and Fagan, 2000). This can be seen as an explanation of both under-tertiarisation and low employment rates in continental Europe (Borzaga and Villa, 1999; Pugno, 2002).

In conclusion, the effects of a growing service sector on disparities in productivity growth across regions differ greatly, depending on the specific activity considered. Knowledge-based services, in general, favor accessibility to the peripheral regions, but the service activities most linked to manufacturing, though enhancing growth, are very concentrated. For personal services Baumol would predict a negative effect on growth, but also a rise in relative prices of these services, so that they may be rationed by consumers. Excessive regulation in these markets, as it has been recognized for continental Europe, acts as a further constraint (OECD, 1991; Koefijk and Kremers, 1996; Pilat, 1996; Pugno, 2002).

Does Out-migration Reduce Overall Employment Rate?

The third weakness in the convergence process as a result of classical dualism is that part of out-migration from agriculture may go to the pool of unemployed or exit from the labor market due to retirement. Figure 4.6, which reports the association between out-migration from agriculture and overall employment rate, shows that there is some truth in this presumption: increases in employment rates are larger where out-migration is smaller.

However, while this relation is statistically significant (r=0.36), it is weakened by the high variability of the Southern European regions. For example, in some Southern regions the high reduction of the agriculture share has been the accompanied by remarkable increases of employment in the service sector, especially public administration (P4, Alentejo +14 per cent points, E11 Extremadura +13 per cent) or tourism (G6, Ionia Nisia +21 per cent, P5 Algarve +30 per cent).

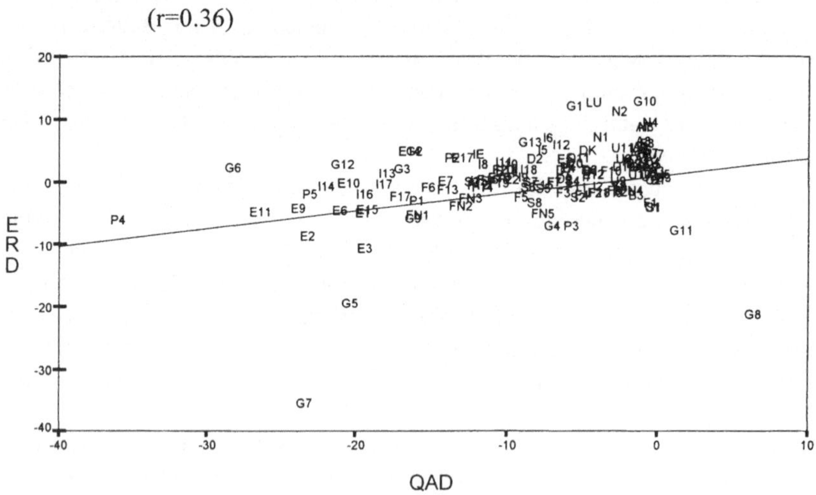

Figure 4.6 Variation 1975-97 of the labor share in agriculture (QAD) and of the overall employment rate (ERD).

One reason for the negative association between out-migration from agriculture and overall employment rate may be due to the difficulties shown by industry in absorbing employment. In fact, during the most recent decades both agriculture and industry have reduced employment throughout the European regions. The decline in agriculture is well-known, and it is analyzed in the previous section, but the extent and spread of the decline in industry is less well-known. During the period 1975-97 industrial employment diminishes in 114 regions, while in 3 regions only it exceeds 1 per cent per year (see also European Commission, 2000). It is interesting to note that this decline takes place in the regions irrespective of their level of per-capita income[19]. Therefore, it cannot be expected that future growth of industrial activity will be able to solve the problem of unemployment. First, growth in industrial value added does not seem to be much correlated with growth of industrial employment any longer. In fact the simple correlation coefficient between the two variables is 0.3 for the period considered (the regression coefficient is 0.33). Secondly, no correlation emerges between growth in industrial value added and the *overall* employment rate (0.19), and between the share of industrial employment and the overall employment rate (0.06). Thirdly, even the increase in competitiveness, as approximated by growth in industrial value added per worker, appears not to favor the overall employment rate (–0.03). These results take national accounts as face value, so that they do not take into account the externalization of services from manufacturing firms, which has been recently an increasing process, as noted above.

By contrast, the service sector has absorbed much employment, and it is expected to have an increasing role to this end (Elfring, 1989; Storrie, 2000). In fact, all regions but four have experienced an increase in employment of market services over 1975-97, and in 92 regions the increase is above 1 per cent per year. Moreover, employment in market services grows both in the poorest regions, and in the richest regions (Dathe and Schmid 2000)[20]. This result is relevant, because it confirms that out-migration from agriculture, which is greater in the poorest regions, may by-pass manufacturing and go directly to services.

The contribution of the service sector to the solution of the unemployment problem can be more properly seen by observing the relationship between the service share in value added and the overall employment rate. Simple correlations show some positive relationship across the European regions (-.01, .15, .35 for the subperiods 1975-83, 1984-91 and 1992-97 respectively; for German regions see Dathe and Schmid, 2000). More precisely, by disaggregating services one finds that the relationship for market services becomes closer, though very much less for Distributive Trades, whereas for non-market services it turns from positive in 1975-83 to practically zero afterwards[21]. These results are only indicative, and reveal that the positive contribution of market services in absorbing unemployment is positive, but is very unsystematic across regions. A general rise in the value added share in market services may tighten the labor market in some areas, while still leaving other areas with great unemployment. Fortunately, metropolitan areas seem to have recently started to delocalize some service activities, but a clear trend is not yet apparent (Illeris, 1996; Mur, 1996).

Different Growth Patterns across European Regions

Our analysis of the growth process across the European regions has called to attention three important factors that have influenced the speed and the direction of the convergence process. The first factor is structural change, whose key mechanism seems to be associated with the shift of labor shares from agriculture towards sectors with different productivity levels (manufacture and services). A second feature we will deal with is the evolution of the employment rate within the convergence process. This is a crucial element for our analysis since, as we have already noticed, convergence in terms of labor productivity may differ from per capita income simply because there are large differences among regions in the levels and evolution of participation and unemployment rates.

A third element is localized technological capacity; i.e. the ability, specific to each region, to create new ideas and to imitate external innovations. This element can both play an independent role in convergence, and interact with the process of dualism-driven convergence by affecting the conditions that allow a successful expansion of the non agricultural sector (see the previous paragraph).

Our analysis in this section aims at sketching the relationships between these three elements in order to draw a final picture of regional growth in Europe based on an exercise in cluster analysis. Let first briefly describe the data and the chosen variables.

Structural change: employment share in agriculture in the initial year 1975 (QA75); variation of the agriculture share over the period 1975-97 (QAD)[22].

Labor market dynamics: variation over the period 1975-97 of the ratio employment /population; for simplicity we refer to this indicator as 'employment rate' (ERD)[23].

Technological capacity: ratio patents/GDP, average value 1985-86 (PY)[24].

Labor productivity: levels of overall labor productivity in the initial (1975) and final (1997) years (Y75, Y97); annual average growth rate of labor productivity over the period 1975-97 (YG).

We now make use of the seven variables listed above to define homogeneous groups of regions using the cluster analysis technique. Table 4.1 reports for each group of homogeneous regions the average values of the included variables; the groups are listed according to the decreasing value of their 1975 labor productivity level; a geographical distribution of the six clusters is displayed in Figure 4.7. The main features of each cluster are discussed below and are determined not only on the basis of the included variables, but also looking at the mean value of other relevant variables within each cluster.

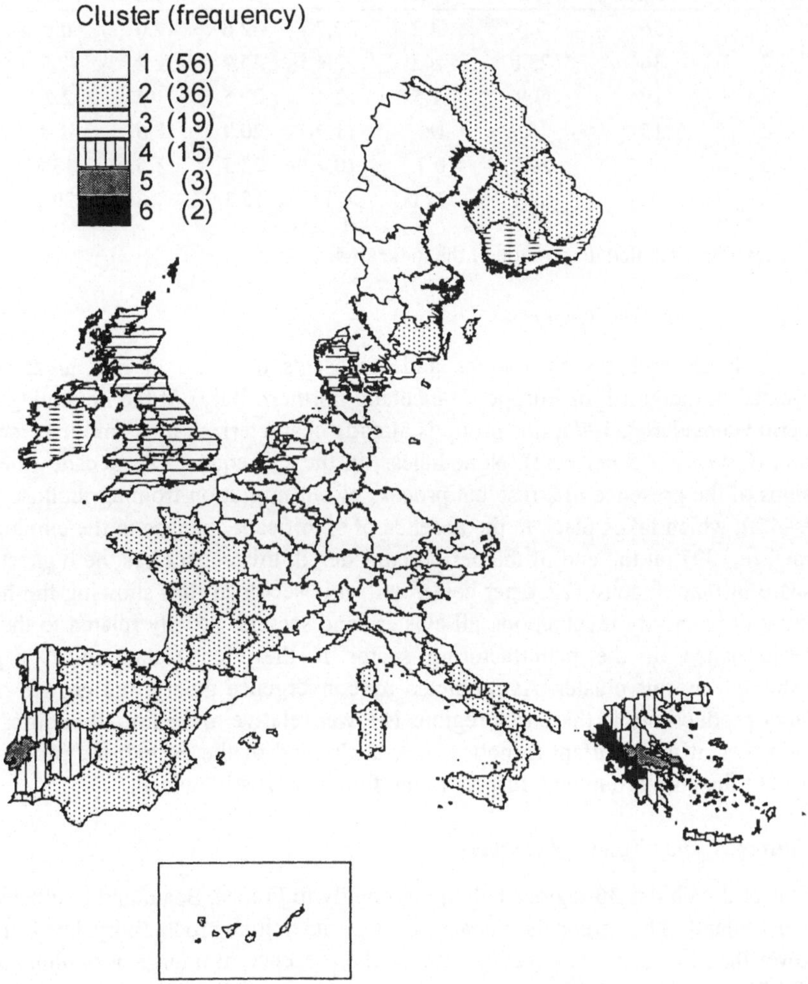

Figure 4.7 Clusters of the European regions.

See Table 4.1 for the included variables.

Table 4.1 European regions growth process. Final cluster centers for the included variables.

Cluster	n. regions	QA75	QAD	Y75	Y97	YG	ERD	PY
1	56	7.5	-4.2	27.7	42.6	2.0	0.0	4.4
2	36	23.8	-14.0	22.4	35.9	2.2	-2.7	1.4
3	19	3.9	-1.5	22.4	29.5	1.2	2.2	5.3
4	15	45.9	-18.5	11.9	20.9	2.6	-1.8	0.1
5	3	20.8	0.7	10.4	22.5	3.6	-13.8	0.2
6	2	58.1	-22.0	6.1	15.3	4.2	-29.2	0.0

See text for a detailed description of the indicators.

Cluster 1: The Core Group

This cluster includes 57 regions and represents the core of rich areas mainly located in the North of Europe, France and northern Italy. At the beginning of the period considered, 1975, this group is already characterized by a "modern" sectoral mix (QA75 = 7.5 per cent). Nonetheless, in the subsequent two decades there are signs of the presence of a residual process of out-migration from agriculture (QAD = -4.2), which takes place in the absence of significant changes in the employment rate. In 1997, at the end of the period considered, this cluster has the highest labor share in manufacture (22.4 per cent), with this sector in turn showing the highest labor productivity level among all clusters and sectors. Strictly related to the good performance of the manufacturing sector is the high technological capacity exhibited by this cluster. As predicted by convergence theory, the growth rate of labor productivity in these rich regions is lower relative to the initially poorer ones. However, it is important to notice that, at the end of the period, the productivity lead of the core group with respect to the followers is still evident.

Cluster 2: The Growing Periphery

Cluster 2 includes 36 regions belonging mainly to France, Spain and Southern Italy and Finland. This group is characterized by an initial productivity level slightly lower than the European average and by the presence of a large agriculture sector (QA75 = 23.8 per cent). Over the period these regions display a strong out-flow of labor from the primary sector: the proportional variation of the agricultural share is equal to -58.8 per cent. In spite of such a strength of out-migration, the decrease of the aggregate employment rate is rather small (ERD = -2.7). A more detailed analysis shows that the general tendency for a decrease of manufacturing labor share here looks less pronounced, probably thanks – among other things – to the presence of a significant technological activity at the local level. The overall productivity growth rate is the highest among the advanced regions (YG = 2,2 per cent). All in all, in this cluster, part of the convergence appears to be compatible with the hypothesis that the dualistic mechanism is at work. From this point of view, a comparison with the characteristics of Cluster 4 is particularly interesting.

Cluster 3: Specialization in Public Services

This cluster includes 19 regions belonging mainly to the North (Brussells, Berlin, Dutch and British regions), the only exception being the capital region of Greece (Attiki). Interestingly, these regions started in 1975 with the same labor productivity level of cluster 2. The common feature of these regions is the low incidence of agriculture even in the mid seventies (QA75 = 3,9 per cent) and the strong specialization in manufacture and services which give rise to a relevant technological capacity (PY = 6). In these regions most of the dualistic transition has already taken place, even though we still notice a reduction of the agricultural share. A very important feature which distinguishes this cluster from all the others is the increase of the overall employment rate (ERD = 2,2). Looking at the sectoral composition of employment in 1997, we find in this cluster the highest share of public services (27 per cent), which seems to have acted as a sponge soaking up the surplus labor. The effects of this process in terms of growth performance are negative: this group displays the lowest growth rate of aggregate labor productivity among all European regions (1.2 per cent). Clearly, dualism-driven convergence is not present, and the gap between these regions and the richer ones seems to have reached a rather stationary level.

Cluster 4: Structural Change and Safeguard of Employment Levels

This cluster gathers 15 Southern European regions which have gone through a strong process of structural change (QAD = -18.5). There are similarities with respect to Cluster 2: a rather large initial agricultural share; a rather fast reduction of the latter during the subsequent period; a limited decrease of the employment rate; a growth rate higher than that of the richer cluster. Here again the dualistic mechanism seems to be at work in generating convergence. However, there are two important (related) differences. The initial gap in labor productivity is much larger, as well as the size of the agricultural sector (46 per cent v 24 per cent). All other things being equal, we would expect a higher rate of change of the agricultural share and a significantly higher aggregate growth rate. Both predictions are rejected by the evidence: the agricultural share decreases in the period at a rate equal to -40.3 per cent (far less than in Cluster 2), and the growth rate is only a little higher than in cluster 2. In other words, regions in this cluster appears to lie below the theoretical relationship behind the dualism driven convergence mechanism previously described. As a consequence, in these regions there seems to exist some potential for convergence associated to the existence of dualistic features not fully exploited. Why this is so is a problem that deserves some attention in future research. For the time being, we should notice that we detect a low level of local technological activity. This might be part of the explanation, as previously suggested.

Cluster 5: Adapt to the Market Openness

This group includes only three southern regions, two Greek and one Portuguese. The structural change process had already started (QA75 = 20 per cent) so that, over the period considered, these regions saw an increment of their labor share in agriculture (QAD = 0.7). Nonetheless, the overall employment rate show a clear reduction (ERD = -13.8) signaling a process of expulsion of redundant labor from other sectors. More specifically, these regions show a reduction of employment in manufacture (-13 per cent points over the entire period) associated with a high growth of labor productivity, as a necessary response to increasing international competition. The effects of this structural adjustment on the aggregate growth rate of productivity are positive (YG = 3.6 per cent) even though lower than in cluster 6. This result give additional support to the idea that the key feature of a structural change growth-enhancing process is the out-migration of labor from agriculture.

Cluster 6: Radical Structural Change

Again this is a very small subset formed of only two Greek regions. In contrast with the previous cluster, here the regions are characterized by a radical decline of the agriculture labor share (QAD = -22), associated with an analogously strong reduction of the employment rate. Such changes allow these regions to obtain the highest increase in agriculture labor productivity (5 per cent annual average) and also significant productivity growth in the non-agriculture sectors. Therefore, the overall productivity growth of these economies is the highest among all clusters (YG = 4.2 per cent).

In conclusion, our cluster exercise confirms the crucial role of the dualistic mechanisms in defining different growth paths (and consequently homogeneous groups of European regions) in terms of both labor productivity growth and employment rate dynamics.

Conclusions

The picture on disparities in productivity growth and in unemployment across European regions shows three main broad characteristics: a slow and not very systematic convergence of labor productivity toward a common level; an even more uncertain convergence of unemployment rates; absence of correlation between growth rates and unemployment.

The literature, both theoretical and empirical, has usually dealt with the two kinds of disparities in a separate manner, and often in aggregate terms, so that a comprehensive explanation has not yet been provided. This paper has offered an attempt to use a unified framework to study both phenomena, by adopting a sectoral perspective, i.e. by considering the relationship between agriculture, industry and services, and their role in enhancing growth and absorbing employment. Our contribution has been to collect and organize different kinds of evidence from the more recent literature, to provide new evidence, and to interpret both the previously known and the new evidence within the same unified framework. To be more specific on this latter point, we should add that we have also pursued an implicit aim – i.e. obtaining an initial assessment of the consistency of our evidence with a specific, multi-sector theoretical framework.

This underlying theoretical framework can be summed up as follows. We think that the observed patterns of aggregate convergence can be better analyzed and understood by taking explicitly account of the underlying sectoral dynamics. First, the reallocation between agriculture and the non-agricultural sectors during the transition of a dual-economy towards its steady-state is potentially a powerful source of convergence; second, the Baumol model gives a useful account of the role that the service sector may play in aggregate growth; third, the well-known Engel's Law links the declining weight of agriculture to the rising weight of services. Clearly, putting these pieces together is not a simple task. To name just one problem, they are based on assumptions about technology and/or preferences that appear to be far from homogeneous[25]. However, combining them is useful as long as we pursue the limited aim of achieving some simple insights of how convergence is obtained within a three-sector framework. The key predictions that can be obtained by this exercise are as follows. Economies which differ in their initial conditions tend to converge in overall economic growth rates, provided that long-run productivity growth is homogeneous across economies and sectors. Convergence is mainly due to that fact that, according to the dualistic model, labor migrates from the least productive sector, since it is attracted by higher values of marginal productivity elsewhere, thus reducing the agricultural sector, consistently with the Engel's law, and feeding the sector crucial for growth, i.e. manufacturing. In fact, this migration does not always translate into a sufficient expansion of the non-agricultural sector, so that a reduction in the labor participation rates often accompanies the process. The more backward regions would then exhibit the largest intersectoral migration, the highest overall productivity growth, and the largest reduction in the employment rates. According to Baumol, labor migrates to services so that a constant share in real expenditure for them is maintained, in the presence of a level of productivity lower than that prevailing in manufacturing. If labor supply is not constraining, employment would rise (Tronti, Sestini and Toma, 2000). Engel's law would emphasize this effect by predicting a rising share in real expenditure for services.

This theoretical framework has not been formally developed in the paper, but the bulk of the empirical findings from the European regions discussed in this paper are broadly consistent with the approach defined above. In fact, most of the European regions seem to follow the predicted pattern of convergence and structural change. For instance, at this stage we have much evidence suggesting that convergence in aggregate productivity is strongly associated with out-migration from agriculture, and that the magnitude of the impact of the latter on aggregate growth depends significantly on which sector absorbs the migrating workers.

The most promising piece of new evidence is perhaps the exercise presented in the fourth section, where we have used cluster analysis to identify subsets of regions homogeneous in terms of variables such as sectoral dynamics, labor market dynamics, and overall productivity growth. The picture that emerges is consistent with the main relationships characterizing the three-sector framework sketched in this paper. Regions that start from a low agricultural share (Cluster 1) are the richest and grow relatively slowly; regions that start from high agricultural shares (both Cluster 2 and 4, although heterogeneous in other respects) are characterized by a fast decline of that share and by higher than average growth rates; in addition to this, these regions show a limited decline in their employment rates. The few remaining regions exhibit rather diverse features, but they can still be grouped into few main clusters, the characteristics of which are again easily interpreted within the proposed framework. In particular, the group specialized in service activities, mainly metropolitan areas (Cluster 3), shows a particularly slow rate of productivity growth and a rising employment rate.

All in all, we think that the evidence discussed in this paper shows the relevance of a sectoral perspective on convergence analysis. By understanding what controls the flows of out-migration from agriculture and their direction (towards manufacturing, services or else) we should be able to better identify the strong and weak points of the overall convergence. Consequently, more research in the same direction, both theoretical and empirical, will certainly be useful especially for those researchers aiming at obtaining well-founded and detailed policy implications on how to strengthen the process leading to smaller regional differentials in the long-run.

Notes

1 This paper has been presented at the XLI Annual Conference of the *Società Italiana degli Economisti*. Financial support provided by Murst (Research Project on 'European Integration and Regional Disparities in Economic Growth and Unemployment') is gratefully acknowledged. We thank *Cambridge Econometrics* for providing us the data on the European regions. We also thank Mario Paffi for excellent research assistance and Dario Paternoster for valuable help with the data. We have also benefited from comments by seminar participants at the University of Modena.

2 Two further distinctions should be made in their application to the European regions: the distinction between income and GDP, and that between resident population and working age population. But they are not yet particularly investigated due to the lack of reliable data.

3 Cfr. Tondl (1999) for an extensive survey and check of the results.

4 Data on employment and value added are from Cambridge Econometrics; value added is in million of ECU 1990 and it has been corrected for PPS. 15 members and 131 regions of the EU are considered, excluding the East part of Germany. The list of the regions appears in the Appendix.

5 Moreover, at a finer level of territorial disaggregation, the richest areas of the Northern regions reveal an increased deviation from the others (Dunford, 1993; Magrini, 1999; Rombaldoni, 1998).

6 The evidence on the effectiveness of unemployment and wages on migration is mixed. The unemployment variable is not significant according to Bentivogli and Pagano (1998) and Neven and Gouyette (1995), but it is significant according to Fagerberg et al. (1997). As for the wage variable, the opposite pattern is detected.

7 This conclusion is confirmed by the absolute β-convergence. In fact, by adopting OLS weighted by the population in the middle of the estimation period (1975-96), the following R^2 can be obtained for per capita Gdp and productivity, respectively: 0.035, 0.17. If the same procedure is applied for the employment rate, a significant *positive* β obtains, with R^2=0.075. If the unweighted OLS is run for the three cases, then the R^2s are 0.073, 0.33, 0.23 respectively, thus confirming the importance of weighting.

8 For an application to the European regions see Fingleton and McCombie (1998).

9 Piacentini and Sulis (2000) find some *negative* correlation between productivity and the employment rate (defined in gaps with the employment average), but *within* the 'Objective I regions'.

10 The correlation coefficients linking the specified variables are the following:

	E/P	g(*E/P*)	*u*
Y/E	-.035	.33	.116
g(*Y/E*)	.053	-.591	-.06

where g(.) stands for growth rate, and the variables are calculated as averages over 1975-97.

11 For the European countries see Doyle and O'Leary (1999).

12 This is of course a very simplified account of the transitional dynamics of the dual economy. See Paci and Pigliaru (1999b).

13 All the correlation coefficients presented in this section are based on 131 observations and are statistically significant at 1 per cent level, unless otherwise specified.

14 Their results also show that by ignoring the dualistic sectoral dynamics, transitional features (that do not determine stationary values) can be wrongly interpreted as permanent ones (that do determine them). Wrong policy implication could then be derived. For instance, in the early phases of the process a large size of the agricultural sector can exert a negative influence on a region's growth rate. However, this influence is *transitory* in the dual economy. Ignoring this feature could lead to a very different interpretation about the role of agriculture in growth.

15 As for the correlation between changes in agriculture and in services shares, its value is -
-.38.

16 A stronger convergence in services than in manufacturing total factor productivity is found for the Oecd countries (Bernard and Jones, 1996b; Gouyette and Perelman, 1997).

17 Not only a large part of transport and communication services should be excluded from the stagnant sector, but also some typical personal services, like some health services, which have benefited from great scientific progress, or like some tourist services.

18 Services provide increasingly inputs and innovations also to themselves. This may create new service products but tends to give rise to geographical concentration.

19 The correlation coefficient between the percentage change in industrial employment and per-capita value added is 0.2 for the period considered.

20 The correlation coefficient between per-capita value added and the employment growth rates of the market services is 0.29.

21 The correlation coefficients are -.22, -.25, -.09 for Distributive Trades, .39, .51, .49 for Transport and Communications, -.24, .03, .34 for Finance and Insurance Services, .21, .40, .46 for Other Market Services, and .09, .12, .01 for non-market services. At the national level, more disaggregated data reveal that within Other Market Services those for producers employ at a very increasing rate, while those for consumers tend to stagnate (European Commission, 1999).

22 We have also considered other indicators of sectoral composition and change relative to manufacture, building, private and public services. However, their inclusion leave almost unchanged the clusters composition, confirming that the key role of structural change is played by the out-flow of labor from agriculture.

23 The complement to the employment/population ratio is a measure of both the unemployment and the participation rates which can be viewed as the two adjustment channels to labor market disequilibrium. Due to the lack of reliable data on unemployment and labor forces at the regional level in Europe, we prefer to use the employment/population ratio as a comprehensive indicator of the labor market characteristics.

24 Patents data are from the CRENoS databank (www.crenos.it) and refer to patent applications to the European Patent Office.

25 Baumol assumes that productivity growth differs exogenously across sectors, while no such difference is present in the dual-economy model used in the third section above; preferences are homothetic in these two models while Engel's law reflects non-homotheticity. More analytical work is clearly needed to assess in depth the complementarity of these three potential components of a more general framework. However, intermediate results are available in several recent papers, for instance Murat and Pigliaru (1998), where some of Baumol's results are obtained in the absence of unbalanced growth.

References

Abraham, F. (1996), 'Regional adjustment and wage flexibility in the European Union', *Regional Science and Urban Economics*, vol. 26, pp. 51-75.

Abraham, F. and van Rampuy, P. (1995), 'Regional convergence in the European Monetary Union', *Papers in Regional Science*, vol. 74, no. 2, pp. 125-142.

Aghion, P.and Howitt, P. (1994), 'Growth and Unemployment', *The Review of Economic Studies*. vol. 61, no. 3, pp. 477-494.

Antonelli, C. (1998), 'Localised technological change, new information technology and knowledge-based economy: the European evidence', *Journal of Evolutionary Economics*, vol. 8, pp. 177-198.

Anxo, D. and Fagan, C. (2000), 'Service employment: a gender perspective', in D. Anxo and D. Storrie (eds), *The job creation potential of the service sector in Europe*, Centre for European Labour Market Studies, Sweden, pp. 83-106.

Baddeley, M., Martin, R. and Tyler, P. (1998), 'European regional unemployment disparities: convergence or persistence?', *European Urban and Regional Studies*, vol. 5, no. 3, pp. 195-215.

Baumol, W. (1967), 'Macroeconomics of unbalanced growth: the anatomy of urban crisis', *American Economic Review*, vol. 57, pp. 415-426.

Bentivogli, C. and Pagano, P. (1998), *Regional disparities and labour mobility: the US vs. the European Monetary Union*, Banca d'Italia (mimeo).

Bernard, A. and Jones, C. (1996a), 'Productivity and convergence across US states and industries', *Empirical Economics*, vol. 21, pp. 113-135.

Bernard, A. and Jones, C. (1996b) 'Comparing Apples to Oranges: Productivity Convergence and Measurement Across Industries and Countries', *American Economic Review*, vol. 86, no. 5, pp. 1216-1238.

Borzaga, C. and Villa, P. (1999), 'Flexibility and the Tertiary Sector', University of Trento, mimeo.

Canova, F. and Marcet, A. (1995), 'The poor stay poor: non-convergence across countries and regions', *Cepr Discussion Paper*, no.1265, November.

Caselli, F. and Coleman, W.J. (2001), 'The U.S structural transformation and regional convergence: a reinterpretation', *Journal of Political Economy,* vol. 109, no. 3, pp. 584-616

Cuadrado-Roura, J., Mancha-Navarro, T. and Garrido-Yserte, R. (2000), 'Regional productivity patterns in Europe: an alternative approach', *Annals of Regional Science*, vol. 34, pp. 365-384.

Dathe, D. and Schmid, G. (2000), 'Determinants of business and personal services: evidence from the German regions', in D. Anxo and D. Storrie (eds), *The job creation potential of the service sector in Europe*, Centre for European Labour Market Studies, Sweden, pp. 183-242.

De Bandt, J. (1988), 'Le débat sur la productivité dans les servics: des problèmes mal posé', *Revue d'Economie Industrielle*, 43.

de la Fuente, A. (1996), 'On the sources of convergence: a close look at the Spanish regions', *CEPR Discussion Paper* No. 1543.

de la Fuente, A. and Freire Seren, M.J. (2000), 'Estructura sectorial y convergencia regional', *Documentos de Economia/2*, Fundacion Caixagalicia.

Decressin, J. and Fatas, A. (1995), 'Regional labor market dynamics in Europe', *European Economic Review*, vol. 39, pp. 1627-1655.

Doyle, E. and O'Leary, E. (1999), 'The role of structural change in labour productivity convergence among EU contries: 1970-1990', *Journal of Economic Studies*, vol. 26, pp. 106-120.

Dunford, M. (1993), 'Regional disparities in the European community: evidence from the Regio Databank', *Regional Studies*, vol. 27, no. 8, pp. 727-743.

Elfring, T. (1989), 'New evidence on the expansion of service employment in advanced economies', *Review of Income and Wealth*, vol. 35, December, pp. 409-440.

Epifani, P. (1998), 'Globalizzazione e divergenza dei tassi regionali di disoccupazione nei paesi dell'Unione Europea', *Liuc Papers*, no. 59, Libero Istituto Universitario Cattaneo.

European Commission (1999), *Services in Europe*, Bruxelles

European Commission (2000), *Sixth Periodic Report on the Social and Economic Situation and Development of Regions in the European Union*, Bruxelles.

Fagerberg, J., B. Verspagen and M. Caniels (1997), 'Technology, growth and unemployment across European Regions', *Regional Studies*, vol. 31, pp. 457-466

Fingleton, B. (1999), 'Economic geography with spatial econometrics: a "third way" to analyse economic development and equilibrium, with application to the EU regions', *European University Institute WP ECO*, No. 99/21.

Fingleton, B. and McCombie, J. (1998), 'Increasing returns and economic growth: some evidence for manufacturing from the European Union', *Oxford Economic Papers*, vol. 50, pp. 89-105.

Gazier, B. and Thevenot, N. (2000), 'Analysing business services employment', in D Anxo and D. Storrie (eds) *The Job Creation Potential of the Service Sector in Europe*, Centre for European Labour Market Studies, Sweden, pp. 243-265.

Gouyette, G. and Perelman, S. (1997), 'Productivity convergence in OECD service industries', *Structural Change and Economic Dynamics*, vol. 8, pp. 279-295.

Illeris, S. (1996), *The service economy. A geographical approach*, London: Wiley.

Koefijk, K. and Kremers, J. (1996), 'Marketing opening, regulation and growth in Europe', *Economic Policy: An European Forum*, no. 23, pp. 443-460.

López-Bazo, E., Vayá, E., Mora, A.J. and Suriñach, J. (1999), 'Regional Economic Dynamics and Convergence in the European Union', *Annals of Regional Science*, vol. 33, pp. 343-370.

Magrini, S. (1999), The evolution of income disparities among the regions of the European Union, *Regional Science and Urban Economics,* vol. 29, no. 2, pp. 257-281.

Mas-Colell, A. and Razin, A. (1973), 'A model of intersectoral migration and growth', *Oxford Economic Papers*, vol. 25, pp. 72-79.

Miles, I. (1993), 'Services in the new industrial economy', *Future*, vol. 22, July/Aug., pp. 653-671.

Mur, J. (1996), 'A future for Europe? Results with a regional prediction model', *Regional Studies*, vol. 30, no. 6, pp. 549-565.

Murat, M. and Pigliaru, F. (1998), 'International trade and uneven growth: A model with intersectoral spillovers of knowledge', *Journal of International Trade & Economic Development*, vol. 7, pp. 221-236.

Nakamura, L. (1997), 'Is the US economy really growing too slowly? Maybe we're measuring growth wrong', *Federal Reserve Bank of Philadelphia Business Review*, vol. 0, March/April, pp. 1-12.

Neven, D. and Gouyette, C. (1995), 'Regional convergence in the European Community', *Journal of Common Market Studies*, vol. 33, March, pp. 47-65.

Ochel, W. and Wegner, M. (1987), *Services Economies in Europe. Opportunities for Growth*, Pinter, London.

OECD (1991), *Economic Survey. Italy*, Paris.

Paci, R. (1997), 'More similar and less equal, economic growth in the European regions', *Weltwirtshaftliches Archiv*, vol. 133, no. 4, pp. 609-634.

Paci, R. and Pigliaru, F. (1997), 'Structural change and convergence. An Italian regional perspective', *Structural Change and Economic Dynamics*, vol. 8, pp. 297-318.

Paci, R. and Pigliaru, F. (1999a), 'European regional growth: do sectors matter?', in J. Adams and F. Pigliaru (eds), *Economic Growth and Change. National and Regional Patterns of Convergence and Divergence*, Elgar, Chelthenham, pp. 213-235.

Paci, R. and Pigliaru, F. (1999b), 'Is dualism still a source of convergence in Europe?', *Applied Economics*, vol. 31, pp. 1423-1436.

Paci, R. and Usai, S. (2000), 'Technological enclaves and industrial districts: an analysis of the regional distribution of innovative activity', *Regional Studies*, vol. 34, pp. 97-114.

Pench, L.R., Sestito, P. and Frontini, E. (1999), 'Some unpleasant arithmetics of regional unemployment in the EU', mimeo.

Piacentini, P. and Sulis, G. (2000), 'Crescita virtuosa e crescita neodualistica nell'ambito regionale: tendenze recenti per le aree europee in ritardo di sviluppo', *Rivista Economica del Mezzogiorno*, vol. 2, pp. 57-98.

Pilat, D. (1996), 'Competition, productivity and efficiency', *OECD Studies*, vol. 0, no. 27, pp. 108-146.

Pugno, M. (2002), 'Under-tertiarisation and unemployment', in R. Balducci and S. Staffolani (eds) *Income Distribution, Growth and Employment*, Edizioni Scientifiche Italiane, Naples (forthcoming).

Quah, D. (1996), 'Regional convergence clusters across Europe', *European Economic Review*, vol. 40, pp. 951-958.

Rombaldoni, R. (1998), 'Core and periphery patterns of regional convergence in Europe', *Rivista Italiana degli Economisti*, vol. 3, no. 3, pp. 419-457.

Siriopoulos, C. and Asteriou, D. (1998), 'Testing for convergence in Greek regions', *Regional Studies*, vol. 32, pp. 537-546.

Storrie, D. (2000), 'Service employment, productivity and growth', in D. Anxo and D. Storrie (eds), *The Job Creation Potential of the Service Sector in Europe*, Centre for European Labour Market Studies, Sweden, pp. 29-58.

Tondl, G. (1999), 'The changing pattern of regional convergence in Europe', *Jahrbuch fuer Regionalwissenschaft/Review of Regional Research*, vol. 19, no. 1, pp. 1-33.

Tondl, G. (1998), 'What determined the uneven growth of Europe's Southern regions?', Paper presented to the 38th Congress of the *European Regional Science Association*, September.

Tronti, L., Sestini, R. and Toma, A. (2000), 'Unbalanced growth and employment in the services', in D. Anxo and D. Storrie (eds), *The Job Creation Potential of the Service Sector in Europe*, Centre for European Labour Market Studies, Sweden, pp. 59-82.

Windrum, P. and Tomlinson, M. (1999), 'Knowledge-intensive services and international competitiveness: a four country comparison', *Technology Analysis and Strategic Management*, vol. 11, no. 3, pp. 391-408.

Appendix: List of the 131 European regions included.

B1	Bruxelles
B2	Vlaams Gewest
B3	Région Wallonne
DK	Denmark
D1	Baden-Württemberg
D2	Bayern
D3	Berlin
D4	Bremen
D5	Hamburg
D6	Hessen
D7	Niedersachsen
D8	Nordrhein-Westfalen
D9	Rheinland-Pfalz
D10	Saarland
D11	Schleswig-Holstein
G1	Anatoliki Makedonia
G2	Kentriki Makedonia
G3	Dytiki Makedonia
G4	Thessalia
G5	Ipeiros
G6	Ionia Nisia
G7	Dytiki Ellada
G8	Sterea Ellada
G9	Peloponnisos
G10	Attiki
G11	Voreio Aigaio
G12	Notio Aigaio
G13	Kriti
E1	Galicia
E2	Asturias
E3	Cantabria
E4	Pais Vasco
E5	Navarra
E6	La Rioja
E7	Aragón
E8	Madrid
E9	Castilla y León
E10	Castilla-la Mancha
E11	Extremadura
E12	Cataluña
E13	Com. Valenciana
E14	Baleares
E15	Andalucia
E16	Murcia
E17	Canarias (ES)
F1	Île de France
F2	Champagne-Ardenne
F3	Picardie
F4	Haute-Normandie
F5	Centre
F6	Basse-Normandie
F7	Bourgogne
F8	Nord - Pas-de-Calais
F9	Lorraine
F10	Alsace
F11	Franche-Comté
F12	Pays de la Loire
F13	Bretagne
F14	Poitou-Charentes
F15	Aquitaine
F16	Midi-Pyrénées
F17	Limousin
F18	Rhône-Alpes
F19	Auvergne
F20	Languedoc-Roussillon
F21	Provence-Alpes-Côte Azur
F22	Corse
IE	Ireland
I1	Piemonte
I2	Valle d'Aosta
I3	Liguria
I4	Lombardia
I5	Trentino-Alto Adige
I6	Veneto
I7	Friuli-Venezia Giulia
I8	Emilia-Romagna
I9	Toscana
I10	Umbria
I11	Marche
I12	Lazio
I13	Abruzzo
I14	Molise
I15	Campania
I16	Puglia
I17	Basilicata
I18	Calabria
I19	Sicilia
I20	Sardegna
LU	Luxembourg
N1	Noord-Nederland
N2	Oost-Nederland
N3	West-Nederland
N4	Zuid-Nederland
P1	Norte
P2	Centro (P)
P3	Lisboa e Vale do Tejo
P4	Alentejo
P5	Algarve
U1	North East
U2	North West
U3	Yorkshire and Humber
U4	East Midlands
U5	West Midlands
U6	Eastern
U7	South East and London
U8	South West
U9	Wales
U10	Scotland
U11	Northern Ireland
A1	Burgenland
A2	Niederosterreich
A3	Wien
A4	Karnten
A5	Steiermark
A6	Oberosterreich
A7	Salzburg
A8	Tirol
A9	Vorarlberg
S1	Stockholm
S2	Östra Mellansverige
S3	Småland Med Öarna
S4	Sydsverige
S5	Västsverige
S6	Norra Mellansverige
S7	Mellersta Norrland
S8	Övre Norrland
FN1	Itä-Suomi
FN2	Väli-Suomi
FN3	Pohjois-Suomi
FN4	Uusimaa
FN5	Etelä-Suomi

Chapter 5

Dynamics and Agents of Regional Growth: The Performance of SME Clusters in Europe

Ayda Eraydın

Introduction

Following the crisis in 'traditional' regional policy in the 1970s, there have been several attempts to theorize the dynamics of territorial/regional development. These attempts evolved under the influence of different perspectives ranging from The New Growth Theory to several theories of territorial development. They have a common feature, however, which is an interest in unveiling the endogenous nature of growth.

Local potential based on small and medium enterprises (SME) and industrial clusters was the core of the regional development literature in the 1980s (Brusco, 1982, 1986; Beccatini, 1991; Schmitz, 1999). This interest continued by means of soft institutional theories in the following decade with increasing emphasis on learning and innovation (Belussi, 1999; Breschi, 2000; Torre and Gilly, 2000; Kirat and Lung, 1999; Maskell and Malmberg, 1999a and 1999b; Amin and Cohendet, 1999). At the same time, economists were interested in explaining contemporary issues via the modification of traditional theories of economic growth. Both of these two theoretical perspectives recently have been criticized due to their limited contribution to regional policy issues. That is why there is an increasing concern to build a 'third way' between the hard theories of economics and the soft theories of territorial development (Plummer and Taylor, 2000).

It is the aim of this Chapter to discuss the relations between regional growth and the factors that provide competitive advantages to regions, such as clustering, innovation and human capital with reference to both territorial models of growth and also the new growth theory of neo-classical economics. Although, these two perspectives have different starting points they have several focal concepts in common, which is used in the empirical work on the European regions. The chapter begins by summarizing the recent theoretical debates on regional economic growth, which concentrate on the dynamics of clustering and the role of human capital in growth process. Secondly, it attempts to explain why and how SMEs became central to the territorial growth agenda. Third, the growth performance of regions as indicated by the concentration of SMEs and their innovativeness are reviewed, using evidence from the European regions. The fourth part of the chapter is devoted to the question why some of these regions experience relatively higher rates of growth than others. The last and concluding part of the chapter reviews the findings with reference to existing theoretical debates and outlines the need to update some of the premises used in recent theoretical work.

New Attempts to Theorize Growth

The first type of new theoretical debate on growth stemmed from the need to revise neo-classical growth theory. Accordingly, New Growth Theory theorists modified the assumption of diminishing returns to capital and introduced monopolistic competition as the underlying market form (Langlois, 2001). With the help of these extensions it then became possible to endogenise technological progress, which is interpreted as the whole collection of accumulable factors of production, such as human capital and the stock of knowledge (Solow, 1994, p. 49). New Growth Theory has attracted wide interest since it is consistent with increasing divergence among the growth rates of countries, instead of convergence as predicted by neo-classical growth theory. Assuming that each unit of capital not only increases the stock of physical capital but also the level of technology for all firms, the new model proposes endogenously defined technological level due to knowledge spillovers (Romer, 1990, 1994). The main argument is summarized by Romer (1994, p. 3), who argues that 'growth is an endogenous outcome of an economic system, not the results of forces impinged from outside'. More recently, this theory, integrating technological progress into the neo-classical growth model, has been transferred to spatial economics. The work pioneered by Krugman (1995), commonly referred to as the New Economic Geography, defines *local externalities* as the resource of increasing returns. According to him the factors of increasing returns are external to a firm but internal to a region. This situation explains the importance of agglomeration economies and how agglomerations sustain increasing returns via knowledge spillovers although he argues that the source is pecuniary not technological externalities.

The same emphasis can be observed in theoretical discourses, popular since the 1970s, that can be grouped together under the title of territorial models of growth, namely innovative milieux, industrial districts, new industrial spaces and learning regions (Eraydın, 2002). These models of territorial development are strongly influenced by the issues raised in institutional and evolutionary economics and the neo-Schumpeterian perspective on the role of innovation and technology, They have slightly different points of emphasis, however, they mainly concentrate on local externalities of learning and innovation.

The industrial district literature emphasizes collective learning based on small firms that are specialized in different stages of production, and their innovative capacities. Belussi (1999, pp. 734-736), based on the experience of Italian industrial districts, lists the factors that enable the collective learning processes and the diffusion of technical change and know-how within local clusters. He emphasises the sunk nature of knowledge, fluid interactions and many channels where information can quickly circulate among the firms in spatial and social proximity, higher levels of inter-firm cooperation, low transaction costs and a stimulating environment for enterprises to adopt innovation process more rapidly. In this approach, in addition to other historical and socio-economic factors within the industrial cluster, the transmission of tacit knowledge, which is facilitated by trust and reciprocity among local firms, gets a special emphasis. The literatures on *high technology industrial clusters or new industrial spaces* also concentrate on local interdependencies and knowledge transfer among firms, while giving special emphasis to research and development (R&D) and institutions that create externalities. In this approach a cluster is a place where knowledge for new products and processes appears and spreads under the existing social regulation mechanisms prominent in that area. According to Scott and Storper (1987, p. 29) social regulations define the new industrial spaces by coordinating inter-firm transactions, organizing local labor markets and supporting community formation and social reproduction. *The theory of regional innovation systems* focuses on the institutional basis of learning following the debate on national innovation systems. The argument indicates that the different kinds of R&D institutions complement and compete with one another in support of learning processes and innovative activities (Gregersen and Johnson, 1997). At the regional scale, Cooke, Uranga and Etxebarria (1997) define an innovative industrial cluster as the area likely to have firms with access to others in similar or complementary sectors as customers, suppliers and partners. They also have access to such knowledge infrastructure as universities, research institutes, contact research organizations and technology transfer agencies. The interactive learning process in these areas are assumed to be promoted by governance structure of business associations, chambers of commerce and public economic development, training and promotion agencies as well as government departments. In *innovative milieux*, learning and innovation depends on the capacity of firms through relationships with other agents within a 'co-operative atmosphere'. Finally, the learning region model integrates these ideas in order to indicate the conditions for building knowledge-based dynamic competitive capacities (Morgan, 1997).

All of these theoretical debates are quite informative, but it is rather difficult to read from these theoretical attempts, as Malmberg (1996, p. 398) has indicated, how the relations hold in an industrial system and difficult to obtain precise knowledge of the dynamics of spatial agglomeration and change. That is also why Krugman (1995) criticized these soft theoretical frameworks due their anti clarity, a view which is also shared by Plummer and Taylor (2000). One thing that is quite obvious in these theoretical debates, however, *is the importance of localized externalities and the factors that enable increasing returns in clusters.*

Emphasis on Clustering and the Assets of Clusters

It is not difficult to understand this concurrence of hard and soft theories of growth. One reason is the relaxation of an important assumption of neo-classical economics by the New Growth Theorists, namely 'once produced knowledge spills easily into the hand of others with zero marginal costs'. The change in this assumption indicates the importance of the cost of knowledge transactions, especially involving transactions of tacit knowledge, and puts agglomeration economies back on the agenda. In fact, there is a wide literature that can be labeled '*proximity dynamics*' (Kirat and Lung, 1999), that discusses this phenomenon. Although sharing the same location does not guarantee the existence of production and knowledge networks and collective learning processes, the literature agrees that proximity facilitates interactive activities (Amin and Cohendet, 1999; Maskell and Malmberg, 1999b), especially learning and innovation. Additionally, proximity provides opportunities for entrepreneurs to specialize and to respond to volatile demand more easily, since it enables interaction and cooperation, an easy information interchange, frequency of interpersonal contacts and higher factor mobility within the boundaries of a local area.

What are major advantages of these clusters? The discussions above clearly show that the advantage of clusters lies in 'relational' aspects and 'institutions' that facilitate these relations. These assets have been defined with the concepts of 'production networks', 'institutional thickness', 'learning' and 'human capital' in the recent literature.

Local production networks are expected to promote local innovative capacity and the dissemination of technology, which are the end results of interactive learning process and face to face relations in local industrial clusters (Digiovanna, 1997). In fact, successful industrial clusters are described as nodes where growth is stimulated by the intensive production networks among specialized industries (Park and Markusen, 1995; Mouleart, Swyngedouw and Wilson, 1988). Besides these production networks (Schmitz, 1990), the social networks are important, where information exchanges are facilitated by various forms of social capital, especially the cultural norms of trust, cooperation and reciprocity (Brusco, 1986; Fukuyama, 1995).

The different studies on territorial development discuss several locally embedded relations that enforce clustering and improve localized and generalized capabilities. It is possible to extend this by indicating the importance of local institutionalization via the concept of institutional thickness (Tödling, 1994), as well as the contribution of central and local government institutions in the development process of regions (Cooke and Morgan, 1994; Stöhr and Pönighaus, 1992; Scott and Angel, 1988; Castells and Hall, 1994; Scott and Storper, 1987; Harrison, 1994a and 1994b; Lin, 1997). In particular the theoretical discussions, which are in much the same spirit as institutional economics, try to define critical institutions influencing the path of growth, including rules, practices, routines, traditions as well as entrepreneurial spirits, culture and other values native to an area.

These assets of clusters are not adequate to sustain their viability in the global economic system. That is why, in the 1980s and early 1990s, the evolution of industrial clusters became a new area of interest extending the context of discussions beyond the localization process. Gordon (1996) claims that the viability of an industrial cluster is a product of their ability to articulate a coherent industrial presence within a global milieu that can be achieved via knowledge and learning. It should be noted that globalization can also act as a process of ubiquitification of many previously localized capabilities, production factors and embedded tacit knowledge (Maskell and Malmberg, 1999b). In that respect learning is the key issue, since it is the source of innovativeness and obviously long-range growth. Learning, however, is a concept which is quite loose and in general human capital is accepted as the core factor that denotes human learning capability and which is used as a proxy for learning and innovativeness.

While many studies emphasize the importance of human capital, Romer (1990, p. S73) made a more definitive statement of the connection between growth and human capital by saying 'stock of human capital determines the rate of growth'. In building this thesis, firstly he defines human capital not as a public good, but as both a rival and excludable good. Human capital can be used either in the final-output sector or in the research sector. He claims that research output depends on the amount of human capital devoted to research as well as on the stock of knowledge available to the person doing research. Secondly, by using human capital as a scale variable, Romer (1990, p. S95) proves that human capital has the effect of quickening the rate of growth.

The Agents of Growth: The Significance of SMEs

In the theoretical debates discussed above, SMEs are explicitly or implicitly defined as the main agents of economic growth (Amin and Malmberg, 1992). Analysis at the firm level and discussions of the contribution of individual small and medium-sized firms to regional growth are very important in this evaluation. The neo-classical perspective emphasizes the importance of SMEs due to their potential for employment generation and comparatively low capital requirement. It has been often claimed that SMEs can use indigenous resources more efficiently and the entrance and exit of SMEs into production activities is comparatively easy. Nevertheless, the importance of these firms is usually tied to their role in labor markets, especially the use of low wage labor market niches.

The main focus of territorial models, however, is the group of SMEs that is closely linked to a geographical area. They define SMEs as the active agents of learning and innovation. *The theory of innovative milieux* defines SMEs as a vital part of production systems. Their privileged relationships form the basis of the milieu, which can be defined by a co-operative atmosphere and by strategic relations (Camagni, 1991). The emphasis on SMEs is clearer in the *industrial district literature* (Brusco, 1982). It stresses collective learning between small firms that are specialized in different stages of production and in their innovative capacities. *The theory of high technology industrial clusters and the new industrial spaces literature*, which concentrates on local interdependencies and knowledge transfer among firms, also emphasize the crucial role of small firms in these clusters. SMEs are also the main focus in the *theory of regional innovation system*, which aims to define the institutional basis of learning. Regional Innovation Systems (RIS) are defined as an innovative industrial cluster of small firms in an area likely to have firms with access to others in similar or complementary sectors as customers, suppliers and partners (Cooke, et al., 1997).

While the theoretical studies emphasize the role of SMEs in economic growth, most of the literature related to the dynamics of clusters provides evidence about individual success stories. These findings, however, are less supported by analytical studies on regions, which include controversial findings on the relations between regional growth and the concentration of SMEs. Using evidence from Italy, Camagni and Capello (2001) asked the question whether regions with a high share of firms have a better performance than others. Their finding is that 'the regions with greater share of small firms are no longer characterized by better performance and employment growth as happened during the seventies'. Additionally, these two researchers found that in some regions good performance was associated with good industrial employment growth, whereas in other regions it was associated with severe employment cuts.

SME Clustering and Regional Growth: Empirical Evidence

This section of the chapter deals with a similar question to that posed by Camagni and Capello (2001) in the European regional context, in order to check the empirical support for the theoretical emphasis on the crucial role of SMEs in the development process. In other words, it tries to answer the question 'whether the performance of European regions with higher shares of SMEs are better than large-enterprise regions or not', which is followed by a preliminary analysis of the innovativeness of different types of regions. The analysis of the factors, which contributed to growth process is presented in the later sections of the chapter.

As with all studies that attempt to study the regions in the European Union, the biggest problem is related to differences in definitions of the main parameters and to the non-standardized data basis. The definition of SMEs is different across Europe, even in the documents that emanate from the various institutions of the European Union. In some documents SMEs are defined as firms with fewer than 250 employees, having an annual turnover of not more than 40 million ECU, and or a balance sheet valuation of not more than 27 million ECU and with less than half owned by a large enterprise (European Commission, 1999). However, in this study we follow the definition given in the report by The European Observatory for

SMEs, in which SMEs are defined as firms that employ 10-499 employees (European Network for SME Research, 1994).

The share of SMEs in total firms has wide variation among the European regions. While in the south of Europe micro enterprises and SMEs are dominant, this picture changes as we move towards northern parts of the Union. According to the reports (European Commission, 1999), there are 18 million enterprises in the Union excluding agriculture and non-market services and out of these 99.8 per cent are enterprises employing fewer than 250 people. These firms are estimated to account for two-thirds of the jobs in EU (excluding agriculture and non-market services) and 55 per cent of turnover. As may be observed, the definition above includes the micro enterprises that employ less than 10 employees. Unfortunately the data on SMEs at the European regional level is very limited and very difficult to find. This situation explains why there are very few cross-regional studies dedicated to SMEs in Europe. In this study also it has not been possible to find the actual data on the number of SMEs or their share in the total number of enterprises for all EU regions. As a result, the analysis presented in this section of the paper is restricted to 74 regions of 5 countries, namely Belgium, Italy, Spain, Portugal and France. The reason why the other European Union countries are not included basically depends on the lack of compatible data for the same years. The data on the share of SMEs is from SME Research Network.

In order to illustrate the relationship between SMEs and regional growth, we firstly present a scatter diagram (Figure 5.1). This diagram shows the distribution of regions according to their relative change in income per capita during 1986-96 period and the share of small firms in total employment at the beginning of the period[1]. The x axis relates to the SME data, comprising firms that employ between 10-499 employees. The y-axis denotes the relative change in income per capita (RC_i) that is calculated as follows:

$$RCI_i = I_{i,1996}/AI_{eu15,1996} - I_{i,1986}/AI_{eu1996}$$

where I_i regional income in purchasing power parity (PPS) and
AI_{eu15} the average income of the 15 European Union countries in PPS

The correlation coefficient of these two variables is equal to 0.3050 (t=2,71) which is statistically significant at the 0.01 level. The visual analysis of the diagram, however, provides more detailed information. Using the shares of employment created by SMEs and the relative change in income per capita data sets, it is possible to identify four groups of regions, categorized according to the averages of the regions studied. The definition of these groups is as follows: GROUP 1: Regions with higher shares of employment created by SMEs and above average changes in relative income per capita, GROUP 2: Regions with lower shares of SME employment than the average, but higher relative change in income per capita, GROUP 3: Regions with lower shares employment by SMEs and relatively slower growth in income per capita and GROUP 4: Regions with high shares of employment in SMEs than the average, but relatively the lower rates of income per capita growth.

The figure clearly shows that the regions with higher shares of SMEs improved their relative income per capita levels within the European Union, whereas regions with lower shares of SMEs in total employment experienced a different growth trajectory. There is a group of regions, with higher shares of employment created by large firms, which were not successful in retaining their earlier positions in the EU in terms of income levels, but others reached higher rates of per capita income growth than the 74 regions average. It is quite interesting to see that there are only two regions with high SME shares in total employment that lost their earlier positions in terms of income per capita.

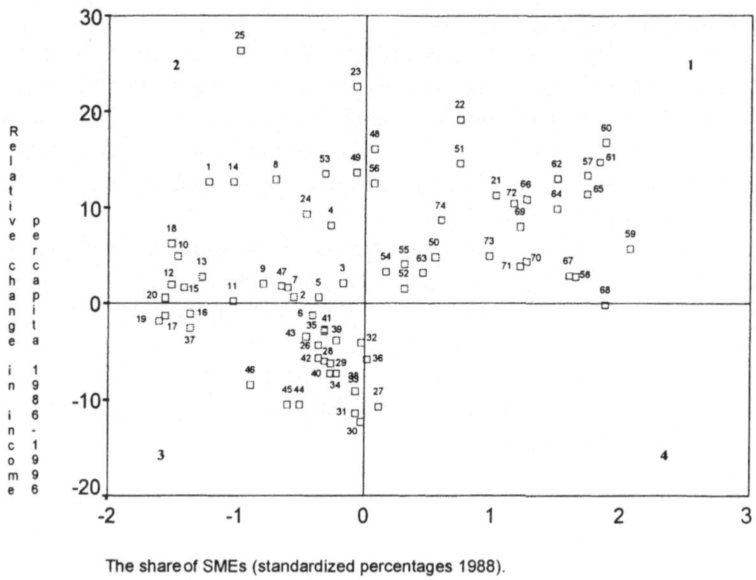

Figure 5.1 The share of SMEs and regional growth.

Source: Data is obtained from European Network for SME Research (1994, 1995) and Eurostat (1997).

Note: See Appendix 1 for the name of the regions indicated in numbers on the graph.

The figure above shows that the regions where SMEs have higher contribution to total employment had a good performance in terms of income growth. Following this evidence, the second issue that needs further attention is whether this growth depended upon the innovative capacity of these regions. In the literature there are contrasting debates on the innovativeness of SMEs. While one group of studies claim that SMEs are more innovative (Acz and Audretsch, 1990; Pavitt et al., 1987), other research findings indicate that innovation by SMEs is somewhat different, occurring 'in an incremental and defensive way introducing small changes in their products and services' (Tödling and Kaufmann, 2001, p. 212). Figure 5.2 presents the distribution of regions based on their shares of SMEs in total employment and patent applications per region. In both of the axes the standardized values are used. The correlation coefficient of these two variables is -0.234 (t=-2.042), which is low but a statistically significant negative relation at the 0.10 level.

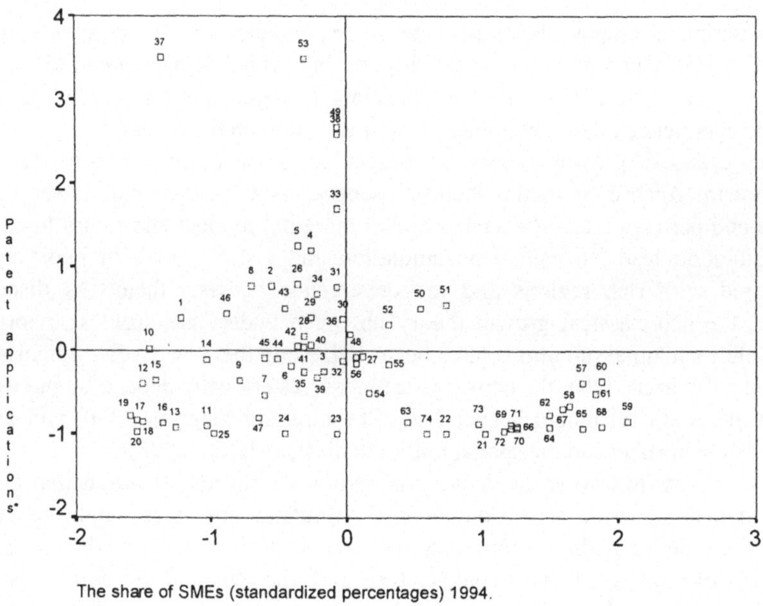

* Standardized values (per million people 1994-95-96 average).

Figure 5.2 The share of SMEs and innovativeness.

Source: Data is obtained from European Network for SME Research (1994, 1995) and Eurostat (1997).

Note: See Appendix 1 for the name of the regions indicated in numbers on the graph.

The distribution of regions in the Figure 5.2 is quite different from the Figure 5.1 distribution. The number of patent applications remains below the average in most of the regions with higher shares of SMEs, while the number of innovative regions with higher shares of SMEs seems to be limited. However, as the low correlation coefficient suggests, there is also an important number of regions with a relatively higher contribution to employment from large enterprises, but with lower innovativeness. It is interesting to see that these findings are supported by the outcomes of the SME Policy and Regional Dimension of Innovation (SMEPOL) and European Regional Innovation Survey (ERIS) Projects. These two European Union projects indicate that SMEs are less engaged in innovation (Tödling and Kaufmann, 2001; Strenberg, 2000). However, there is a need to be careful when analyzing patent data, since many small firms are reluctant to apply the European Patent Office (EPO), due to the high cost and lengthy procedures.

Growth, Innovation and Human Capital in SME Clusters

The descriptive graphs above provide some evidence on the relatively higher growth performance of many SME clusters, but which is not enhanced by their innovative activities. This situation prompts a major question, 'why do some regions experience relatively higher rates of growth than the others?'.

Neo-classical growth theory is based on a decreasing returns to scale mechanism. According to the theory, countries and regions with lower capital stocks and per capita income have a higher marginal product and return to capital. This situation leads to capital accumulation and faster growth in poor regions compared with rich regions and to convergence between them. As discussed earlier, the neo-classical growth theory has been widely criticized at theoretical level and its main assumptions have been revized by the New Growth theorists. It has been also argued that the convergence measures critically depend on the way in which the empirical model is specified (Cheshire and Magrini, 2000) and on the chosen time horizon and the spatial unit of analysis (Martin, 1998).

That is why, following the debates on regional/territorial growth, actual growth performance is viewed as the outcome of a multivariate process and the aim is focused on defining the various determinants of growth. In fact, the increasing mobility of traditional locational factors and the removal of some resource bottlenecks changed the factors that define the growth potential of regions. It is true that the emphasis in growth theories on economic and technological factors had led a certain neglect of social forces, but recently there is increasing concern about the role social conditions in economic growth performance (Rodriquez-Pose, 1998).

As the discussions on the last decade clearly stressed, there is need for a clearer understanding of processes in terms of their impact on economic growth. Endogenous growth theories and territorial models emphasize the role of certain variables on the economic growth process, such as physical and human capital accumulation, clustering, innovation and institutionalization for knowledge creation. The importance of these factors, however, needs to be tested with the help of cross-country studies, since individual case studies can be quite misleading.

In this study a model is defined so as to analyze the factors that contributed to convergence of the regional income per capita during 1986-96 period and which contributed to divergence.

The model is; $RCI_i = \beta_0 + + \beta j\ X_{ij,t0} + \varepsilon_{i,j,t0}$

where $RG_{ij} = (I_{i,t1}/AI_{eu15,it1,} - I_{i,t0}/AI_{eu,t0})$ is the relative change of income per capita by regions during 1986-96 period, $\beta_{j,\ j=1....k}$ are unknown parameters, $X_{ij,t0}$ are explanatory variables in region i at time t_0 and $\varepsilon_{i,j,t0}$ denotes random error terms. The variables are presented in Table 5.1. The explanatory variables used in order to explain regional growth differentials represent different facets of growth defined in theoretical discussions.

Table 5.1 Definition of the variables used in regression analysis.

THEORETICAL CONCERNS		EXPLANATORY VARIABLES
Convergence		INCOME86: The relative income per capita in 1986 (EU average=100)
Clustering		SHARESME: The share of SMEs in the regions in 1988
Innovation and learning		EXPRD: The share of R&D expenditures as a % of GDP (Spain, 1989; France, 1991; Belgium, 1989; Italy, 1994; Portugal, 1990)
Human capital	Educational attainment	HIGHEDU: The level of educational attainment of population between 25-59 years old in higher education institutions (% of total) 1986-87
	Research oriented personnel	SHARERD: % of R&D personnel in active population (for Spain, 1989, Italy, 1994; France, 1991; Belgium, 1994; Portugal, 1990)
Local human resource base		POP1564: The share of active population (15-64 ages) in total population 1990
Inadequate job opportunities and structural problems		UNEMP87: The rate of unemployment in 1986-87
National impact/national dynamics		NATIMPACT: The rate of growth in country in which region occurs

The first variable is the relative income per capita levels (standardized measures) of regions at the initial period. Following the neo-classical framework a negative relation between the income levels and growth rates are expected. Although there is a well developed critical literature relating to this issue there are also many studies that provide evidence that supports the neo-classical approach.

One important study is by Sala-i-Martin who showed that over a long period (1950-90) a pattern of convergence emerging across Europe. Similarly the analysis of 104 regions by Martin (1998) indicates convergence between European regions, albeit at a lower pace. In fact, there is also counter evidence indicating the divergence among European regions. Moreover, it is possible to see that the convergence between countries can overshadow the divergence inside the countries. In fact, there are many studies that indicate the convergence between countries and regions in Europe, but the consequences are increasing regional inequalities within certain countries. The OLS results for the 74 regions between 1986-96 period given below also show a negative relation.

There is, however, still need to define another explanatory framework based on different determinants of regional growth. In this model the central thesis of endogenous growth theory is taken as a starting point and the growth determinants are defined as, externalities due to the clustering of small and medium enterprises, the innovative nature of firms and organizations, a strong institutional basis that support learning and innovative activities and the availability of human capital, including local human resources. The main hypothesis is that higher rates of growth can be achieved in regional industrial clusters with an innovative nature and possessing higher amounts of human capital. The most appropriate variables are selected on the basis of the underlying theory and according to the data that is available for empirical analysis.

The variable reflecting the regional clustering of firms is the share of SMEs in total employment. This choice reflects therefore the extent to which small and medium enterprises dominate the local economic structure of regions. Theoretically, many small and medium sized firms sharing the same location enables the development of production and other types of networks, which will generate important externalities to firms in the process of learning, adaptation and facing external shocks. It is obvious that the type of SMEs, ranging from traditional to high technology, is important in defining the newly generated comparative advantages of different regions. Nonetheless, there is a strong expectation that clustering will make a positive contribution, with a strong body of empirical support coming from data for individual regions.

The second component of growth that has received wide attention in recent years is innovation. Innovation, which can lead to monopolistic conditions for firms and organizations, provides certain advantages to innovative agents compared with others. It is obvious that due to communication and information networks it not easy to protect advantages, due to the ubiquitification process of knowledge. Recently, besides technical innovations there is an increasing concern for innovations related to social organizations, however it is very difficult to identify the latter. The same problem holds, but even more so, for the technical type of innovation. Although patents are used as a proxy for innovation, many studies indicate that firms and people are reluctant to apply to patent offices for various reasons. That is why, although there may be a strong positive relation between growth and innovation, it is difficult to find the evidence.

The recent literature is keen on the role of institutions, especially the ones that are designed to support innovative activities. The importance of institutions is measured across regions by the ratio of R&D expenditures as a per cent of GDP. It is assumed that R and D expenditures represent the focus and involvement of different economic agents within regions, and it is for this reason that R&D expenditure as a percentage of GDP is taken as the third variable.

The fourth group of variables is related to human capital. As discussed earlier there is a heavy emphasis on human capital both in the New Growth Theory and in various territorial models of growth. It is usually defined as a proxy for learning, new knowledge generation and innovation, which are believed to promote growth. Human capital denotes a special segment of human resource. In the economics literature there is high level of consensus about the positive role of human capital in growth. Similarly, in recent debates about territorial development, there is a special concern about the role of human capital. The various definitions of human capital, however, are highly differentiated. Firstly, human capital is defined through educational attainment (Barro, 1991). Education facilitates an understanding of the society and the world people live in and allows them to articulate their present and future conditions. In fact, specialized educational institutions, training establishments (Scott and Storper, 1987; Lyons, 1995) and teaching programs that are set up in the community are important elements of local reproduction and economic growth (Capecchi, 1989; Schmitz and Musyck, 1994). In particular, universities are defined as critical institutions for generating human capital. They play several different roles in the development process, such as generating knowledge both in basic and applied science, training the labor force that is crucial for new technologies, and acting as entrepreneurs by means of supporting their research spin-offs into a network of industrial firms and business ventures (Castells and Hall, 1994). In the analysis, the share of people between 25-29 age group that have attained access to higher education institutes is defined as the first of two variables devoted to showing the potential of human capital in different regions.

Secondly, human capital is defined with reference to learning and innovation. Learning is not restricted to education and R&D activities, but covers knowledge creation and improvement through learning-by doing, learning by interacting and learning by imitating. The learning capacity of an agent is described as 'the capacity to create, acquire and transform knowledge and upgrade its skills, expertise and competencies to fulfil its objectives in a fast changing and turbulent economic environment' (Jin and Stough, 1998). That is why in the recent past there has been strong support to both private and public R&D activities, although not all learning activities end up with innovations. In fact, although several studies describe successful examples of regional growth based upon increasing R&D, it is difficult to say that how far these examples conform to the basis of the new model of economic growth. In the OLS analysis, the ratio of R&D personnel in the active population is used to represent human capital engaged in research and development.

The third interpretation of human capital is related to the enterprise culture (Plummer and Taylor, 2000). In fact the number of new enterprises is one of the indicators that explains how far human capital is engaged directly in the process of income generation and growth. However, the new firm formation across the regions were not available across the regions.

The other two variables are related to the labor force available in regions. In the literature, the attitude towards the contribution of human resources is not consistent. Romer (1994) claims that large amounts of human resource make no contribution to growth, contrary to classical arguments that emphasize the importance of available manpower in the growth process. Even when one considers high technology firms one sees that they require important amounts of non-skilled labour force at several stages of the production process, so it is not possible to disregard the availability of human labor as an asset.

In this analysis unemployment rates are used as an indicator of structural problems of the regional economy. Although in the neo-classical framework unemployment rates indicate labor waiting for new jobs and eager to accept lower wages, it is evident that in most of the cases there is an inconsistency, or mismatch, between the labor demanded and the labor force that is available.

The last variable used in the analysis is the relative change of income per capita with respect to EU average over the period 1986-96 period. This variable is added to see whether the growth performance of countries has any significant impact on regional performance. One way to approach this question is to add country dummies in the regression. However in this study, underlying differences in policy and institutions and economic cycles that influence differential national rates of growth are represented by a continuous variable, similar to the study by Cheshire and Magrini (2000). Since the number of countries is limited, being only five, the contribution of this variable to the model should be evaluated carefully.

Several models are tested in this analysis, four of which are presented in Table 5.2, namely the convergence model, the best- fit model, the general model and the general model with a dummy variable for national growth rates. The convergence hypothesis is supported by the findings of all models. The variable, the income per capita index for 1986, has a negative sign as expected in the hypothesis. It implies that lower income regions have the tendency to grow faster. It is also statistically significant at the 0.001 level. This convergence can be due to different factors including government policies and the regional policies of the European Union, since many of the programs and funds the Union are directed to lower income regions of the European periphery[2]. Having controlled all these effects, in this analysis the main concern is to define the regionally specific variables that contribute the explanation of growth differentials.

The stepwise regression analysis defines a best fit model accounting for 49,5 per cent of the relative change of income per capita between the regions during 1986-96 period. The value of $F(5,72)=13,114$ (significant at 0.001 level) provides strong evidence in favor of the hypothesis that this set of variables accounts for statistically significant amount of variability. In this model four region specific variables, namely the percentage of R&D personnel in active population, population in the active age group, the share of SMEs in total employment and unemployment levels at the beginning of the period are statistically significant with signs as expected.

Those regions with higher amounts of R&D personnel are predicted to have higher rates of growth. Similarly those regions with higher shares of SMEs have higher estimated rates of growth, which enable them to improve their relativities in terms of income per capita. The variable that indicate the ratio of population in active age groups (POP1564) has also a positive sign, which indicates the regions with higher human resources are predicted to have higher rates of growth. On the other hand, the share of unemployed in the total population has a negative sign showing that the regions with higher unemployment rates are predicted to have lower economic growth performance. This is also an expected outcome since as defined earlier the high unemployment rates indicate some structural problems and loss of vitality in the economy of regions. The other two variables were not statistically significant and excluded from the model due to multicollinearity problem between high education and the share of SMEs (R=0.523) and between the R&D expenditures and the share of R&D personnel in active population (R=-0.672).

The general model (Model 3), which includes all variables explains 51,9 per cent of the relative change of income per capita between the regions during 1986-96 period, which is slightly higher than the previous model. Nevertheless the two factors included in the model do not change the sign of the other coefficients and the level of significance of the variables included in the model except the significance of the variable on the share of SMEs. It is interesting to note that high education is not statistically significant in this model. This situation implies that the high access to higher education institutions may be over emphasized in territorial models of growth, or at least that among the sample regions, high levels in higher education have had a limited impact on growth. The same finding occurs when we consider R&D expenditures. Obviously, it is surprising to have a negative sign for R&D expenditure, which was intended to capture the impact of efforts at creating an innovative environment. The important emphasis on research and innovation, however, is reflected by the variable defined as the share of R&D personnel in active population, which is positive and statistically significant.

In fact, among the European countries, national economic policies still account for important differences, which have important impact, as predicted by the model, on the regional growth performances of the five countries studied. The correlation coefficient (R^2) between the regional rates of income growth and national income growth rates is equal to 0,41. In fact, in order to find out whether the national rates of growth are important in the growth rates of regions, a dummy is added to the equation. After including this new variable, the set of variables now accounts 58,8 per cent of the relative change in income per capita during the same period. In this new model two variables, income per capita at the base period and share of R and D personnel in total population, are statistically significant as well as the dummy variable representing national growth rates. The significance of the other variables are reduced after introducing the dummy variable (see Table 5.2). This change is quite understandable since the variance in the shares of SMEs by region and unemployment levels by region are quite related to the economic structure of the country.

Table 5.2 OLS analysis: Per capita GDP growth 1986-96.

Variables	MODEL 1: Convergence	MODEL 2: Best fit	MODEL 3: All variables	MODEL 3: All variables+ National dummy
(Constant)	15,635 (4,383)***	-132,162 (4,438)***	-120,72 (-3,761)***	-6,6145 (-1.927)*
INCOME86	-1,41 (-3,586)***	-,305 (-6,745)***	-0,294 (-5,804)***	-0,156 (-2,460)**
SHARESME		,121 (2,527)**	0,061 (1,044)	-0,07396 (0,604)
EXPRD			-3,387 (-1,632)	-4,047 (-1,277)
HIGHEDU			0,177 (1,246)	0.286 (1,821)**
SHARERD		3,678 (2,010)**	5,972 (2,2077)**	4,531 (1,821)*
POP1564 (1990)		2,424 (5,082)***	2,271 (4,416)***	1,284 (2,263)**
UNEMP87		-,574 (-3,179)**	-0,620 (-3,353)***	-5.99 (-3.469)***
NATIMPACT				1,735 (3,259)**
R	0,389	0,703	0,721	0,767
R2	0,152	0,495	0,519	0,588
F-test	F(1,73)= 12,856***	F(5,72)= 13,114***	F (7,72)= 10,036***	F(8,72)= 11,409***

Notes: t values are in brackets.
* Statistically significant 0.10 level.
** Statistically significant at 0.05 level.
*** Statistically significant at 0.01 level.

There are various criticisms that can be made of OLS models that attempt to analyze growth (Cheshire and Magrini, 2000). The scepticism depends on whether the OLS models appropriately reflect underlying theories and/or the data used are appropriate. Taking all the weaknesses of linear regression models into consideration, nevertheless the findings still provide important clues regarding our understanding of real life experiences. In fact, the analysis presented provides evidence which supports the main theoretical arguments that have dominated the recent literature. They indicate the importance of human capital engaged in research and development, and the role of clustering and human resources as factors affecting the growth performance of the regions of the Southwest European countries, namely Spain, Portugal, Italy, France and Belgium.

Following on from this analysis, further insight is gained by using similar models in order to explain the growth dynamics of the three Groups of Regions[3] which were defined earlier (see Appendix 2). Using only two variables, we can account for 47,1 per cent of the relative change of regional income growth rates among the regions of Group 1. These two variables are the share of active population in total employment and the rate of unemployment. What is interesting in this, apart from the impact of the level of unemployment, is the negative sign of the active population. In the analysis of Group 2, none of the models pass the F-test, indicating the inadequacy of these variables as explanations of the relative change of income in the regions, which are characterized by relatively higher shares of large firms and relatively higher growth rates. It is of some interest that innovation, R&D and human capital do not explain a substantial amount of variation in growth rates between these regions. Controversially for Group 3, only one variable, the share of SMEs, accounts for 28,4 per cent of the income growth differentials, which is statistically significant. In this group of regions, with relatively larger enterprises but lower relative change in income per capita, having small enterprises seems a disadvantage for growth.

Conclusive Remarks: Empirical Results and Theoretical Explanations

There are several important findings deriving from the empirical studies presented in this paper. What do these findings mean in terms of the ongoing theoretical debates? Firstly, the figures show that there is a statistically significant positive relation between the share of SMEs and the relative income growth rates among the European regions. It means that, although there is increasing scepticism about the sustainability of growth in SME regions and their performance in adapting to the changing economic conditions (Glasmeir, 1991, 1994; Staber, 1997), the empirical findings do not support this scepticism. According to empirical estimates most of the regions with higher shares of SMEs have performed quite well, although the relation is not very strong. Obviously, the figures do not define any causal relations, but they provide a useful insight into what puts regions on different growth trajectories.

In contrast, these are other findings that do support increasing scepticism about SME clusters, namely the negative relation between innovativeness (the number of patent applications) of regions and their shares of SMEs in total employment. Obviously, however, one might question the extent to which patent applications reflect the innovativeness of firms or clusters of firms. As Paci and Usai (2000) explain, it remains true that firms, especially small and medium-sized firms, are reluctant or do not have adequate information to apply to the European Patent Office. That is why the existing analysis provides only a very rough picture.

Thirdly, the paper aims to define the main factors that explain the growth performance of regions. The theoretical framework created an impetus for the analysis of the relation between growth and several region specific factors, such as innovativeness, the externalities associated with clustering, human capital and human resources. Four different regression models are used to identify the significant factors accounting for regional growth differences among 74 regions in 5 European countries. The results of the analysis show there is convergence among these regions, a propensity which is supported by higher levels of human capital devoted to R&D activities, the tendency to cluster and higher activity levels. Higher unemployment levels, which indicate economic problems and the non-vitality of the local economy, is seen to have a negative effect on regional growth rates.

These three sets of findings provide several hints about the future conduct of theoretical debates and they emphasize the need for further across-country studies. At present most studies are based on individual regions and most of them are descriptive in nature, although there is an increasing interest in quantitative analysis (Cheshire and Magrini, 2000; Martin, 1998; Rodriquez-Pose, 1998). These are obviously very helpful, but on the other hand they are misleading since they overemphasize some issues which may be irrelevant for other regions. On the other hand, there is some, albeit limited, interest amongst economists in regional growth issues, although it is often said that 'the world is becoming a mosaic of regions', so this interest should grow. The findings of the present study show that some of the core issues raised by theoretical discussions and by studies based on casual observation are not actually supported by empirical evidence. In saying that we should be aware of the need for refinement of both data and of analytical techniques. However, as Plummer and Taylor (2001) state, this situation should not stop us emphasising the need to re-evaluate theoretical discussions and attempting to fill the gap between descriptive studies and abstract models of economic growth.

Notes

1 It was not possible to find 1986 figures.

2 Informal analysis of the residuals does not suggest the presence of spatial autocorrelation among the residuals, although we would want to look at this issue in more detail subsequently to see if this materially affects the conclusions drawn from our preliminary regression analysis.

3 Since Group 4 has only two regions, it is not included in the statistical analysis.

References

Acz, Z.J. and Audrecht, D.B. (1990), *Innovation and Small Firms*, MIT Press, Cambridge MA.

Amin, A. and Cohendet, P. (1999), 'Learning and adaptation in decentralised business networks', *Environment and Planning D: Society and Space*, vol. 17, pp. 87-104.

Amin, A. and Malmberg. A. (1992), 'Competing structural and institutional influences on geography of production in Europe', *Environment and Planning A*, vol. 24, pp. 401-416.

Barro, B.J. (1991), 'Economic growth in a cross section of countries', *Quarterly Journal of Economics*, vol. 106, no. 2, pp. 407-444.

Becattini G. (1991), 'The industrial district as a creative milieu', I.G. Benko and M. Dunford (eds) *Industrial Change and Regional Development*, Belhaven, London, pp. 102-114.

Belussi, F. (1999), 'Policies for the development of knowledge-intensive local production systems', *Cambridge Journal of Economics*, vol. 23, pp. 729-747.

Breschi, S. (2000), 'The geography of innovation: A cross-sector analysis', *Regional Studies*, vol. 34, no. 3, pp. 213-229.

Brusco, S. (1982) 'The Emilian model: productive decentralization and social integration', *Cambridge Journal of Economics*, vol. 6, pp. 167-184.

Brusco, S. (1986), 'Small firms and industrial districts: The experience of Italy', in E. Keeble and E. Wever (eds), *New Firms and Regional Development*, Croom Helm, London, pp. 184-202.

Camagni, R. (1991), 'Local milieu, uncertainty and innovation networks: Towards a new dynamic theory of economic space' in R. Camagni (ed), *Innovation Networks*, Belhaven, London, pp. 121-144.

Camagni, R. and Capello, R. (2001), 'Innovation and performance of SMEs in Italy: The Relevance of Spatial Aspects', *Competition and Change*, vol. 3, pp. 69-107.

Capecchi V. (1989), 'The Informal Economy and the development of Flexible Specialization in Emilia-Romagna', in A. Portes, M. Castells and L.A. Benton (eds), *The Informal Economy Studies in Advanced and Less Developed Countries*, Johns Hopkins University Press, Baltimore, pp. 189-215

Castells, M. and Hall, P. (1994), *Technopoles of the World*, Routledge, London and New York.

Cheshire, P and Magrini, S. (2000), 'Endogenous processes in European regional growth: Convergence and policy', *Growth and Change*, vol. 31, no. 4, pp. 455-480.

Cooke, P. and Morgan, K. (1994), 'Growth regions under duress: Renewal strategies in Baden-Württemberg and Emilia Romagna', in A. Amin and N. Thrift (eds), *Globalisation, Institutions and Regional Development in Europe*, Oxford University Press, Oxford, pp. 91-117.

Cooke, P., Uranga, M.G. and G. Extebarria (1997), 'Regional innovation systems: Institutional and organisational dimensions' *Research Policy*, vol. 26, pp. 475-491.

Digiovanna, S. (1997), 'Industrial districts and regional economic development: A regulation approach', *Regional Studies*, vol. 30, pp. 373-386.

Eraydın, A. (2002), 'Building up competence, institutions and networks in order to catch up in the knowledge economy' in R. Hayter and R. Le Heron (eds), *Knowledge, Territory and Industrial Space*, Ashgate, Aldershot, pp. 67-87.

European Network for SME Research (1994), *The European Observatory for SMEs: Second Annual Report*, Report Submitted to Directorate General XXII, ENSR.

European Network for SME Research (1995), *The European Observatory for SMEs: Third Annual Report*, Report Submitted to Directorate General XXII, ENSR.

Eurostat (1997), *Regions: Statistical Yearbook*, EU, Luxembourg.

Fukuyama, F. (1995), *Trust: The Social Virtues And The Creation Of Prosperity*, The Free Press, New York.

Glasmeir, A. (1991), 'Technological discontinuities and flexible production networks: The case of Switzerland and the world watch industry', *Research Policy*, vol. 20, pp. 469-485.

Glasmeir, A. (1994), 'Flexible districts, flexible regions? The institutional and cultural limits to districts in an era of globalization and technological paradigm shift', in A. Amin and N. Thrift (eds), *Globalisation, Institutions and Regional Development in Europe*, Oxford University Press, Oxford, pp. 118-146.

Gordon, R. (1996), 'Industrial districts and the globalization of innovation: Regions and networks in the new economic space', in X.Vence-Deza and J.S. Metcalfe (eds), *Wealth from diversity*, Kluwer, Rotterdam, pp. 103-133

Gregersen, B. and Johnson, B. (1997), 'Learning economies, innovation systems and European integration', *Regional Studies*, vol. 31, no. 5, pp. 479-490.

Harrison, B. (1994a), 'The Italian industrial districts and the crisis of cooperative form: Part I'. *European Planning Studies*, vol. 2, pp. 3-22.

Harrison, B. (1994b), 'The Italian industrial districts and the crisis of cooperative form: Part II'. *European Planning Studies*, vol. 2, pp. 159-174.

Jin, D.J. and Stough, R. (1998). 'Learning and learning capability in the Fordist and post-Fordist age: an integrative framework', *Environment and Planning A*, vol. 30, pp. 1255-1278.

Kirat, T. and Lung, Y. (1999), 'Innovation and proximity: Territories as loci of collective learning process', *European Urban and Regional Studies,* vol. 6, pp. 27-38.

Krugman, P. (1995), *Development, Geography and Economic Theory*, MIT Press, Cambridge.

Langlois, R.N., 2001, 'Knowledge, consumption and endogenous growth', *Journal of Evolutionary Economics*, vol. 11, pp. 77-93.

Lin, C. Y. (1997), 'Technopolis development: An assessment of the Hschchu experience', *International Planning Studies*, vol. 2, pp. 257-272.

Lyons, D. (1995), 'Agglomeration economies among high-technology firms in advanced production areas: The case of Denver Boulder', *Regional Studies*, vol. 29, pp. 265-278.

Malmberg, A. (1996), 'Industrial geography: agglomeration and local milieu', *Progress in Human Geography*, vol. 20, pp. 392-403.

Martin, P. (1998), 'Can regional development policies affect growth and geography in Europe?', *World Economy*, vol. 21, no. 6, pp. 757-775.

Maskell, P. and Malmberg, A. (1999a), 'Localised learning and industrial competitiveness', *Cambridge Journal of Economics*, vol. 23, pp. 167-185.

Maskell, P. and Malmberg, A. (1999b), 'The competitiveness of firms and regions: Ubiquitification and the importance of localized learning', *European Urban and Regional Studies*, vol. 1, pp. 9-25.

Morgan, K. (1997) 'The learning region: Institutions, innovation and regional renewal', *Regional Studies*, vol. 31, pp. 491-503.

Mouleart, F., Swyngedouw, J. and Wilson, A. (1988), 'Spatial Responses to Fordist and Post-Fordist Accumulation and Regulation', *Papers of the Regional Science Association*, vol. 64, pp. 11-23.

Paci, R. and Usai, S. (2000), 'Technological Enclaves and Industrial Districts: An analysis of the regional distribution of innovative activitiy in Europe', *Regional Studies*, vol. 34, pp. 97-114.

Park, S.O. and Markusen, A. (1995), 'Generalizing New Industrial Districts - A Theoretical Agenda and an Application from a Nonwestern Economy', *Environment and Planning A*, vol. 27, pp. 81-104.

Pavitt, K. Robson, M. and Towsend, J. (1987), 'The size distribution of innovating firms in the UK 1945-84', *Journal of Industrial Economics*, vol. 45, pp. 297-306.

Plummer, P. and Taylor, M. (2000), 'Theory and Praxis in Economic Geography: Enterprising and local growth in a global economy', paper presented to *The Wisconsin Economic Summit*, November 29-December 1, Wisconsin.

Plummer, P. and Taylor, M. (2001), 'Theories of local economic growth (part 1) concepts, models and measurement', *Environment and Planning A*, vol. 33, pp. 219-236.

Rodriquez-Pose, A. (1998), 'Social conditions and economic performance: The bond between social structure and regional growth in Europe', *International Journal of Urban and Regional Research*, vol. 22, no. 3, pp. 443-460.

Romer, P.M. (1990), 'Endogenous technological change', *Journal of Political Economy*, vol. 98, no. 5, pp. S71-S102.

Romer, P.M. (1994), 'The origins of endogenous growth', *Journal of Economic Perspectives*, no. 1, pp. 3-22

Schmitz, H. (1990), 'Small firms and flexible specialization in developing countries', *Labor and Society*, vol. 15, no. 3.

Schmitz, H. (1999), 'Collective efficiency and increasing returns', *Cambridge Journal of Economics*, vol. 23, pp. 465-483

Schmitz, H. and Musyck, B. (1994), 'Industrial Districts in Europe - Policy Lessons for Developing-Countries', *World Development*, vol. 22, pp. 889-910.

Scott, A.J. and Angel, D.P. (1988), 'The global assembly-operations of US semiconductor firms: a geographical analysis', *Environment and Planning A*, vol. 20, pp. 1047-1067

Scott, A.J and Storper, M. (1987), 'High technology industry and regional development: A theoretical critique and reconstruction', *International Social Science Journal*, vol. 112, pp. 215-232

Solow, R.M. (1994), 'Perspectives on Growth Theory', *Journal of Economic Perspectives*, vol. 8, no. 1, pp. 45-54.

Staber, U. (1997), 'Specialisation in a declining industrial district', *Growth and Change*, vol. 28, pp. 475-495.

Stöhr, W. B. and Pönighaus, R. (1992), 'Towards a data-based evaluation of the Japanese technopolis policy and organizational infrastructure on urban and regional development', *Regional Studies*, vol 26, pp. 605-538.

Strenberg, R. (2000), 'Innovation networks and Regional Development- Evidence from the European Regional Innovation Survey (ERIS): Theoretical concepts, methodological approach, empirical basis and introduction to the theme issue', *European Planning Studies*, vol. 8, no. 4, pp. 389-408.

Tödling, F (1994), 'The uneven landscape of innovation poles: local embeddedness and global networks', in A. Amin and N. Thrift (eds), *Globalisation, Institutions and Regional Development in Europe*, Oxford University Press, Oxford.

Tödling, F. and Kaufmann, A. (2001), 'The role of region for innovation activities of SMEs', *European Urban and Regional Studies*, vol. 8, no. 3, pp. 203-215.

Torre, A. and Gilly, J. P. (2000), 'On the analytical dimension of proximity dynamics', *Regional Studies*, vol. 34, pp. 169-180.

Appendix 1 The Names and Numbers of the Regions that are Included in the Statistical Analysis

1	Veneto	38	Rhone-Alpes
2	Piemonte	39	Limousin
3	Marche	40	Poitou-Charentes
4	Emilia-Romagna	41	Basse-Normandie
5	Lombardia	42	Bretagne
6	Toscana	43	Midi-Pyrenees
7	Umbria	44	Aquitaine
8	Friuli-Venezia Giulia	45	Languedoc-Roussillon
9	Abruzzo	46	Provence-Alpes-Cote d'Azur
10	Liguria	47	Corse
11	Puglia	48	Limburg
12	Valle d'Aosta	49	Antwerpen
13	Molise	50	Oost-Vlaanderen
14	Trentino-Alto Adige	51	West-Vlaanderen
15	Lazio	52	Liege
16	Campania	53	Brabant Wallon
17	Sardegna	54	Hainaut
18	Basilicata	55	Namur
19	Sicilia	56	Luxembourg
20	Calabria	57	Navarra
21	Norte	58	Pais Vasco
22	Centro	59	La Rioja
23	Alentejo	60	Cataluna
24	Lisboa e Vale do Tejo	61	Madrid
25	Algarve	62	Aragon
26	Franche-Comte	63	Asturias
27	Champagne-Ardenne	64	Cantabria
28	Lorraine	65	Castilla-La Mancha
29	Haute-Normandie	66	Castilla y Leon
30	Picardie	67	Comunidad Valenciana
31	Centre	68	Murcia
32	Pays de la Loire	69	Galicia
33	Alsace	70	Andalucia
34	Bourgogne	71	Baleares
35	Nord-Pas-de-Calais	72	Extremadura
36	Auvergne	73	Canarias
37	Ile de France	74	Ceuta y Melilla

Appendix 2

Group of Regions 1:

Model	Variables	B	Std. Error	t	Significance
1	(Constant)	111,758	43,592	2,564	,019
	POP1564 (1990)	-1,540	,642	-2,398	,026
2	(Constant)	213,430	50,252	4,247	,000
	POP1564 (1990)	-2,845	,698	-4,076	,001
	UNEMP87	-1,413	,474	-2,982	,008

R^2=0,471 F (2,21)=8,476 (significant at 0,995 level).

Group of Regions 2:

Model	Variables	Coefficients	Std. Error	t	Significance
1	(Constant)	12,671	26,726	,474	,641
	INCOME86	5,569E-02	,142	,391	,700
	PERRD	7,877	5,710	1,380	,185
	EXPRD	-4,458	6,145	-,725	,477
	ACTIVITY	-,132	,561	-,235	,817
	SHARESME	5,894E-02	,119	,493	,628
	UNEMP87	-,243	,255	-,954	,353
	HIGHEDU	-,228	,464	-,492	,628

R^2= 0.317 F(7,25)=1.195 (0.355).

Group of Regions 3:

Model	Variables	Coefficients	Std. Error	t	Significance
1	(Constant)	1,145	2,478	,462	,649
1	(Constant)	1,145	2,478	,462	,649
	SHARESME	-,209	,073	-2,887	,009
	SHARESME	-,209	,073	-2,887	,009

R^2=0,284 F(1,22)=8,335 (significant at 0,99 level).

PART II: SMEs AND REGIONAL DEVELOPMENT AT THE NATIONAL SCALE

Chapter 6

Accounting and Modelling SMEs in the Regional Economy

Bjarne Madsen and Chris Jensen-Butler

Introduction

There are two principal areas of interest concerning the role of SMEs in national and regional economies. First, accounting for the contribution of SMEs and related issues concerning their demographics over time, constitutes one field of interest. The second relates to a theoretical understanding of the role of SMEs in national, regional and inter-regional production systems. Here, a key issue is the extent to which SMEs both create and use positive externalities, which have consequences both for costs and productivity. This in turn is closely related to regional and spatial issues. The substantial interest in clusters, at present observable throughout Europe, reflects these issues. The configuration of SMEs in space is argued to affect their performance, through a variety of mechanisms, of which knowledge spillover and learning effects are often argued to be primary.

The present paper addresses both of these issues within a common modelling framework and demonstrates the close links between an accounts-based approach and a theoretical approach, which attempts to model, identify and measure externality effects. The framework presented is based upon a Social Accounting Matrix (SAM) approach, at a spatially disaggregated level. This permits us to address the problems related to accounting for the contribution of SMEs in a national, regional and interregional setting. However, it also transpires that this approach provides a unique framework in which the theory of production of ideas and innovation, related in turn to training and education can be operationalized. The present paper concentrates on the first issue, namely establishment of a set of consistent (SAM based) interregional accounts where the SME sector can be clearly identified. A number of central ideas concerning the second issue are presented in the SAM context, though these are at present less well developed.

SAM as a Tool for Analysis of SMEs

Analysis of the interrelations between the SMEs and regional economies involves a number of choices, both in terms of study method (such as case-studies, comparative studies, modelling) and in terms of data and data collection. The methodological approach is not determined independently, but is intertwined with the problem of selection and constructing or collecting data. Data construction and analysis are, in fact, very interrelated. In this paper the SAM framework is presented as an efficient tool for selection and building consistent data and as an implicit framework for modelling SMEs in regional economy.

Different approaches to the study of the role of SMEs in the regional economy can be identified. The first is the case study type where data used for case studies are, in principle, one off, and do not have to be comparable with other data on SMEs – including official data. The second type of study, the comparative study (across country, sector or time-series) requires that SME-data is comparable. Data comparability means that data production must be of high quality and follow the same standards, like the classification and measurement principles for economic activities set up by international institutions, such as the EU or the UN. Finally, for modelling exercises – both macro- and microeconomic modelling – the data must also fulfil certain fundamental accounting rules, such as sales by sector must be equal to expenditure by sector. In a firm demographic model, which is a part of an extended SAM, the number of firms at the end of a period must be equal to the number of firms in the beginning of the period adding new firms (entries) and subtracting dead firms (exits) during the period.

It is advisable that in general follow international classification principles, in order to ensure a high degree of comparability between countries or sectors and over time. Even for case studies, it seems preferable, if possible, to follow these principles, although for new types of data and new information, it almost by definition is impossible to follow standards which are non-existent.

It is also preferable that data meet the same demand for consistency required for modelling applications. Even though it is not necessary to know both supply and demand by commodity produced by SMEs, inconsistency between supply and demand raises the question of quality of data for all types of studies. If data do not meet the demand-supply restrictions either demand-side or supply-side data must be wrong. A decision has to be taken concerning which data source is most reliable. Therefore, even though consistency checks for data seem to be unnecessary in a number of cases, it is preferable that data also meet this kind of quality requirement.

In this paper Social Accounting Matrices are presented both as an accounting framework for data on SME in the regional economy and as a basic modelling tool. A SAM is a general macroeconomic accounting and modelling framework, which in a systematic way describes economic activities in a given geographical area. A SAM for a country is based on the national accounts, but provides a more extensive description of economic activities than the national accounts. The national accounts are in fact a subset of the SAM. In the United Nations' recommendations for setting up national accounts recommendations for building SAMs are presented (UN 1993). As a consequence, the data which fits into a SAM-framework meets the demands for comparability and consistency.

The SAM framework provides a modelling tool to answer one set of questions about the role of SMEs in the national and regional economy. These questions concern the nature and strength of backward and forward linkages from SMEs in the national and regional economy. SAM-based models provide a detailed mapping of regional linkages. The standard SAM model is based upon a set of independent agents and behaviour is modelled using linear relations and a limited number of explanatory variables.

SAM, Externalities and SMEs

As well as being an accounting framework, a SAM is also a theoretical framework for analysis of the role of actors and institutions in regions' economies, including the role of SMEs. These firms exist in a world where externalities exist and indeed, one of the main reasons why there is substantial interest in the role of SMEs in the economy is their contribution to the creation of, and their use of externalities. This implies a shift in analytical focus to a world where actors are no longer independent and where behavioural relationships are non-linear.

It is customary to distinguish between *pecuniary* and *technological* externalities (Scitovsky, 1954). Pecuniary externalities arise when input prices vary with the amount of output produced. For example, if input prices fall with increasing output in a given industry, then the industry is a decreasing cost industry. This can occur because of scale economies in the production of inputs. Technological externalities arise because of spillover effects between actors. SAM-based models can address both types of externality, as discussed in the section on SMEs and externalities below.

In the first section below a SAM for one region is presented. The SMEs and large enterprises are included in the SAM-framework as sub-sectors of the production account and as sub-sectors in the institutional account. The inclusion of the SMEs in the SAM is examined. In the second section below the SAM accounting scheme is transformed into a macroeconomic modelling framework, which forms the basis for regional general equilibrium models. The role of SMEs in the modelling framework is presented. The firm demographic model is presented as a part of the regional general equilibrium model. Inclusion of the firm demographic model transforms the SAM-based model into a dynamic model. In the following section the interregional SAM is presented. In the interregional SAM the SMEs become a part of an interregional and international economy. In the interregional SAM, interregional and international commodity trade, commuting in the factor market and investments become a part of the environment for the SMEs. In next section, treatment of externalities in the SAM and the model is discussed.

In the final section, characteristics of SMEs in Denmark at the national level are presented and work with setting up SAM at the regional level and without subdivision of economic activities by scale is examined.

The One Region SAM

Introduction

A SAM is a comprehensive accounting system for transactions between different actors in an economy. Actors can be different types of production units, institutional units etc. SMEs can be defined both as actors in the production account and in the institutional account.

In the UN recommendation for national accounts a social accounting matrix is defined as 'the presentation of SNA's accounts in a matrix which elaborates the linkages between a supply and use table and institutional sector accounts' (see chapter XX in UN 1993). Compared with the traditional input-output tables, the SAM is a more extensive and developed description of the (regional) economy (Hewings & Madden, 1995).

In traditional (regional) input-output tables, the interrelations between final demand and production and between production and intermediate consumption are accounted for. Eventually, the input output-relations can be accounted for in make and use tables, where the make tables show the commodity composition of production by sector, whereas the use tables show the commodity composition of demand by component of demand[1].

In the SAM there is not only a link between production and intermediate consumption, but it also accounts for the link between production units and institutional units, or, formulated in macroeconomic terms, between income and final demand (induced effects). The demand circle in the traditional input-output table from production to intermediate consumption and back to production has been extended to a circle including the link from factor income in production to institutional income and from institutional income to final demand. In the SAM these linkages are normally both detailed and well-developed.

From an SME point of view, the SAM seems to be a more relevant accounting system than traditional national accounts. This is because SMEs can be defined as actors both in the production account and in the institutional account.

The One Region SAM

To show the structure of the SAM, and the inclusion of SMEs means that a slightly adjusted version of the table from the presentation of the SAM in UN (1993) is used. On the basis of the UN table (see Table 20.4), the structure of the one-region SAM including SME actors is presented.

The SAM is built on principles similar to an input-output table, where revenue flows are to be found on rows and expenditures are in the columns. By definition, the sum of revenues is equal to the sum of expenditures. An example illustrates these accounting principles. The row for Production (2), which is divided into SMEs and large enterprises, shows that production activities gain revenues from sale of goods and services ($T_{2,1}$). Total revenue (y_2) is shown in the right hand column. The column for Production (2) shows total expenditure on Generation of income ($T_{3,2}$), on Other taxes and subsidies on production, on Goods and services (intermediate consumption) ($T_{1,2}$) including taxes, net, on products and depreciation of fixed capital ($T_{8,2}$). Total expenditure (y_2^T) is to be found in the last row. It is by definition true that $y_2 = y_2^T$.

Table 6.1 A one-region SAM for a closed economy.

		Goods and services	Production	Generation of income	Allocation of primary income	Secondary distribution of income	Use of (adjusted) disposable income	Capital	Fixed capital formation	Financial	Total
			1 | 2		1 | 2	1 | 2					
Goods and services			$T_{1,2}$				$T_{1,6}$	$T_{1,7}$	$T_{1,8}$		y_1
Production	1 2	$T_{2,1}$									y_2
Generation of income			$T_{3,2}$								y_3
Allocation of primary income	1 2	$T_{4,1}$		$T_{4,3}$	$T_{4,4}$						y_4
Secondary distribution of income	1 2				$T_{5,4}$	$T_{5,5}$					y_5
Use of (adjusted) disposable income						$T_{6,5}$	$T_{6,6}$				y_6
Capital							$T_{7,6}$	$T_{7,7}$		$T_{7,9}$	y_7
Fixed capital formation			$T_{8,2}$					$T_{8,7}$			y_8
Financial								$T_{9,7}$			y_9
Total		y_1^T	y_2^T	y_3^T	y_4^T	y_5^T	y_6^T	y_7^T	y_8^T	y_9^T	

1) SME = Small and medium size enterprises.
2) LE = Large enterprises.

There is an in-built causal structure in the SAM: Considering only flows inside region 1, there is a relation from 'Production' (2) to 'Generation of income' (3), $T_{3,2}$, which shows the payment of production activities to factors of production. Next, there is a flow from the 'Generation of income account' to the 'Allocation of primary income', that is from production factors to institutions: to households and to companies ($T_{4,3}$). There are also links from the 'Allocation of primary account' to 'Secondary distribution of income' ($T_{5,4}$). This transformation includes the transfers between institutions, like taxes and income transfers redistributing income between households, firms and government. Third, households and other types of institutions satisfy wants through the 'Use of disposable income' ($T_{1,6}$). A share of the disposable income is used for savings, which is revenue for the capital account ($T_{1,7}$). Capital accounts use the savings for gross fixed capital formation ($T_{8,7}$) and for the financial account ($T_{9,7}$). Wants are linked to commodities ($T_{1,6}$), which in turn are linked to Activities ($T_{2,1}$), which completes the demand circle.

The SMEs in the Social Accounting Matrix

The term SME is often used for different types of activities. In the SAM, the SME – sector can be seen as part of the production account and the institutional account.

Looking at the SMEs as part of the production account, the SMEs can be defined as production units with a turnover of less than a given magnitude per unit per year or with an employment level of less than a critical level per production unit. The production activities are assigned to the place of production for the production unit and can be further sub-divided into relevant sectors.

The SMEs can also be seen as part of the institutional account. The institutional account includes;

- the non-financial corporate sector;
- financial institutions;
- insurance companies and pension funds;
- general government;
- private, non-profit institutions;
- the household sector.

The SME can, in principle, be treated as a subset of each of these institutional sectors. Most of the SMEs are part of the household sector and the non-financial corporate sector. SMEs in the institutional account relate to the place of residence of the institutional unit.

Production Units and Firm Demography

Production changes from year to year. These changes reflect the fact that production from one period to the next increases because of newcomers and decreases because of production unit exits. Therefore, the SAM can be seen as an accounting system for newcomers and for production unit exits. The structure of the SAM for these marginal production units can be used to characterize changes in the economy. A demographic accounting system can be set up for production in existing production units, together with newcomers and production unit exits. This demographic system can register changes in terms of turnover, value added, capital equipment, employment etc.

The SAM also includes information on investment. Investment is demand for commodities which are used in accumulating capital for production. The capital accumulation in newcomer production units and capital depreciation in production unit exits characterizes the new production.

As SMEs are an important part of new arrivals (and production unit exits) a demographic accounting system for production units using the SAM-structure is a valuable tool in the analysis of the role of SMEs in the growth of regional economies.

SMEs in the Regional Economy

The role of SMEs in the regional economy can be analysed using the fundamental structure of the economy embedded in the regional economy and represented in the SAM. To this end a simple regional general equilibrium model is presented.

Introduction

Implicitly, the social accounting matrix (SAM) includes the two fundamental causal structures which drive the regional economy and which are at the core of a regional general equilibrium model.

On the one hand the SAM includes a cost – price circle: Prices in production are determined for both SMEs and other production units by adding up production costs. The production costs include intermediate consumption, wage cost and profits. The commodity prices are determined through the distribution of sector prices to the commodities produced in the sectors. Markets prices are determined by adding the cost of transporting commodities to the market and by adding sales costs and commodity taxes. Prices of commodities for intermediate consumption enter into the production of other commodity, closing the cost-price circle.

On the other hand, the traditional demand – production – income – demand circle is a part of the SAM: The production sector, subdivided into SMEs and other production units, receives income from sales of commodities. The factor account receives factor income from the production account. The institutional sectors, subdivided into SMEs and other institutional units earn income, which are transferred from the factor account. Finally, the commodity account sells commodities to the institutional account. Through this chain of interaction, which forms a real circle, the SAM reflects traditional Keynesian demand theory.

Putting the two circles together, the skeleton of a general equilibrium model has been established. The exact formulation of the model depends on how the cost-price variables determines the variables in the real circle, for example, how the export of commodities is determined by domestic prices, foreign prices, foreign income etc.

Two Circles in Detail

A verbal and graphic description of the model follows. For a mathematical presentation, see Madsen and Jensen-Butler (2001).

Figure 6.1 shows a stylized version of the cost and price circuit in the regional general equilibrium model. The circle follows the formation of prices from the adding up process of cost in the production process to the market (where transport cost and commodity taxes are included) and further to place of residence including transport costs related to shopping. The horizontal dimension is spatial: place of work, place of residence and place of demand. Production activity is related to place of work. Factor rewards and income to institutions are related to place of residence and demand for commodities is assigned to place of demand. The vertical dimension follows with its five-fold division the general structure of a SAM model. Production is related to activities; factor incomes are related to i) activities by sector ii) factors of production by qualification, sex and age and iii) institutions (households and firms) iv) demand for commodities is related to wants (aggregates of commodities or components of final demand and intermediate consumption); v) commodities, irrespective of use. The production sector has been further subdivided into SMEs and other production units. The institutional sector has also been subdivided into SMEs and other firms.

In cell AE (see figure 6.1) sector basic prices (in current prices) are determined by costs (intermediate consumption, value added and indirect taxes) excluding transport costs. Moving anti-clockwise through a reverse Make matrix, sector prices by sector are transformed into sector prices by commodity, again in current prices (from AE to AV). In the trade model lying between AV and DV, transport costs related to trade are added transforming the value of commodities into basic prices including transport costs. These are then transformed into market prices through inclusion of retailing and wholesaling costs and indirect taxes (from DV to DW). This transformation takes place using a reverse Use matrix. Prices for intermediate consumption enter as a production cost in production (from DW to AE), closing the cost-price circle. Finally, private consumption is transformed from place of demand to place of residence in market prices, including transport costs (from DW to BW). Through all of these steps, current prices are used.

Figure 6.2 shows a stylized version of the real circle in the general equilibrium model. The real circuit corresponds to a straightforward Keynesian model and moves clockwise. Starting in cell AE in the upper left corner, production generates factor income in basic prices including the part of income used to pay commuting costs. This factor income is redistributed from activities to factors (cell AE to cell AG), where the labour force is divided into qualification, sex and age groups. Factor income is then transformed from place of production (AG) to place of residence (BG) through a commuting model. In this process, transport costs are subtracted from factor income. Disposable income is calculated in a sub model where taxes are deducted and transfer and other incomes are added. Disposable income is distributed from factors (BG) to households and firms (BH). This is the basis for determination of private consumption in market prices, including transport, by place of residence (BW). Private consumption is assigned to place of demand (DW) using a shopping model. In this process transport costs related to shopping are subtracted. Private consumption, together with intermediate consumption, public consumption and investments, constitute the total local demand for commodities (DV) in basic prices, through a Use matrix. In this transformation from market prices to basic prices (from DW to DV) commodity taxes and trade margins are subtracted. Local demand is met by imports from other regions and abroad in addition to local production. Through a trade model, exports to other regions and production for the region itself are determined (from DV to AV). Adding exports abroad, gross output by commodity is determined. Through a Make matrix the cycle returns to production by sector (from AV to AE).

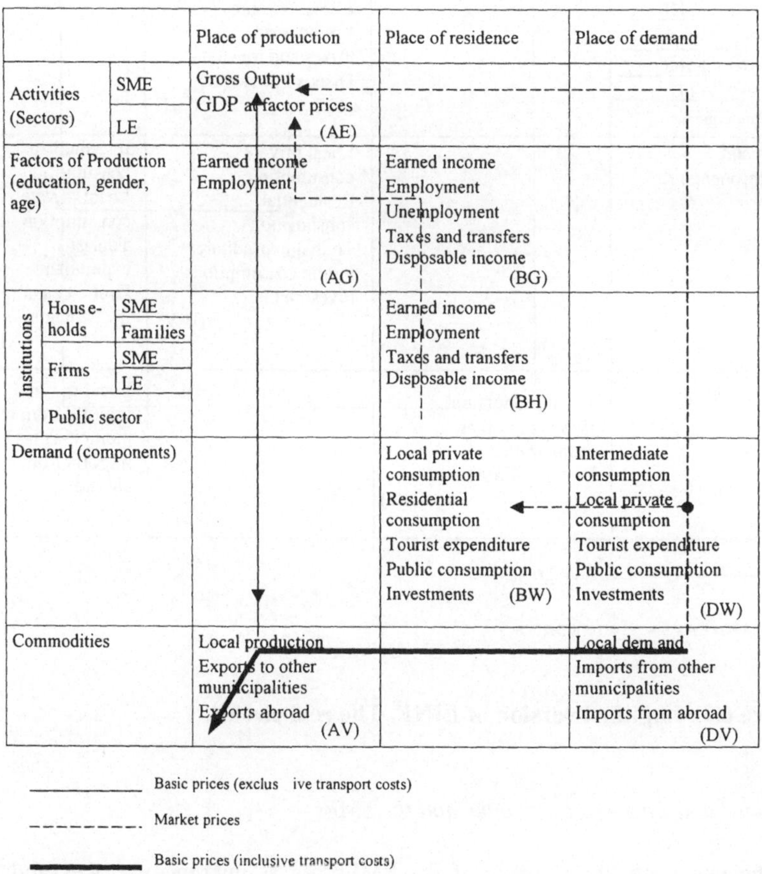

Figure 6.1 Simplified version of LINE. The cost price circuit.

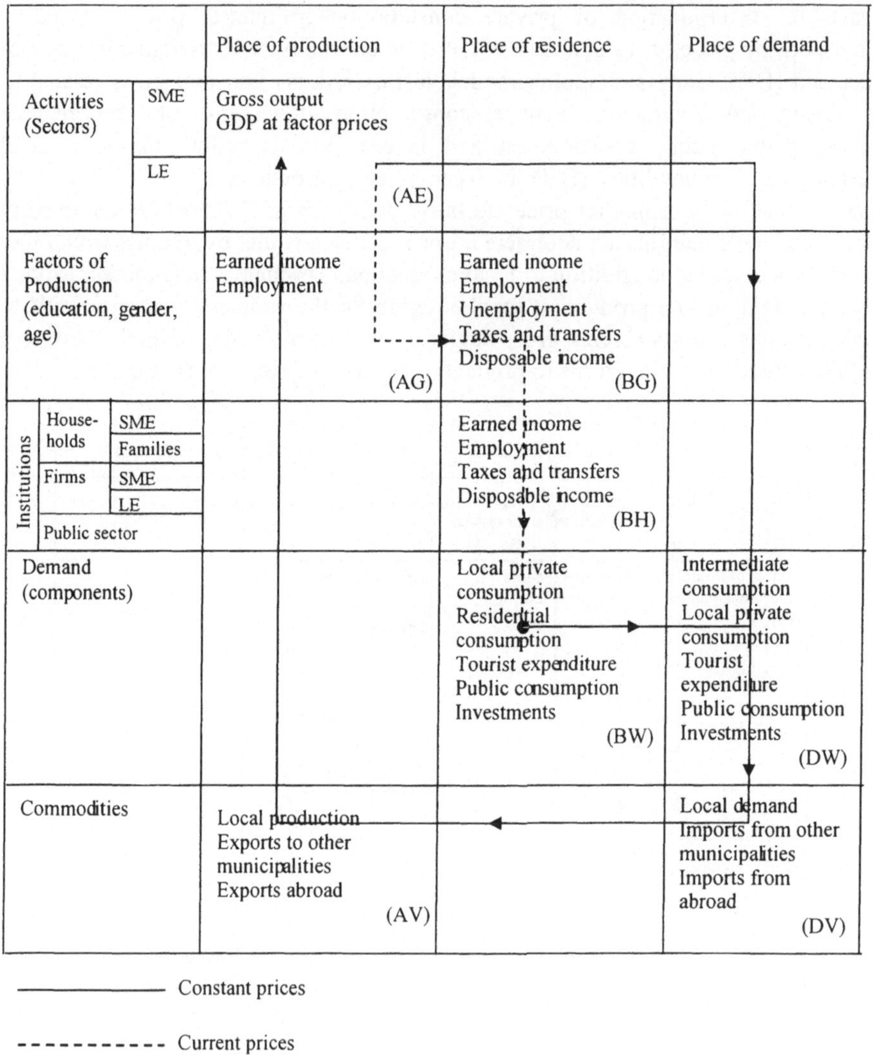

Figure 6.2 Simplified version of LINE. The real circuit.

Forward and Backward Linkages and the SMEs

On the one hand, the impacts of the SMEs are a function of prices and other qualities and characteristics of the commodities produced by them. The positive effects of the production or the *forward linkages* of the SMEs is a function of a number of factors: First, the productivity of the SMEs determines the cost of production and in turn production prices. Productivity is a function of the production in the firm, but is also a function of the environment in which production takes place. If the SMEs are located in a local production environment with positive spillovers or externalities, productivity will, other things being equal, be higher. These issues are discussed in the section on SMEs and externalities below. Costs of production are also determined by labour costs, capital costs as well as prices of intermediate products. Second, the strength of forward linkages depends on good access to markets. These can be products destined for final demand or intermediate consumption.

The impacts of SMEs depend on the other hand on the demand effect of these production activities or on the *backward linkages* of the SMEs. First, there are the intermediate consumption impacts of the SMEs. Second, there are the induced effects from SMEs working through labour demand and income.

SMEs and the Interregional Environment

The SME works not only as a local production or institutional unit. The SME is part of an interregional economy, where the interregional labour market supplies the SMEs with labour, SMEs supply to the interregional commodity market and demand commodities from other actors, including SMEs. Also interregional institutional systems, where the SMEs plays an important role, are involved in the allocation of investment and capital for the SMEs.

In this section, the interregional SAM is presented as an accounting system, which in a systematic way, whilst maintaining fundamental supply and demand restrictions, can present a picture of interaction between the SMEs and form the basis for modelling their interrelationships in the regional and interregional economy.

The Interregional SAM

The one-region SAM can be extended with interregional and international transactions showing interaction with other regions and with abroad. The extensions imply changes in the format of the one-region SAM presented in the section above. First, interaction between the region and other regions and between the region and the rest of the world has been added to the table as extra rows and columns. Second, the denomination and the classification of actors have been changed in order to come as close as possible to the tradition in the construction of interregional SAMs (see for example Round 1995 and Thorbecke 1998).

To illustrate the structure and format of an ideal interregional SAM a two-region SAM with a foreign sector is presented in Table 6.2.

Table 6.2 An interregional SAM with 2 regions and a foreign sector.

		Region 1								Region 2								Rest of World	Total
		1	2	3	4	5	6	7	8	9	10	11	12	13	14	15	16	17	
Region 1																			
Commodities	1								$T_{1,8}$	$T_{1,9}$								$T_{1,17}$	y_1
Activities 1)	2	$T_{2,1}$									$(T_{2,10})$							$(T_{2,17})$	y_2
Factors	3		$T_{3,2}$									$T_{3,11}$						$(T_{3,17})$	y_3
Institutions: Households 3)	4			$T_{4,3}$	$T_{4,4}$	$(T_{4,5})$	$T_{4,6}$						$(T_{4,12})$					$(T_{4,17})$	y_4
Institutions: Companies 2)	5			$T_{5,3}$	$(T_{5,4})$	$(T_{5,5})$	$(T_{5,6})$							$(T_{5,13})$				$(T_{5,17})$	(y_5)
Institutions: Governments	6	$T_{6,1}$	$T_{6,2}$	$T_{6,3}$	$T_{6,4}$	$(T_{6,5})$	$T_{6,6}$								$(T_{6,14})$			$(T_{6,17})$	(y_6)
Capital	7		$T_{7,2}$		$T_{7,4}$	$(T_{7,5})$	$T_{7,6}$									$(T_{7,15})$		$(T_{7,17})$	(y_7)
Wants	8		$T_{8,2}$		$T_{8,4}$		$T_{8,6}$	$T_{8,7}$									$T_{8,16}$	$T_{8,17}$	y_8
Region 2																			
Commodities	9	$T_{9,1}$															$T_{9,16}$	$T_{9,17}$	y_9
Activities 1)	10		$(T_{10,2})$							$T_{10,9}$								$(T_{10,17})$	y_{10}
Factors	11			$T_{11,3}$							$T_{11,10}$							$T_{11,17}$	y_{11}
Institutions: Households 3)	12				$(T_{12,4})$							$T_{12,11}$	$T_{12,12}$	$(T_{12,13})$	$T_{12,14}$			$(T_{12,17})$	y_{12}
Institutions: Companies 2)	13					$(T_{13,5})$						$T_{13,11}$	$(T_{13,12})$	$(T_{13,13})$	$(T_{13,14})$			$(T_{13,17})$	y_{13}
Institutions: Governments	14						$(T_{14,6})$			$T_{14,9}$	$T_{14,10}$	$T_{14,11}$	$T_{14,12}$	$(T_{14,13})$	$T_{14,14}$			$(T_{14,17})$	y_{14}
Capital	15							$(T_{15,7})$			$T_{15,10}$		$T_{15,12}$	$(T_{15,13})$	$T_{15,14}$			$(T_{15,17})$	(y_{15})
Wants	16								$T_{16,8}$		$T_{16,10}$		$T_{16,12}$		$T_{16,14}$	$T_{16,15}$		$T_{16,17}$	y_{16}
Rest of World	17	$T_{17,1}$	$(T^{17,2})$	$(T_{17,3})$	$(T^{17,4})$	$(T^{17,5})$	$(T^{17,6})$	$(T^{17,7})$	$T_{17,8}$	$T_{17,9}$	$(T_{17,10})$	$T_{17,11}$	$(T_{17,12})$	$(T_{17,13})$	$(T_{17,14})$	$(T_{17,15})$	$T_{17,16}$		(y_{17})
Total		y_1^T	y_2^T	y_3^T	y_4^T	(y_5^T)	(y_6^T)	(y_7^T)	y_8^T	y_9^T	y_{10}^T	y_{11}^T	(y_{12}^T)	(y_{13}^T)	(y_{14}^T)	(y_{15}^T)	y_{16}^T	(y_{17}^T)	

Notes: ( ) Data in brackets are not included in the interregional SAM for Denmark. 1) Divided into SMEs and large enterprises. 2) Divided into SMEs as firms and large companies. 3) SME is a part of the household account.

The one-region SAM (the north-west quadrant of the table) consists of the following accounts:

- Commodities (in the one-region Table 6.2 called 'Goods and services');
- Activities (in the one-region Table 6.2 called 'Production');
- Factors (in the one-region Table 6.2 called 'Generation of income');
- Institutions (in the one-region Table 6.2 divided into two accounts – 'Allocation of primary income' and 'Secondary distribution of income') which do not have the division in a distribution and redistribution account, but have instead been divided into
  - households
  - companies
  - governments;
- Wants have been separated out of the commodity account in order to account demand for commodities in composite commodities and to distinguish between market prices (Wants) and basic prices (Commodities).

The illustrative interregional SAM consists of

- intraregional SAMs (see Table 6.2);
- interregional matrices showing interaction between region 1 and region 2;
- import matrices and 2 export matrices.

For each actor, there are interregional and international links. The transformation between regions takes place in two steps. In the case of factor income flows from region 1 to region 2, this is done in the following two steps: First, factor income in region 1 is transferred to the factor account in region 2. Second, factor income is distributed to the household sector in region 2. Therefore, commuting is represented as an intermediate calculation which transfers revenues to factor accounts in region 2 ($T_{11,3}$). Looking at international interaction, some of the factor income is transferred to institutions (households or companies) abroad ($T_{17,3}$) and some factor income is received from abroad ($T_{3,17}$). For other actors similar transfers from one account to the same account in another region or to abroad take place.

It is also the case here that the production account is subdivided into SMEs and other production units and the institutional account is subdivided into SMEs and other firms.

Interregional and International Interaction in the SAM

The commodity account shows interregional and international trade with commodities and the transformation to the production account. This transformation is divided into two steps: First, commodity demand by place of demand is moved to place of production through intraregional, interregional and international trade:

Commodities transferring sales from region 2 ($T_{1,9}$) and from abroad ($T_{1,17}$) to region 1 are interpreted as exports to other regions and foreign export. Imports of commodities from region 2 ($T_{9,1}$) and from abroad ($T_{17,1}$) are shown in the commodity account column. The commodity account is measured in basic prices. Second, commodity production is direct revenue from sales in the activity account at place of production.

In principle, the activity account can also show interregional and international transfer of activities. If an activity is divided into units, then the interaction can show how production tasks are transferred from one region to another. Often interregional transfer of production activities does not take place, because interchange of production activities is accounted for as trade in commodities. Activities are measured in basic prices.

Factor income for mobile factors is transferred to institutions in two steps: First, factor income is transferred from one region to another: For production, in-commuting gives jobs/income to the labour force in other regions ($T_{11,3}$) and countries ($T_{17,3}$), whereas out-commuting to other regions ($T_{3,11}$) and abroad ($T_{3,17}$) gives jobs/income to the labour force in the residence region. Putting the matrices for intra-regional commuting ($T_{3,3}$ and $T_{11,11}$) together with the 4 external matrices forms the total commuting matrix. Second, factor income is transferred to the institutions in the region itself. Factor income is defined in factor prices.

Examining the institutional sectors (households and companies, both of which include SMEs, and government) interaction between households takes place in two steps: First interregional, and second inter-institutional. Looking at interregional interaction, interregional ($T_{12,4}$,$T_{13,5}$ and $T_{14,6}$) and international ($T_{17,4}$, $T_{17,5}$ and $T_{17,6}$) transfers of institutional income not used in the region (other current transfers and capital transfers) are made to institutional sectors in other regions or abroad. In SAM this type of interaction is not accounted. Second, transfers between institutions are accounted in the one-region SAM – see the section above.

Next, disposable income from institutions is used to buy composite commodities or wants. Here, again, the transformation to the wants account is accounted for in two steps: First, interregional transfer, where wants transferred from region 2 ($T_{8,16}$) and from abroad ($T_{8,17}$) to region 1 are shopping activities in region 1, where demand originates in region 2 and abroad. Wants originating in region 1 and going to region 2 ($T_{16,8}$) and abroad ($T_{17,8}$) is shopping going out of region 1. Second, wants inside the regions are allocated to the commodity account, as described in the section above.

The matrix, which can be put together from these 8 sub-matrices, forms an interregional/international shopping matrix ($T_{8,8}$, $T_{16,8}$, $T_{8,16}$, $T_{16,16}$, $T_{17,8}$, $T_{17,16}$, $T_{8,17}$, $T_{16,17}$).

In this context, shopping is broadly defined and includes:

- intermediate consumption (where origin: place of production, destination: place of demand);

- private consumption (divided into local private consumption and tourist expenditure, where origin: place of residence, destination: place of demand);
- public consumption (where origin: place of residence, destination: place of demand);
- investment (where origin: place of residence/production, destination: place of demand).

In the SAM only shopping for private consumption is accounted for. Wants are measured in market/buyers prices. Finally, income which is not used, is accumulated in the capital account. In this process savings are also transferred to other regions and abroad. In SAM savings are only accounted for as a residual.

SMEs and Externalities

The previous sections have described the way in which a SAM-based modelling approach can be used to identify and model the effects of forward and backward linkage impacts from SMEs on a one-region and multiple region economy. It was assumed implicitly that production units and institutional actors were independent, ie that their behaviour did not affect each other, except through the market. It was also assumed that industries are of the constant cost type.

It is commonly argued that a significant feature of the development of SMEs in an economy is that they both promote the development of, and are able to use, positive externalities, which serve to raise productivity and lower costs.

Pecuniary Externalities

Pecuniary externalities, as noted above, arise when input prices vary with the amount of output produced. For example, if input prices fall with increasing output in a given industry, then the industry is a decreasing cost industry. Thus, growth of numbers of SMEs in a given sector can create pecuniary externalities. This effect may be reinforced when the regional dimension is introduced. The effects can occur because of scale economies in the production of inputs.

Pecuniary externalities can be introduced through the use of non-linear production functions, whose parameters are estimated using cross sectional data from the SAM. The equations derived from this exercise can substitute the purely linear relationships in the basic SAM.

Technological Externalities

Technological externalities, as with pecuniary externalities, result in a downward shift of the industry average cost curve. A classical positive technological externality is knowledge spillovers between firms. A large pool of production units will potentially create a larger spillover effect than a small pool. The size of the pool which is accessible for production units is in part a geographical question, reflecting the current interest in clusters and industrial development. Thus, transport and access costs play an important role in determining benefits arising from these externalities.

There are fundamentally two different approaches to modelling technological externalities in the SAM framework. The first approach is similar to that used for pecuniary externalities: the SAM contains cross sectional data which permits estimation of productivity as a function of accessibility to a common idea pool, which can be assumed to depend upon sectoral specialization, labour qualifications, and other sector. These relations can be included in the SAM-based model, which describes regional prices and competitiveness. Improving accessibility to a knowledge pool and increasing the number of SMEs in the pool will have measurable positive regional economic effects.

The second approach is beyond the scope of this paper, but an outline can be provided. The SAM-based accounting and modelling approach includes flows and stocks of ideas, treated as commodities, where in the production account, ideas are produced, and in the production and institutional account, ideas are demanded and consumed.. For non-traded ideas (which have a public or semi-public good character) the SAM can be extended. This development is, however, difficult, but perhaps not impossible. A demographic model for ideas based upon SAM accounting principles, including untraded ideas, can account for and model changes in the stock of ideas, which together with the number of knowledge workers, affects production.

Modelling the Performance of SMEs in Denmark

The Danish SAM and the LINE model as used in empirical analyses in Denmark contains a basic division into 275 local authorities. For each, there is a division into 12 industries, 7 age, 2 sex and 5 education categories for factors of production. Households are divided into four categories by type and there are 20 commodity categories. SAM-K contains data for each year from 1970 until 1999.

The SAM framework and the LINE model which is described theoretically above containing a division of production units and firms by size has not yet been made operational, though this can be added. Basic information on the SME as a part of the production account and as a part of the institutional account is available in the Danish data registers.

Characteristics of SMEs in Denmark

Even though a SAM with a subdivision of production and firm accounts is not yet available, it is possible to give a more partial and not fully consistent description of SME characteristics using ordinary production and accounting statistics for Danish production. In the Danish statistical system, the EU standard definition of fewer than 250 employees cannot be used, because of confidentiality problems. In the following, a threefold division has been used:

- Small firms (fewer than 50 employees);
- Medium sized firms (50-99 employees);
- Large firms (100 employees and above).

Table 6.3 shows the general characteristics of SMEs in Denmark.

Table 6.3 Characteristics of Danish firms (1999).

	Small firms	Medium sized firms	Large firms	Total
Number of firms	98.5%	0.8%	0.8%	100.0%
Turnover	48.8%	9.1%	42.1%	100.0%
Employment	31.0%	6.8%	62.3%	100.0%
Export	25.3%	9.0%	65.7%	100.0%
Gross profits	67.7%	4.9%	27.3%	100.0%
Gross investment	48.8%	7.1%	44.1%	100.0%

Source: Statistics Denmark (2001).

In terms of numbers, Small firms are completely dominant. However, measured by all other indicators, they have a lesser role. In particular, large firms have a large share of both employment and exports. However, the effect of size varies by industry.

Table 6.4 Turnover by numbers of employees by sector 1999 (million Dkr; 1 Euro = 7.42 DKK).

	Small firms	Medium sized firms	Large firms	Total
Primary sector	2.55	0.77	0.91	2.38
Industry	1.04	1.03	1.25	1.17
Construction	0.92	0.97	1.12	0.98
Commerce	2.58	2.92	2.62	2.63
Transport	1.42	1.33	1.45	1.44
Finance/Business service	1.52	0.78	0.40	0.85
Total	1.50	1.27	0-64	0.99

Source: Statistics Denmark (2001).

Table 6.4 shows that turnover per employee for industrial firms increases with size, whilst in the financial and business sectors the reverse is the case. This is because of the effects of scale economies in industry, whilst smaller firms employing highly educated labour are common in the financial and business service sectors. For the remaining sectors, except the primary sector (mainly agriculture), turnover per employee does not vary strongly with firm size. Almost all agricultural enterprises are very small, but inside the category of small firms there is a positive relationship with size.

Table 6.5 Export in relation to turnover by sector 1999 (%).

	Small firms	Medium sized firms	Large firms	Total
Primary sector	8.5%	16.4%	46.6%	9.4%
Industry	21.4%	39.2%	57.4%	47.1%
Construction	1.4%	1.5%	4.1%	2.1%
Commerce	11.9%	17.3%	11.0%	12.1%
Transport	18.1%	18.0%	41.8%	33.7%
Finance/Business service	5.8%	14.1%	16.6%	9.3%
Total	11.1%	21.3%	33.5%	21.4%

Source: Statistics Denmark (2001).

Table 6.5 shows that in general, export's share grows with increasing size, which reflects the export of mass-produced commodities for intermediate and final consumption. Smaller firms tend to be suppliers to larger export-orientated firms.

Table 6.6 Gross profits in relation to turnover by sector 1999 (%).

	Small firms	Medium sized firms	Large firms	Total
Primary sector	11.0%	-3.2%	2.8%	10.7%
Industry	9.1%	5.6%	6.1%	6.7%
Construction	11.7%	3.7%	2.1%	8.3%
Commerce	5.0%	2.7%	2.3%	3.9%
Transport	12.0%	4.2%	6.2%	7.7%
Finance/Business service	25.1%	4.8%	3.8%	18.0%
Total	9.5%	3.7%	4.4%	6.8%

Source: Statistics Denmark (2001).

Table 6.6 shows that gross profit as a share of turnover seems to be markedly higher for small firms as compared with larger firms, for all sectors. Gross profits do, however, tend to be volatile, from year to year and sector by sector, so caution should be exercised in relation to drawing general conclusions.

Table 6.7 Gross investment per employee (DKK 1000, 1 Euro = 7.42 DKK) 1999.

	Small firms	Medium sized firms	Large firms	Total
Primary sector	30.0	37.9	2.6	29.6
Industry	57.1	41.6	49.3	50.4
Construction	45.1	19.3	31.4	38.9
Commerce	18.0	16.4	16.8	17.4
Transport	50.8	26.3	55.0	52.1
Finance/Business service	105.8	88.3	100.6	103.0
Total	39.1	30.7	40.9	39.1

Source: Statistics Denmark (2001).

Table 6.7 suggests that investment in the small and the large firms is more important than in the middle group. It should also be remembered that the capital/labour ratio varies substantially between sectors. Investments are also very volatile from years to year.

Conclusion

A main conclusion of this paper is that the social accounting matrices are relevant tools for building high quality and consistent data on SMEs in the regional economy. Additionally, the SAM-framework is an appropriate tool for modelling the impacts of SMEs in the regional economy. On the basis of a detailed description in the SAM of two important processes in the regional economy a) cost – prices – cost and b) demand – production – income it is possible to set up simple or more advanced interregional general equilibrium models to analyse the interrelations between the SMEs and the regional economy. The introduction of the concepts forward and backward linkages and the regional and interregional externalities are important in the analysis of the role of SMEs. The SAM accounting and modelling tool has a considerable potential value with respect to the systematic inclusion of externalities into the study of SME performance and their role in the economy. Basic data concerning Danish SMEs have been presented, which constitutes the context for modelling the performance of SMEs.

Note

[1] The make and use tables will be presented in detail as part of the social accounting matrix in this chapter.

References

Hewings, G.J.D and M. Madden (eds) (1995) *Social and Demographic Accounting*, Cambridge University Press, Cambridge.

Madsen B., Jensen-Butler, C. and Dam, P.U. (2001a) *The LINE-model*, AKF Forlaget, Copenhagen.

Madsen, B., Jensen-Butler, C. and Dam, P.U. (2001b) *A Social Accounting Matrix for Danish Municipalities, SAM-K*. AKF Forlaget, Copenhagen.

Scitovsky, T. (1954) *Two Concepts of External Economies*, Journal of Political Economy, 62: 143-151.

Statistics Denmark (2001) *Generel Erhvervsstatistik* (2001:19) Danmarks Statistik, Copenhagen.

Thorbecke, E. (1998) 'Social Accounting, matrices and social accounting analysis', in W Isard et al., *Methods of interregional and regional analysis*, Ashgate, Aldershot, England.

United Nations (1993) *System of National Accounts 1993*, Brussels/Luxembourg, New York, Paris, Washington, D.C.

Chapter 7

Norwegian Regional Development and the Role of SMEs

Steinar Johansen

Introduction

Norway is a relatively rich country in the sense that you will find Norway at the top of lists of countries, with a high standard of living. These statistics do not reveal the regional problems we have in Norway, which are relatively different from the ones we find in many other countries. During the past fifty years or so, Norway and the other Scandinavian countries have developed an integrated public-private society, where re-distribution of income has been emphasized. This has contributed to securing a certain distribution of wealth, between wage earners and benefit receivers, between poorer and richer regions and so on. Given the total wealth of Norway, which also is an oil exporting country, poverty problems in an international sense do not exist.

The Norwegian economy runs at almost full capacity, at least compared to many other countries. This implies low unemployment rates. At the same time, it implies structural change and centralization of jobs. In Norway, population densities are very low in the peripheries, and jobs centralization can easily result in migration towards the centres and, in turn, to de-population of the peripheries. De-population, as well as the causes of this problem, including regional production, industrial structure and job opportunities, is the main problem of regional development in Norway.

This paper is therefore focused on discussing the term 'regional development', and the factors that influence regional development in Norway. We try concentrating on the following important questions:

- What are the regional development issues in Norway, and to what extent do these differ from issues of regional development in other countries? How can we define the term regional development in this context, especially the relationship between regional (economic) growth and the more general term 'regional development'?

- Which are the most important preconditions for regional development in Norway? Is firm size relevant and important, or are there other factors that have more influence on development?

The first part of the first question, as well as the second question, will be discussed in some length in the following sections of the paper. We want to try answering the second part of the first question here. What is the relationship between regional development and regional growth? Firstly, we have to look into the term 'regional', which of course is an interesting term to write lengthy papers about. We will not do that here. The basic question is why we are interested in regions at all. A very simple, but yet an illustrative, answer is that people live there, companies produce their goods and services there, and markets are (partly) there. Most economic activities are, in other words, located to regions, people live in regions, and goods, services and people travel within and between regions. These activities occur in space (and time) and not in a one-dimensional, national spot. This is a brief and popular explanation for why we are interested in regions and regional development, and this leads us to the main question of what regional development means.

Many textbooks on regional development do not discuss this term explicitly, and implicitly they often assume that regional development and regional economic growth are similar expressions. The question is: are they, or should they be, similar expressions? Our answer is that regional economic growth can be very different from regional development, but that regional growth in some cases can be a predominant factor determining regional development. Growth can be measured in different ways. In many cases, growth is measured as growth in regional GDP (which can be named regional domestic product or RDP), in other cases it can be measured as growth in value added of the businesses in the region, as growth in export incomes, or as growth in personal incomes. These definitions of growth are different, but essentially they measure in one way or another how the regions themselves generate incomes that can be spent within or outside the region.

If we accept that we are interested in regions because people live there, and because companies are active there, the term development could and should be used more widely than the term growth. It would include, among other things, variables that are connected to quality of life (soft variables), rather than only to standard of living (RDP, income and other hard variables). The determinants of regional development would, in this sense, have to be more widely defined than the determinants of regional growth. There is a potential conflict between goals connected to regional economic growth in the narrow sense and goals connected to regional development.

This also implies that a national policy for redistributing regional income, for instance to achieve a even income distribution, would contribute to regional development in the weaker regions, but could at the same time contribute to reducing growth measured in standard terms both in weaker and stronger regions.

This might be especially relevant for countries like Norway, which has become rich partly from extracting and exporting oil, and where national income and GDP growth depend on this (which is not produced in a standard region) as well as on the aggregate regional growth. There is, in other words, more income to redistribute than the sum of incomes of all regions.

If we accept that regional development and regional growth are not necessarily the same things, we have a broader view on regional development. We have to include more than the regions themselves, and how they cope, in the discussion. In particular, distributive policies and issues connected to these will be very relevant for development issues. In Norway, we find especially that the public sector, as a provider of services, as a distributive body and as a partner with the private sector, is very important.

Regional Issues of Norway

Norway is a relatively large country, situated at the northernmost periphery of Europe. The geography is harsh, with mountains and fjords, and relatively few people live in Norway. However, Norway is, and has always been, relatively rich on natural resources, such as fish, minerals, energy, forests and so on. The last thirty years or so, oil extraction has become an increasingly important activity for the Norwegian economy. Norway has become one of the richest countries in the world, with a relatively active, re-distributing state. This mixed economy is often referred to as the 'Scandinavian Welfare State Model', or simply the Scandinavian Model. It includes an extensive social security system, and the government influences resource allocation both directly (rules and regulations) and more indirectly (incentives). In addition, the public sector produces many goods and services that probably would be produced by the private sector in more liberal economies, especially in peripheral regions.

In this paper, we focus on regional development, and the link between SMEs and regional development. Some of the regional issues or problems in Norway differ quite substantially from the problems we find in many other countries, and especially within the European Union (EU), but some are more similar. One important regional issue is the issue of viable, or sustainable, regions all over the country. This is connected to industrial development and regional growth, and in this sense quite similar to regional policies in the rest of Europe. The other main issue for regional policies is the population pattern. Being a relatively large country, but with few people (Annex 1, Table 7.2a), it has been very important to try preventing de-population of the periphery. This is quite unlike regional policies in other countries, maybe except Sweden and Finland. In other countries, industrial decline, high unemployment rates and low income (or major differences in these indicators across the country), factors that might be referred to as 'poverty problems', have been more important regional issues beside the question of regional growth. Compared to other countries, it is very difficult to claim that such poverty problems exist in Norway.

Traditionally, the Norwegian economy has been resource based, and dominated by primary industries (fishing, agriculture, forestry) located close to where the resources could be found, in what we now would call the peripheral areas. During the 20th century, the manufacturing sector started evolving in the cities, and in small industrial towns, and out-migration from the peripheral areas commenced. Productivity growth in resource based industries implied a decreasing need for labour in the peripheral areas, at least in the long run. Markets for services are comparatively small in the peripheries, given the few people living there, and the nature of services (which are difficult to export). Both these points lead therefore, to the fact that industrial development, where more and more jobs are found within the production of services, leads to a centralization of jobs.

Table 7.1 illustrates the current (1998) situation on the structural differences between regions in Norway. The table is based on indices, showing the employment share in each region in relation to the national share. An index of 100 means that the share is the same as the national average, while a smaller (or greater) figure shows the relatively lower (or higher) importance of a sector in the region. The figures illustrate that employment in central parts of the country (main cities and their surroundings) is dominated by private services (which are oriented towards people and production). All regions outside the most central ones are dominated by production of goods (in the primary or secondary sectors) and public services. The above mentioned decreasing need for labour within the production of *goods*, and the small growth in labour demand due lack of markets for *services*, have been countered by a growth within public sector employment in the 1970s and 1980s.

The problem of centralization, however, is the problem of de-population of the peripheral areas, and congestion of the core parts of the country. This problem can be divided into several categories. First, we have the continuing restructuring of the economy. Within production of primary or secondary goods, investment in machinery tends to decrease the need for labour, even if production continues at the same pace as before. Given the localization of these sectors, this implies reduced demand for labour in the peripheries. Parallel to this, the demand for labour increases in the services sector. As the services sector is located in primarily the core of the country, demand for labour rise more in the more urbanized, more developed core areas. This leads to job centralization, which in turn might lead to job related migration of the population from the peripheral areas to the main centres. Second, we have a change in the birth rates, which can be explained by the fact that women now are older when they have their first child. There are many reasons for postponing reproduction, and one of them is that women today choose higher education. Migration from the peripheral areas to the main centres of the country has been on-going for many decades, but in earlier times the rate of reproduction in the peripheries was high enough to secure a relatively stable population. Since the rate of reproduction has fallen, and the age structure is more favourable in the main centres, we will have an automatic centralization of the population *even without migration*. This is a new situation in Norway. The risk of de-population is, in other words, more evident today than earlier, which leads us to believing that Norway's regional problems will be greater in the future than they have been in the past.

Table 7.1 Employment by sector and type of region 1998. Index: national share = 100.

	Primary	Secondary	Personal services	Industrial services	Public services	Sum (per cent)
Main city regions	28	81	113	143	91	43,6
City regions	97	116	95	76	105	36,9
Village regions	175	118	88	54	109	6,9
Small village regions	233	116	86	51	106	7,0
Countryside	426	99	65	42	118	5,6
Sum (per cent)	4,3	23,3	30,4	13,9	28,0	100

Note: Types of regions are defined in Annex.

Source: Labour market statistics from PANDA.

Norwegian Policies – General Principles

This line of argument is, of course, based on the fact that Norway's situation in many respects differs from that of other countries. Norway is, on the one hand, not a member of the EU. This means, in principle, that Norwegian policies can be defined within the nation. However, Norway has signed a treaty with the EU (the EEA – the European Economic Area). This treaty means that Norway has to adapt to European rules of competition, in exchange of access to the European market. Norwegian authorities are quite good at adapting European rules and regulations, often quicker than the EU member states themselves.

On the other hand, (a) Norway is (in many respects) a relatively rich country. One could argue that most of the wealth comes from the oil, which is probably true. At the same time, (b) the public sector plays a very active role in developing the country, as an owner, an employer, a buyer and a regulator. Policies are, in other words, very important, and probably more important than in other, more liberal, economies. However (c), the role of the Government and of policies is gradually changing. Adapting to international treaties is one factor, but also liberalization, globalization, decentralization and New Public Management influence the Government's role in development generally, and within regional development more specifically. These three factors, together with the aims for regional policies, sum up most of the framework for regional policies in Norway.

- Norway has become a relatively wealthy country, especially during the past thirty years. There are several reasons for this, it is not simply the discovery of huge oil reserves. However, the oil has been an important factor in recent years. This has led to positive 'balances'; the fact that the trade balance is positive and there are tax revenues from oil has produced a surplus in the public sector as well. The public sector's assets are growing, even if the public sector is spending a lot of money, and the economy runs at more or less full capacity. A relatively expansive economic policy leads to structural change at an increased pace. Many experts argue that government spending, with relatively low rates of unemployment, leads to over-investment and over-employment in the non-competitive (private as well as public) services sector. In the long run, they claim, there is a risk that this could lead to vanishing competitive goods-producing sector, and a risk of the arrival of the so-called 'Dutch Disease' as the competitive sector is crowded out of the economy. We can already see signs of this, with increasing wage rates driven by the non-competitive sector, increased factor cost in the competitive sector (without a matching increase in productivity growth) and a very strong currency making Norwegian products extremely expensive abroad.
- As mentioned earlier, the Scandinavian Model is based on distributive measures. This implies a mixed private-public economy, based on markets for most commodities, but also on the government taking an active role in economic life. One of the important contributions the Government has made, is that it has maintained a tradition of keeping unemployment low, even during the recession of the 1970s. In this period, investments in the oil industry were among the things that kept the economy running. At the same time, the public sector expanded all over the country, with an increased production of public services directed towards the population. Recessions do happen in Norway as well however, but they are relatively minor compared to other countries. An expansive economic policy during recessions, and now, when we have become a relatively wealthy state, has contributed to re-allocation of resources particularly in the context of regional policies. Now, the investments in the oil sector are starting to pay off (Norway is becoming wealthy), and the problem of avoiding unintentional structural change (see first bullet point above) by spending too much money, is coming increasingly into focus.
- During recent years, several factors have contributed to changing the public sector's role in the economy. Among the important ones is the EEA and EU regulations, which limit the extent to which the public sector can participate in economic life. Trends towards liberalization of the economy can, however, be explained both by the increased internationalization and by a more liberal view

on things within politics as well as economics, at least when it comes to leaving more resource allocation to the market and less to distributive measures. In the light of this, the production of many formerly publicly produced goods is becoming privatized. Goods and services still produced by the public sector are to a certain extent becoming allocated to users through some sort of simulations of markets, instead of using more old-fashioned distribution mechanisms (New Public Economy). The economic argument for doing this is to make the economy more efficient (there are additional political arguments, which might be just as important), but in some cases administering these simulations and privatizations can be relatively costly.

The three points above summarize the situation for policies in Norway. They explain why, and under which conditions, the public sector has become very important, and point to some of the reasons why distributive measures might be reduced in the future. This is also one of the reasons why a paper on regional development (and SMEs) in Norway would be impossible without discussing the public sector's role.

Since the war, regional issues have been important in Norway, and the re-distributive state has influenced the allocation of resources and incomes between regions. In the beginning, the rebuilding of the country after the war, especially the northernmost parts of the country, was the main task. The Government gradually found that some parts of the country would need extra support even after everything had been rebuilt, to avoid *unwanted centralization* as well as *de-population of the peripheries*, but also to provide a more even *income distribution*. In this sense, the Government provided relatively more infrastructure in the peripheral areas, in addition to contribute to building a national manufacturing sector in small industrial towns. This was thought of as being economically efficient, in the sense that it would contribute to a better allocation of resources *where people lived*. As welfare goals became increasingly important from the 1960s on, and as the markets for welfare services were very small in the peripheral areas, the Government started providing welfare services through local Governments (municipalities). This services provision also contributed to increasing the size of and the number of opportunities within local labour markets, even in peripheral areas, and centralization was reduced in the 1970s. In this period, the arguments for regional policy supporting the peripheral areas were changed, and they now have become more distributive. Today, regional equality still is important, and the provision of services is one of the fields in which the Government is active. The people should have access to the same services wherever they live. We still have the political aim of preserving the population pattern (preventing de-population of the peripheries), but more and more emphasis within regional policies is now being put on regional sustainable growth and on endogenous factors (and less emphasis is being placed on a national-regional income distribution). This implies that policies turn in the direction of increased growth, and that distributive matters get a lower priority. However growth based mostly on the regions' own resources and competence could lead to a polarization of regions, where core regions become richer, while periphery regions become poorer. In turn, this could lead to increased centralization and de-population of the peripheries.

Firm Size and Regional Development

In the above sections, I have argued that the public and private sector in Norway are woven tightly together, and especially that the public sector is important in the peripheries. Therefore, a discussion about regional development in Norway cannot be held without including the re-distributive state and discussing the aims for regional policy and the role of the public sector. In light of this, I have also argued that regional growth (in an economic sense) is something other than regional development, but that growth sometimes is a predominant need for regional development.

In Norway, a large company is a company with more than 100 employees. Small companies have less than 20 employed, while micro companies have less than five. This means that medium sized companies have between 20 and 100 employees. Around 200,000 companies have registered employment in Norway (in all, there are 480,000 registered companies – more than half have zero employment). Of these, around 1,400 are *large*, 96 per cent are *small*, and 80 per cent are *micro*. This is at the national level. One small company of course employs less people than a large one. The number of employees in small (less than 20) companies is, on total, about the same as the number of employees in large (more than 100) companies. Turnover per employee (one of many productivity measures) is slightly larger in large companies than in small ones.

When discussing firm size and regional development, we are really discussing whether there is a causal relationship between their sizes and development. This can be done in several ways. Employment in *small and medium sized* companies is, in total, larger than in large enterprises. SMEs, in other words, employs more people (and they also have a larger total turnover than the large ones). In this sense, SMEs are more important than large companies. However, we have not argued that there is a causal relationship between company size and development (employment, turnover). This is only an observation. More interesting is the question, what are the characteristics of SMEs (except size) compared to larger companies?

The most striking characteristic is that *SMEs are very different*. We find SMEs in all sectors, producing different products. Some SMEs produce for the home market and some produce export goods, some produce goods and some produce services, some are solvent and some are not, some are new and some are old, some are labour intensive and some are capital intensive, the productivity varies, and different SMEs have different market positions. These differences make analysing all SMEs within the same framework very difficult. Are there *any* similarities between SMEs?

One important similarity is probably that in larger companies, the distance between the workers and the management is greater, and that this distance decreases in smaller companies. In smaller companies, it is easier for everyone to see what is going on, and the interests of the workers and the management will probably coincide more. These reasonably tight networks within SMEs could contribute to generating a good climate for innovation and growth. On the other hand, the existence of large research departments is less likely in SMEs than in larger enterprises, which means that some innovation processes are more difficult.

Another similarity is probably that the SMEs are more flexible, as changes in production processes or systems require fewer people changing jobs and probably fewer changes in the capital stock. However, this has a reverse side as well, as smaller companies have fewer legs to stand on and are therefore more sensitive to exogenous changes in the economic conditions that create the framework within which they operate. Smaller companies also have fewer opportunities for short and long term cross-subsidising activities within the companies. They, in other words, have to be more aware of costs in production processes than larger companies do, at least if they want to survive in the long run.

Empirical evidence shows that SMEs are flexible. SMEs are born and die all the time, entrepreneurs seem to change companies several times, and they are innovative. We could conclude the discussion here, by saying that size matters, and that SMEs are important for development, and also for regional development.

However, several factors have not yet been mentioned. The *size structure varies across industrial sectors*, the *industrial structure varies in a centre-periphery perspective* (Table 7.1), the *size of the companies varies regionally* within the same industry and the *importance of the public sector* (which is not included in the figures on companies' sizes above) *varies regionally*[1].

The *industrial characteristics* show that companies, generally, are smaller when they are involved in the production of services and in primary production, than when they are in the manufacturing sector. In other words, regions where the manufacturing sector is relatively important would, on average, have larger enterprises than regions that are characterized by primary production and services. This might also imply that company size on average would *decrease* in the long run, as the economy is becoming more service oriented.

However, *regional characteristics* are also important, as the average size of companies *within the same industry* varies regionally. This applies especially to companies specialising in the production of services[2]. These companies are, on average, larger in the core areas of the country than in peripheral areas. Some of the reasons for this can be that the size of the home markets are bigger in the main centres, that the access to (educated) labour is greater, and that there can be certain scale effects in such areas. These scale effects are probably connected to administrative costs per employee, concentration and market power within certain types of specialized services, and bigger profits earned when the company is large. This could imply that company size *within the services sector* would *increase* on average, as the economy becomes more service oriented and centralization continues.

The final point is that the *public sector* is relatively more important in peripheral areas than in the main centres of economic activity. One of the important reasons for this is that the size of markets in the peripheries is not sufficient for private production of these services. The regional distribution of the public sector is partly a political choice, and as I have pointed out in the previous sections, the general trends towards liberalization and privatization are present in Norway. Therefore, it is difficult to know whether the regional distribution of the public sector will be controlled to the same extent in the future as it has been in the past.

This section has shown that the size of private companies matters, that the size varies across industries and regions, and that the public sector is important. Norwegian regional development issues are connected to de-population as well as growth. All in all, different companies (and the public sector) serve different purposes all over the country. More important than companies' sizes is, therefore, their functions within the local and regional economy. In order to get a well functioning and growing economy, and subsequently regional development, all or most functions have to be present. Company size is secondary, but it is a fact that most companies are small, and that they are smaller in the peripheries (except large, manufacturing plants) than in core parts of the country. Therefore, SMEs will continue to be important for regional development in Norway in the future as they have been in the past.

Some Conclusions

Many factors influence regional development. In this paper, I have focused on company size, and on the public sector including policy preferences, but I have also mentioned some other factors briefly.

Regional development is not the same as regional growth. Distributive measures are also very important, either we re-distribute wealth or we distribute wealth that comes from outside (in the case of Norway this obviously means distributing revenues generated by off-shore oil production activities). Therefore, growth itself cannot explain regional development. I think it is very important to remember that the aim of growth (regionally or nationally) is increased welfare, and not increased profits. Sometimes, the market does not provide the desired allocation of resources, and policies are used to intervene. Such interventions are very important in Norway, where the public and the private sectors are very tightly intertwined. However, new trends and conditions might influence this in the future. New regional problems might arise, regions might, in line with liberal trends, be left more to themselves in the future and so on. This, we do not know yet.

However, if this happens, the importance of markets and private enterprises might increase, and welfare provision might become more dependent on endogenous factors and on regional growth than on distributive factors. In this sense, small and medium sized enterprises can possibly become increasingly important, both in central and peripheral parts of the country. On the other hand, lack of markets might lead to increased centralization in such a scenario. Politicians in Norway agree, at least pragmatically, that de-population is undesirable, and they might still use a distributive policy in the future. The question is, will it work? I will not try to answer that question here, but simply point to the fact that market forces are strong, structural, industrial and demographic features differ, and we might see increased centralization in Norway in the future irrespective of political priorities.

Notes

1 Detailed charts on these issues can be found in Spilling, O: *Fakta om små og mellomstore bedrifter 2000* (Facts on SMEs 2000), Fagbokforlaget, Bergen, 2000.

2 Large, manufacturing enterprises are located in certain locations, where they have been located for many years. These locations are outside the main centres, but not in the most peripheral parts of the country.

Annex: Dividing the Country into a Core-Periphery Dimension

Table 7.1a Principles for dividing the country into regions.

Name of region	Type of region	No of inhabitants in centre	Max travel distance to centre (minutes)	No of workers in labour force
Periphery 1	Countryside	< 2000	30	< 2000
Periphery 2	Countryside	< 2000	30	2000-20000
Not central 1	Small village regions	2000-5000	30	< 6000
Not central 2	Small village regions	2000-5000	30	6000-20000
Middle central 1	Village regions	5000-15000	45	< 6000
Middle central 2	Village regions	5000-15000	45	6000-20000
Central 1	City regions	15000-50000	60	< 20000
Central 2	City regions	15000-50000	60	20000-60000
Central 3	City regions	15-50000	60	60000-200000
Very central 1	Main city regions	> 50000	75	60000-200000
Very central 2	Main city regions	> 50000	90	> 200000

In this table, the country's 435 municipalities are aggregated into 11 (5 if we use the second column) regions using a core-periphery dimension. The criteria applied are the number of inhabitants living in (or the size of) the main centre, max travel distance to the main centre in minutes and the number of workers in the labour force in the municipalities that are employed there. The geographical dimension is not taken into consideration. A municipality is associated with the largest centre, if there are two different centres near by. The bottom line of the table represents the most central municipalities (around Oslo), while the top of the table represents the very periphery of the country. The number of municipalities, the population and the population densities in each region are shown in Table 7.2a. There are a total of 435 municipalities, 4.4 million people and an average population density of 14.5 inhabitants per square kilometre. The table shows that there are substantial differences between the core and periphery regions.

Table 7.2a Number of municipalities and inhabitants in five types of regions 1998.

Name of region	No of municipalities	No of inhabitants (000)	Population densities (inh/sqkm)
Countryside	143	301	2.3
Small village regions	60	333	4.9
Village regions	46	335	8.7
City regions	143	1807	28.1
Main city regions	43	1670	266.0

Chapter 8

Regional Development and SMEs in Ireland

Edgar Morgenroth and Eoin O'Malley

Introduction

Throughout most of the 1990s, GDP growth in Ireland far exceeded that of other European countries. While this exceptional growth performance allowed Ireland to converge rapidly to the EU average per capita GDP, it was also accompanied by a growing divergence between Irish regions with respect to per capita GDP. Consequently there has been renewed interest in the question of regional disparities within Ireland with the publication of a number of research papers. This interest in regional development has also been reflected in a greater emphasis on regional policy. Thus, the National Development Plan for the period 2000-06 has a strong focus on regional development and the Irish Government is currently drawing up a national spatial strategy that will crucially influence the geography of development.

In order to explain the type of differences in growth rates that have been observed within Ireland and elsewhere, recent economic literature has focused on models of endogenous growth. In contrast to the older growth models such as the Solow-Swan model which explained sustained economic growth simply through technical progress, the sources of which were not specified (see Solow, 1956), these models have endogenized mechanisms that overcome diminishing returns and therefore would result in sustained growth. Without technical progress the earlier models predict that growth will eventually cease due to the diminishing returns to capital. Furthermore, in these models policy measures only have a temporary effect on the growth rate which changes only along a transition path until a new steady state is reached. In the endogenous growth literature a number of different factors have an important impact on the growth rate. For example technical progress is to a large extent driven by research and development (R&D) activities. This has been incorporated into growth models as the accumulation of knowledge (e.g. Romer, 1986) or improvements in the quality of intermediate inputs (e.g. Aghion and Howitt, 1992, 1998). Another avenue that has been explored is the effect of public infrastructure, which is typically modelled as an additional input in the production function (Barro, 1990; Futagami et al., 1993). Public infrastructure raises the marginal product of private capital thus sustaining growth. An important feature of these models is the existence of externalities from knowledge and infrastructure due to their public good characteristics. While these models offer interesting insights into the mechanisms which determine growth, only a few contributions are concerned with market structure and growth while the particular role of small and medium sized enterprises appears to have been ignored.

The literature on firm size and R&D does allow for a link between firm size and growth and this has been utilized in the new growth literature. Perhaps the earliest contribution to the literature on firm size and innovation was that of Schumpeter (1942) who argued that larger firms had an advantage over smaller firms in innovating which would lead to the concentration of economic power in a few giant corporations. This argument is plausible if innovation is subject to very high set up costs which could only be borne by large firms, or if R&D is subject to increasing returns to scale. However, the opposite could also hold if, for example smaller firms are more flexible to the demands of the marketplace which would allow them to innovate more rapidly such that they overtake the incumbent larger firms. The ideas of Schumpeter have been applied in a formal setting by Aghion and Howitt (1992, 1998), who model innovation as a sequence of quality improvements in intermediate inputs such that the previous technology becomes obsolete – a process of creative destruction. In their basic models the innovation fully supersedes the previous technology and yields monopoly rents to the innovator until a new innovation supersedes the old one. Furthermore, an innovation in one firm also helps others to innovate further. This basic structure implies that innovation is motivated by monopoly rents and it is thus the pursuit of monopoly rents that lead to growth. This clear result is however not entirely reflected in the empirical literature. For example, Nickel (1996) finds that productivity growth is positively related to the degree of competition. Blundell, Griffith and van Reenen (1995) found that dominant firms innovate more but that concentration reduces innovation. However, other research has found that in sectors which are concentrated, have high levels of R&D and which are capital intensive large firms tend to innovate more while small firms innovate more in sectors which are dominated by large firms and in which skilled labour is important (see Acs and Audretsch, 1988). In order to make their model conform more with these empirical findings Aghion and Howitt (1998, Chapter 7) further develop their basic model. For example they recast the innovation process from one of leap-frogging to one of step-by-step innovation where the existing innovators are not overtaken by new innovators and where a higher degree of competition forces firms to innovate more in order to stay ahead of the competition.

Separately from the growth literature described above the relationship between firm size and firm growth has also been investigated. For example firms may go through a life cycle which runs from birth to maturity with an intermediate stage of take off during which firms grow most rapidly, with slower growth that may be unrelated to size at maturity. Along a similar vein Jovanovic (1982) proposed a model where firms learn whether they are efficient or not through a learning process which predicts that firm growth decreases with size once the age of the firms are held constant. This suggests that smaller firms will grow faster than larger ones and are therefore important in driving regional growth. However, alternative theories predict that firm growth is independent of size such that Gibrat's law holds. Overall this brief discussion of the theoretical models on firm size and growth suggests that the question as to whether small and medium size enterprises contribute more to regional growth is largely an empirical question, since these theoretical models are not giving one definite answer.

In the case of Ireland, the role of small and medium sized enterprises (SMEs) in regional development has not been examined extensively. There is little existing literature that explicitly examines the general significance of SMEs in regional development and growth in Ireland. But there are existing studies on two related areas. First, there are studies on regional disparities and regional convergence/divergence in Ireland – without reference to SMEs or firm size. And second, there are studies that refer to the contribution of different types and/or sizes of firm to growth – but usually without much reference to the regional dimension within Ireland. In this chapter, we first outline briefly some findings of existing studies on each of these two areas in turn. We then aim to build further on these findings, concentrating more directly on the role of SMEs in regional and national development and making use of more up-to-date information.

Regional Disparities and Regional Convergence/Divergence in Ireland

Before turning to the results of existing studies it is useful to review how Ireland is divided into regions. The traditional Irish administrative units are the counties. For domestic planning purposes these have been grouped into eight Planning Regions (NUTS III regions) which are administered by Regional Authorities since 1994[1]. Two of these planning regions, the Mid-East and Dublin regions, are often jointly referred to as the Greater Dublin Area. In the past Ireland was not divided into sub-national NUTS II regions for EU Structural Funds purposes. However more recently the country has been split into two NUTS II regions namely the Border, Midlands and West (BMW) region and the Southern, Eastern and Dublin (SEAD) region which comprises the other five Planning Regions (Dublin, Mid-East, South East, South-West and Mid-West) (Figure 8.1).

The focus of much of the recent research on regional disparities has been aimed at identifying whether the poorer regions (NUTS III) are improving their relative position with regard to output measures (see for instance Boyle, McCarthy and Walsh (1999), O'Connor (1999a) and O'Leary (1999)). This is an interesting issue since Ireland as a whole has grown rapidly during the 1990s and has converged to the average EU per capita GDP. In general this work has found that the regions are diverging since about 1990 in terms of Irish per capita gross value added (GVA), but all regions are converging towards the EU average or have surpassed the EU average (Dublin and the South West). The divergence within Ireland in the 1990s is easily seen in Figure 8.2, which also shows that there was no general divergence in the previous period.

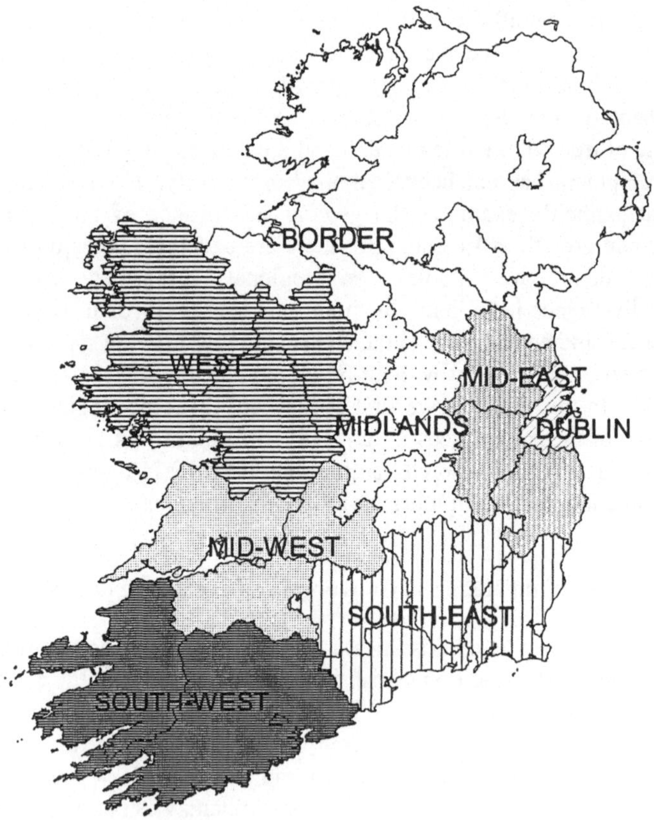

Figure 8.1 The Irish planning regions.

However, this literature has not focused on the explanations for divergence in the 1990s (e.g. O'Connor, 1999a, 1999b, 1999c). One exception is the paper by Boyle, McCarthy and Walsh (1999) who, following the methodology used by Fitz Gerald, Kearney, Morgenroth and Smyth (1999), decomposed the regional variation in per capita GVA into productivity, the employment rate, the participation rate and the dependency ratio. Their results show that the regional variation is largely explained by differences in productivity and that these differences are in turn due to productivity differences in industry and services.

O'Leary (2001) also uses this type of decomposition, although he applied it to a measure of regional income which nets out the effects of transfer pricing. His main findings were that there is an increasing income-output gap due to profit outflows and divergence in the participation and dependency rates. However, divergence has been dampened by strong labour productivity and employment growth.

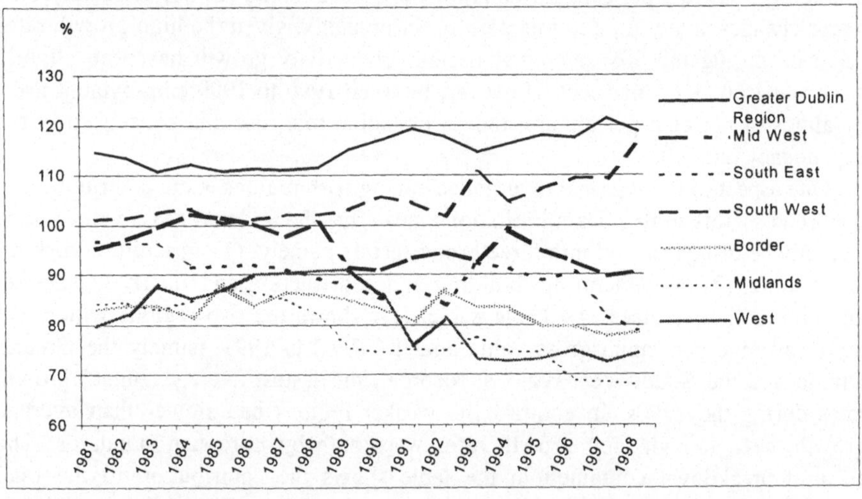

Figure 8.2 The evolution of indices of regional gross value added per capita as measured against the national average from 1981 to 1998 (State=100).

Source: CSO Regional Accounts various issues and ESRI calculations.

Differences regarding the manufacturing sector were explored in Bradley and Morgenroth (2000). Their paper showed that with regard to a number of performance indicators the differences within the regions (at county level) are greater than those between the regions. More recently, Morgenroth (2001) carried out an analysis of the Dublin and Mid-East regions which included a detailed analysis of the manufacturing sector in these regions that focused on sectoral specialization and clustering. This research found large differences between counties regarding their concentration of employment in fast growing sectors that explain much of the differences in performance. However, neither of these papers examined differences in the size distribution of firms at the regional or county level.

Much of the detailed work that will be presented in this chapter relies on data on manufacturing only and is further limited since, at the regional level, only employment by class size is available. While this clearly limits the analysis valuable insights into the importance of small and medium sized enterprises for regional development in Ireland can nevertheless be made. There are two reasons why the focus on employment only and manufacturing is not as limiting as might be expected.

Employment growth rather than productivity growth has been the major driving force of the recent high growth and convergence period of the Irish economy. In general productivity growth in the Irish economy has been strong for over 30 years averaging close to 3 per cent per annum from 1960 and this has not been subject to major changes at any time in this period. Surprisingly, given the high growth rates achieved during the 90s, over that period productivity growth has been slightly slower at around 2.5 per cent. However, between 1990 to 1999 employment grew by almost 4 per cent per annum, the participation rate rose and consequently the dependency rate fell.

One aspect of the regional divergence among Irish regions is the contribution of the broad sectors to this. Data limitations mean that the regional gross value added can only be disaggregated into three broad sectors namely; (1) agriculture, forestry and fishing, (2) manufacturing, building and construction and finally (3) market and non-market services. As Table 8.1 clearly shows the two regions which had above average per capita gross value added (GVA) in 1991, namely the Greater Dublin and the South-West regions, recorded the fastest average annual growth rates during the 1990s. In contrast the weaker regions had slower than average growth, even though their growth rates were high by European standards. The sectoral breakdown contained in the table shows the contribution to the total growth rate. This takes into account the fact that economic activity is not split evenly between the three broad sectors. Overall, agriculture declined over that period, while both services and manufacturing grew strongly.

Table 8.1 Average annual growth rates of Total Regional Gross Value Added (GVA) for the period 1991-99 and sectoral decomposition.

	Agriculture, Forestry & Fishing	Manufacturing, Building and Construction	Market and Non-market Services	Total
Border	-0.2	2.1	3.2	5.0
Midlands	-0.6	3.2	2.9	5.5
West	-0.2	2.9	3.9	6.6
Greater Dublin	-0.1	4.0	4.4	8.4
Mid-West	-0.4	3.6	3.5	6.7
South-East	-0.6	3.5	3.4	6.3
South-West	-0.5	6.5	3.6	9.6
State	-0.2	4.0	3.9	7.7

Source: CSO Regional Accounts.

In order to get a better understanding of the influence of the different growth rates at the sectoral level on the pattern of regional divergence, one can simply subtract the national average growth rate for each sector from the growth rate of that sector in each region. The results are shown in Table 8.2. The table shows that for the Border and West regions manufacturing contributed most to the negative divergence, while for the South-West manufacturing contributed most to the positive growth performance. In the case of the Midlands, Mid-West and South-East, manufacturing and services contributed roughly equally to the poorer performance of these regions, while only in the case of the Greater Dublin region did the effect of services dominate in contributing to divergence above the average growth rate. Thus, while services do impact on the relative growth performance of the regions, manufacturing seems to play a more important role in driving their relative performance.

Table 8.2 Relative GVA growth rates and sectoral contributions to total GVA growth.

	Agriculture, Forestry & Fishing	Manufacturing, Building and Construction	Market and Non-market Services	Total
Border	0.0	-1.9	-0.7	-2.7
Midlands	-0.3	-0.8	-1.0	-2.2
West	0.0	-1.1	0.0	-1.1
Greater Dublin	0.2	0.0	0.5	0.7
Mid-West	-0.1	-0.4	-0.4	-1.0
South-East	-0.4	-0.5	-0.5	-1.4
South-West	-0.2	2.5	-0.3	1.9

Source: CSO Regional Accounts.

Contribution to Growth by Different Types of Enterprise

There is an existing literature that has examined the different contributions of Irish indigenous (meaning Irish-owned) enterprises and foreign-owned multinational enterprises (MNEs) to industrial development in Ireland. The foreign MNEs are of course generally large international firms, and the subsidiaries that they control within Ireland are also relatively large so that 69 per cent of their employment in Ireland is in large enterprise units with over 250 employees. In contrast, only 20 per cent of employment in Irish indigenous industry is in such large enterprises while the remaining 80 per cent is in SMEs with less than 250 employees (*Census of Industrial Production 1999*, Table 18). Thus, this area of literature concerning foreign MNEs and Irish indigenous firms gives some indications about the relative contributions of large companies and SMEs to industrial development. It has been found that, since substantial inflows of foreign direct investment began in the 1960s, foreign MNEs have consistently made the major contribution to growth of manufacturing employment, output and exports. Consequently, by 1999, foreign-owned MNEs accounted for 49 per cent of manufacturing employment and 76 per cent of manufacturing gross output in Ireland.

For much of the time from the mid-1960s until the late 1980s, Irish indigenous manufacturing had little growth or actual decline in employment and relatively low growth of output (O'Malley, 1989, chapter 6). However, beginning in the late 1980s this changed, and Irish indigenous manufacturing had relatively strong growth in employment and output by international standards. Nevertheless, the growth of indigenous industry still lagged significantly behind the average growth rate for all industry in Ireland because of the even higher growth rates recorded by the foreign MNE sector in Ireland (see Tables 8.3 and 8.4). Thus, even in this period of relatively strong growth for Irish indigenous industry compared to other countries, it appears that the foreign-owned MNEs – consisting mainly of larger firms – contributed more to industrial growth.

Table 8.3 Annual average percentage change in manufacturing employment, Ireland, EU and OECD, 1980-88 and 1988-96.

1980-1988		1988-1996	
OECD	-0.6	**Ireland – All**	**1.5**
EU (15 countries)	-1.5	**Irish Indigenous**	**0.8**
Ireland – All	**-2.2**	Japan	0.0
Irish Indigenous	**-3.2**	USA	-0.6
		Australia	-0.6
		United Kingdom	-1.9
		EU (15 countries)	-1.9
		Canada	-2.0

Source: O'Malley (1998), Table 6.

While there is quite a substantial literature that makes distinctions between foreign-owned MNEs and Irish indigenous industry, most of this does not refer to the regional dimension within Ireland. One exception is an article by O'Malley (1994) which shows that, in the 1960s-80s, employment in foreign-owned MNEs tended to go disproportionately to the least industrialized regions. Thus, by 1989, foreign-owned MNEs generally accounted for a higher than average percentage of industrial employment in the regions that had been least industrialized in 1960, such as the West, Midlands and North-West. At the same time foreign-owned MNEs generally accounted for a lower than average percentage of industrial employment in the regions that had been most industrialized in 1960. Foreign MNEs, therefore, which were mostly large enterprises, tended to contribute to convergence in regional levels of industrialization in the 1960s-80s.

Table 8.4 Average annual percentage change in volume of manufacturing production, Ireland, EU and OECD, 1985-87 and 1987-95.

1985-1987		1987-1995	
Ireland – All	**6.6**	**Ireland – All**	**9.9**
OECD	2.4	**Irish Indigenous**	**4.0**
EU	2.1	OECD	2.0
Irish Indigenous	**0.6**	EU	1.7

Source: O'Malley (1998), Table 9.

Although it is not clear from this what exactly were the implications for regional convergence or divergence measured in terms of output or income per capita, it seems very likely that foreign MNEs either contributed to convergence or at least helped to offset other tendencies towards divergence in the 1960s-80s.

As outlined above, when one looks at the relative contributions of Irish indigenous and foreign-owned firms to industrial growth at the national level, it is clear that the foreign MNEs – the larger enterprises – generally contributed most. A somewhat different light is cast on this by studies that looked at the contribution of different size classes of firm *within* indigenous industry, leaving aside the foreign MNEs, in the 1970s and 1980s. For example, O'Malley, Kennedy and O'Donnell (1992) found that smaller size classes contributed most to indigenous employment growth and larger size classes contributed least over a long period until about 1987, although that pattern showed signs of changing in 1987-90. Thus, Table 8.5 shows a clearly superior employment growth performance by smaller size classes and a clearly inferior performance by larger size classes in the period 1973-87, in a context of overall decline in indigenous employment. However, in the next three years 1987-90, in a context of overall growth in employment, the record of the smallest size class weakened substantially while that of the largest size class improved and the performance of the medium-size class was the best of all. In about half of the individual sectors this change was even more marked in 1987-90, with strong employment growth occurring in both the medium and large size classes while there was virtually no growth in the small size class.

During the 1980s there was considerable interest in Irish industrial policy circles in the question of scale and what was happening to the size structure of indigenous industry. The decline of the larger firms and the relative rise of smaller firms during much of the 1970s and 1980s came to be seen as a problem that policy must aim to correct. The reason was because this was occurring in a context when Ireland was still adjusting to the introduction of free trade, with the removal of previous protection against imports (Ireland joined the EEC, as it then was, in 1973). The decline of larger firms was happening particularly in internationally traded sectors of industry that were characterized by economies of scale, and it was seen as indicating that many Irish firms did not have an adequate scale and structural strength required to compete successfully in such industries. An influential report by the Telesis Consultancy Group (1982) to the National Economic and Social Council identified this as a key issue, and the same report also pointed out that much of the growth among smaller firms was happening in naturally small-scale activities that inevitably serve only limited local markets. Such small 'non-traded' activities had a significant degree of natural protection against distant competitors so that they did not have to face the challenge of international competition. They could be expected to grow quite readily whenever there was growth in domestic demand, but they could not be expected to make a further independent contribution to economic growth.

Table 8.5 Average annual percentage employment change in indigenous manufacturing, by size class.

Employment Size Class	1973-87	1987-90
Less than 50	1.2	0.3
50-199	-1.9	2.7
200 or more	-6.3	-1.5
TOTAL	-2.2	0.7

Source: O'Malley, Kennedy and O'Donnell (1992), Table 2.15.

Reflecting this understanding of the situation, an official report from the Department of Industry and Commerce (1990, p. 52) highlighted as an objective of industrial policy for Irish-owned industry the need to 'build companies of sufficient quality, scale and strength to win and sustain profitable positions in their chosen international markets'. It was argued that this should take priority, rather than providing unnecessary and often wasteful support to small firms or new start-ups that would never engage in internationally traded activities.

Having briefly outlined the findings of some existing studies, the rest of this chapter builds further on these findings by adding new and more up-to-date analysis that concentrates more directly on the role of SMEs in national and regional growth. Since the available data that is suitable for this purpose refers to manufacturing industry, we concentrate on developments in the manufacturing sector.

SMEs in Regional and National Manufacturing Growth

Growth by Size Class at the National Level

Table 8.6 shows annual average rates of change in total manufacturing employment, for Ireland as a whole, by size class, over the years 1973-99. We have divided this period into four sub-periods with different overall experiences of manufacturing employment change. In 1973-79 there was fairly strong employment growth, followed by sustained decline in 1979-87, modest recovery in 1987-93 and strong growth in 1993-99.

Table 8.6 Average annual percentage change in total manufacturing employment, by size class, 1973-99.

Employment Size Class	1973-79	1979-87	1987-93	1993-99	1973-99
Micro (<10)	6.0	3.1	-3.5	-1.9	1.0
Small (10-49)	2.5	-1.2	-0.2	1.6	0.5
Medium (50-249)	2.1	-2.5	1.3	1.5	0.3
Large (250+)	-0.6	-6.1	1.8	6.1	-0.3
TOTAL	1.3	-3.1	0.8	2.9	0.2

Source: Derived from Forfas annual employment survey.

Note: The data are classified by size of establishment or local unit, rather than whole enterprises.

The right-hand column in Table 8.6 shows that over the whole period 1973-99 employment in the smaller size classes grew by most while employment in the larger size classes grew by least. However, there was a clear and very marked change in this pattern within the period 1973-99. At the start, in 1973-79, and again in 1979-87, the smaller size classes tended to grow faster than the larger ones. But there was a change after that. In 1987-93, and even more markedly in 1993-99, the larger size classes tended to grow faster than the smaller ones. Thus, the experience in this regard changed considerably over time.

We must be careful, however, about the interpretation of the data in Table 8.6. It has sometimes been pointed out that an increase in employment in the small size class, for example, does not necessarily mean that small firms were entirely responsible for that increase. It could be the case that some larger firms became smaller during the period concerned and finished up in the small size class, thereby generating the increase in the small size class. Similarly, if employment in the large size class increases, this is not necessarily caused by large firms alone. It could be that some smaller firms grew considerably in the period concerned so that they finished up in the large size class, and this could generate an increase in the large size class. For this reason, it has been argued, a given employment increase in the small size class, for example, does not necessarily mean that small firms contributed that employment growth.

This point, which is known as the 'size distribution fallacy', was considered in some detail in the Third Annual Report of the European Observatory for SMEs (EIM/ENSR, 1995, Appendix to Chapter 3). It was concluded that the argument is theoretically valid, although it is not necessarily of any real empirical significance. For example, a Swedish study was quoted which found that in practice very small numbers of enterprises (less than 2 per cent) appeared to cross the size class boundaries, so that the size distribution fallacy was virtually irrelevant empirically. Having examined employment data by size class for 12 members of the EU plus four other European countries, EIM/ENSR (1995, Chapter 1) concluded that crossing of size class boundaries by enterprises was of little empirical significance for their analysis of European employment trends by size class.

In the case of our data on manufacturing in Ireland, however, it is clear that we cannot ignore the size distribution fallacy, because there are indications that substantial numbers of establishments have crossed size class boundaries at times. For example, in 1979 there were 174 large establishments with 250 or more employees, but the number of these fell to 113 by 1987, a decline of 35 per cent. If we look at Irish-owned firms only, the number of large establishments fell from 82 in 1979 to 33 in 1987, which was a 60 per cent decline. It is likely that some of those departing from the large size class simply closed down. But it is only reasonable to assume that quite a significant proportion of establishments that were large in 1979 dropped into smaller size classes by 1987, thereby improving the growth rate of the smaller size classes in 1979-87.

In the period 1973-79 the number of large establishments increased by just 3 per cent, and in 1987-93 the number increased by only 7 per cent. However, there was a much greater change in the period 1993-99 when the number of large establishments rose by 36 per cent. It can be observed, therefore, that in the period of sharpest employment decline (1979-87) and in the period of strongest employment growth (1993-99), the number of large establishments changed substantially indicating that there was probably significant crossing of size class boundaries occurring. In 1993-99 the big increase in the number of large establishments would have been partly caused by new large start-ups, particularly new branches of foreign-owned MNEs. Nevertheless, it is reasonable to assume that a significant part of this increase would have been caused by smaller establishments growing into the larger size class, particularly in the case of Irish indigenous industry which recorded an increase of 31 per cent in the number of large establishments.

This chapter aims to investigate what has been the contribution to growth from firms of different sizes. Given the indications that significant numbers of firms have crossed size class boundaries at times, we cannot simply accept the type of data shown in Table 8.6 as providing the definitive answer to this question. To take account of this problem, Table 8.7 presents the results of a different type of analysis. To derive this table, establishments were classified by size at the start of the first year, and percentage growth rates were calculated for each size class in the first year. Then the establishments were reclassified according to their size at the start of the second year, and percentage growth rates were calculated for each size class in the second year. This procedure was repeated for every individual year so that establishments were always classified according to their size at the beginning of each year. The average growth rates shown in Table 8.7 are the average of the individual yearly growth rates calculated in this way for each size class.

Table 8.7 Average annual percentage change in total manufacturing employment, with annual reclassification by size class.

Employment Size Class	1973-79	1979-87	1987-93	1993-99	1973-99
Micro (<10)	8.3	2.3	4.0	5.9	4.1
Small (10-49)	1.0	-3.9	-0.9	2.2	-0.7
Medium (50-249)	-0.3	-5.7	-1.4	1.3	-1.8
Large (250+)	-3.5	-6.3	-0.7	1.0	-2.7
TOTAL	1.3	-3.1	0.8	2.9	0.2

Source: Derived from Forfas annual employment survey.

Note: The data are classified by size of establishment or local unit, rather than whole enterprises.

With this procedure, if an establishment crosses a size class boundary, say from ‘medium’ to ‘large’ in 1996, it is classified as medium up to 1996 and as large after 1996. The fact that it crosses the boundary within the period 1993-99 does not reduce the growth rate of the medium class for the period 1993-99, as it would in Table 8.6. And the fact that it crosses the boundary does not increase the growth rate of the large class in 1993-99 (except to the extent that the establishment really does grow while it is actually within the large class after 1996).

It is worth noting that, with this procedure, new start-ups during a given year are not included in any size class in that year because they have no employment at the start of the year. They are first included in a size class in the following year, based on their employment size at the start of that year. However, new start-ups in a given year are included in total employment at the end of that year, so that they do add to total employment growth for that year although they do not add to the growth of any individual size class in the year concerned.

Comparing Table 8.7 and Table 8.6, it can be seen that the figures for total employment in the bottom row are the same in both tables, as would be expected[2]. Table 8.7 is also similar to Table 8.6 in so far as the right-hand column again shows that, over the whole period 1973-99, the smaller size classes grew by most while the larger size classes grew by least. In the case of Table 8.7, we can safely interpret this as meaning that smaller existing firms contributed more than larger existing firms to employment growth over the period as a whole. It is noticeable that the 1973-99 figure for 'micro' firms is a good deal higher in Table 8.7 than in Table 8.6, while the figures for the other size classes are lower in Table 8.7 than in Table 8.6. This probably indicates that the micro figure in Table 8.6 tended to be reduced as a result of firms growing into other size classes. The other size classes in Table 8.6 would have been boosted to some extent by this effect, and also by the inclusion of some new start-ups each year whereas the entry of new start-ups during a given year does not boost the growth rates of size classes in Table 8.7.

Table 8.7 is similar to Table 8.6 in the sense that the smaller size classes grew by most while the larger size classes grew by least in the first two sub-periods, 1973-79 and 1979-87. However, while, this pattern was completely reversed in the two later sub-periods in Table 8.6, this is not the case in Table 8.7. The pattern is only partially reversed in 1987-93 in Table 8.7, with the largest size class having a stronger performance than the small and medium classes but not stronger than the micro class. And in 1993-99 in Table 8.7, the smaller size classes once again grew faster than the larger size classes. If we combine the micro, small and medium size classes into one category of SMEs, the existing SMEs had a stronger growth performance than existing large firms in 1973-79, 1979-87 and 1993-99, using the methodology of Table 8.7. However, in 1987-93 the existing large firms had a stronger performance than existing SMEs, using that methodology. Thus, while it can be said that existing SMEs contributed more to employment growth than existing large firms most of the time, there can be no general rule that this has to be the case at all times.

A final point worth noting here is that particularly fast employment growth was seen in the large size class in 1993-99 in Table 8.6, but this is not repeated in Table 8.7. This means that much of that growth in the large size class in Table 8.6 was caused, not by growth of existing large firms, but rather by new large start-ups and by smaller firms growing into the large size class.

Table 8.8 shows employment change by size class for Irish indigenous manufacturing alone, leaving out the foreign-owned MNEs, using the same methodology as in Table 8.6. The overall trends here are weaker here than in the case of total manufacturing, as can be seen by comparing the bottom rows of Table 8.8 and Table 8.6. This reflects the fact that Irish indigenous industry had persistently slower growth than the foreign-owned MNEs in Ireland.

Nevertheless, other aspects of Table 8.8 are similar to Table 8.6. Thus, the right-hand column of Table 8.8 shows that over the whole period 1973-99 the smaller size classes of Irish indigenous industry grew by most while the larger size classes grew by least. But, as in the case of total manufacturing, there was a marked change in this pattern within the period 1973-99. In the period 1973-79 and again in 1979-87, the stronger growth of the smaller size classes of indigenous industry in Table 8.8 was very clear. However, this pattern changed in 1987-93 when the smallest size class had the weakest growth while the medium size class had the strongest growth. Subsequently, in 1993-99, a complete reversal of the earlier pattern was established, with the larger size classes having the fastest employment growth while the smaller size classes had the slowest growth. Thus, there was considerable change in this respect over time.

Table 8.8 Average annual percentage change in Irish indigenous manufacturing employment, by size class.

Employment Size Class	1973-79	1979-87	1987-93	1993-99	1973-99
Micro (<10)	6.1	3.0	-3.4	-1.8	1.1
Small (10-49)	2.5	-1.7	0.1	2.1	0.5
Medium (50-249)	-0.1	-4.1	1.0	2.5	-0.5
Large (250+)	-2.7	-10.7	-0.3	2.7	-3.5
TOTAL	0.2	-4.1	0.0	2.0	-0.8

Source: Derived from Forfas annual employment survey.

Of course Table 8.8 is subject to the same caveat concerning interpretation that applies to Table 8.6. Because of the likelihood of significant numbers of establishments crossing size class boundaries within periods, it cannot be said that the growth of a particular size class in Table 8.8 accurately reflects growth by firms of that size. To take account of this point, Table 8.9 shows changes in Irish indigenous manufacturing employment with reclassification by size class every year, using the same methodology described above with respect to Table 8.7.

Comparing Table 8.9 and Table 8.8, it can be seen that the figures for Total indigenous employment in the bottom row are the same in both tables, as expected. Table 8.9 is also similar to Table 8.8 in the sense that the right-hand column shows that, over the whole period 1973-99, the smaller size classes of Irish indigenous industry grew by most while the larger size classes grew by least. Since this is true of Table 8.9, we can interpret this to mean that existing smaller indigenous firms did contribute more than existing larger indigenous firms to employment growth over the period as a whole.

Table 8.9 is also similar to Table 8.8 in the sense that the smaller size classes grew by most while the larger size classes grew by least in the first two sub-periods, 1973-79 and 1979-87. However, while this earlier pattern was partially reversed in 1987-93 and completely reversed in 1993-99 in Table 8.8, this is not the case in Table 8.9. In Table 8.9, the earlier pattern is partially broken in 1987-

93 in so far as the performance of the large firms is stronger than that of the medium-size firms. But apart from this, the smaller indigenous firms in Table 8.9 tended to do better than the larger ones in 1987-93, and this was unambiguously the case in the final period 1993-99. Thus it can be said that, for the most part, existing smaller indigenous establishments tended to contribute more to employment growth than existing larger indigenous establishments.

Table 8.9 Average annual percentage change in Irish indigenous manufacturing employment, with annual reclassification by size class.

Employment Size Class	1973-79	1979-87	1987-93	1993-99	1973-99
Micro (<10)	4.8	0.3	-1.5	3.1	1.6
Small (10-49)	-0.1	-5.4	-1.6	1.5	-1.7
Medium (50-249)	-2.4	-7.8	-2.9	0.0	-3.6
Large (250+)	-3.9	-8.1	-2.4	-1.9	-4.4
TOTAL	0.2	-4.1	0.0	2.0	-0.8

Source: Derived from Forfas annual employment survey.

Incidentally, it was noted above that the Department of Industry and Commerce (1990) stated that it was an objective of industrial policy for Irish-owned industry to build larger indigenous companies. Table 8.8 serves to confirm that this objective was being achieved in the 1990s, since the strongest growth was occurring in the largest size classes of indigenous industry. Table 8.9 does not contradict this conclusion. What Table 8.9 does is to show that much of that growth in the larger size classes was not caused by growth of existing larger firms. Instead, much of that growth must have been caused by smaller firms growing into the larger size classes, and perhaps to some extent by new relatively large start-ups.

Table 8.10 shows employment change by size class in foreign-owned industry in Ireland, using the same methodology as in Tables 8.6 and 8.8. In this table, the right-hand column shows that the medium and large size classes in foreign-owned industry grew faster than the smaller size classes over the whole period 1973-99. There was quite an amount of variation in this regard between the different sub-periods. The fastest growth in 1973-79 occurred in the medium-size class. In 1979-87, the smallest size classes grew by most while the largest size classes grew by least, and in 1987-93 and 1993-99 this pattern was reversed with the largest size classes growing by most while the smallest size classes grew by least. Apart from the first period 1973-79, therefore, this pattern of change between sub-periods in foreign-owned manufacturing was similar to that for total manufacturing seen in Table 8.6.

In the case of foreign-owned manufacturing, however, it should be noted that the micro and small size classes are of rather little importance. These two size classes together accounted for no more than about 10 per cent of total foreign-owned employment throughout the period, compared to 30 per cent or more in Irish indigenous industry. This relative insignificance of the micro and small size classes in foreign-owned industry means, of course, that foreign establishments were always highly concentrated in the larger size classes. We also know that foreign-owned industry had consistently faster growth than Irish indigenous industry, so that the foreign firms were becoming an increasingly important component of total manufacturing. This trend alone would have tended to contribute increasingly to faster growth among the larger size classes than among the smaller size classes at the level of total manufacturing. This tendency would have been present even if there had been little change in the size structure within foreign-owned industry.

Table 8.10 Average annual percentage change in foreign-owned manufacturing employment, by size class.

Employment Size Class	1973-79	1979-87	1987-93	1993-99	1973-99
Micro (<10)	3.7	3.6	-5.6	-2.6	0.0
Small (10-49)	2.7	1.5	-1.4	-1.0	0.5
Medium (50-249)	6.3	-0.3	1.6	0.4	1.8
Large (250+)	1.6	-3.2	2.6	7.3	1.6
TOTAL	3.4	-1.5	1.7	3.9	1.6

Source: Derived from Forfas annual employment survey.

Table 8.10 is naturally subject to the same caveat concerning interpretation that applies to Tables 8.6 and 8.8. Because establishments may have been crossing size class boundaries, it cannot be said that the growth of a particular size class in Table 8.10 properly reflects growth by establishments of that size. To take some account of this point, Table 8.11 shows changes in foreign-owned manufacturing employment with reclassification by size class every year, using the same methodology that was used above for Tables 8.7 and 8.9.

At first sight, perhaps the most remarkable feature of Table 8.11 is the extremely high growth rates for the micro size class in all periods, which is very different from the performance of the micro size class depicted in Table 8.10. This has to mean that some micro-size firms were growing rapidly into larger size classes throughout the period. To put this in perspective, it should be borne in mind that the micro size class in foreign-owned industry was always very small, with less than 700 jobs at all times. When substantial new foreign establishments first start up, there would generally be a time, however brief, when they initially employ less than 10 people even if it is planned from the start that they will quickly recruit some hundreds of employees. All that would be required to generate the micro class growth rates seen in Table 8.11 would be for one or two such substantial new start-ups to be captured in their initial phase in the micro class at the time when the employment survey was carried out each year. In view of the numbers of substantial new foreign start-ups in most years, this would not be an unlikely occurrence, which means that the growth rates for the micro size class seen in Table 8.11 are not as extraordinary as they might seem.

Table 8.11 Average annual percentage change in foreign-owned manufacturing employment, with annual reclassification by size class.

Employment Size Class	1973-79	1979-87	1987-93	1993-99	1973-99
Micro (<10)	67.2	43.0	44.8	66.0	54.3
Small (10-49)	7.2	4.1	2.4	5.8	4.8
Medium (50-249)	3.4	-2.8	0.3	2.9	0.7
Large (250+)	-3.2	-5.1	0.0	1.9	-1.9
TOTAL	3.4	-1.5	1.8	3.9	1.6

Source: Derived from Forfas annual employment survey.

In Table 8.11, the right-hand column shows that, over the whole period 1973-99, the smaller foreign-owned establishments grew by most while the larger ones grew by least. This is almost the opposite of the pattern seen in 1973-99 in Table 8.10. This means that the superior growth performance of the larger size classes in 1973-99 in Table 8.10 was not being caused by a superior growth performance by existing larger foreign-owned establishments. Instead, much of the growth in the larger size classes in 1973-99 in Table 8.10 had to be caused by new relatively large start-ups and by smaller firms growing into the larger size classes.

A similar point applies to the different sub-periods. Looking at the sub-periods in Table 8.11, it can be seen that in every sub-period the smaller establishments grew by most while the larger ones grew by least. This means that smaller existing foreign establishments always contributed more to employment growth than larger existing foreign establishments. In those sub-periods when the large or medium-size classes grew by most in Table 8.10, this cannot have been mainly caused by growth of existing large or medium-size establishments. Instead, much of such growth in the larger size classes in Table 8.10 was caused by new relatively large start-ups or by smaller firms growing into the larger size classes.

In the case of Irish indigenous industry, we considered that this type of effect was likely to be caused more by smaller firms growing into the larger size classes rather than by new large start-ups. In the case of foreign-owned industry, however, it is quite clear that there have been many new relatively large start-ups over the past few decades, so that this must have been a major source of the growth of the larger size classes seen in Table 8.10. Thus, it is indeed clear from Table 8.11 that smaller existing foreign establishments contributed more to employment growth than larger existing foreign establishments. But the importance of new large foreign start-ups is such that it cannot be said, in an overall sense, that smaller foreign establishments were more important for growth than larger foreign establishments.

Before concluding this section, it should be said that our analysis of trends by size class has focused on employment trends because the most suitable data source available to us for this purpose is the Forfas Employment Survey, which does not include data on output or production. To give some assurance that there is generally a broad correspondence between employment trends and output trends by size class, Table 8.12 shows annual average growth rates by size class for both gross output (in current values) and employment, in total manufacturing in Ireland in the 1990s. The data in Table 8.12 are taken from the annual Census of Industrial Production.

Table 8.12 Annual average percentage change in gross output (current values) and employment, by size class, total manufacturing, 1991-99.

Employment Size Class	Gross Output	Employment
<20	2.1	-0.1
20-49	7.1	2.1
50-99	4.7	1.0
100-199	12.7	2.5
200-499	14.4	2.6
500+	24.9	9.2

Source: Derived from annual Census of Industrial Production.

It can be seen in Table 8.12 that, in terms of gross output, the larger size classes grew by most while the smaller size classes grew by least, in 1991-99, with the exception that the 20-49 size class was out of line with this pattern. The employment column in Table 8.12 follows the same pattern, with larger size classes growing by more than smaller size classes except for the 20-49 size class being again out of line. This also corresponds reasonably well with the employment trends shown for the 1990s in Table 8.6 above, derived from the Forfas employment survey.

Growth by Size Class at the Regional Level

This section examines patterns of growth by size class at the regional level within Ireland. Table 8.13 shows several aspects of manufacturing employment growth in the regions in the period 1973-79. (Note that the Greater Dublin region includes Dublin and Mid-East combined). In this table, the regions are ranked according to their rate of manufacturing employment growth at that time, with the fastest growing regions placed at the top of the table. The table attempts to address the question whether there has been some relationship between regional growth performance and SMEs.

First, we can ask were the regions that had the fastest growth in this period, as shown in column 1, also regions in which SMEs were particularly important, as shown in column 2. There does appear to be such a pattern to some extent. The West and Midlands at the top of the table had the highest proportions of their employment in SMEs at the start of the period, while the South-West and Greater Dublin regions at the bottom of the table had among the lowest proportions of their employment in SMEs.

This is no more than a preliminary indication, however, since it may not necessarily be the case that SMEs were responsible for higher growth rates in the faster growing regions. To take this a step further, we can ask a second question - whether the regions with the fastest growth experienced particularly rapid growth among their SMEs or among their large firms. To answer this question, the last two columns of Table 8.13 show two different measures of employment growth by region and size class in 1973-79. The first of these, labelled (i), measures growth as the difference between employment in a size class in the first year of the period and employment in the same size class in the final year of the period. This way of measuring growth by size class is similar to that used at the national level in Tables 8.6, 8.8 and 8.10 above. Using this indicator, it can be seen in the bottom row of Table 8.13 that the overall pattern at national level in 1973-79 was that employment in the large size class declined a little while employment in the SME size class increased[3]. Therefore it is not surprising to find that in five of the seven regions employment in the large size class grew more slowly than in the SME class. But the two regions that were exceptions to this were the two with the fastest overall growth, the West and Midlands. Thus in these cases, the relatively fast growth performance occurred in the large class more than the SME class.

However, as was already discussed above when considering the national level, one needs to be careful when using this way of measuring growth by size class. If significant numbers of firms are crossing size class boundaries, it could be that much of the growth of a smaller size class is caused by larger firms declining into that class, or much of the growth of a larger size class could be caused by smaller firms growing into it. Therefore we include a second way of measuring employment growth by size class, labelled (ii), in the last column of Table 8.13. This is the average of the yearly growth rates in employment by size class, with establishments being reclassified by size class in every individual year. This way of measuring growth by size class is the same as that used at the national level in Tables 8.7, 8.9 and 8.11 above.

Table 8.13 Manufacturing employment change by region, SMEs and large establishments, 1973-79.

Region	Change in manufacturing employment % p.a., 1973-79	SMEs' share of employment (%), 1973	Size Class	Employment change, % p.a., 1973-79 (i)	Employment change, % p.a., 1973-79 (ii)
West	7.3	81.0	SME	4.7	2.9
			Large	16.0	10.6
Midlands	5.7	77.1	SME	5.6	4.2
			Large	5.9	-9.8
South-East	3.2	65.7	SME	3.9	1.8
			Large	1.6	-1.0
Mid-West	2.4	45.4	SME	8.1	2.8
			Large	-3.8	-7.2
Border	1.2	68.5	SME	2.0	0.4
			Large	-0.6	-5.6
South-West	0.7	55.8	SME	1.9	-0.3
			Large	-0.9	-2.1
Greater Dublin	-0.4	54.8	SME	0.7	-0.6
			Large	-1.8	-4.1
IRELAND	1.3	59.3	SME	2.5	0.7
			Large	-0.6	-3.5

Source: Derived from Forfas annual employment survey.

Notes: In the second to last column, employment change (i) is based on the difference between employment in a size class in the first year and employment in the same size class in the final year of the period. In the last column, employment change (ii) measures the average of the yearly changes in employment by size class, with establishments being reclassified by size class in every individual year.

Using this indicator, it can be seen in the bottom row of Table 8.13 that the pattern at national level in 1973-79 was that employment in large firms declined while employment in SMEs increased. Furthermore, in six of the seven regions, employment in the large size class grew more slowly than in the SME class. But the one region that was an exception to this was the one with the fastest overall growth, namely the West, where there was much faster growth among large firms than among SMEs. In the case of the Midlands, there was faster growth in the large size class than in the SME class according to measure (i) whereas SMEs performed much better than large firms according to measure (ii). This means that the growth of the large size class seen under measure (i) was greatly influenced by smaller firms growing into the large class or by new large start-ups, as opposed to existing large firms.

Table 8.14 Manufacturing employment change by region, SMEs and large establishments, 1979-87.

Region	Change in manufacturing employment, % p.a., 1979-87	SMEs' share of employment (%), 1979	Size Class	Employment change, % p.a., 1979-87 (i)	Employment change, % p.a., 1979-87 (ii)
Mid-West	0.0	62.5	SME	1.3	-1.7
			Large	-2.5	-3.7
Midlands	-1.5	76.7	SME	0.1	-3.6
			Large	-8.9	-4.5
West	-2.2	69.6	SME	-2.7	-3.9
			Large	-0.9	-4.5
Border	-2.3	71.8	SME	-0.8	-3.8
			Large	-6.9	-7.2
South-East	-2.5	68.6	SME	-2.4	-4.5
			Large	-2.6	-4.0
South-West	-3.1	59.9	SME	-1.5	-3.9
			Large	-5.9	-6.9
Greater Dublin	-4.6	58.5	SME	-2.3	-5.6
			Large	-8.6	-7.4
IRELAND	-3.1	63.5	SME	-1.6	-4.4
			Large	-6.1	-6.3

Source: Derived from Forfas annual employment survey.

Notes: In the second to last column, employment change (i) is based on the difference between employment in a size class in the first year and employment in the same size class in the final year of the period. In the last column, employment change (ii) measures the average of the yearly changes in employment by size class, with establishments being reclassified by size class in every individual year.

Table 8.14 is similar to Table 8.13 but it refers to a later period, 1979-87, when there was a substantial decline in employment at the national level. Here we see that there appears to be a preliminary indication of some relationship between relatively good regional growth and the relative importance of SMEs, although this is weaker than in Table 8.13. The two regions with the greatest proportion of their employment in SMEs, Midlands and Border, ranked second and fourth out of seven in terms of employment change. At the same time, the two regions with the smallest proportion of their employment in SMEs, Greater Dublin and South-West, had the poorest employment performance with substantial employment decline.

Table 8.15 Manufacturing employment change by region, SMEs and large establishments, 1987-93.

Region	Change in manufacturing employment, % p.a., 1987-93	SMEs' share of employment (%), 1987	Size Class	Employment change, % p.a., 1987-93 (i)	Employment change, % p.a., 1987-93 (ii)
Border	2.2	80.7	SME	-0.5	-0.5
			Large	10.7	5.1
Mid-West	2.1	69.4	SME	1.4	0.0
			Large	3.6	0.0
West	1.7	66.4	SME	1.6	-0.1
			Large	2.0	0.3
South-West	1.2	68.3	SME	1.4	-0.2
			Large	0.8	-1.3
South-East	0.4	69.0	SME	-0.5	-1.0
			Large	2.3	-0.3
Midlands	0.3	87.5	SME	-0.7	-1.8
			Large	6.4	-0.5
Greater Dublin	-0.4	70.5	SME	0.2	-2.0
			Large	-1.9	-2.5
IRELAND	0.8	71.8	SME	0.3	-1.1
			Large	1.8	-0.7

Source: Derived from Forfas annual employment survey.

Notes: In the second last column, employment change (i) is based on the difference between employment in a size class in the first year and employment in the same size class in the final year of the period. In the last column, employment change (ii) measures the average of the yearly changes in employment by size class, with establishments being reclassified by size class in every individual year.

Looking at the second to last column in Table 8.14, it can be seen that the employment performance of the SME size class was considerably stronger than that of the large size class at the national level according to measure (i). The same was also true of every region except the West, which was close to the middle of the range among regions in terms of overall employment performance. According to measure (ii) SMEs again had a somewhat stronger performance than large firms at the national level. This was also true of all regions except the South-East, which was close to the middle of the range in terms of employment performance. Thus, the general picture here is one of SMEs performing better than larger firms across nearly all regions, with the exceptions being neither particularly strong nor weak in terms of overall performance.

Table 8.15 refers to the next period, 1987-93, when there was moderate employment growth at the national level. Here it is difficult to discern any relationship between regional growth and the relative importance of SMEs, partly because SMEs' share of employment was so similar at about 66 to 69 per cent in most of the regions at the start of this period. The Midlands and Border regions had a substantially higher share of their employment in SMEs, but one of these had the strongest overall growth while the other was the second weakest.

Looking at the second to last column in Table 8.15, we see that the large size class grew faster than the SME size class at the national level, according to measure (i). This was also true of five of the seven regions. The two exceptions in which the SME size class grew faster than the large class, South-West and Greater Dublin, did not have a particularly strong overall growth performance. Measure (ii) in the last column of Table 8.15 shows a stronger performance by large firms than by SMEs, at the national level and in five of the seven regions. The two exceptions were the South-West and Greater Dublin again, two regions that did not have a relatively strong overall growth performance. Thus the general picture in 1987-93 was almost the opposite of 1979-87, in the sense that the large size class did better than the SME size class across most regions, while the regions that were exceptions to this did not perform particularly well. There was no real indication of a special contribution from SMEs to regional growth in this period.

Table 8.16 covers the period 1993-99, which was a time of exceptionally strong growth at the national level. There is little indication here of a relationship between regional growth and the relative importance of SMEs. Most of the regions had much the same proportion of their employment in SMEs, at about 65 to 69 per cent. The two regions that had a greater share of their employment in SMEs, the Midlands and Greater Dublin, were at about the middle of the range in terms of overall growth performance.

The second to last column in Table 8.16 shows that the large size class grew much faster than the SME size class at the national level, according to measure (i). The same observation applies to all of the regions except the Border region, which had the weakest overall growth. In contrast, measure (ii) in the last column of Table 8.16 shows that SMEs grew faster than large firms at the national level, when firms are classified by their size in every year. Clearly, therefore, much of the growth of the large size class seen according to measure (i) came from SMEs growing into the large size class and also from new large start-ups. Measure (ii) in the last column of Table 8.16 also shows that SMEs grew faster than large firms in five of the seven regions. But the two regions that were exceptions to this, with faster growth coming from large firms, were the West and Mid-West, which were also the two regions with the fastest overall growth.

Table 8.16 Manufacturing employment change by region, SMEs and large establishments, 1993-99.

Region	Change in manufacturing employment % p.a., 1993-99	SMEs' share of employment (%), 1993	Size Class	Employment change, % p.a., 1993-99 (i)	Employment change, % p.a., 1993-99 (ii)
West	4.9	65.8	SME	2.5	3.5
			Large	8.9	3.6
Mid-West	4.6	66.6	SME	1.1	2.4
			Large	10.3	4.7
Greater Dublin	3.1	73.1	SME	1.2	2.1
			Large	7.5	1.3
Midlands	2.8	82.2	SME	1.6	1.9
			Large	7.6	-3.3
South-West	2.5	69.0	SME	1.4	1.4
			Large	4.8	1.1
South-East	1.7	65.3	SME	0.9	1.9
			Large	3.1	-1.3
Border	0.9	68.8	SME	0.9	1.1
			Large	0.8	-2.6
IRELAND	2.9	70.0	SME	1.3	1.9
			Large	6.1	1.0

Source: Derived from Forfas annual employment survey.

Notes: In the second to last column, employment change (i) is based on the difference between employment in a size class in the first year and employment in the same size class in the final year of the period. In the last column, employment change (ii) measures the average of the yearly changes in employment by size class, with establishments being reclassified by size class in every individual year.

To conclude this section, we have examined patterns of growth by size class at the regional level, in four different periods, to see whether there was a relationship between regional growth and SMEs. The outcomes are rather mixed. For one period, 1979-87, we can conclude with little qualification that SMEs did make an especially important contribution to regional growth performance. For another period, 1987-93, we can draw the opposite conclusion, that large firms made the greater contribution to regional growth. The conclusions on the other two periods are more ambiguous. In both cases, there was at least evidence that existing SMEs grew faster than existing large firms in most regions (as shown by measure ii). On the other hand, in the fastest growing regions existing large firms grew faster than existing SMEs. In addition, it is very likely that new large start-ups made an important contribution, particularly in 1993-99 in view of the big gap between the growth of large firms recorded under measure (i) and measure (ii). Overall, therefore, we have not found compelling evidence that SMEs have generally had an especially important role in regional growth.

Foreign-Owned Firms and Regional Growth

If there has not been a generally strong relationship between size class and regional growth trends, one might ask are there other factors, apart from size class, that should be considered when analysing regional growth trends in order to attain a better understanding. It is not our intention to consider this question in detail here, since there are many other factors that might potentially be of some importance. But we can make a few observations concerning the apparent importance of paying some attention to nationality of ownership of industries and related characteristics.

For example, it was shown in Tables 8.13 and 8.14 that the regions with the poorest industrial employment growth performance from 1973 to 1987 were Greater Dublin and the South-West. Table 8.15 showed that Greater Dublin continued to have the poorest growth performance from 1987 to 1993, although the South-West began to do better in that period. Greater Dublin and the South-West have the two largest urban areas in the country, Dublin and Cork, and they had the major concentrations of older Irish-owned industries that had been developed with the help of protection against imports up to the 1960s. Many of these older Irish-owned industries did not fare well when this protection was removed during the late 1960s and 1970s. It seems that their decline was part of the reason for the relatively poor performance of Greater Dublin and the South-West at that time and for some time afterwards. This factor would not have had a comparable influence on other regions.

There were also a limited number of foreign-owned firms among the older protected industries, and they too tended to be concentrated in Greater Dublin and the South-West which had the principal local markets for their products. But when foreign direct investment became a really significant feature in Ireland from the

1960s onwards, it mainly went into starting up new industries that were producing very largely for export markets, and these new industries were more geographically dispersed around the country. Table 8.17 shows the percentage of employment in foreign-owned manufacturing that was located in each region in five different years. It can be seen that there were some quite significant changes in the regional distribution of foreign-owned industry over the period 1973-99.

It is of particular interest to note that the regions that had the fastest overall growth in total manufacturing employment in any given period were always regions that gained an increase in their share of foreign-owned industrial employment. And conversely, the regions that had the poorest total employment growth performance in a given period were always regions that had a decline or no growth in their share of foreign-owned industrial employment. Thus, trends in the location of foreign-owned industry seem to have been important determinants of the relative growth performance of different regions.

For example, it was shown in Table 8.13 that the West and Midlands had the fastest growth in total manufacturing employment in 1973-79, and it can be seen in Table 8.17 that these regions had a substantial increase in their share of foreign employment in that period. Table 8.13 showed that Greater Dublin and the South-West had the weakest growth in total manufacturing employment in 1973-79, and Table 8.17 shows that these regions had a declining share of foreign employment in the same period. In the next period, 1979-87, it was the Mid-West and Midlands that had the fastest overall growth and a rising share of foreign-owned employment, while Greater Dublin and the South-West had the weakest growth and a falling share of foreign-owned employment. Similar remarks concerning the connection between regional share of foreign-owned employment and regional growth also apply to the periods 1987-93 and 1993-99.

Table 8.17 Percentage distribution of employment in foreign-owned manufacturing, by region, 1973-99.

Region	1973	1979	1987	1993	1999
Border	12.8	12.0	10.3	13.0	10.6
Greater Dublin	46.7	38.8	34.4	30.8	32.7
Mid-West	9.6	9.9	14.1	14.5	15.9
Midlands	2.3	5.0	6.2	6.2	4.7
South-East	6.2	8.9	11.3	10.9	9.9
South-West	17.4	16.5	14.7	15.8	16.0
West	4.9	8.9	9.0	8.8	10.3
TOTAL	100	100	100	100	100

Source: Derived from Forfas annual employment survey.

It is also noticeable that, compared to earlier periods, the South-West began to have stronger overall industrial employment growth and a rising share of foreign-owned employment in 1987-93 and 1993-99, while a similar improvement on both counts occurred in Greater Dublin in 1993-99. Thus, in the 1990s, foreign-owned firms were going increasingly to these more highly developed regions, in contrast to previous trends. Furthermore, foreign-owned firms in these regions in the 1990s had substantially higher net output per employee than those in the less-developed Border, Midlands and West regions. Therefore the shift by foreign firms towards favouring locations in the more highly developed Greater Dublin and South-West regions was probably a significant factor in causing the divergence in regional gross value-added per capita that occurred in the 1990s, as seen in Figure 8.2 above.

The reason for this locational shift has not been explored in great detail, but it is probably related to the fact that new foreign investment in Ireland in the 1990s increasingly went into high technology industries such as electronics, software and pharmaceuticals. These industries had significant requirements for higher level skills that are found most readily in the larger urban areas. There are also indications that some aspects of agglomeration economies were developing with respect to these industries (Barry, Bradley and O'Malley, 1999), which would have tended to make them increasingly concentrated in the more favourable locations.

Conclusion

In this chapter we have sought to establish whether SMEs made a particularly significant contribution to growth at the regional and national levels in Ireland, focusing on trends in manufacturing industry. The findings are a little complex, but they do not amount to consistent evidence in support of the special importance of SMEs. At the national level, it was found that the smaller size classes grew faster than the larger size classes in two out of four periods, while the larger size classes grew faster than the smaller ones in the other two periods. However, we also pointed out that, in Ireland, growth by a particular size class of firms over a period of years is not necessarily a good reflection of growth by firms of that size, because of the possibility of significant numbers of firms crossing the size class boundaries. When we used a different methodology, reclassifying firms by their size class at the start of every individual year, we found that existing SMEs grew faster than existing large firms in three out of four periods, while the opposite was the case in one of the four periods. Given that new large start-ups also made a further independent contribution to growth, there appears to be no general rule that SMEs contribute more to growth than large firms.

At the regional level also, the findings are rather mixed. For one of the four periods, we concluded that SMEs did make an especially important contribution to regional growth, but for another period we drew the opposite conclusion, that large firms made the greater contribution to regional growth. The conclusions on the other two periods are more ambiguous. In both cases, there was at least evidence that existing SMEs grew faster than existing large firms in most regions. On the other hand, in the fastest growing regions existing large firms grew faster than existing SMEs. In addition, it is very likely that new large start-ups made an important contribution. Overall, therefore, we have not found convincing evidence that SMEs have generally had an especially important role in regional growth in Ireland.

Leaving aside considerations of size class, we found that the regions that had the fastest overall growth in total manufacturing in any given period were always regions that gained an increase in their share of foreign-owned industrial employment. And conversely, the regions that had the poorest total manufacturing growth performance in a given period were always regions that had a decline or no growth in their share of foreign-owned industrial employment. Thus, trends in the location of foreign-owned industry seem to have been important determinants of the relative growth performance of different regions.

Notes

1 The Planning Regions are defined as: Border (Donegal, Sligo, Leitrim, Cavan, Monaghan and Louth), Dublin (Dublin, Dun Laoghaire-Rathdown, Fingal and South Dublin), Mid-East (Meath, Kildare and Wicklow), Midlands (Longford, Westmeath, Offaly and Laois), Mid-West (Clare, Limerick and Tipperary N.R.), South-East (Carlow, Kilkenny, Tipperary SR., Wexford and Waterford), South-West (Kerry and Cork) and West (Mayo, Roscommon and Galway).

2 Actually, the different methods of calculating these two sets of figures do produce small differences in the results, but these differences are so small that they are not evident when the figures are rounded to one decimal place as in Tables 8.6 and 8.7.

3 SMEs are defined here as establishments with less than 250 employees, while the large size class includes those with 250 or more.

References

Acs, Z., and Audretsch, D. (1988), 'Innovation in large and small firms: an empirical analysis,' *American Economic Review*, vol. 78. pp. 678-690.

Aghion, P. and Howitt, P. (1992), 'A model of growth through creative destruction,' *Econometrica*, vol. 60, no. 2, pp. 323-351.

Aghion, P. and Howitt, P. (1998), *Endogenous Growth Theory*, MIT Press, Cambridge (MA).

Barro, R. (1990), 'Government spending in a simple model of endogenous growth,' *Journal of Political Economy*, vol. 98, pp. 103-125.

Barry, F., Bradley, J. and O'Malley E. (1999), 'Indigenous and foreign industry: characteristics and performance', in F. Barry (eds), *Understanding Ireland's Economic Growth*, Basingstoke, Macmillan, and NewYork, St. Martin's Press, pp. 45-74

Blundell, R., Griffith, R. and van Reenen, J. (1995), 'Dynamic count data models of technological innovation', *Economic Journal*, vol. 105, pp. 333-344.

Boyle, G., McCarthy, T. and Walsh, J. (1999), 'Regional income differentials and the issue of regional equalisation in Ireland', *Journal of the Statistical and Social Inquiry Society of Ireland*, vol. 152, pp. 155-199.

Bradley, J. and Morgenroth, E. (2000), 'Celtic cubs? Regional manufacturing in Ireland', in D. Duffy, J. Fitz Gerald, I. Kearney and D. Smyth (eds), Medium-Term Review 1999-2005, *Medium Term Review Series No. 7.* Dublin: Economic and Social Research Institute, pp. 155-174. Department of Industry and Commerce (1990), *Review of Industrial Performance 1990*, Stationery Office, Dublin.

EIM/ENSR (1995), *The European Observatory for SMEs, Third Annual Report*, Zoetermeer, EIM.

Fitz Gerald, J., Kearney, I., Morgenroth, E. and Smyth, D. (1999*), National Investment Priorities for the Period 2000-2006*, ESRI Policy Research Paper No. 33, Economic and Social Research Institute, Dublin.

Futagami, K., Morita, Y. and Shibata, A. (1993), 'Dynamic analysis of an endogenous growth model with public capital', *Scandinavian Journal of Economics*, vol. 95, no. 4, pp. 607-625.

Jovanovic, B. (1982), 'Selection and evolution of industry', *Econometrica*, vol. 50, pp. 649-670.

Morgenroth, E. (2001), *Analysis of the Economic, Employment and Social Profile of the Greater Dublin Region*, ESRI Books and Monograph Series Paper No. 161, Economic and Social Research Institute, Dublin.

Nickel, S. (1996), 'Competition and corporate performance', *Journal of Political Economy*, vol. 104, pp. 724-746.

O'Connor, F. (1999a), 'Regional variation in economic activity: Irish regions', ESRI Seminar Paper presented at the Economic and Social Research Institute, Dublin, 4th of April.

O'Connor, F. (1999b), 'An econometric model of regional activity in Ireland', paper presented at *the 13th Annual Conference of the Irish Economic Association*, Westport, Co. Mayo 23-25 of April.

O'Connor, F. (1999c) 'The Irish regions: review and medium-term forecasts 1996- 2005', *ESRI Working Paper* No. 120.

O'Leary, E. (1999), 'Regional income estimates for Ireland, 1995', *Regional Studies*, vol. 33, no. 9, pp. 805-814.

O'Leary, E. (2001), 'Convergence in living standards among Irish regions: the roles of productivity, profit outflows and demography', *Regional Studies*, vol. 35, no. 3, pp. 197-206.

O'Malley, E. (1989), *Industry and Economic Development: The Challenge for the Latecomer*, Gill and Macmillan, Dublin.

O'Malley, E. (1994), 'The impact of transnational corporations in the Republic of Ireland', in P. Dicken and M. Quevit (eds), *Transnational Corporations and European Regional Restructuring*, Netherlands Geographical Studies 181, Utrecht.

O'Malley, E. (1998), 'The revival of Irish indigenous industry 1987-1997', in T.J. Baker, D. Duffy and F. Shortall (eds), *Quarterly Economic Commentary*, April, Economic and Social Research Institute, Dublin, pp. 35-62. O'Malley, E., Kennedy, K.A. and O'Donnell, R. (1992), *The Impact of the Industrial Development Agencies*, report to the Industrial Policy Review Group, Stationery Office, Dublin.

Romer, P. (1986), 'Increasing returns and long run growth', *Journal of Political Economy*, vol. 94, pp. 1002-1037.

Schumpeter, J. (1942), *Capitalism, Socialism and Democracy*, Harper, New York.

Solow, R. (1956), 'A contribution to the theory of economic growth', *Quarterly Journal of Economics*, vol. 70, pp. 65-94.

Telesis Consultancy Group (1982), *A Review of Industrial Policy*, National Economic and Social Council, Dublin.

Chapter 9

Small and Medium-Sized Business as a Regional Development Factor in Lithuania

Vytautas Snieška, Regina Virvilaitė, Jūratė Banytė, Vaida Kvainauskaitė and Asta Savanevičienė

Introduction

The world-wide globalization of economies as well as the science-based development of economies have had a direct effect on regional development. In this context, regional economic development analysts have put forward four alternative ideas concerning what key conditions are needed for development to occur and what methods are needed to assure that it does. The key conditions range from injecting new investment, to providing labour training, to preserving a natural resource base, to changing the psychological mindset (Krugman, 1995; Rodrik, 1997; Sen, 1992; Todaro, 1997).

Economists, in general, have proposed various strategies to assure that development does occur. These have included, but are not limited to, creation of backward and forward linkages among firms (Hirschman, 1958), promotion of a structural change from agricultural to an industrial manufacturing and service economy (Lewis, 1995), formation of industrial complexes (Isard, 1975), and creation of clusters of firms to achieve agglomeration effects (Porter, 1990).

In the opinion of many economists, a typical development path for a national economy in its initial stage involves inter-regional divergence and the movement of factors of production, the outcome being that the most developed centres benefit. Within this process, we consider the development of small and medium-sized business (SMB) to be a regional development factor (Scott, 1995). Divergence theories as described by Rodrik (1997) as well as Swan (1995) emphasize the possibility of attracting SMBs that plays the role of service enterprises in the formation of growth poles.

The regularities of regional development described by these authors are expected to appear in Lithuania as well. One such regularity and one of the subjects of regional development should be the dynamic development of SMBs. The SMB is of huge importance to the economic development of the country, however, the role of the Lithuanian SMB in the development process has never been analysed.

The aim of this article is to determine whether the present characteristic features of SMB development in Lithuania are in line with the features characteristic to the contemporary economic development, described in the economic development models mentioned above.

Regional Economic Development Models and SMB

One of the earliest regional economic development and growth theorists, Marshall (1898) focused on factors determining the location of industries such as 'agglomeration' and 'spill over effects' meaning scale effects external to the SMBs, but favourable to all companies in a region's 'industrial district'. Schumpeter (1934) gave a prominent role to SMBs when explaining that the economic growth of a country is related to their ability to turn inventions into profitable, commercial innovations. The Heckscher-Ohlin theorem of comparative advantages assumed that a region's production and trade pattern is determined by its relative supply of various factors of production. Solow (1957) and Denison (1962) pointed out the importance of the technological residual in the production function for the regional economic growth.

After the 1980s a number of important contributions determining the regional development theories have occurred. Economists gave most of their attention to the analysis of divergence theories. They distinguished two classes of theory. One class marked by extreme views, states that economic development may result in the rapid emergence of sharp differences among regions whereby rich regions develop fast, while poor ones remain in the same stage of development or even decline. Other theories express moderate views and claim that economic development does not result in a visible decrease in regional differences.

Cumulative growth theory is the best example of divergence theories. This theory is based on the critics of relative superiority theory that is usually applied to international trade (Rodrik, 1997). According to cumulative growth theory, market forces do not guarantee even distribution of production factors or income, because richer regions attract capital, qualified labour force, and other production factors to the disadvantage of poorer regions. In such a case two closed cycles are formed as follows: a beneficial one, in which the richer regions attract all the necessary production factors and develop more rapidly, and regional differences become more visible. On the other hand, however, cumulative development may result in the lessening of the economic benefits associated with developing agglomerations, which at some certain point later starts to hinder speedy economic development. In such a case divergence produces not only negative social consequences (the living standard in peripheral regions is lower than in the centre), but economic consequences as well, since production factors are not effectively used. Lets assume, that in the peripheral regions as well as in the centre the difference between the labour demand and supply increases: in the centre capital may be ineffectively used due to the lack of sufficient labour, while in the periphery there may be a lack of qualified labour (Alden and Boland, 1996; Hardy, 1995).

Another popular divergence theory is growth pole theory, which states that economic development concentrates in the most urbanized areas. The theory rests on the ability of the main industry sectors to attract the related (service) enterprises and form the growth pole (Swan, 1995). The ability to attract the so-called related enterprises creates favourable conditions for the development of SMB. A pole could be described as a cluster of specialized industries or service enterprises, which due to the above-mentioned agglomeration and localization effects, is capable of speedy economic development.

In this context it is important to classify the factors, which influence the regional development. Debates on factors that influence regional development have turned into active discussion among the supporters of exogenous and the supporters of endogenous economic development. Such a division is directly related to regional development policies, because this issue raises a question of what should be the basis for regional development: attraction of foreign capital (external economic development) or development of local human resources and promotion of SMB (internal economic development). The second view that emphasizes the importance of local human resources and creation of favourable conditions for SMB, which is related to EU structural policy, is becoming more and more popular.

The SMB Role in Regional Development of Lithuania

Preconditions for Regional Development in Lithuania

Regional development concept has been alive in Europe for several decades and is marked by changes in mode, measures, and priorities, but it has only recently been an issue in Lithuania. In the opinion of Brazas (1998), regional development received little attention in the years immediately following the restoration of Lithuania's independence mainly because Lithuania is a small country in which regional development issues have traditionally been a minor consideration. Secondly, regional differences were overlooked due to the emphasis on the analysis of the general economic environment of the country. Moreover, it is commonly accepted that regional differences in Lithuania are not very distinct, although they have had a tendency to increase. On the other hand, it is difficult to test the accuracy of this statement due to the lack of statistical data. However, despite the above mentioned restrictions we will try to point out some of the structural peculiarities of the regions.

The actions of the former Soviet Union made a huge impact on the structure of regions of present day Lithuania. Firstly, in the context of regional policy,

Lithuania was regarded as an autonomous unit of the Soviet Union. Due to its comparatively small spatial extent Lithuania was not divided into smaller independent territorial-administrative units, and this limited the development of various instruments for regional development within the country. Secondly, Soviet regional policy was based on the idea of the redistribution and channelling of financial resources from richer to poorer areas. Accordingly Lithuania, which was one of the richer Soviet countries, consistently featured as one of those areas that donated financial resources to the less well-off parts of the Soviet Union. Such an experience of the past naturally promoted negative opinions on regional development after the restoration of independence.

The fact that regional development was and very often is identified, as territorial planning is another relic of the former Soviet Union. The first steps in the field of territorial planning were made in the early 60s. The regional development plan of the republic was drawn up during the years 1962-64 for the period up to the year 1980. On the basis of this plan the present urban structure of the country was formed. Territorial plan considered the objective of universal industrialization of all the Soviet countries, which led to a relatively dispersed pattern of distribution of industry and the emergence of regional differences. As a result of this plan, ten centres were developed. Five of them were already big cities such as Vilnius, Kaunas, Klaipėda, Šiauliai, Panevėžys, and the other five were expected to grow rapidly in the future – Alytus, Marijampolė, Plungė, Utena, Tauragė. In 1994, on the basis of these ten cities, the boundaries of the regions were established. Subsequent analysis will be based on the supposition that the regional boundaries will in the future remain the same as they presently are.

It is obvious that the rise of regional differences in Lithuania was mainly influenced by decisions made by the Soviet regime about the development of the individual industry sectors and about their location. This is an important point since most of the theories of regional development do not pay much attention to this type of factors that give rise to the regional differences at the outset.

Means of Regional Development in Lithuania

Taking into account the strategic directions of the Lithuanian SMB development, one of the main means of regional development is differentiated activity by the state that is directed towards the creation of balanced social-economic development conditions in all the Lithuanian regions, with the emphasis on the importance of human resources and creation of favourable conditions for SMB. Such a conception of regional development is of a progressive nature because it is directed towards the creation of favourable conditions for development and not towards direct redistribution based on providing compenzation to the poorer regions to the disadvantage of the richer ones. At present the issue of regional differences in Lithuania is not yet widely discussed, however, the analysis of them as well as the study of regional development trends could help to identify the directions of the general economic and social development in the country.

Thinking on the conditions of Lithuania priority should be given to promotion of growth poles with SMBs in the field of regional development. The speedy development of the growth poles during a short period of time may result in the widening of regional differences, however, over the longer period it could create conditions for the inter-regional convergence within the country. Lithuania has favourable conditions for such a regional development scenario because a comparatively decentralized urban system allows us to expect that speedy economic development during a short period of time will not cause lessening of agglomeration economies, which is the main negative aspect of the growth poles policy.

It is important to ensure that existing economic trends help the formation of several growth poles in Lithuania and interrupt the earlier *bad* cycle of development, which favoured only the growth of Vilnius to develop rapidly. Such a tendency is evident from the distribution of direct investments in Lithuania. For example, in the year 1998 direct foreign investments in Vilnius accounted for 51 per cent of the total direct foreign investment in Lithuania, while in the year 2000 this figure reached 60 per cent of the total direct foreign investment in Lithuania (Tiesioginės užsienio investicijos Lietuvoje, 2000). Thus, the attraction of foreign investment, which due to the lack of local investments becomes an important source of capital, and its diversion to the growth poles outside Vilnius, could be considered as one of the means of regional development in Lithuania.

SMB as a Basis for Regional Development

In order to create successful growth poles, the state emphasizes the importance of creating favourable conditions for SMBs. This principle is considered to be more effective than interventionist policies directed to eradication of income differentials among regions. Weak consumer purchasing power raises in the prices of raw materials, less business turnover, a lack of capital, and various bureaucratic procedures all slow the rate of SMB development as well as increase regional differences.

In order to achieve effective regional development, it is important to assess the opportunities that exist for the economic development of SMBs, as well, as promote the growth of poorly developed regions, these two things go hand-in-hand. Regarding regional development, we advocate that the regions should be divided into the following two main groups namely regions requiring *special* promotion and the regions requiring *normal* promotion.

The regions can be grouped according to the two following factors:

- *Level of unemployment* – in other words the status of the region with respect to direct and indirect unemployment (number of unemployed, number of people who work part time, number of people who search for a job, etc.);
- *Attractiveness of the region* – this is a complex indicator designed to describe the qualitative status of the region taking into consideration the market potential, level of infrastructure development, etc.

In addition, attention could be focused on the promotion of certain innovative activities, and on the promotion of SMB that are oriented to export.

General Social-Economic Characteristics of Business Conditions in Lithuania

Since independence Lithuania has achieved a significant progress while stabilizing the economy and undertaking structural reforms, the implementation of the main economic reforms having established the conditions for constant growth in the economy. The economy started to recover in 1994 and grew for several of the subsequent years. The real GDP (Gross Domestic Product) increased 3,3 per cent in 1995, 4,7 per cent in 1996 and 7,3 per cent in 1997. So the average annual increase of Lithuania's real GDP was 5 per cent between 1995-98. More recently, this progress ground to a halt because of the Russian crisis. As Lithuania is very dependent on exports to Russia and other CIS countries, the decline in the economies of these countries caused a decrease in exports and in real GDP in 1999. Real GDP has decreased by 4,1 per cent, but the year 2000 marked a changing point, after which we have seen a recovery.

These statistical data reflect the reality of the Lithuanian economy, which can be explained in the following way: firstly, Lithuania is very strongly dependent on employment in the agricultural sector, where significant unstable tendencies are recognized. Secondly, the service sector has expanded lately, but differently from that in EU. In Lithuania it is domestic demand, and not international trade in services, which influences the development of the service sector most of all. Thus an important aspect of the economy is the independence of the industry. Therefore, in our opinion, seeking to explain general social-economic SMB development conditions in Lithuania, we propose to analyse two factors, those are: the situation in Lithuania's industry and foreign trade patterns.

Industry is still a very important branch of Lithuania's economy, even if the share of general added value has decreased from 1/3 in the beginning of 1990 to 1/5 in 2000. One sixth of the country's labour force is working in industry.

Comparing with EU countries, the following sectors of Lithuania's economic structure are bigger: agriculture and food industry; textile and clothing industry; wood treatment and related fields, which use wood products and transport. Production for a large volume of the above mentioned sectors and are the biggest or one of the biggest when one compares Lithuania with other European countries.

Lithuania is close to Italy, Portugal and Spain using this criterion when one considers the garment industry. In the Lithuanian garment industry the production of quality and competitive goods is related to investment in technologies, management structures and communication. 18 per cent of the textile industry and 20 per cent of the garment industry enterprises are small (in Lithuania enterprises that have less than 9 employees are small, enterprises that have from 10 to 49 employees are middle sized- definitions adopted by an small and medium-sized enterprises development law in 1998). 4,4 per cent of textile industry workers work in such enterprises.

Light industry (especially the garment industry) has been an export leader for several years despite Russia's crisis some years ago. Its trade balance has constantly been positive, but the opportunities for light industry are not fully utilized and it faces problems just like other Lithuanian industries. The garment industry's activity and development problems can be divided into five groups: legal, technological, financial, social and economic. The study of the garment industry's social and economic problems highlights the necessity of restructuring industrial enterprises.

The restructuring of enterprises is coming along satisfactorily, but the connections between industries are weak (there aren't enough local resources for the flax industry, though there are the basic conditions for this industry's development, but this isn't being supported. The flax is imported from France and Belgium). The garment enterprises prefer foreign suppliers for their flexibility instead of Lithuanian producers, but such an approach increases the costs of production. Meanwhile industry's competitive position depends on the development of strong clusters – a same-line-of-business cooperative network, in which each involved enterprise's exertion adds to a synergy effect.

Generalizing Lithuania's industrial situation in the context of integration into the EU, we have to emphasize that the main factors, which determine the current development of Lithuania's industry, are:

- backward industrial structure, there are not enough enterprises receptive to scientific developments;
- poor labour productivity in many sectors;
- significant dependence upon cheap Russian materials;
- lack of professional and managerial competence;
- poor cooperation among various economic areas;
- poor infrastructure for business services;
- poorly developed financial services sector, with too-high interests rates on capital borrowing.

Thus, seeking to survive in conditions of rapidly increasing competition, Lithuania's industrial enterprises need to create the whole complex of relative competitive advantages. That requires not only real technical know-how, but also very high managerial and marketing competence. Many Lithuanian enterprises are not ready for that and they will have to implement a lot of important changes in order to make the necessary transition, such as changing:

- from physical production to business and information services;
- from cheap supplies to effective capital;
- from industrial areas to competitive clusters;
- from a regional to a global market.

One of the most important factors, which have influenced the recovery of the economy, has been foreign trade. From 1992 to 1998 Lithuania's export volume has increased by a factor of four. However, import volumes were even bigger than export volumes and that produced an increasing foreign trade deficit.

Also it is important to indicate that recent data on Lithuanian foreign trade in 1998 and 1999 show a change in the pattern of foreign trade. Up to 1998 the main partners of Lithuanian foreign trade were the CIS countries but more recently it is the EU countries that have become the main export markets.

Exports to EU countries exceeded the symbolic 50 per cent mark in the first quarter of 1999, and that accounted for 52,2 per cent of the whole Lithuanian exports, indicating a change in the geographical structure of trade. Germany became the main foreign trade partner with Russia now in second place.

With regard to recent trends in Lithuania's foreign trade the following conclusions can be made:

- The Russian financial-economic crisis and reduction in demand in the CIS countries had a major impact on Lithuania's the main export markets;
- The strengthening of the dollar in relation to the Euro and rouble has decreased the competitiveness of our exports to Eastern and Western Europe;
- The protectionist policies of the CIS countries has limited the exports of Lithuanian products to these markets;
- Export duties on Russian oil and gas exported to Lithuania and the rise of these products' prices in global markets increased production costs.

The comprehensive analysis of Lithuanian foreign trade allows us to state that export growth rates were decreased not only by Russia's crisis, but also because of an unstable legal base and information maintenance problems.

Study of Lithuanian SMB at a Regional Level

The Analysis of the Main Economic Indicators of SMB at a Regional Level

Small and medium-sized enterprises (SMEs) are the most dynamic and constantly changing group of enterprises, the middle chain in the structure of the economy that has a decisive influence on the growth of the economy and on the stability of social relations in Lithuania (the term 'SME' we use to emphasize the nature of economic organization as unit). SMEs do not require much capital; they react quickly to the changes in the market and have powers of flexible adaptation. They also possess an ability to compete with large state enterprises, and are able to provide services to big enterprises. Moreover they are associated with the development of usually better quality new products, new services or manufacturing processes, and are a suitable structure for family businesses, while providing opportunities to improve the qualifications of specialists. The establishment and promotion of the activities of SMEs is therefore the basis of Lithuanian regional development as well as one of the main sources of new jobs.

In order to show the role of SMB at a regional level in greater detail, we will refer to a survey carried out by the Department of Statistics (Lietuvos ekonomikos apžvalga, 1998, 1999 and 2000), which provides the main indices of regional development. Figure 9.1 illustrates the uneven distribution of the Gross Domestic Product (GDP) in the regions in the period of the years 1996-2000. In the Vilnius region it increased over the period to accounted for 33.1 per cent of GDP, in the Kaunas region GDP was rather stable although it fell to 19,6 per cent, and in the Klaipėda region – it was about 12 per cent of the total GDP over the period of the year 1996-2000. The smallest shares were in the Tauragė region (2 per cent), the Marijampolė region (3 per cent) and the Alytus region (4 per cent).

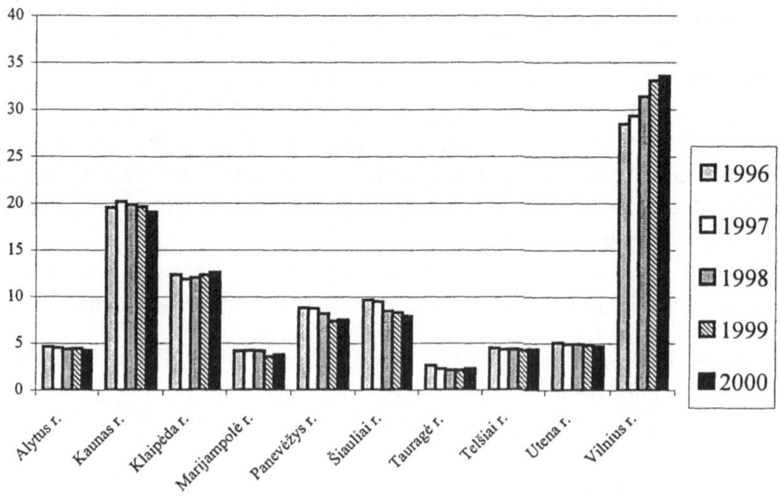

Figure 9.1 Distribution of the gross domestic product (GDP) in the regions of Lithuania during the period 1996-2000, by percentage.

Source: Lietuvos ekonomikos apžvalga, 1998, 1999 and 2000.

Figure 9.2 shows that the Gross Domestic Product (GDP) per person has the highest value in the Vilnius and Klaipėda regions and has increased in the Vilnius region by 3 per cent and in the Klaipėda region by 2 per cent in the period of the years 1996-2000. The smallest shares were in the Tauragė and Marijampolė regions where it decreased by 1 per cent in both regions during the period 1996-2000.

The survey reveals that distribution of SMEs in the regions of Lithuania is not even. In late 2000, more than a half of them (51,7 per cent) were located in the Vilnius and Kaunas regions (Figure 9.3). The growth of those two economic indicators in these regions was due to the concentration of industry and investments, which promotes the establishment and development of SMEs as well as maximizes their importance as service enterprises.

Small and medium-sized business contributes a lot to the establishment of new jobs. This is illustrated by the fact that in the territories with low unemployment the number of SMEs per 1000 of citizens is higher then the number of SMEs in the territories with high unemployment.

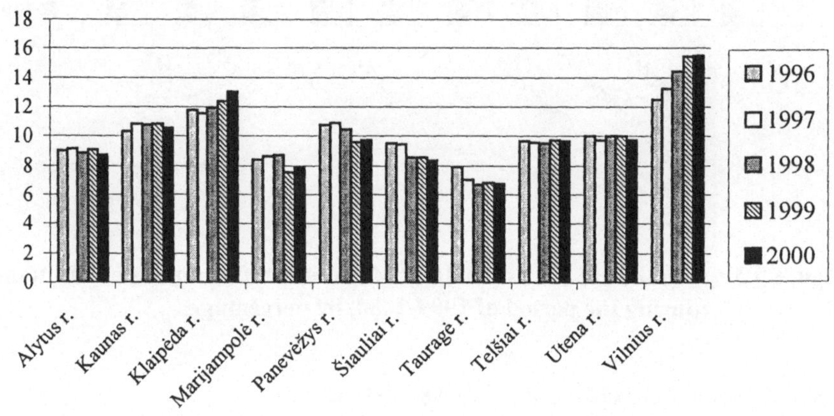

Figure 9.2 Distribution of the gross domestic product (GDP) per capita in the regions of Lithuania during the period 1996-2000, by percentage.

Source: Lietuvos ekonomikos apžvalga, 1998, 1999 and 2000.

In late 2000 the number of SMEs per 1000 citizens was highest in the Vilnius (17,4 per cent) region which also had a the level of unemployment equal to 9,9 per cent and in Klaipėda (15,9 per cent), where the the level of unemployment was 11 per cent. The lowest number of SMEs per 1000 citizens was to be found in the regions of Utena (10,2 per cent), unemployment (11,7 per cent), Alytus (10,2 per cent), unemployment (16,1 per cent), and Marijampolė (10,3 per cent, unemployment 16,2). The growth of the number of SMEs in the region of Klaipėda could be explained by the activities of the Klaipėda port, which created favourable conditions for the activities of SME, and the development of SMBs due to the provision of tourism services in recreational locations.

In addition, the level of unemployment is higher in the regions in which local authorities did not set SMB promotion funds. For example, in the region of Marijampolė as many as four municipalities out of six had no such funds, which explains why it has the highest level of unemployment in the region and a comparatively low number of SMEs per 1000 of citizens (10,3 per cent).

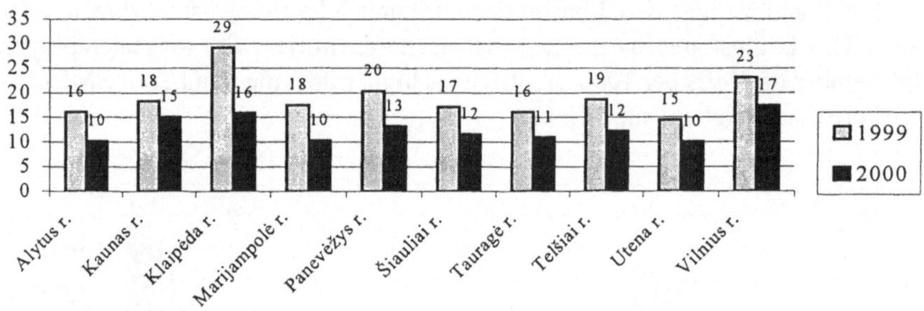

Figure 9.3 Number of SMEs per 1000 of citizens in the regions of Lithuania during the period of 1999-2000, by percentage.

Source: Lietuvos ekonomikos apžvalga, 1998, 1999 and 2000.

With regard to the total number of SMEs, we find that in Lithuania SMEs are being actively set up where there exists urban investment and regions that are 'business friendly', meaning that they possess a well developed institutional business infrastructure, and scientific, technical and intellectual potential. In the year 2000 the greatest number of SMEs was established in the regions of Vilnius (34,9 per cent) and Kaunas (18,3 per cent), while the number of newly established SMEs in other regions was lower in comparison with the number that had gone out of business (Figure 9.4). The following factors are the reasons why the number of newly established SMEs has tended to decrease:

- Amendments to the rules governing the issue of patents and activities according to patents. On 28 December 1999 the Government of the Republic of Lithuania adopted Resolution no. 1491 which stated that patents could be issued to individual persons only.

- Simplification of the procedure for de-registration and liquidation of enterprises. On 13 July 2000 the Seimas of the Republic of Lithuania adopted the Provisional Law on Simplified De-registration of Enterprises.
- Growth in labour costs. The Law adopted by the Seimas of the Republic of Lithuania on 29 December 1999 prescribed rates for state social insurance contributions that the total share of the state social insurance contribution of the insured making up 31 per cent, and the share of the state social insurance contribution for the insured making up 3 per cent. The approved rates increased the burden of taxes and caused a rise in the price of labour.
- Tax increase. Amendment to the Law on State Social Insurance effective from 1 January to 3 July 2000 committed owners of private enterprises to paying for insurance not on the basic pension, but according to income received, which increased the burden of taxes for private enterprises.
- Introduction of additional taxes. On 12 September 2000 the Seimas adopted the Law on the Guarantee Fund. It provides that all the enterprises registered in compliance with the procedure established in laws of the Republic of Lithuania are obliged to pay 0.2 per cent of the staff remuneration before taxes to the Guarantee Fund.
- Introduction of additional bureaucratic barriers in labour relations (employment certificate, notification of unpaid leave provided, notification of monthly insured income amounts to retired persons).
- Emergence of big trade networks in the trade sector. Big trade networks took advantage of economies of scale in order to reduce their costs and price of production. The result was that some SMEs were not able to offer competitive prices and had to terminate their activities.

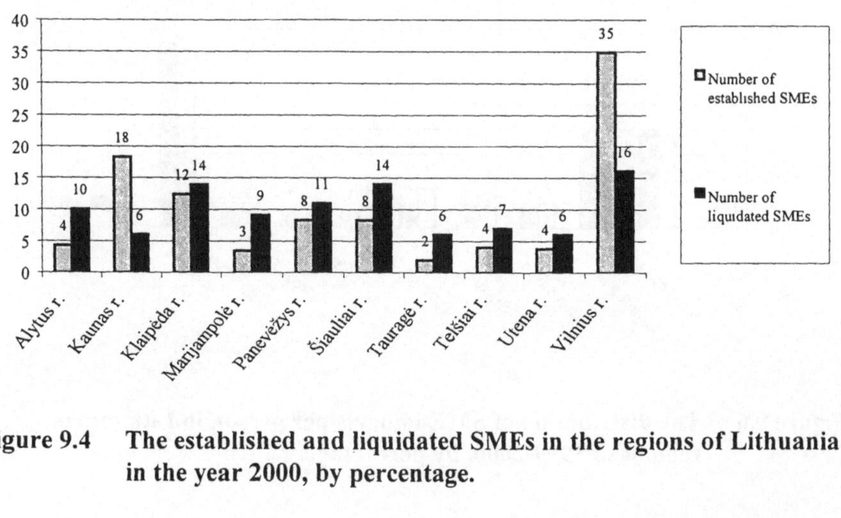

Figure 9.4 The established and liquidated SMEs in the regions of Lithuania in the year 2000, by percentage.

The distribution of SMEs by region is somewhat different when we look at those that are engaged in foreign trade. The largest number of SMEs is located in the Vilnius region (35 per cent SME in Lithuania), so that SME exports per person in this region amounts to (about one third of Lithuania's total exports of SMEs per person in the year 1999 2000 (see Figure 9.5). On the other hand, SME exports per person in regions such as Alytus, Marijampolė, Panevėžys, Šiauliai and Utena have tended to decline as a result of the economic crisis in Russia, which has reduced commercial contacts involving business partners in Russia.

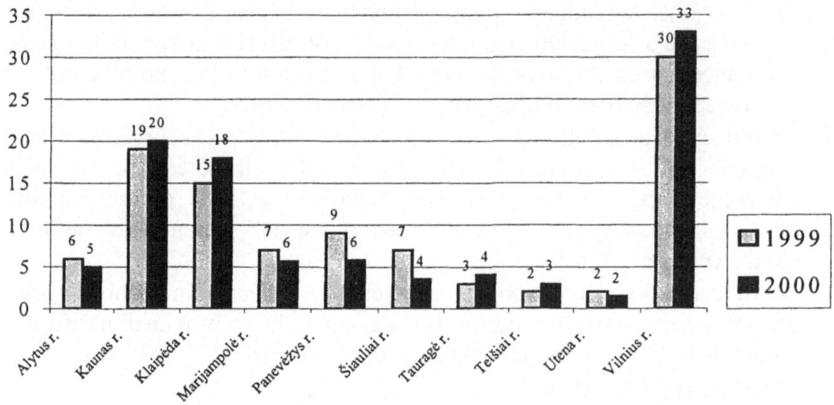

Figure 9.5 The distribution of SME exports per person in Lithuanian regions in 1999-2000, by percentage.

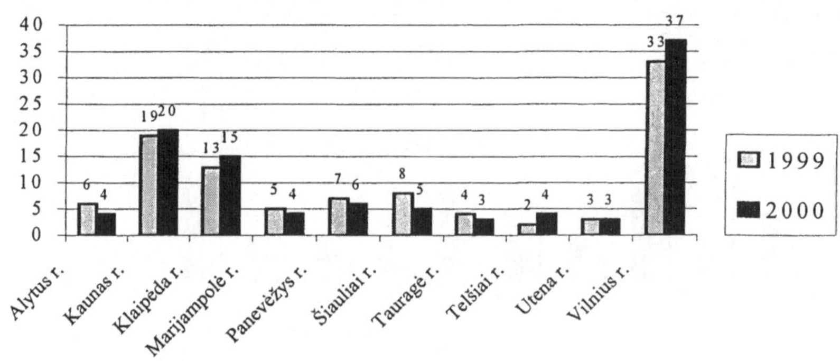

Figure 9.6 The distribution of SME imports per person in Lithuanian regions in 1999-2000, by percentage.

The greatest number of enterprises that import are located in the region of Vilnius, the smallest share located in the regions of Tauragė, Telšiai and Utena (see Figure 9.6).

The regional analysis of the main economic indicators relating to SMBs clearly distinguishes the Vilnius and Kaunas regions from the rest. The development of SMBs in the Vilnius region was encouraged by the distribution of investments (in 1998 direct foreign investment in the Vilnius region made up more than a half of the total direct foreign investment in Lithuania), reflecting the ability of the main industrial sectors and state enterprises to attract the so called service enterprises as well as create favourable conditions for the formation of growth poles. The development of SMB in the Kaunas region was influenced by the good geographical location of the region, and by the comparatively high concentration of science-based activity with good potential for commercial application and the introduction of innovations.

Evaluation of Support for the Development of SMB in the Regions

Data used in this section were compiled from survey 'Trends of SMB development in Lithuania', which conducted in the year 1999-2000. The survey collected information related to changes of SMB environment, identification of obstacles for SMB development, businessmen opinion about main forms of SMB support providing by Lithuania's government. In total, about 1500 respondents were surveyed.

According to the theoretical analysis, the assessment of regional development trends and determination of regional differences are related to the identification of regions requiring special promotion and regions requiring normal promotion. However, the lack of statistical data does not allow us to make this type of classification. Thus, in order to establish what are the trends in the development of regional differences and to analyse the factors that influence them in greater detail, we will make use of the following:

- Tax concessions for business start-ups;
- Credits on favourable terms;
- Improvement of tax administration;
- Provision of information to the business people.

Survey data (see Table 9.1) revealed that for the business community, the most important form of support is tax concessions for business start-ups, an initiative supported by 58 per cent of respondents. Comparing the 1998 and 1999 data indicate that the importance of tax concessions has declined by 4,3 per cent. In 1998, 65,5 per cent of the respondents in the Šiauliai region thought that tax concessions were the most important form of support for SMBs while as many as 78,3 per cent were of this opinion in the Tauragė region. However in 1999 the percentages in support of tax concessions fell, for instance it was 62,9 per cent in the Alytus region and 70,6 per cent in the Kaunas region.

Credits on favourable terms received different levels of support in different regions, with any given region's proportion changing over time. For example, in 1998 only 6,7 per cent of the business community respondents of the Tauragė region supported favourable credits terms as a form of SMB support, however, in 1999 this figure reached 37,5 per cent. In 1999 easy credit was positively evaluated in the Alytus (41,7 per cent), Telšiai (40,8 per cent), and Utena (39,4 per cent) regions, but only 26.9 per cent of respondents in the Klaipėda region favoured this form of support.

Likewise the importance of improving tax administration was evaluated differently in different regions. In 1998 the supporters of tax administration improvement ranged from 15,6 per cent (the Alytus region) to 32 per cent (the Marijampolė region). In contrast in 1999 the percentages ranged from 13,8 per cent (the Telšiai region) up to 34,5 per cent (the Marijampolė region). It is possible that this variation by region and over times was influenced by the varying popularity of the tax collection methods that were used.

Table 9.1 Differences by regions in evaluations of the importance of different forms of business support for the acceleration of SMB development.

Regions	Tax concessions		Credits on favourable terms		Improvement of tax administration		Provision of information	
	1998	1999	1998	1999	1998	1999	1998	1999
Alytus	75	62,9	25,6	41,7	15,6	11,1	0	28,6
Kaunas	73,6	70,6	33,6	27,6	16,7	27,1	4,5	20,5
Klaipėda	77,9	67,7	28,1	26,9	14,6	19,4	29,2	21,6
Marijampolė	65	64,4	21,9	31	32	34,5	18,2	37,5
Panevėžys	68,7	63,6	35,5	28,6	16,3	23,1	7,4	28,6
Šiauliai	65,5	67,6	36,8	28,8	18,7	16,9	28,1	9,5
Tauragė	78,3	68,6	6,7	37,5	20	25	0	14,3
Telšiai	67,4	67,7	32,4	40,8	29,6	13,8	30	14,3
Utena	78	67,9	27,3	39,4	13,6	24,1	23,1	14,3
Vilnius	72,3	69,2	29,1	33,3	23	19	7,6	19,6
Total	72,2	67,9	30,9	31,7	19,4	21,4	12,9	19,8

Note: The values show percentage of the total surveyed businessmen in the regions who evaluate the define form of business support as important.

The survey reveals even sharper differences in opinions of the respondents about the value of the provision of information to the business community as a form of SMBs promotion. In 1998 none of the respondents from the Alytus and Tauragė regions indicated that information provision was important. However, in 1999 there was a radical shift in opinion in the Alytus region, with the level of support rising from zero to 28,6 per cent. In the same year the number of people who indicated provision of information as an important form of promotion in the Marijampolė region reached 37,5 per cent.

The study shows that because of the varying levels of support for SMB development expressed by the respondents in different regions, it is difficult to identify the regions that need special attention and difficult to evaluate the usefulness of the regional development measures. However, we should emphasize that regional differences in Lithuania are comparatively minor, and this means that a policy that aims to create favourable conditions on a fairly even basis across all regions should be feasible.

Conclusions

At present the view that emphasizes the importance of local human resources and creation of favourable conditions for SMB and which rests upon the goals of the EU's structural policy is becoming more and more popular in Lithuania. The issue of regional differences in Lithuania is not yet widely discussed, however, the analysis of them as well as the study of regional development trends at the initial stage in Lithuania may help to identify directions of the general economic-social development of the country.

While creating more favourable conditions for SMB at a regional level it is important to consider the fact that the growth of regional differences indicates the lack of attention on the regional development in Lithuania. On the other hand, the weak purchasing power of the consumers, the rise of prices of raw materials, the drop of business turnover, the lack of capital, and various bureaucratic procedures slow the rate of SMB development as well as increase regional differences in Lithuania.

The analysis of the main economic indicators of SMB indicates a clear distinction of the Vilnius and Kaunas regions from all the rest due to investments, concentration of science potential, ability of the main industry sectors and enterprises to attract the so called service enterprises as well as create favourable conditions for the formation of growth poles. However, the number of SMEs tends to decrease due to various bureaucratic procedures, the weak purchasing power of the consumers, the lack of capital, etc.

Differences by regions in evaluations of the importance of different forms of business support for the acceleration of SMB development are not essential. So there is no need for different attitudes in different regions in selecting of SMB support forms.

Rather unfavourable social and economic conditions due to extreme differences in volumes comparing direct investments to the capital city (Vilnius) region and to the other parts of Lithuania for the activities of SMB hinder effective growth and development of SMB in the peripheral regions. That limits the participation of SMB in the promotion in Lithuania of more effective forms of economic development that are described in modern models of development.

The failure to solve the problems of SMB promotion results in slower economic development in Lithuania and a limited possibility for the convergence of regional development.

References

Alden, J. and Boland, P. (1996), *Regional Development Strategies: a European Perspective*, Regional Studies Association, London.

Brazas, A. (1998), *Europos Sąjunga: Struktūriniai Fondai ir Regioninė Politika*, Vilnius, Pradai.

Denison, E.F. (1962), 'United States economic growth', *Journal of Business*, vol. 35, pp. 17-29.

Hardy, S. (1995). *An Enlarged Europe: Regions in Competition*, Jessica Kingsley Publishers Ltd., London.

Hirschman, A.O. (1958), *The Strategy of Economic Development*, Yale University Press, New Haven, CT.

Isard, W. (1975), *Introduction to Regional Science*, Englewood Cliffs, NJ: Prentice-Hall. Inc.

Krugman, P. (1995), *Development, Geography and Economic Theory*, The MIT Press, Cambridge, MA.

Lewis, W.A. (1995), *The Theory of Economic Growth*, George Allen and Unwin, London.

Lietuvos Ekonomikos Apžvalga (1998), Statistikos departamentas prie LRV.

Lietuvos Ekonomikos Apžvalga (1999), Statistikos departamentas prie LRV.

Lietuvos Ekonomikos Apžvalga (2000), Statistikos departamentas prie LRV.

Marshall, A. (1898), *Principles of Economics*, Edited by C.W. Guillebaud (1961), Macmillan, London.

Porter, M.E. (1990), *The Competitive Advantage of Nations*, The Free Press, New York.

Rodrik, D. (1997), *Has Globalization Gone Too Far*?, Institute for International Economics, Washington, DC.

Schumpeter, J. (1934), *The Theory of Economic Development*, Harvard University Press, Cambridge.

Scott, J. (1995), *Development Dilemmas in the EC*, Open University Press, Buckingham.

Sen, A. (1992), *Inequality Re-examined*, Harvard University Press, Cambridge, MA.

Solow, R. (1957), 'Technical change and the aggregate production function', *Review of Economics and Statistics*, no. 39, pp. 35-48.

Swan, D. (1995), *The Economics of the Common Market*, Penguin Books, New York.

Todaro, M.P. (1997), *Economic Development*, 6th ed., Addison Wesley, London

Tiesioginės užsienio investicijos Lietuvoje (2000). Statistikos departamentas prie LRV.

Chapter 10

The Role of SMEs in the Regional Development of the Czech Republic

Vaclav Beran and Jana Frková

Introduction

> One of the most fateful errors of our age is the belief that 'the problem of production' has been solved.
>
> E.F. Schumacher 1973

The goal of this chapter is to compare the economic development of the regions in the Czech Republic in relation to small and medium-sized enterprises (SMEs). SMEs have an important function for the socio-economic development of regions. They also create specific positive economic 'spin-off' effects for regions, in the form of employment, tax income to municipal budgets and social stability. As E.F. Schumacher (1999) suggested in his monograph, SMEs might be an answer to modern economic problems, as he also indicated in his earlier book *Small is Beautiful*, written in the 1970s. Nowadays, solutions seem to be more complicated (Fingleton, 2001) since there is a need to deal with three or four different types of *capital*. The economic nature of *ecological*, *social*, *human* and *business* capital is more complicated than it was in 1973, when Schumacher's idea was first published.

The first section of this chapter introduces Czech regional policy and the situation that existed before and after the transition of the economy. The second section focuses on *the role of SMEs in the Czech economy*. It provides a short history of SMEs, followed by a comparison of small and large businesses in relation to regional development. The third section, SMEs Sector Segmentation and Development in the Czech Republic, analyses the sectoral distribution of SMEs. The next section deals with government policies in the Czech Republic related to SMEs, followed by the last section on *obstacles to further SMEs development in the Czech Republic*. The main argument in this section is that restricting the development of a market economy creates obstacles for entrepreneurship.

Regions and Regional Policy of the Czech Republic

The change of the political system in the Czech Republic at the end of 1980s was marked by uncertainty about planning methodologies, which restricted the implementation of national and regional plans. The central government, however, maintained its power, partly because of the abolition of regional governments at the beginning of 1990s, and the governmental attitude towards regional policy matters remained largely unchanged. State intervention was considered to be the best way to make a quick transition from a planned to a market economy.

Nevertheless, some aspects of the transformation process led to severe economic problems that were associated mainly with the growth of employment opportunities. These problems were the substantial decline of heavy industry, the reduction of agricultural sector employees, the very low inter-regional mobility of the labour force, and serious environmental problems. The suspiciously low level of unemployment (around 4%) at the beginning of the 1990s raised questions about the reliability of unemployment figures as an accurate economic indicator. In fact, the Czech situation was a specific one. The low levels of unemployment rates were due to the existence of latent unemployment, especially in the form of over-manning in the state-owned heavy industry companies, which was tolerated to avoid potential political consequences (Beran, 2000).

Regional policy in the Czech Republic, up to the year 1990, is associated with a massive redistribution and reallocation of resources. No systematic regional policy was articulated during the 1980s in order to tackle the numerous problems in the sphere of regional development. Subsequently the *Principles of Government Regional Economic Policy* Act of 1992 defined regional policy as an activity to support the effective functioning of the market economy, taking into account the regional economic differences. The policy was clearly oriented toward the support of small and medium-sized enterprises and the improvement of infrastructure. Therefore it can be regarded as a regional industrial policy. The role of the state remained essential and it did not even include proper co-ordination with the relevant ministries concerned with regional issues, or with other potential partners at the regional and municipal levels. In 1996, the newly formed Ministry for Regional Development was given coordinating role with the aim of securing the state's regional policy.

It was only in April 1998 that the general rules governing the implementation of regional policy were set out in the new *Principles of regional policy*. This document did not bring concrete solutions to regional problems, but rather it temporarily put in place the missing legislation. It has a broader approach, however, compared with the government principles of 1992. The regional policy is understood as consisting of guidelines for state actions, and the aims of regional authorities are defined as follows: To contribute to the balanced and harmonious development of regions in the Czech Republic, to reduce the differences of economic development between regions and to improve the regional economic and social structure.

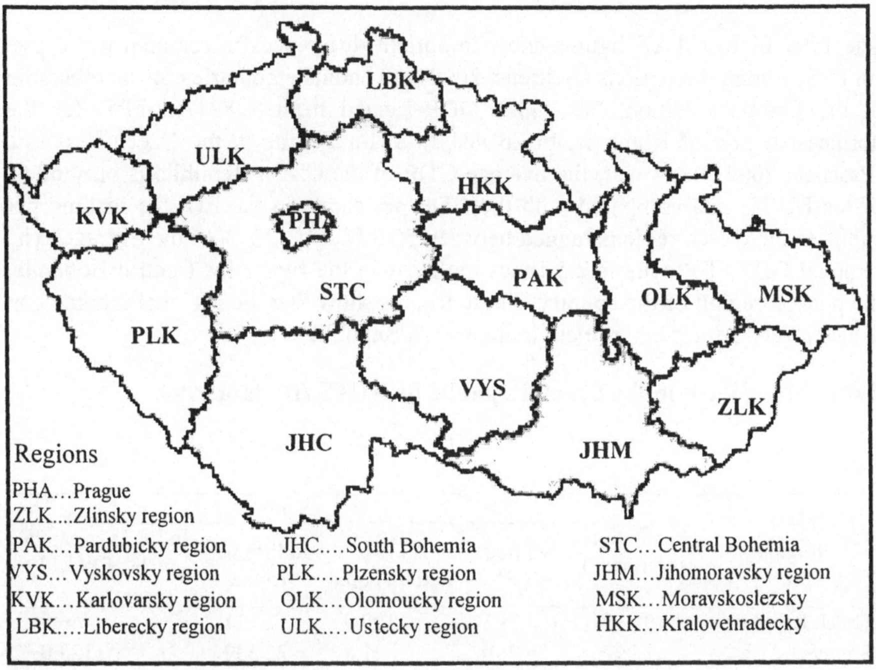

Figure 10.1 Regions NUTS III in the Czech Republic and their names.

The new regional policy was designed by taking into consideration the basic principles of the structural policy of the EU and the overall aim of economic and social cohesion. Additionally, following the directions of the EU in 1.1.2001 the new regional structure was formed. In this new regional division of the country, 14 NUTS III regions and 8 NUTS II regions have been designated by the Parliament. Figure 10.1 shows the partitioning of the national territory into NUTS III regions.

The Principles of the Government Regional Policy already defined two types of problematic regions, namely structurally-deficient regions and lagging regions. The regions with structural problems were defined as regions with high concentrations of traditional industry, high levels of urbanization and unemployment. On the other hand, lagging regions were characterized as regions with low standards of living, high levels of employment in the primary sector, low population density and also unemployment above the average (Frkova, 1999). These regions were mostly rural areas with a lower level of urbanization and economic development. Accordingly, a specific program has been developed for the 18 different problem territories.

The Regional Problem

The 1999 EUROSTAT figures show important differences in regional per capita (in PPS) among the regions (Behrens, 2002) of candidate countries for membership of the European Union. Per capita GDP ranged from 3 871 in PPS, for the northeast region of Romania, to 26 961 PPS, for Prague in the Czech Republic (Pasanen, 2002). However, the average GDP of the Czech Republic is only 66 % of the EU 15; and compared with the GDP per capita in the EU, the income per capita in the Czech regions ranged between 50.3 % and 123 % of the average. The regional GDP of Prague is 2,5 times higher than the figure for Central Bohemia, the poorest region of the country. These figures show that the regional income gap is also a very important problem in the Czech Republic.

Table 10.1 GDP in the Czech Republic by NUTS III, data 1999.

Regions	Population (thousands)	GDP			
		Million PPS*	As % of national total	In PPS per capita	In PPS per capita in % of EU 15 average
Czech Republic	10 315	123 897	100.0	12 011	66.2
Prague	1 207	26 961	21.8	22 332	123.0
Central Bohemia	1 106	10 095	8.1	9 128	50.3
South Bohema	627	6 808	5.5	10 864	59.8
Plzensky	555	6 747	5.4	12 159	67.0
Karlovarsky	305	3 261	2.6	10 688	58.9
Ustecky	825	9 218	7.4	11 171	61.5
Liberecky	429	4 323	3.5	10 075	55.5
Kralovehradecky	554	5 771	4.7	10 423	57.4
Pardubicky	510	5 233	4.2	10 264	56.5
Vyskovsky	523	5 026	4.1	9 611	52.9
Jihomoravsky	1 140	12 866	10.4	11 282	62.1
Olomoucky	645	6 557	5.3	10 159	56.0
Zinsky	600	6 069	4.9	10 109	55.7
Moravskoslezsky	1 288	14 962	12.1	11 613	64.0

* PPS - Purchasing Power Standard.

Source: The Czech Statistical Office 2001.

Table 10.1 in the last column shows the differences in GDP per capita (in PPS) between regions (Rathouska, 2002). In the distribution of regional income per capita, an absorption effect typical of large cities is evident in the concentration of companies in Prague, which sucks in substantial economic potential from the surrounding areas. The regions where larger cities are located also have higher GDP per capita. This situation can be noted in the Plzen region (per capita GDP 67 in PPS per capita in % of EU 15 average), the Ostrava region (64,0) and the Brno region (62,1), where the large cities are located. Prague has another specific advantage in being an administrative centre, including the institutions of government and also the headquarters of international corporations.

Each region has its individual characteristics. Even in some basic respects (unemployment, salaries and wages, etc.) the differences are quite extensive. Unfortunately, these differences have been increasing in the past few years in terms of GDP per capita, average salaries and employment. The main characteristics of the regional disparities in the Czech Republic are demonstrated by the data given in Table 10.2.

The difference between the capital city, Prague, and the other regions, in terms of living standards, shows a strong polarization. In the disadvantaged regions, such as the Vyskovsky region, the GDP per capita declined from 98,2 % of the Czech average in 1995 to 88 % in 1998. This region also has a relatively low number of entrepreneurs out of the total population (13,0 %). It is a typical agricultural area. Another region with a low percentage of entrepreneurs (13,0 %) is North Moravia and Silesia, which also has a high unemployment rate (15,13 %). This region was formerly significant as a leader of heavy industry and black coal mining, but now it has lost this role, due to industrial decline. On the other hand, the highest unemployment rate is in the Usti region (16,15 %). Usti is a typical economically weak or lagging region, where the new environmental measures have had a negative effect on brown coal mining within the region.

Prague is the only region that has experienced a significant growth of GDP in the 1995-98 period (9,4 % growth in 3 years). In Prague, there is the largest number of entrepreneurs in the total population (21 %). The very low unemployment rate in Prague (3,42 %) is related to its relatively higher level of entrepreneurial activity. Furthermore, there are significant differences in the average gross monthly wages between the regions. Wages in Prague (18 865 CZK) are 40 % higher in comparison with the national average (13 484 CZK). The lowest wages are in the agricultural region named Vyskovsky, in south Moravia.

The Czech experience shows that some regions need extensive industrial restructuring, especially the North Bohemia and North Moravia regions. There has been a failure to implement the quick and effective structural changes, which are needed in these regions.

On the other hand, there is a wide variation in infrastructural facilities and human capital between the regions. The districts lying on the north-eastern borders of the Czech Republic, in particular, are lagging behind. There are important differences in the share of university-educated people between the two biggest cities (Prague and Brno) and other regional capitals. Inadequate transport connections, particularly involving the north-eastern regions of Moravia and Silesia, the trans-European motorway and railway systems and the capital city explain the limited interest of foreign investors in this region.

Table 10.2 Regional comparisons in 2000.

REGIONAL COMPARISONS	Unit	Czech Republic	Regions													
			PHA	STC	JHC	PLK	KVK	ULK	LBK	HKK	PAK	VYS	JHM	OLK	ZLK	MSK
Growth GDP 1998/95		98,2	109,4	101,9	96,3	96,9	89,4	96,9	96,3	91,0	90,0	88,0	96,9	93,0	94,7	92,5
Private entrepreneurs in business as per Trades Licensing Act		1 624 445	258474	183855	100025	85595	48786	112625	75048	88456	71714	68069	172150	93692	95604	166353
Entrepreneurs in % of populations	%		21,0	16,5	16,0	15,0	16,0	13,6	17,5	16,0	14,0	13,0	15,0	15,0	16,0	13,0
Area	km²	78 866	496	11 015	10 056	7 561	3 314	5 335	3 163	4 758	4 519	6 925	7 066	5 140	3 964	5 554
Population																
Mid-year population	th. Persons	10 273	1 184	1 113	626	552	305	827	429	551	508	521	1 137	642	598	1 280
Migration increase/decrease	‰	0,6	-1,5	5,9	0,8	0,9	-1,0	0,8	1,3	-0,1	0,7	-0,2	0,7	0,4	0,7	-1,4
Gross domestic product (1999)																
Share of the region in GDP	%	100,0	24,6	9,1	5,5	5,2	2,4	6,6	3,5	4,7	4,2	4,1	10,0	4,9	4,8	10,4
GDP per capita	CZK	190 750	408259	159813	170696	184811	157259	155305	161031	168764	160563	152820	171977	148455	158124	159690
	EUR	5 358	11 468	4 489	4 795	5 191	4 417	4 363	4 523	4 741	4 510	4 293	4 831	4 170	4 442	4 486
Labour																
Average monthly gross wage of employees	CZK	13 484	18 865	13 429	12 551	12 829	12 119	12 646	12 435	12 312	11 917	11 721	12 534	11 892	12 114	12 966
Unemployment rate (31 Dec)	%	8,78	3,42	6,80	5,82	6,47	8,02	16,15	6,44	5,89	7,87	7,48	9,35	11,87	8,14	15,13
Average number of employees	th. Persons	3 120	468	295	191	177	92	234	128	172	153	158	334	182	173	364
Registered job applicants (31 Dec)	Persons	457 369	21 832	38 160	18 498	18 535	13 174	66 572	14 016	16 643	19 896	19 402	54 005	38 092	23 935	94 609
Vacancies (31 Dec)		52 060	4 906	8 241	3 168	3 431	1 542	2 798	3 649	5 031	3 661	2 638	4 396	3 684	1 942	2 973

Source: Czech Statistical Office 2001.

The Role of SMEs in the Czech Economy

SMEs are an important element in the Czech economy. The long history of SMEs, however, shows considerable changes in the role of SMEs in the economic development of the country. In the first half of the last century, small enterprises played a pioneering role both in Czech industry and in Central European industry generally. Hardworking craftsmen and professionals had a high reputation during the first wave of development of newly-founded industrial enterprises. This situation continued before, during and after World War II. Small enterprises showed little change, during this period, either in terms of structural characteristics or in terms of productivity. This period was shaped by demand conditions. In spite of political changes, i.e. nationalization in the 1950s, the character of the market did not change. The supplier driven market dominated, notwithstanding nationalization, the planning system, and the state regulations which provided the legal framework for economic activity. Until the 1960s, economic units consisted of small working groups. To summarize, the organization of production changed only slightly during the first economic wave of the 1955-62 period.

The political changes in the country did however negatively affect economic motivation and the entrepreneurial spirit. The relative increase in economic growth during the first waves of nationalization was followed by economic distress and stagnation. Economists warned about the decreasing labour productivity at that time and this led to the initiative known as the New Economic System (NES) which was set up as a way of increasing the efficiency of the economy. The implementation of the NES, however, was far from successful in accelerating further economic progress.

During this period, industry accepted orchestrated action with enthusiasm, and started to assimilate the flood of new investments. The development took the form of massive large-scale industrialization. This second wave of industrialization was connected with the centralization of industrial capacity in large-scale organizations. The monopoly of large-scale industry was established at that time, which had the main responsibility for supplying goods for the whole state. At this point in time, there existed only about two hundred state enterprises in each industrial branch, such as construction, the chemical industry, the machinery industry etc. The main result of this policy was the disappearance of SMEs as an economic category in the planned economy, while the development of large-scale plants and concentration in certain economic sectors dominated the growth process. This process was partially successful, in its first phase, but the resources of qualified labour were very quickly exhausted, and industry began to suffer from lack of motivation, which later led to the ineffectiveness of industrial activities. The amount of value added per worker was unknown, in a planned economy, but in reality it was very low. Innovations in industrial management decreased to a critical point and the implementation of new products became very difficult. The management of state-owned enterprises was not interested in taking new steps towards innovative action. As a result, the planned economy faced the necessity of initiating several changes and establishing a new economic milieu.

The new wave of SME development began in 1989. The economic system changed from a planned to a pluralistic market-driven economy. This change was accompanied by the reinvention of SMEs as microeconomic entities, after the dismantling of the state-owned industry. However, the growth of SMEs seems to be still in progress. In 2000, the self-employed constituted the largest proportion of SMEs, that is 76 % of the total number of small and medium-sized firms. The share of SMEs in GDP reached 40,2 % in 2000. The highest shares belonged firstly to *wholesale and retail* trade (35,9 % of GDP) and secondly to *services* (19,26 % of GDP).

As indicated in Table 10.3, there are visible differences in output per employee between small (0-249 employees) and large (more than 250 employees) businesses, ranging between 1552,6 t. CZK in large enterprises and 1186,0 t. CZK in small firms. This situation means that the larger firms are 31 % more productive than the SMEs. However, the difference in labour costs per employee is smaller. The average wages are only 22 % higher in large enterprises. The picture changes completely if we look at the need for fixed capital in order to create one job. In small enterprises, there is a need for 92,7 thousand CZK (that is about 2 897 thousand EUR) in order to generate one job, whereas large enterprises have to invest more than twice that amount (199,3 thousand CZK, that is 6 228 thousand EUR), which amounts to a more than 215 % larger fixed capital need than smaller firms.

Table 10.3 Structure and economic power of businesses in industry (1999).

	Total	Businesses 0-249 employees	Businesses 250 + employees
Number of active businesses	7623 42	760892	1450
Number of employees in th.	3084	1834	1250
Output per employee (thousand CZK)	1334, 6	1186,0	1552,6
Value added per employee (thousand CZK)	435,4	385,1	509,2
Labour costs per employee (thousand CZK)	157,4	144,7	176,1
Investment per employee (thousand CZK)	135,9	92,7	199,3

Source: Czech Statistical Office 2001.

The comparison of value added per employee and labour cost per unit of output, given in Table 10.4, shows that there are no significant differences between small and large enterprises, but there are considerable differences in the need for investment in order to create industrial output. Small businesses are less capital-intensive (0,08) than larger ones (0,13).

What do all these figures mean? Firstly, large businesses are more productive, have higher value added per employee, and also higher wage levels. Besides, the difference in productivity is higher than the difference in wages, which identifies a possible profitability gap between large and small firms. Similarly, there are massive differences in investment equipment per employee. A large enterprise needs more than 2,1 times more investment assets than a small one. These figures indicate that the advantage of large firms, in terms of productivity, is the result of the use of more advanced equipment in the work place. Table 10.4 assures us that economic outputs per unit are relatively well-balanced and there is no substantial difference between small and large enterprises. Nevertheless, there are also other assets and advantages which small enterprises possess, such as flexibility and the ability to adapt to volatility in the market, etc.

Table 10.4 The comparison of small and large enterprises according to performance indicators.

Indexes	Value added per unit of output	Labour costs per unit of output	Investment per unit of output
Total units	0,33	0,12	0,10
Businesses 0-249 employees	0,32	0,12	0,08
Businesses 250 + employees	0,33	0,11	0,13

Another category of enterprises, which is very important in the Czech Republic, is the self-employed. The number of self-employed per 1000 inhabitants ranges between 111 and 228 across the different regions, while the EU average only amounts to 43 employees per 1000 inhabitants. The high number of self-employed can be explained by the possibility to work for oneself while still being employed in a company. Statistics relating to this type of work are not available, but estimations indicate that half of the self-employed are also employees.

The Sectoral Distribution of SMEs and Development in the Czech Republic

There are considerable differences between economic sectors, in terms of the share of value added in total production. Table 10.5 shows differences in terms of the share of value added in the total value added generated by SMEs among the main sectors of the economy (Rathauska, 2002). The highest value added within production was created in the *Restaurants and trade* sector and the second highest was in *Market services*. The lowest ratio belongs to the *Construction* sector.

Table 10.5 Comparison of sectors.

SMEs in (year 2000)	SMEs total production (million CZK)	SMEs total value added (million CZK)	Share of value added on production (%)
Industry	739 877	202 278	27,3
Non-financial institutions and households	2 202 402	645 052	29,3
Construction	316 688	66 479	21,0
Agriculture, forestry and fishing	120 426	36 527	30,3
Restaurants and trade	356 839	179 387	37,2
Transport, storage and communications	163 669	28 109	17,2
Market services	379 216	132 272	34,9

Table 10.6 The shares of SMEs in total production and value added.

SMEs in (year 2000)	Share of SMEs on total production	Share of SMEs on total value added	Relative differences
Industry	34,2	34,7	0,5
Non-financial institutions and households	54,2	53,7	-0,5
Construction	74,8	77,4	2,6
Agriculture, forestry and fishing	83,4	81,6	-1,8
Restaurants and trade	88,3	85,3	-3
Transport, storage and communications	46,2	23,9	-22,3
Market services	87,8	82,4	-5,4

Source: Czech Statistical Office 2001.

More importantly, the shares of SMEs in different economic sectors also display considerable variation (Table 10.6). The largest share of SMEs in total production is in the *Restaurants and trade* sector and the lowest in *Industry*. Besides, the difference between the share of SMEs in total production and value added becomes quite considerable in different sectors. For example, in the *Transport, storage and communications* sector there is a gap between the share of production (46,2 %) and value added (23,9 %). This means that this sector is not able to create sufficient value added and is not competitive enough.

According to the shares given in Table 11.6, it can be seen that SMEs in construction are the most competitive.

If we compare the value added of production in particular sectors, over a six-year time period, it is possible to observe the declining trend in all the sectors (Table 10.7). The reason for this situation is that the value added growth index for the 1995/2000 period was 1,38 while the intermediate consumption growth index reached 1,72 in the same period (Rathouska, 2002).

Table 10.7 Value added share on production (%) - time series 1995 to 2000.

SMEs in 1995-2000	1995	1996	1997	1998	1999	2000
Industry	30,7	29,4	26,7	26,6	27,8	27,3
Non-financial institutions and households	35,4	34,9	28,7	30	29,4	29,3
Construction	30,5	27,8	24,9	23,4	22,3	21
Agriculture, forestry and fishing	38,5	35,8	27,2	30,2	29,8	30,3
Restaurants and trade	43,5	42,8	35,3	38,5	37,6	37,2
Transport, storage and communications	22,1	24,5	18,9	17,9	16,7	17,2
Market services	40	42,2	31,5	36,2	34,1	34,9

Source: Rathouska, 2002.

Further information is given in Table 10.8. There is need to pay more attention to the indicator 'the share of value added in investment' since investment has a multiplier effect on production. One unit of investment creates more than seven units of value added in the construction sector. The main reason is that *Construction* has a high share of value added in production and at the same time it has the highest increase in the price index for the 1995-2000 period (about 10 %). Other sectors have lower price index growth and need higher investment input. The general trend in the Czech Republic's economic development explains the changes in the share of value added in investment during the 1995-2000 period, which are given in Table 10.8. Figure 10.2 presents the index of GDP per capita during the 1995-2001 period and predictions for the 2002-04 period. This figure shows the recession which occurred between 1996-98, which was due to the fast growth of domestic consumption, a high import deficit, and the relatively low productivity growth in the industry and services sectors. This pattern of growth in GDP is reflected in the growth of the sectors described in Table 10.7 and Table 10.8.

Table 10.8 Value added share in investment (%) 1995-2000.

SMEs in 1995-2000	1995	1996	1997	1998	1999	2000
Industry	3,36	3,80	3,02	3,51	2,65	3,77
Non-financial institutions and households	3,79	3,62	2,72	3,37	3,04	3,65
Construction	7,32	8,50	6,21	7,43	7,42	7,64
Agriculture, forestry and fishing	2,48	2,12	1,19	2,02	2,18	2,44
Restaurants and trade	4,08	4,09	2,61	3,70	3,84	4,80
Transport, storage and communications	2,98	3,10	2,13	2,92	2,31	2,17
Market services	3,77	2,80	2,22	2,69	2,55	2,69

Source: Rathouska, 2002.

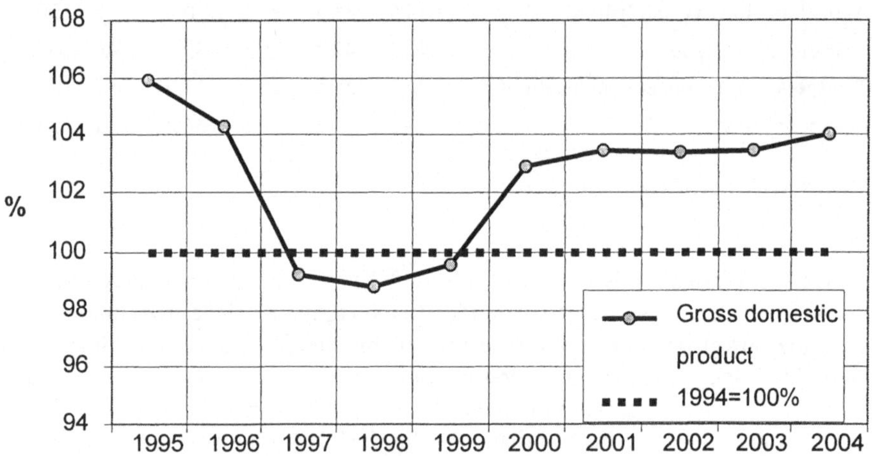

Figure 10.2 Real growth of GDP in transition period of CR.

Measures Supporting SMEs for Regional Development

Although SMEs are flexible in their production organization, they are confined to certain localities, due to the immobility of their main resources. Individuals linked to SMEs are connected to their place of residence, housing, etc. That is why large enterprises prefer to locate their factories according to a range of regional conditions, but small enterprises are more dependent on business opportunities in their region. The transaction costs are relatively high for small firms. These constraints mean that regions without an attractive environment for business have to create acceptable conditions for small businesses, if they are looking for sustainable development (Fingleton, 2001).

In the near future, due to their proximity to the developed countries of the European Union, the Czech regions are expected to get an influx of capital and know-how, which will aim to utilize the available qualified labour force. Also, after accession to the European Union, new opportunities in the unified market may have a positive impact on several regions, and the financial support which will be provided by European Union programs may lead to the acceleration of the restructuring process in industry and agriculture. A prerequisite for these growth scenarios is the incorporation of SMEs into the restructuring process, as one of the major sources of innovation, although many of the changes so far have been focused on large-scale industry. There are several points that the new policies need to take into account. Firstly, industrial centers, functioning as development poles, are important in the creation of seedbeds for SMEs. Secondly, the trans-border cooperation of local manufacturing industry, agriculture and tourism in border regions is vital in acquiring the structural funds of the European Union. Thirdly, the existing government policies intended to support SMEs in the Czech Republic should be used more effectively. The Ministry of Industry and Trade sets up special programs every year for the support of SMEs. If they are to make use of the existing incentives, SMEs are expected to fulfil several conditions, such as that they must employ less than 250 employees, annual sales must not exceed 250 million CZK (7 million EUR), and they must be independent units (no more than 25 % of capital may owned by a company which is not an SME. There are also programs financed by the state budget; and assistance is provided in certain fields, such as facilitating access to financial sources (the programmes *Guarantee, Credit, Market*, etc.), employment support (the programme *Special*), reinforcing their position in the market and improving competitive advantage (*Cooperation, Design, Consultancy*, etc.), regional programmes (*Region, Regeneration, Village, Mobile Salesroom*, etc.), and so on. Also, banking and financial schemes exist for the support of SMEs. The *Small Loan Program* is a financial subsidy for the financing of development projects. The range of this loan is from 0,3-1 million CZK, the maturity is 4 years, and the interest rate is the prime rate plus 1 %. On the other hand, the industry program that has been announced by the Ministry of Industry supports subprogrammes called *Transfer* and *Quality*. The aim of this programme is to introduce new technologies and products, which are expected to initiate R&D activities, in collaboration with domestic universities, or using external suppliers. The *Transfer* programme pays up to 50 % of the accepted proposals to a maximum of 3,5 million CZK on projects (1 million EUR). The aim of *Quality* is to support projects which specialize in information technology (IT) development and information control systems, test systems, methodology and diagnostics. *Quality* pays up to 50 % of the approved proposals to a maximum of 200 000 million CZK on projects (7 000 EUR).

There are 29 *Regional Advisory and Information Centres* (RPICs) and 5 *Business Innovation Centres* (BICs) in the Czech Republic, for the purpose of supporting the innovative capacities of firms. RPICs mostly provide advisory services for entrepreneurs, such as help in establishing new companies, assistance in making business plans, mediating bank credits, creating new jobs, providing information about support programs available in their region, organizing educational seminars for entrepreneurs, etc. *Business Innovation Centres* (BICs) are focused especially on supporting innovative businesses, the transfer of technologies from abroad, the implementation of R & D outcomes, and making use of the possibilities provided by the European network of business and innovation centres, in addition to basic advisory services. Their special task is to provide support for companies placed in so-called business incubators. The standard services provided by RPICs and BICs are introductory consultation, business advisory services, subsidies for innovative firms in *incubator centers*, as well as the training of entrepreneurs. The amount that was allocated from the state budget for the support of SMEs was quite low, approximately 1 million EUR, and obviously such a low level of financial help cannot do much to promote SMEs. At the regional level, municipal authorities do not have any resources to promote SMEs in their region, due to financial conditions.

The support system designed for SMEs in the Czech Republic seems well defined, well advised and well coordinated. Low financial resources, however, are the main obstacle to the realization of its intended purpose. Obviously, the development of the regions has to be seen as a result of increasing market relations and not necessarily of the state's economic policy. In this process, SMEs play an important role in regulating the market consisting of large enterprises, especially in the service sectors and in innovative production activities. Nevertheless, SMEs have to act very carefully. One large mistake or wrong decision might be a serious threat to them. Therefore, the management of small enterprises have to behave more carefully than large enterprises.

Therefore it is necessary to develop more effective methods of helping small businesses. A small enterprise is influenced not only by the local economic conditions, but also by external forces. The impact of national macro-economic conditions is usually unavoidable. In Figure 11.3, there is a schematic example of the development of an enterprise within the framework of local conditions.

Obstacles to Further Development of SMEs in the Czech Republic

The economic environment in the Czech Republic is characterised by an improving, but still imperfect, legal framework, continuing privatization, and insufficient adaptability to world market conditions. In recent years, the national economy has suffered from the lack of domestic capital, low levels of investment in industry and the general decrease of fixed capital investment rate.

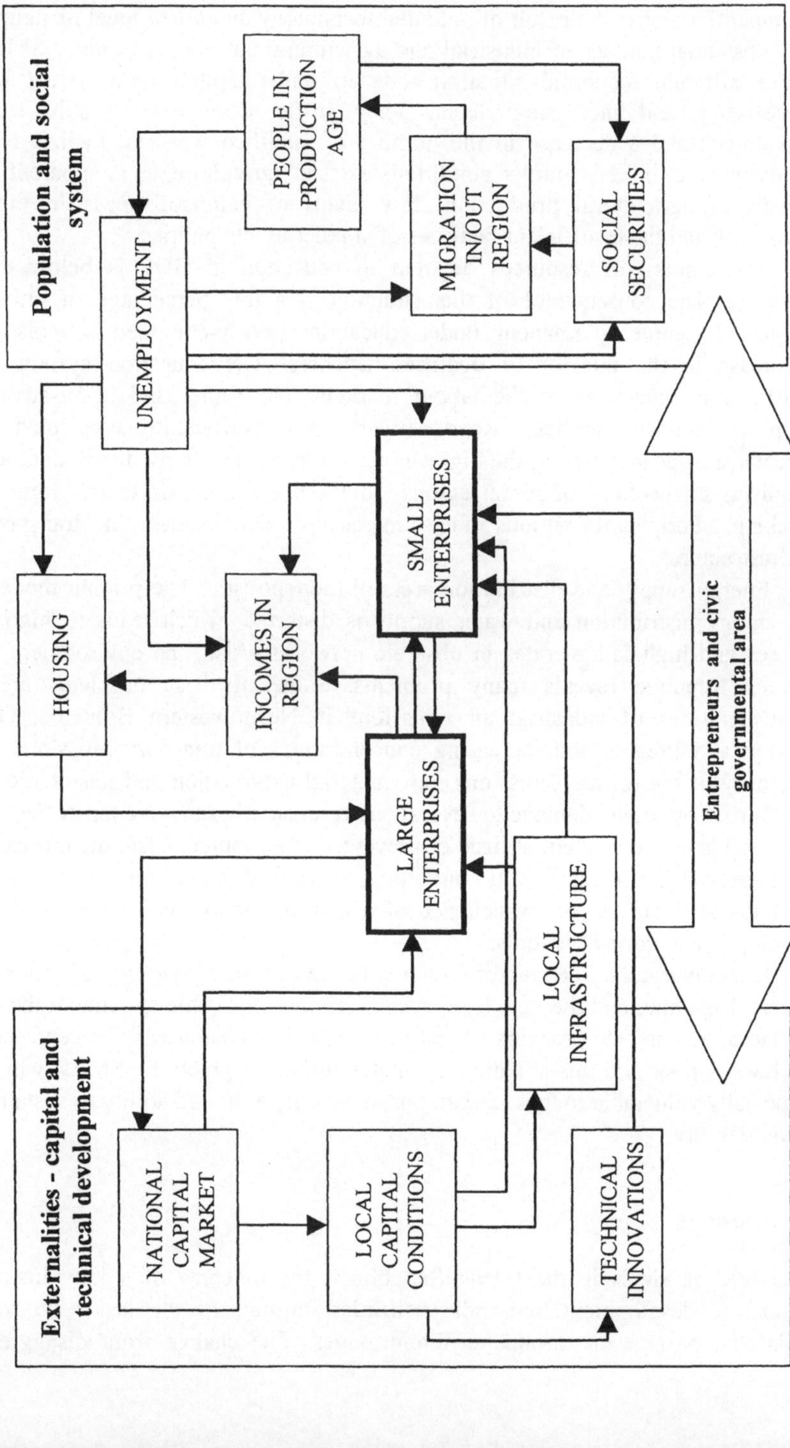

Figure 10.3 Scheme of Dynamic Development model of regional growth (main elements).

In general, economic potential is relatively limited. The low level of competitiveness is the result of outdated technology and a low level of innovation. A substantial number of industrial and agricultural enterprises (mainly SMEs) are in a difficult economic situation, due to under-capitalization, latent or real insolvency and increasing debts. They suffer from unfavourable technical conditions and a decrease in the number of qualified workers. In-firm research activities are limited. Similar conditions exist in agriculture, as is apparent in low levels of agricultural production, low levels of competitiveness in the rural economy and the insufficient facilities of smaller municipalities.

The amount of resources devoted to education in GDP is below the EU average. The consequence of this situation is a low percentage of university-educated people, permanent under-education, poorly-equipped schools and a decrease in the number of qualified teachers. The education system is not sufficiently connected to the labour markets. The same kind of disadvantages appears in utility services. Road networks are insufficiently connected to the greater European network, the highway networks are unevenly distributed, and the highway connections of some regions (southern Bohemia, northern Moravia) are lacking. Peripheral regions face increasing deficiencies in transportation infrastructure.

Energy supply and distribution are still monopolistic. The pricing model used in energy distribution and water supply is distorted, which leads to high water losses and high failure rates in obsolete networks. Also, the environment in the Czech Republic reveals many problems. Some of these problems are high concentrations of industrial air emissions in North-western Bohemia, Ostrava region and Prague, and increasing concentrations of transport emissions in the majority of big towns. Emissions, raw material exploitation and unsuitable forms of tourism are doing damage to several environmentally sensitive territories. Waste disposal is not controlled, utilized or prevented at its source. Also, the utilization of non-renewable sources is still continuing, as well as a preference for 'pipe-end' technologies, etc., as a consequence of a lack of, or low efficiency of, suitable economic and normative tools.

In summary, the free market economy has been running for only 10 years in the Czech Republic, and the new legal system has not been able to remove the habits of the past. The entrepreneurs do not respect business standards. The enforcement of laws is poor and this situation facilitates dishonest practices. SMEs, which are especially vulnerable to these conditions, have only a limited ability to sustain their own viability.

Conclusions

The role of SMEs in the Czech Republic is the outcome of a long history of economic development and industrialization throughout the last century. The industrial basis went through different stages. The change from disaggregated small-scale manufacturing to relatively concentrated industry, on a private basis, which was the experience of the first half of the last century, was followed by the concentration of state-owned enterprises in the planned economy. The deregulation and privatization of the last decade, however, led to the revitalization of entrepreneurship and the creation of many small or middle-sized enterprises. The market driven economy promptly highlighted enterprises' weak and strong points and the regional context of entrepreneurship became an important indicator of economic performance.

SMEs are important segments of the economic landscape of the Czech Republic, since half of economic production is attributable to SMEs (52,85 %). The main concentration areas of SMEs are *Agriculture, forestry and fishing, Restaurants and trade*, *Market services*, and *Construction*, in which sectors the share of small and medium-sized firms in total production is higher than 80 %. However, the share of SMEs in total manufacturing production is only 35.25 %, according to 2000 figures. This outcome, and several of the problems in manufacturing, are the result of the policies followed in the *planned economy*. The main problems are low economic efficiency, suppression of interest in innovation and technical progress, low productivity, high percentage of wages in the value of production, etc.

Currently, the incentives to growth have been oriented not only to large-scale industry, services and other segments of the economy, but also to small and middle-sized enterprises. The support provided for the factors promoting development has led to the rediscovery of SMEs as an important instrument of economic progress (Beran, 2001). The ability of SMEs to operate within the new global economy is more limited, since globally operating enterprises have a greater ability to succeed in the global market and to deal with economic problems. However, there is a need to balance business opportunities between *large* and *small or medium-sized* enterprises, in order to initiate and sustain regional development. It should not be forgotten that SMEs are important not only for their role in economic growth, but also for their contribution to the strengthening of social cohesion.

In spite of the lower value added per worker created by SMEs, the welfare attributes of small entrepreneurship make SMEs important for local and regional development. From the economic point of view, large public enterprises may have a comparative advantage compared with small ones, since they can support the unemployed and the socially handicapped, but SMEs are able to substitute for several public social services in the regions (Eraydın, 2001). That is why SME support schemes are cheaper than direct payments of social services and unemployment benefits by governments. SMEs are crucial in the development of the regions. The investment requirements of SMEs are only half as demanding as the investment requirements of large-scale enterprises. Apart from this aspect of SMEs, they are more flexible and have an ability to create changes and innovations. That is why SMEs are the subject of attention, not only in the Czech Republic, but also in the European Union.

References

Behrens, A. (2002), 'Regional gross domestic product in candidate countries 1999', www.europa.eu.int/comm/eurostat/.

Beran, V. (2000), *Development Strategies II: Regions and Municipalities*, CTU Prague.

Beran, V. (2001), *Management of sustainable live cycle development of regions and their buildings structures*, CTU Prague.

Czech Statistical Office (2001), *Small and Medium Sized Enterprises in Industry*, Czech Statistical Office, Prague.

Eraydın, A. (2001), 'Regional development in Turkey: Development factors', *Cost A17 Workshop*, Ankara.

Fingleton, B. (*2001*), 'Implementation of production functions for regional analysis', *Cost A17 Workshop*, Ankara.

Frkova, J. (*1999), The Individual Enterprise*, CTU Prague.

Pasanen, J. (2002), 'The GDP of the candidate countries', www.europa.eu.int/comm/eurostat/.

Rathouska, B. (2002), *Selected economic results of small and medium-sized enterprises in the CR in 1995-2000*, Czech Statistical Office.

Schumacher, E.F. (1999), *Small is Beautiful: Economics as if People Mattered: 25 Years Later*, Hartley & Marks Publishers Inc.

PART III: CASE STUDIES ON SMEs AND REGIONAL DEVELOPMENT

Chapter 11

The Changing Role of SMEs in the Regional Growth Process: The Case of Denizli

Bilge Armatlı Köroğlu and Burak Beyhan

Introduction

In recent debates, SMEs have been defined as the leading agents of economic growth. The traditional model of growth based on state intervention and the external transfer of capital and knowledge has been increasingly challenged by the endogenous growth approach based on the decisive role and capacity of small and medium-sized enterprises. The analysis of the evolution of local economic systems reveals that the role of SMEs in economic growth is subject to transformation in the face of changing global conditions. This transformation is such that SMEs have employed different adoption mechanisms, by which they have not only sustained their livelihood but also challenged the substantive economy of their respective territories as a result of competing with their global rivals.

In this context, the aim of this Chapter is to unveil the changing role of SMEs in local economic growth, with special reference to the case of Denizli, which has experienced remarkable economic development in the last two decades. As has been pointed out above, one of the major distinctions between the old and the new group of approaches and theories is the increasing importance assigned to SMEs. Among the new theories and approaches, the industrial district approach has a leading role, because of its ability to explain the nature of complex relationships among SMEs. In industrial district debates, SMEs have been defined as the main agents of economic growth due to their role in employment generation and flexible production relations. In recent studies pertaining to this approach, the relationship between SMEs and economic growth are analysed in relation to collaborative relations, sectoral specialization, cultural characteristics and attributes of knowledge.

In the last two decades, Turkey has witnessed the emergence of new industrial growth nodes in which SMEs have played vital roles in fostering local economic growth. Before the 1980s, regional economic growth had mainly depended on the state's income redistribution and welfare policies. During this inward-oriented policies era a few metropolitan regions dominated Turkey's industrial production. However, after 1980, it became difficult to sustain interventionist state policies within the context of globalization processes and state-led development strategies were replaced by market-directed and export-oriented policies. In this context, some less developed areas have exhibited rapid increases in manufacturing activities, showing the potential of areas outside the major industrial metropolises (İstanbul, Ankara, İzmir and Bursa). There are many industrial districts, the so-called 'Anatolian Tigers', which are located in different parts of Turkey: Denizli in the Eagean region, Çorum, Konya and Kayseri in central Anatolia, and Gaziantep and Kahramanmaraş in south-east Anatolia (see Figure 11.1). They have some important common characteristics: a rapid increase both in the number of firms and employees in manufacturing industry, the domination of small firms and their network relations and a specialization in labour intensive sectors. In particular, textiles and clothing have developed as the leading sectors of growth and have become the most important export sectors in these districts (Eraydın, 2002). Most notably, Denizli has a strong reputation for its remarkable success in textile production and exports.

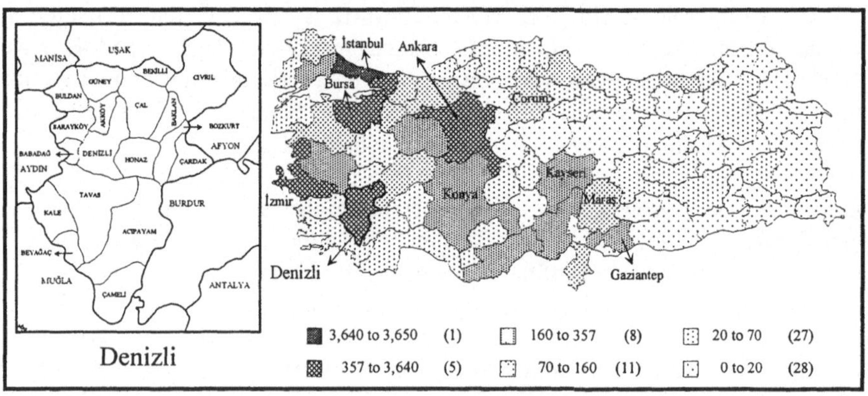

Figure 11.1 Number of establishments in manufacturing by the provinces in Turkey and districts of Denizli with strong tradition in textile industry, 1999.

Source: Unpublished manufacturing statistics, State Institute of Statistics (SIS).

Note: The shaded areas on the map, located on the left-hand side of the figure, show the districts, among which the darker ones have a strong tradition of textile production.

This Chapter assesses the experience of Denizli, which has achieved remarkable economic growth in the last two decades. What is observed in Denizli is a continuous growth process, in which SMEs have played quite important roles in the growth of the textile industry and the transformation of Denizli as a whole. What is striking about the economic growth of Denizli is that, at the beginning of the 1970s, it was a backward region of Turkey, with little anticipation that it would become a focal point for growth. The unprecedented economic growth of Denizli owes much to its specialization in textile production, through which it has been articulated into the global production networks and markets since the early 1980s. With the impetus created by the demand in international markets for the products (especially textile products) of Denizli, between 1980 and 1996, Denizli's share of the total number of firms in Turkey increased from 1.34 per cent to 2.32 per cent. During the same period, Denizli's share of the number of employees increased from 0.93 per cent to 1.60 per cent (Eraydın, 2002). Moreover, SMEs are an important component of the industrial structure of Denizli, accounting for around 90 per cent of all establishments during the period between 1992 and 1997. However, within the same period, the share of SMEs with respect to the number of employees increased from 45.91 to 50.40 per cent (Table 11.1). Also, below the level of SMEs, in 1992 there were 4869 micro firms employing less than 10 workers each.

What follows is a historical analysis of this economic growth, with a special emphasis on the contexts within which conditions of economic growth reveal themselves. For this purpose, the remaining part of the Chapter is arranged into four main subheadings that discuss the transformation of the role of SMEs in the economic growth process. The first two parts summarize the roots of economic growth and the role of SMEs in this process, from the early years of the Turkish Republic to the 1980s. The third part focuses on the peaceful relations between small and large firms, in order to integrate with the global production networks in the 1980s. In the fourth part, the textile boom of the 1990s is analysed as a transformative pressure on the textile production organization and institutional structure. Finally, after revealing the basic characteristics of the transforming nature of the role of SMEs in the growth process, the concluding section remarks on some of the issues concerning the future economic growth of Denizli.

Building the Tradition of Collective Action and the Promotion of Local Clustering in Denizli

Success stories are not built on a tabula rasa. A rich institutional and historical background can be observed in nearly all of the successful industrial districts (see, for example the watch industry of the Swiss Jura Arc (Glasmeier, 1991; Maillat, et al., 1995), the machinery industry of Jæren in Norway (Hassink, 1997), the electronics and computer industry of Silicon Valley in USA (Saxenian, 1985 and 1991)). Parallel to this, it comes as no surprise that artisanal textile (fabric) production in Denizli has a strong tradition. It can even be traced back to the Greco-Roman period (Mutluer, 1995; Batmaz and Özcan, 1998). Towards the end of the Ottoman period, and during the early Republican period, there were some production units operating in a capitalist way, but the artisanal form of (textile) production was still dominant in Denizli (Pınarcıoğlu, 2000; Erendil, 1998). In especially mountainous regions of the province, where the land is not suitable for agricultural production, for many centuries the economy was inevitably restricted to artisanal textile production. According to the first industrial census, conducted in 1927, there were 1581 establishments in all the sectors in Denizli (Mutluer, 1995). The number of establishments operating in the textile sector was 423 (Erendil, 1998; Pamuk, 1998).

In less developed regions, the transition from the artisanal form and traditional sectors of production to the modern form and sectors of production required a strong impetus, created by either the public or the private sector. The roles played by public enterprises in the Mezzogiorno of Italy and in the steel industry of France illustrate this trend (Dunford, 1988). Not only state holding companies, but also large MNCs and state-supported firms, provide small and medium-sized entrepreneurs with the transformative pressure to upgrade their technological level. The role played by Toyota in the Chukyo region of Japan (Edgington, 1999), and state-owned or supported semiconductor companies in the Malaysian state of Penang (Doner and Hershberg, 1999), and in Hsinchu Science City of Taiwan (Lin, 1997), illustrate this second trend. In the early years of the Republican Period, the opportunities available for such a transition and transformation in Denizli were very limited. During the 1930s, the state opened four cotton yarn factories but none of them was located in Denizli (Pınarcıoğlu, 2000).

At first glance, the fact that Denizli did not receive important public investments directed towards industrial production might be considered as a negative factor for the economic development of the province. But, as Şengün (1998) argues, in the 1930s and 1940s this situation, giving rise to cooperatives, helped the formation of an entrepreneurial spirit and economic growth in Denizli. Indeed, from 1930s onwards, many small textile producers in Denizli had established cooperatives, with the backing of the state, in order to protect themselves from the tradesmen who controlled the textile production. At the end of 1930s, there were 5 textile cooperatives in Denizli (Mutluer, 1995). During the II.World War, the number of textile cooperatives in the centre of the province increased to 16, because Sümerbank[1], which was given the responsibility of preventing the black market conditions in cotton yarn provision caused by the war, employed the cooperatives for the distribution of cotton yarn (Erendil, 1998). With the help of the cooperatives, small textile producers in Denizli began to learn collective responsibility and develop a tradition of mutual trust and support, which has played an important role in the growth of Denizli (Eraydın, 2002; Erendil, 1998).

The collaboration between Sümerbank and the cooperatives had also been extended to the development of local clustering. Indeed, the contribution of public enterprises to the development of local clustering is very important. Although, in the early years, these initiatives are important for the formation of local clustering, in the subsequent years they tend to create some drawbacks, too. What was observed in Denizli illustrates this trend. After the World War II, the state decided to open five new cotton yarn factories. In 1953, one of these factories was established in Denizli province center (Mutluer, 1995). During the 1950s and early 1960s, small textile producers in Denizli benefited very much from this factory. But, in 1964, the factory established by Sümerbank began to produce fabric and initiated printing and dyeing operations (Erendil, 1998), and, as a result, small textile producers in Denizli, compared with the other districts that specialized in the textile production, were no longer able to get cotton yarn as cheaply and easily as before (Eraydın, 2002). Although, in the late 1960s, this hindered the operations of many small textile producers in Denizli (Eraydın, 2002), subsequently, in the 1970s, a few private sector firms started to establish new cotton yarn factories and also provide small firms with modern cotton yarn treatment (Pınarcıoğlu, 2000).

In the early 1960s, electricity also began to be used in Denizli province center. This led to the first great technological transformation in the textile industry of Denizli: a lot of electrically-driven looms were bought from Bursa and Adana (Erendil, 1998; Pamuk, 1998). Together with the existence of the Sümerbank factory, this paved the way for the development of Denizli province center as the center of textile production in the province. As a result, Denizli has attracted people from its textile districts, especially Babadağ. During the 1960s many small but modern textile firms were established in Denizli province center (Pınarcıoğlu, 2000). Even local producers started to produce their own electrically-driven looms. Not only small but also factory-sized establishments emerged during this period, thanks to the possibility of increasing production, due to the widespread use of electricity, and the existence of strong family ties (Erendil, 1998, p. 182). According to the industrial census conducted in Denizli in 1964, there were 626 wage workers, employed by 13 private textile firms (Pınarcıoğlu, 2000). These relatively large firms were the first attempts at capital accumulation by the members who could establish their own family firms in the following years (Erendil, 1998). During this period, in Denizli, the relationship between producers was very dense. As the textile industry was relocated and concentrated in the province center, trade also became very important and attractive for the textile producers.

Denizli as a Growing Node

During the 1970s, Denizli experienced remarkable progress with regard to investments, which was triggered by two important factors. Firstly, in 1973, Denizli was designated as a province having priority for development (Mutluer, 1995). This has been a policy of the state to support industrial development in the lagging regions of the country since the 1970s[2]. As Eraydın (2002) argues, the inclusion of Denizli among the first priority regions was primarily aimed at the elimination of the problems associated with the extension of the cotton yarn production of Denizli Sümerbank factory into the fabric production and printing-dyeing operations. The second important factor in the economic development of Denizli in the 1970s, was the external transfer of capital by local people. Investments realized by the Turkish emigrants working abroad (especially in Germany) were crucial for Denizli (Eraydın, 2002; Pınarcıoğlu, 1998 and 2000)[3]. During the period between 1971 and 1982, approximately 20 firms were established in Denizli as multi-partner workers' enterprises[4]. Although only a limited number of these firms operated in the textile sector, and most of them were unsuccessful (Erendil, 1998; Mutluer, 1995), the experience accumulated through these investments helped the transfer of technical know-how from abroad to Turkey and created an atmosphere of local entrepreneurship (Pınarcıoğlu, 1998 and 2000)[5].

Taken together with the family groups who had accumulated capital in the previous periods, the factors mentioned above gave rise to the emergence of new firms, in quite different sectors, ranging from electronics to the textile and food industries. It can be argued that, in this period, Denizli experienced relative sectoral diversity. Between 1971 and 1979, the number of firms operating in Denizli and employing more than 10 workers increased from 34 to 95 (Erendil, 1998). But only 21 of firms employing 2,500 workers operated in the textile industry (Pınarcıoğlu, 2000; Pamuk, 1998). As Pınarcıoğlu (2000) argues, and as is also evident from the studies of Mutluer (1995), Pamuk (1998) and Erendil (1998), among the newly established textile firms three were of crucial importance for the economic development of Denizli. These firms can be considered as mounting a challenge to Sümerbank, which, during the 1950s and the early 1960s, had dominated the cotton yarn provision and treatment of the province. Two of these firms, the one established in 1975 by the Turkish emigrants working abroad, and the other one established in 1977 by a family from Babadağ, were producing cotton yarn. The third one, Denizli Dyeing and Printing Factory, founded by 174 partners (including both textile producers and tradesmen), was the first big private establishment providing the small textile producers with modern cotton yarn treatment, dyeing and printing facilities.

One of the most important characteristics of Denizli, which was sustained up to the 1980s, and should be emphasized in relation to economic growth and SMEs, is the homogeneous identity that it possessed (Eraydın, 2002; Erendil, 1998). Compared with the other provinces of Turkey, until recently, Denizli did not receive important migration from other parts of the country. In the 1970s, 93 per cent of the population was born in the province center. Until the 1980s, Denizli was able to attract people only from its own hinterland (especially Babadağ), to which, as Işık and Pınarcıoğlu (1996) argue, Denizli owes much of its social cohesion and economic growth. The textile producers who migrated to the province center from Babadağ helped the creation of an atmosphere of local collaboration. In other words, the homogeneous population of Denizli – homogeneous in terms of ethnicity – also reflects 'the homogeneous structure of textile producers in Denizli', which played a crucial role in the growth of Denizli as an important node of textile production, both in Turkey and in international markets.

The Integration to Global Production Networks

In the beginning of the 1980s, Turkey started to implement export-oriented development policies. The central government provided new incentives and institutional supports for foreign trade. As a consequence of these policies, in 1986, Turkey became one of the most important textile exporting countries, and small firms became the agents of this integration process. During this period, 'the export-oriented policies have created the favourable conditions for the rapid transformation in the textile sector and export activities in Denizli' (Erendil, 1998, p. 189).

In Denizli, a few textile producers, who had strengthened their position in terms of capital accumulation and marketing relations in the previous period, entered into the export markets (Erendil, 1998). In this process, trade firms, operating in İstanbul and aiming at fulfilling the subcontracting requests of western enterprises (particularly in textiles), played quite important roles (Işık and Pınarcıoğlu, 1996). During this period, some enterprises attended foreign fairs with their samples, among which there was sufficient demand for towels in export markets (Pınarcıoğlu, 2000)[6]. In the foreign fairs, enterprises perceived the demand for bathrobes and updated their production organization accordingly. The relatively higher value of bathrobes gave an opportunity to some firms to set up new units and to transform themselves into relatively large-scale firms in time.

These relatively large firms, which played a leading role, have been important in generating growth motivation and in the internationalization process, and have become the initiators of local transformation and specialization in towel and bathrobe production (Pınarcıoğlu, 1998). These firms, which had founded subcontracting relations with western enterprises in the textile industries, drew many medium-sized firms into the export-oriented production field (Pınarcıoğlu, 1998). This interactive environment has attracted a large number of small firms and led them to benefit from the opportunities provided by the town. Therefore, it has also been noted by Erendil (1998) that the major facilitator of this process can be defined as 'following successful examples'. According to the literature on Denizli, the total production capacity of export firms was not enough to meet the demands of export markets, and, most of the time, the labour-intensive stages of production have been subcontracted to small firms.

The leading firms of Denizli, producing for the global markets, were forced to improve their technology and quality to adapt to international production standards. Consequently, Denizli has upgraded its production technology in a step-by-step fashion, from large firms to small ones. Some leading 'firms started to invest in machinery, especially the second-hand machinery from Italy and started to export basically home furnishing products (bed sheets and other fabrics) to

Middle-Eastern countries and EU countries' (Erendil, 1998, p. 192). Small firms were also able to upgrade to the minimum level of technology required for the export markets through, again, the second-hand market that has been created by the local large and medium-sized firms, that either renewed their stock of machinery or enlarged their production capacities (Eraydın, 2001). This upgrading process has resulted in a local technological configuration such that the levels of technology employed in large and small firms were more or less complementary or similar to each other, which played a very important role in the establishment of the subcontracting relationships between large and small firms (Kazdağlı, 1998; Aslanoğlu, 1998).

In this transformation process, the cooperation which was established among the small and medium-sized firms, has been the driving force behind the rapid growth in Denizli. Cooperation was built upon both the formal relations and the informal relations, such as friendship, kinship and membership of the same town. Being from the same area, or being from the same family, has always been very important in the establishment and the growth of firms (Eraydın, 2002), especially among the textile producers born in Babadağ. The partnerships and mutual aids in the form of provision of information and capital were very dense among the producers from Babadağ (Erendil, 1998). In addition, within the context of relationships between compatriots, they have helped each other in the export markets.

In this respect, a general strategy that was widely used by the textile producers in Denizli, during the 1980s, has been the establishment of partnerships on a temporal basis. Partnerships have been formed both between members of the same family and the same town, due to similar backgrounds and trust-based relations, formed in Denizli in previous periods (Eraydın, 2001). On the other hand, the 1980s could be considered as the initial stage of the process of integration into global production networks. In this process, the relations between small and large firms were generally constructed through sub-contracting relations, which depended on the collaborative tradition in textiles and the relatively homogeneous local environment. These egalitarian subcontracting relations among small and large firms have been lost, in the later stages of growth, and the role of SMEs in the growth process has transformed Denizli.

The Consequences of the Export Boom: The Decline of Cooperative Relations

By the end of the 1980s, Denizli had increased its exports, but the boom came in the first half of the 1990s, with the help of local opportunities and state incentives in the textile sector. During the period of the export boom, catching up with international standards in the quality of products became crucial. But, at the beginning of the 1990s 'the quality of production in Denizli stayed behind the requirements of the international market' (Eraydın, 2001, p. 6). For this reason, leading firms started to modernize their machinery, by importing automatic looms, in the so-called second technological transformation. In this technological renewal, as in the case of the first one, the state took on important responsibilities, such as decreasing the minimum investment requirements for an investment incentive certificate, at the beginning of the 1990s (Erendil, 1998). Therefore, this provided an opportunity for many small and medium-sized firms to benefit from these incentives (Pınarcıoğlu, 2000) to update their machinery, as well as large entrepreneurs.

Table 11.1 The number of establishments and employees in the textile sector of Denizli compared with the total of all sectors according to the size of the establishments.

Year	Size of Establishment	Number of Establishments	Number of Textile Establishments	Number of Employees	Number of Textile Employees
1980	Total	117	29	7452	3865
1985	Total	115	37	9679	4302
1990	Total	99	36	12201	6638
1992	Small (10-49)	108	47	2304	959
	Medium (50-249)	44	24	4495	2682
	Large (249+)	16	12	7174	5423
	Total	168	82	13973	9114
1997	Small (10-49)	296	182	6500	4042
	Medium (50-249)	100	67	10859	7637
	Large (249+)	31	27	17080	15213
	Total	427	276	34439	26892
1998	Small (10-49)	241	144	6029	3651
	Medium (50-249)	93	63	10337	7192
	Large (249+)	37	32	20214	18068
	Total	371	239	36580	28911
1999	Small (10-49)	228	133	5479	3231
	Medium (50-249)	94	61	10679	6918
	Large (249+)	36	32	19034	17277
	Total	358	226	35192	27426

Source: SIS, Unpublished manufacturing statistics (only establishments with more than 10 employees are included).

With the export boom, many new entrepreneurs, who were from different provinces, and even from non-textile-oriented professions (such as medicine), entered the market, in order to benefit from the opportunities in the town. Consequently, the number of firms and employees, and the amount of textile exports from Denizli, increased sharply in the 1990s. As it can be seen from Table 11.1, between 1990-92 the number of establishments increased from 99 to 168, and nearly 49 per cent of them were textile firms in 1992. In the same period, the number of textile employees increased from 6638 to 9114. Table 11.3 shows that the region's textile industry recorded an impressive growth rate between 1992 and 1997, which reveals an increasing specialization in textile-related industries.

As can be observed in Table 11.2, the average size of firm changes within the limits of the medium-sized firms (50-249 employees). The average size of firm in the textile industry is larger than the average of total manufacturing sectors, due to the labor-intensive nature of textiles. Nearly 44 per cent of textile employment in 1997 was in firms with less than 250 employees. In other words, it is possible to argue that the number of small and medium-sized firms in textiles has dramatically increased between 1992 and 1997. Consequently, Table 11.3 illustrates the fact that small firms in textiles, and all other manufacturing sectors, recorded impressive growth rates, in terms of number of firms and employees, compared with medium-sized and large firms.

Table 11.2 The share of establishments and employees in the textile sector of Denizli and average firm sizes.

Years	Share of Textile Establishments (%)	Share of Textile Employees (%)	Average Firm Size	Average Firm Size in Textiles
1980	24,79	51,87	64	133
1985	32,17	44,45	84	116
1990	36,36	54,41	123	184
1992	48,81	65,23	83	111
1997	64,64	78,09	81	97
1998	64,42	79,03	99	121
1999	63,13	77,93	98	121

Source: Calculated from Unpublished manufacturing statistics, SIS.

In this rapid growth, the micro firms entering the market have evolved, according to different scales, from small to large ones. Erendil (1998) explains this asymmetry by defining two different types of producers found in Denizli. The first type of producers uses old technology and produces low-quality goods for domestic markets. The second type of producers employs modern technology and produces high-quality goods for international markets. The increasing gap between these two different types of producers has had quite a negative effect on the horizontal network relations, and it has brought about an asymmetric environment, which has led to the domination of a small number of large firms in Denizli.

Table 11.3 The growth rates of firms and employment in manufacturing and textile industry.

Years	Size of Establishment	Growth Rate of Firms (%)		Growth Rate of Employment (%)	
		Total Industry	Textile Industry	Total Industry	Textile Industry
1980-1985	Total	-1,71	27,59	29,88	11,31
1985-1990	Total	-13,91	-2,70	26,06	54,30
1990-1992	Total	69,70	127,78	14,52	37,30
1992-1997	Small (10-49)	174,07	287,23	182,12	321,48
	Medium (50-249)	127,27	179,17	141,58	184,75
	Large (249+)	93,75	125,00	138,08	180,53
	Total	154,17	236,59	146,47	195,06
1997-1999	Small (10-49)	-22,97	-26,92	-15,71	-20,06
	Medium (50-249)	-6,00	-8,96	-1,66	-9,41
	Large (249+)	16,13	18,52	11,44	13,57
	Total	-16,16	-18,12	2,19	1,99
1980-1999	Total	205,98	679,31	372,24	609,60

Source: Calculated from Unpublished manufacturing statistics, SIS.

In the 1990s, the leading firms extended their customer base in Europe and USA. This expansion of demand required faster and better-quality production (Pınarcıoğlu, 2000). Therefore, a tendency emerged for big firms to integrate all the complementary parts of the production in the firm (Erendil, 1998). Inadequate quality and time constraints, especially in periods of high demand, could be seen as the main reasons for these kinds of integration and technological upgrading, supported by the policies of the state. The use of automatic shuttleless looms forced entrepreneurs to decrease subcontracting relations, and this caused a structural transformation. However, during the 1980s, most of the production had been carried out using shuttle looms, in small and large firms, and no major problems had been experienced between the subcontractor and subcontracting firms. In order to meet the increasing quality expectations, in the 1990s, export firms preferred integrated production, instead of subcontracting, as small subcontractors had problems with satisfying the quality requirements of the upper segments of the European market.

In Denizli, the emergence of leading firms had been considered as the force which led SMEs to integrate into the global production networks, in the initial stages of growth. In the same way, although large firms are not a large proportion of the firms in Emilia-Romagna, their importance to the economic growth of the region should not be underestimated (Digiovanna, 1996). However, in the second part of the 1990s, the domination of large firms become obvious, and small firms have been forced into a minor position in Denizli. In this growth process, network relations have become much more loose and fragmented due to the power struggle among the firms (Pınarcıoğlu, 2000). Since the middle of the 1990s, the necessity for collective action in global export markets has diminished, as the demand has been guaranteed by the large firms. Similar events have been experienced in Italian industrial districts. Harrison (1994a, 1994b) concluded from his survey that leading powerful firms threaten the collaborative nature of inter-firm relations in Italian districts. Cooke and Morgan (1994) also emphasized that corporate hierarchies appear in the industrial districts because of growing concentration of capital. In some cases, new vertical networks have begun to replace the traditional horizontal networks of collaboration. In this process, small establishments have become more vulnerable, compared with the big firms, due to the lack of financial resources, lack of adequate skills, and lack of supporting institutions (Özcan, 1995; Erendil, 1998). However SMEs, with their flexible characteristics, still have a significant place in employment and production processes. In this context, it is important to discover new production strategies for sustaining collaboration among small and large firms.

All these problems experienced by the SMEs during the period of domination by large firms gave rise to new form of collaborative action in Denizli, which depends on a solidarity and trust tradition. In 1993, a many-partnered foreign trade company: the Aegean Ready-Garment Producers Association (EGS) was founded by small enterprises to compete with the leading large firms (Eraydın, 2002). EGS was initiated by 464 small producers, and the percentage of producers from Denizli in this cooperative was very high (57 per cent). In this cooperative, each member's share could not be more than 3 per cent. With its roles and values, EGS could be considered as a capitalist form of the traditional cooperatives (Pınarcıoğlu, 1998). The aim of this company has been to provide services, such as export, transportation, and insurance. In these services, collective companies have been formed, while the member firms remained autonomous. In 1996, a bank and a trade firm were founded to solve the financial and export-related problems. The success of the EGS model originated from supplying the major needs of small producers, which depended upon solidarity, mutual trust and the self-help tradition. Therefore, this organization shows that today capitalist institutions and organizations are starting to take the place of traditional communitarian relations.

During the 1997-99 period, macro-economic problems were experienced by the Turkish economy, as a result of the world economic crisis that began in Russia and East Asia. In this period, industrial production and exports were negatively affected by the decreasing demand in national and international markets (Eraydın, 2002). After 1997, due to the effects of the economic crisis, and the changing strategies of large firms, most of the firms, especially the small ones that produced for domestic markets, had been negatively affected, and the number of SMEs and employees began to decrease (Table 11.1). A large number of newcomers, from different occupations, could not survive in the crisis era, because of the lack of experience to deal with the crisis. Moreover, entry into, and existence within, the market was no longer as easy as it used to be. As can be seen from Table 11.3, the growth rates of SMEs, in the period between 1997-1999, were negative in all manufacturing and textile industries. However, in this period, large firms sustained a positive growth rate that was lower than the one experienced in the previous period (1992-97).

In the late 1990s, parallel to these developments, it seemed difficult for the town to continue to articulate with the global textile networks, as a producer of towels and bathrobes. In this period, the EGS lost its collaborative structure, and also its power, in Denizli. Although the share of each member could not be more than 3 percent, the dominance of large firms had became obvious in the decision making process in the EGS. Conflicting interests could not survive within the same institutions, so different power groups constituted their own institutions, in order to maintain and increase growth rates within the highly competitive crisis era. Under these conditions, many small communities that were newly emerging caused an institutional split in Denizli (Eraydın, 2002). Small firms and large firms belonged to different collaborative associations and institutions, due to having different aims and problems. Since the beginning of the 1990s, the number of associations which contain mostly small enterprises have increased. The most important group among them is MUSIAD (Independent Entrepreneurs Association), members of which have a tendency to implement the rules of Islam in economic activities.

After the 1990s, in this fragmented collaborative environment, it became difficult to depend on existing local potential. Moreover, it was obvious that the existing products and production practices of Denizli were inadequate for the updating of competitive power in global markets. Therefore, ready-made garments started to be an important product in the later years of growth in Denizli. Recently, most of the entrepreneurs in Denizli, especially the second generation that studied in the management field in US and European universities, have tried to reorganize production, and have understood that management and marketing have been as important as production in economic growth. Schmitz (1999) also argues that traditional industrial districts, focusing on labor-intensive exports, may not automatically lead to sustainable growth, and that a shift to other stages, such as design or marketing, is required.

Conclusion

In the globalization process, adapting to changing conditions and increasing competitive power become more important for growth nodes. Although, in the technologically advanced countries of Europe, the role of SMEs has gradually shifted from the provision of flexibility to the production of knowledge, in the technologically less advanced countries, located at the periphery of Europe, SMEs are still seen as a factor of flexibility. Indeed, the increasing importance assigned to SMEs in high-tech clusters in Europe stems from their knowledge creation capacity. But, in peripheral countries, the role of SMEs is still evaluated in relation to flexible production organization, employment generation, cost minimization and non-unionization.

The economic growth experienced in Denizli points to a success story associated with the dominance of SMEs. But what is evident from this Chapter is that the role of SMEs in the economic growth of Denizli has gradually changed from a dominant position to a minor position. Between 1930 and 1950, the dominance of SMEs was due to the limited opportunities available for capital accumulation. In the earlier years, this paved the way for more collaborative type of relations such as the cooperatives of the 1930s. With the impetus of the first technological renewal and the Sümerbank cotton yarn factory in the 1950s and 1960s, entrepreneurs began to achieve important capital accumulation, challenging their substantive economy. This pre-take-off period had witnessed the establishment of the first large private establishments in Denizli. But the predominance of SMEs in textile production had continued during these years. From the 1970s until the 1980s, the capital accumulation among SMEs had further intensified, and the number of large establishments gradually increased. The 1980s could be seen as the period of integration into the international markets, within which small and large firms have a complementary position in sustaining economic growth. The textile boom of the 1990s could be seen as a period in which there was pressure to transform the organization and institutional structure of textile production. In the most recent years of global integration, the export success, which required increasing output and quality of product, led to the emergence of large vertically integrated firms, due to the inadequate complementary services in Denizli.

The evolution of local economic systems is associated with the changing nature and role of SMEs in the economic growth process. Although, in earlier periods, it is the limited opportunities available for capital accumulation that creates advantages for SMEs over large firms, in subsequent periods, associated with increasing opportunities for capital accumulation, it is the already established production networks among SMEs, and between SMEs and large firms, that sustains the importance of SMEs in the growth process. The vertical integration process prevailing in the textile industry tends to undermine the relative importance of SMEs, but the flexibility that they provide still seems to be an important ingredient in the sustained local economic growth.

The path-dependent characteristics of Denizli are very evident in its specialization in the textile industry. Although it has benefited very much from this path-dependency, its future is very uncertain. The recent increase in quotas has so far helped avoid any negative aspects associated with this path-dependency, but ultimately these seem unavoidable. However, it should also be noted that Denizli might well survive along this path, if it explores other areas, such as the garment-clothing and fashion-based sectors. The economic growth of Denizli has culminated in a situation in which it is no longer possible to sustain the existing path of specialization with any visible profitability. The urgent need to reflect on this is not only a result of the objective evaluation provided by this Chapter, but also an issue subject to consensus among the economic actors of Denizli, who should immediately take initiatives to create an alternative economically sustainable path for their region to follow.

Notes

1 In the early years of the Turkish Republic, a kind of private sector-led economic development policy was adopted. But the great depression of the 1930s necessitated the direct involvement of the state in industrial production. During the great depression, the Turkish Republic took important measures in order to guarantee and sustain the economic development of the country. Because of the limited capital accumulation by the private sector, the state had to intervene in the economic system through the establishment of state enterprises, each of which was responsible for the production of different industrial products. Sümerbank, established in 1933, was one of these state enterprises, responsible for textile production in Turkey.

2 Similar support schemes can also be observed in other developed and developing countries. Indeed, state incentives are very important for the development of backward regions. The case of the Mezzogiorno in Italy and the steel industry in France illustrate this very well (Dunford, 1988). Among other incentive tools, special tax treatments have a widespread applicability all around the world, especially in technology-oriented sectors and regions (see for example Wang and Wang (1998: 686-687), Castells and Hall (1994), Fujita (1988: 575) and Lin (1997: 264)). The incentive tools granted to investors range from exemption from customs duties and fund levies, investment allowances, Value Added Tax deferral for imported and locally purchased machinery and equipment, to cheap credits.

3 The potential significance of immigrants for economic development in the countries of origin is well documented in the literature (see for example Portes, Haller, and Guarnizo (2001), Thomas-Hope (1999) and Peleikis (2000)).

4 Although, within the context of economic transnationalism, it is possible to observe capital movements from the developed countries to the less developed countries, through the agency of immigrants, the type of remittances experienced in Denizli seem to be unique, in many respects, because of their collectivist nature, which may be attributed to its distinct socio-cultural characteristics.

5 As Portes, Haller, and Guarnizo (2001) argue, at present, the increase of migrant remittances has caught the attention of the respective sending governments. Indeed, many developing countries have initiated programmes to attract the investment of their respective diasporas (the case of Jamaica (Peleikis, (2000) illustrates this very well).

6 Similarly to the case of Denizli, in Sinos Valley, local enterprises did not just wait for opportunities to export. They invited foreign buyers and foreign journalists to visit their national shoe fair, in which they promoted Brazilian shoes to the global export markets (Schmitz, 1995).

References

Aslanoğlu, M. (1998), 'Esnek uzmanlaşma yaklaşımı açısından Denizli havlu dokuma sanayinin analizi', *21. Yüzyıla Doğru Denizli Sanayi Sempozyumu*, pp. 185-190.

Batmaz, N. and Özcan, A. (1998), 'Denizli sanayinin yapısal özellikleri ve sorunları', *21. Yüzyıla Doğru Denizli Sanayi Sempozyumu*, pp. 302-313.

Castells, M. and Hall, P. (1994) *Technopoles of the World*, Routledge, London and New York.

Cooke, P. and Morgan, K. (1994), 'Growth regions under duress: Renewal strategies in Baden Württemberg and Emilia-Romagna', in A. Amin and N. Thrift (eds), *Globalisation, Institutions and Regional Development*, Oxford University Press, pp. 91-174.

Digiovanna, S. (1996), 'Industrial districts and regional economic development: A regulation approach', *Regional Studies*, vol. 30, no. 4, pp. 373-386.

Doner, R.E and Hershberg, E. (1999), 'Flexible production and political decentralization in the developing world: Elective affinities in the pursuit of competitiveness?' *Studies in Comparative International Development*, vol. 34, no. 1, pp. 45-83

Dunford, M.F. (1988), *Capital, the State, and Regional Development*, Pion Limited, London.

Edgington, D.W. (1999), 'Firms, Governments and Innovation in the Chukyo Region of Japan', *Urban Studies*, vol. 36, no. 2, pp. 305-339.

Eraydın, A. (1998), 'Yeni Sanayi Odaklarının Ortaya Çıkmasında Kamunun Düzenleme ve Destekleme Biçimlerinin Katkısı', Paper presented to *Yeni Yerel Sanayi Odakları Semineri* organized by State Planning Organization, State Institute of Statistics and Turkish Capital Market Board, Ankara.

Eraydın, A. (2002), 'The Local Embeddedness of Firms in Social Networks in Turkish Industrial Districts: The Changing Roles of Networks in Local Development', in M. Taylor (eds), *Embedded Enterprise and Social Capital: International Perspectives*, Ashgate, Aldershot.

Erendil, A. (1998), 'Using Critical Realist Approach in Geographical Research: An Attempt to Analyze the Transforming Nature of Production and Reproduction in Denizli', Unpublished Ph.D Thesis, Middle East Technical University, The Department of City and Regional Planning.

Fujita, K. (1988), 'The Technopolis - High Technology and Regional-Development in Japan' *International Journal of Urban and Regional Research*, vol. 12, no. 4, pp. 566-594.

Glasmeier, A. (1991), 'Technological discontinuities and flexible production networks: The case of Switzerland and the world watch industry', *Research Policy*, vol. 20, pp. 469-485.

Harrison, B. (1994a), 'The Italian industrial district and the crisis of co-operative from: Part:I', *European Planning Studies*, vol. 2, no. 1, pp. 3-22.

Harrison, B. (1994b), 'The Italian industrial district and the crisis of co-operative from: Part:II', *European Planning Studies*, vol. 2, no. 2, pp. 159-174.

Hassink, R. (1997), 'What does the learning region mean for economic geography?', Paper presented to *Regional Studies Association 'Regional Frontiers' EURRN European Conference*, 20-23 September, Frankfurt (Oder), Germany.

Işık, O. and Pınarcıoğlu, M. (1996), 'Two faces of local transformation: The case of Denizli, Turkey', *City*, 3-4, pp. 63-70.
Karaalp, İ. and Batmaz, N. (1998), 'Denizli ekonomisinin sanayileşme süreci ve dış ticaretteki payı', in C. Küçüker (eds), *Anadolu'da Hızla Sanayileşen Kentler: Denizli Örneği*, Türkiye Ekonomi Kurumu, Ankara, pp. 101-105.
Kazdağlı, H. (1998), 'Yeni bölgesel gelişme yaklaşımları doğrultusunda Denizli ekonomisi', in C. Küçüker (eds), *Anadolu'da Hızla Sanayileşen Kentler: Denizli Örneği*, Türkiye Ekonomi Kurumu, Ankara, pp. 83-93.
Küçüker, C. (1998), *Anadolu'da Hızla Sanayileşen Kentler: Denizli Örneği*, Türkiye Ekonomi Kurumu, Ankara, pp. 1-14.
Lin, C.Y. (1997), 'Tehnopolis development: An assessment of the Hsinchu experience' *International Planning Studies*, vol. 2, no. 2, pp. 257-272.
Maillat, D., Lecoq, B., Nemeti, F. and Pfister, M. (1995), 'Technology district and innovation: The case of the Swiss Jura Arc' *Regional Studies*, vol. 29, no. 3, pp. 251-263.
Mutluer, M. (1995), *Gelişimi, Yapısı ve Sorunlarıyla Denizli Sanayii*, DSO Yayınları, İzmir.
Özcan, G.B. (1995), *Small Firms and Local Economic Development*, Avebury, London.
Pamuk, Ş. (1998), 'Denizli ve Gaziantep'te sanayileşmenin yakın tarihi, 1900-1980', Paper presented to *Yerel Sanayi Odakları Uluslararası Semineri*, 23-25 September, Ankara.
Peleikis, A. (2000), 'The emergence of a translocal community: The case of a South Lebanese Village and its migrant connections to Ivory Coast' in Cahiers d'etudes sur la Mèditeranèe`orientale et le monde turco-iranien, No. 30, pp. 297-317.
Pınarcıoğlu, M. (1998), 'Peripheral development and the rise of entrepreneurialism: The characteristics of Anatolian Tigers and a comparison between the local textile and clothing industries of Bursa and Denizli', Paper presented to *the 3rd erc METU International Conference in Economics*, organized by the Economic Research Center, Middle East Technical University, 9-12 September, Ankara, Turkey.
Pınarcıoğlu, M. (2000), *Development of Industry and Local Change*, METU, Faculty of Architecture Press, Ankara.
Portes, A., Haller, W. and Guarnizo, L.E. (2002), 'Transnational entrepreneurs: An alternative form of immigrant economic adaptation', *American Sociological Review*, vol. 67, no. 2, pp. 278-299.
Saxenian, A.L. (1985), 'The genesis of Silicon Valley' in P. Hall and A.R. Markusen (eds), *Silicon Landscapes*, Allen & Unwin Inc., Boston, pp. 20-34.
Saxenian, A.L. (1991), 'The origins and dynamics of production networks in Silicon Valley', *Research Policy*, vol. 20, no. 5, pp. 423-437.
Schmitz, H. (1995) 'Small shoemakers and Fordist giants: Tale of a supercluster', *World Development*, vol. 23, no. 1, pp. 9-28.
Schmitz, H. (1999), 'Global competition and local cooperation: Success and failure in the Sinos Valley, Brazil', *World Development*, vol. 27, no. 9, pp. 1503-1514.
Şengün, İ. (1998), 'Denizli ekonomisine tarihsel bir bakış', in C. Küçüker (eds), *Anadolu'da Hızla Sanayileşen Kentler: Denizli Örneği*, Türkiye Ekonomi Kurumu, Ankara, pp. 94-96.
Thomas-Hope, E. (1999), 'Return migration to Jamaica and its development potential', *International Migration*, vol. 37, no. 1, pp. 183-207.
Wang, J. and Wang, J. (1998), 'An analysis of new-tech agglomeration in Beijing: a new industrial district in the making?', *Environment and Planning A*, vol. 30, pp. 681-701.

Chapter 12

Small Entrepreneurs in Međimurje: Between Tradition and Challenges of New Forms of Cooperation

Drago Čengić

Introduction

In the past few years, despite the general public dissatisfaction with the first ten years of development of Croatian capitalism (Meštrović and Štulhofer, 1998; Čengić and Rogić, 1999; Franičević, 2001), more and more frequently the local media also carry stories about successful entrepreneurs. The successful ones very often feature craftsmen and entrepreneurs from *Međimurje county*, a county situated in north-eastern Croatia. Unfortunately, Croatia lacks the systematic and empirically sound research which could give reliable answers to various questions concerning local entrepreneurs' success and failure. This paper attempts to give answers to at least some of the questions which could be posed. For the most part, the economic and sociological analyses carried out so far on small and medium-sized enterprises has dealt only with isolated aspects of the problem. While economists have mostly been oriented towards issues relating to the development potential of newly established companies, the identification of obstacles to development, and the incentive role of the state, sociologists have, to a certain extent, been engaged in studies relating to the social origins and the management legitimacy of the newly emerged managerial and entrepreneurial élite (Bartlet and Franičević, 1999; Bateman, 2000; Sekulić and Šporer, 2000; Bartlet and Bukvić, 2001; Čengić and Rogić, 2001; Županov, 2001).

In this paper we will review some of the present findings and hypotheses relevant to this study.

1. According to some development analyses of small and medium-sized enterprises (SME) (Bartlett and Franičević, 2001; Kovačević and Obadić, 2001), there are some counties/regions in Croatia that are far ahead in terms of SME development. 'The success of small enterprises in these regions, before the market economy emerged, was found in three production segments: plastics production, the electronics industry and the more advanced stages of metal production' (Kovačević and Obadić, 2001, p. 2635). Moreover, these analyses also imply: a) that small and

medium-sized enterprises in individual border regions (such as Međimurje, Varaždin and Istria counties) largely owe their development to their proximity to a border (in these particular cases, Slovenia, Austria, Hungary and Italy), b) that it might be expected that cross-border areas will more rapidly attract foreign investment (Bartlett and Franičević, 1999), and c) that from the long-term perspective, among the main reasons for the dynamic development of SMEs in these parts of Croatia, the following factors are most responsible: 'economic openness, business tradition and appropriate environment'. Do these theses also hold good in Međimurje county?

2. One group of analysts dealing with the SME sector considers that some of their characteristics are typical of those present in most post-socialist countries. On the basis of some findings from the early nineties, Brezinski and Fritch (1996; also Bartlett and Prašnikar, 1995; Bartlett and Franičević, 1999) note: a) that out of the total number of small and medium-sized enterprises established, the number actually doing business is relatively low, b) that those operating businesses are very small enterprises (in terms of the number of employees and the capital employed), c) that they are mostly engaged in small retail businesses, trade and services and much less in manufacturing, d) that they are closely connected with the grey economy, and e) that there is a division into two groups, one that hardly survives in the market, and another that has a certain development potential. According to Bartlett and Franičević (also Franičević and Bartlett, 2001), these are also characteristics of small and medium-sized enterprises in Croatia. The question as to which of these characteristics are present in small and medium-sized enterprises in Međimurje is the subject of our analysis.

3. If small and medium-sized enterprises are also categorized by their development potential, the question arises as to the barriers which hinder their normal growth in individual post-socialist countries. Starting from the fact that small and medium-sized enterprises in post-socialist countries have failed to create an adequate number of jobs, and from the theories of SME growth, Bartlett and Bukvić (2001) have divided growth barriers into five categories. These are institutional barriers, external (market) barriers, financial barriers, barriers of an internal nature (relating to company characteristics) and social barriers.

We have made an attempt to find out what type of enterprises in Međimurje are in the majority – 'survival enterprises' or 'enterprises with a tendency to growth' and what types of barriers will hinder their development in the near future. Also, regarding the role of the state and the local political élite, the question is how the state might stimulate enterprise development: only through macro-economic regulations (by protecting macro-economic stability) or, in addition, by specific entrepreneurship development policies at both the local and national levels (industrial policy, other specific policies) (Bateman and Vehovec, 1999; Bateman, 2001).

Taking into account the fundamental findings from previous analyses and (rather meagre) research, we will try, by studying one Croatian region, to find out to what extent those findings support the empirical data available to us. *Therefore the purpose of this paper is – by using Međimurje as a case in point – to identify key sociological and cultural values and economic aspects of entrepreneurship development up to now, as well as the main factors affecting future development of SMEs in this part of Croatia.* We will try to answer some of the previously posed questions, specifically:

a) To what extent the past development of entrepreneurship in Međimurje, a county which has borders with other countries, has been generated from inside Croatia itself, and to what extent it has been instigated and sustained by favorable market conditions abroad?
b) To what extent, if any, have any of 'the typical characteristics of post-socialist SMEs', identified in the analyses of Brezinski and Fritsch, also been present in the Međimurje region?
c) To what extent are the businessmen from Međimurje 'survival entrepreneurs', or 'entrepreneurs with a tendency to growth'? What regulations do they expect from the state in the near future?
d) Is there any cooperation and, if there is, what is the form of cooperation between small and medium-sized enterprises, and between SMEs and large companies, both from Croatia and abroad? Are small and medium-sized enterprises of this type open to the development of common entrepreneurial networks, as a prerequisite for successful business operations?

Having these objectives in mind, in the following pages we will present a few relevant issues. Firstly, we will have a look at some characteristics of the Međimurje county and our sample of enterprises/entrepreneurs. After that, we'll outline the development of entrepreneurship in Međimurje from a socio-cultural perspective, giving a socio-cultural and economic profile of entrepreneurs, entrepreneurs' perception of barriers to growth, and their perception of the market and of cooperation between entrepreneurs. Finally, our tentative conclusions will be elaborated in the concluding notes.

Some Characteristics of the Međimurje Economy

Međimurje county is situated in the north of the Republic of Croatia, between two large rivers, the Mura and the Drava. It has borders with the Republic of Slovenia on the west and northwest, and with the Republic of Hungary in the northeast (Figure 12.1).

To the south, it borders on Varaždin county and to the southeast on Koprivnica-Križevci county. It occupies a territory of over 730 square km and has 120.000 inhabitants, with an average population density of 165 inhabitants per square kilometre, the highest in the whole of Croatia, and almost double the average population density in Croatia. In terms of territory, Međimurje county (from now on: Međimurje) is the smallest of the all 21 of Croatia's counties. Administratively, it is divided into 21 municipalities and 3 towns (Čakovec, Mursko Središće and Prelog). The town of Čakovec (about 20.000 inhabitants) is the capital of Međimurje county.

Figure 12.1 The geographical position of Međimurje county in Croatia.

According to official reports, the economy of Međimurje 'is predominantly of a traditional, labor-intensive and export-oriented nature'. Measured by the total income and number of employees, *manufacturing industry, trading, construction industry and agriculture dominate* (see Table 12.1) (Međimurska županija, 2001; http://www.hgk.hr/komora/hrv/zupkom/Cakovec). The number of employees in all the enterprises in Međimurje amounts to 21.519 employees, of which 53.64 per cent are employed in the manufacturing industry, 16.62 per cent in trading, 14.29 per cent in construction, and 5.51 per cent in real estate and other business activities. If unemployment and commodity trade with foreign countries (exports) are taken as two relevant criteria in assessing the economy of Croatian counties, the situation in Međimurje is as follows.

At the end of the year 2000, in the Republic of Croatia, there were 378.535 unemployed persons; in other words, the (official) unemployment rate in December 2000 was 22.6 per cent, or the highest in all the transition countries. According to the 1998-2000 data, the unemployment rate increased in all the counties to an index ranging from 110.5 in Zadar County (on the Adriatic coast) to 154.0 in Krapina County (north-west Croatia).

With its share of 2.2 per cent of the overall number of unemployed in Croatia in the year 2000 (8.305 persons), and its slightly more moderate unemployment growth rate (index of 119.09 in the period from 1998 to 2000) as compared with the average unemployment growth rate in the country (index of 125.04),

Međimurje county's problem of unemployment is less pronounced than in other Croatian counties. This is partly due to the economic structure of the county, partly to the privatization model applied, and definitely to the fact that this part of the country was not exposed to war and destruction during the aggression of Serbia and Yugoslavia between 1991 and 1995 (HGK, 2001; ZAP, 2001; HGK-ŽGK, 2001).

Table 12.1 Total revenues and employment by economic activity in Međimurje county, 2000.

Economic activity	*Total revenue*	*Employees*
Agriculture, hunting and forestry	5,17 %	2,78 %
Mining and quarrying	0,00 %	0,00 %
Manufacturing	39,57 %	53,64 %
Electricity, gas and water supply	1,95 %	1,23 %
Construction	9,60 %	14,29 %
Wholesale and retail trade	34,24 %	16,62 %
Hotels and restaurants	0,69 %	1,43 %
Transport, storage and communication	2,08 %	2,32 %
Financial intermediation	0,78 %	0,24 %
Real estate, renting and business activities	4,29 %	5,51 %
Education	0,60 %	0,27 %
Health and social work	0,41 %	0,35 %
Other community, social and personal service activities	0,62 %	1,32 %
Total	*100,00%*	*100,00%*
Values	682 (million of USD)	21.519 (number of employees)
Share on Croatia	**1,93 %**	**2,92 %**

Source: ZAP/Payment System Service (Financial statements for 2000), Main Office in Zagreb, 2001.

According to the international trade data, Međimurje with its 3.3 per cent share of overall exports in 1999, ranks seventh among the 21 counties (see: ZAP, 2001). However, all the counties which are ahead of Međimurje, in terms both of territory and population (1991 census), are several times larger than Međimurje. These proportions also confirm the fact that the Međimurje economy is a vital part of the whole economic structure in Croatia.

Sampling Procedure and Data Gathering

When we look at the local economic structure, at the micro-analytical level, first of all we need to know how many enterprises are really active. The Payment System Service data show that, of all the registered legal entities, about 1.450 business entities in Međimurje, under various forms of ownership, are active. Of this number, according to the criteria used for categorizing companies, 66 are large or medium-sized enterprises, while the remainder are small enterprises. Skilled tradesmen must be added to this group. There are 1950 skilled tradesmen in Međimurje: 30 per cent are accounted for by the production sector, 25 per cent by services, 21 per cent by trading, 12 per cent by transport etc. (Obrtnička komora Međimurske županije, 2001). As to *the type of activity*, of the total number of legal entities in the county, 20 per cent are in the manufacturing industry, 38 per cent in trading, 12 per cent in the construction industry, 13 per cent in the real estate business, 3 per cent in farming, 4 per cent in hotels and restaurants, 5 per cent in traffic, storage and communications etc.

As to the *size of enterprises* (Table 12.2), small enterprises (up to 50 employees) employ 31.44 per cent of the labor force, medium-sized enterprises (51 to 250 employees) employ 26.49 per cent, and large enterprises (over 251 employees) employ 42.07 per cent of the total labor force in Međimurje county.

Table 12.2 Distribution of employees according to the size of enterprises in Međimurje county in 2000.

Enterprise size	*Number of enterprises*	*Share (%)*	*Number of employees*	*Share (%)*
0	136	9,39 %	0	0,00 %
1–5	901	62,18 %	1.979	9,20 %
6–20	288	19,88 %	2.942	13,67 %
21–50	58	4,00 %	1.844	8,57 %
51–250	49	3,38 %	5.700	26,49 %
251–500	9	0,62 %	3.244	15,08 %
501–1000	8	0,55 %	5.810	26,10 %
Total	**1.449**	**100,00 %**	**21.519**	**100,00 %**

Source: ZAP/Payment System Service (Financial statements for 2000), Main Office in Zagreb, 2001.

In terms of *the number of employees*, 95.4 per cent of enterprises are small, since they employ up to 50 employees; 3.4 per cent are medium-sized enterprises (51 to 250 employees), and only 1.2 per cent of them are large enterprises, employing over 250 employees (Table 12.2). We note here that entrepreneurship includes not only small and medium-sized enterprises, but also numerous handicraft trades, some of which, in Croatia today, employ over a hundred employees.

For the purpose of defining a sample of handicraft trades and small and medium-sized enterprises, for the sake of our empirical research, we have used two sources: a) the register of companies in the Croatian Chamber of Commerce – The County Chamber in Čakovec (N = 1466, data from 2000) and b) the Međimurje Craftsmanship Register (30 tradesmen, data from 2001). On the basis of these sources, we have selected 230 enterprises, and conducted an opinion poll of their owners and managers. Data collecting was mostly carried out in January, but partly in February 2002. In addition to a questionnaire, the data were also obtained through interviews with individual entrepreneurs, tradesmen, members of the Međimurje Entrepreneurial Centre, Međimurje county, the Chamber of Crafts and Trades, and some other consultants.

Table 12.3 Sample structure of enterprises by institutional type of entrepreneurship and activity (%).

Type of entrepreneurship (legal form)	%	Craft/enterprise activity	%
1. craft	15.0	1. production/manufacturing industry	24.9
2. limited liability co., joint stock co.	81.3	2. construction	15.5
3. farming and other	3.7	3. trade and services	46.5
		4. other activities	12.7
N = 213			

Altogether, 213 questionnaires were collected, and 15 in-depth interviews (on several occasions) were carried out (sample structure in Table 12.3). We believe that, for the type of activity, our sample mirrors relatively faithfully the structure of the economy in Međimurje, in terms of the activities of the craft entrepreneurs/enterprises.

Table 12.4 Number of employees (owners included) (in %).

	%	*M*	*St.d.*	*Mode*	*Median*
1. 1 to 10 employees	56.4	41.5	122.2	3.0	10.0
2. 11 to 49 employees	31.8				
3. 50 and over	11.8				
minimum = 1, maximum = 1028					

As regards the size of the enterprises that we used in our sample of tradesmen and other entrepreneurs, more than half were so-called *micro enterprises.* The final data show that 56.4 per cent were craft business/enterprise owners having less than 10 employees (Table 12.4). Following these were typical representatives of small enterprises, having from 11 to 50 employees (31,8 per cent), and 11.8 per cent owners of medium-sized enterprise.

Development of Entrepreneurship in Međimurje From a Socio-Cultural Viewpoint

One of the special characteristics of Međimurje is – in our opinion – the fact that the development of post-socialist entrepreneurship relied heavily on the rich tradition of craftsmanship which existed before and during socialism. That development depended mostly on the former Yugoslav market and only to a moderate extent on foreign markets (neighbouring countries). This hypothesis relies on data relating to the history of craftsmanship in this area (Obrtnička komora Međimurske županije, 2001) and the specific mentality of the environment. According to the observations of Jokić-Horvat (1992), since ancient times, the population of Međimurje has been very autonomous relative to the central authorities, regardless of whether such authorities were Austro-Hungarian, Hungarian, or Croatian. Three components are worth noting here.

Firstly, through the acculturation processes, the local Croatian population (mostly farmers) were subject *to certain Protestant worldviews.* For example, Juraj IV Zrinski[1] granted (after 1589) to the inhabitants of a settlement located in front of the Čakovec fortress, the privilege to engage in various crafts and trades. 'As Juraj IV Zrinski was a Protestant, his rather rigid code of living, his dedication to work and vocation, and above all his attempt to somehow set living standards by written and unwritten rules, heavily influenced patterns of living and the value system of the then peasants and citizens' (Jokić-Horvat, 1992, pp. 230-231).

Secondly, the period under the Austro-Hungarian monarchy significantly influenced the development of craft trades and, and particularly the emergence of the first craft-guilds: during the reign of Maria Theresa the first craft-guild statutes appeared. Thirdly, although the autochthonous population was exposed to different foreign influences, it was not inclined to either resistance or rebellion. It developed 'a specific mentality and way of living such that it successfully resisted the extreme influence of other cultures, and accepted rational patterns of living which did not pay much attention to the awareness of mythical, historical, or similar factors. The lack of natural resources created behavioral patterns which were governed by values aimed at individualism, and which relied on hard work and frugality' (Jokić-Horvat, 1992).

If these hypotheses are true, then our subjects will be more inclined to individual and rational values, which do not glorify a mythical image of the world, but instead regard work as a source of prosperity and happiness for the individual. What do our data show?

Firstly, a relatively large number of the respondents (63.4 per cent) believe that entrepreneurship in Međimurje is the most developed in the country. Still, almost a quarter of them (22.5 per cent) do not share this view, or are incapable of giving an assessment. The main reasons for such an opinion, as we will see later, are linked with today's perception of the barriers to enterprise growth and the general perception of the social environment.

Secondly, key reasons for the development of entrepreneurship in Međimurje are related to four significant factors; they are: 1) the hard work and diligence of local people, 2) the tradition of manufacturing craftsmanship/entrepreneurship in families, 3) the knowledge and skills acquired during their work abroad, and 4) the ability of local people to understand the needs of their customers and consequently develop new needs in their customers (Table 12.5).

Table 12.5 Perception of reasons for entrepreneurship development in Međimurje (in %).

Rank	Yes	No
1. hard work and diligence of local people	83,6	16,0
2. tradition of manufacturing crafts/entrepreneurship in the family	49,8	49,8
3. knowledge acquired during their work abroad	39,4	60,1
4. [cap]ability of local people to understand and to develop new needs in their customers	37,6	62,0
5. available capital in local people	18,8	80,8
6. favourable geographical position along the border/exposure to external influences	9,9	89,7
7. availability of infrastructure utilities (electricity, gas, water, sewage system)	4,7	94,8
8. encouragement of craft/entrepreneurship development even [back] in socialism	4,2	95,3
9. readiness of entrepreneurs for mutual cooperation	3,8	95,8
*. Do not believe that entrepreneurship is very much developed	8,0	91,5

Looking only at the three highest ranked items, we may say that they reflect a widespread collective experience of the Međimurje population. Also, they support our assumption that there is a significant tradition of family manufacturing crafts in this region. Thus, entrepreneurs from Međimurje – very much aware of their tradition – believe that entrepreneurship development in their region is based primarily on their own hard work and diligence, and that of their parents, and also on the knowledge and skills that were brought from abroad (by their fellow countrymen) as specific cultural capital (Obrtnička komora Međimurske županije, 2001). Before starting their own business, 13.2 per cent of our respondents worked abroad for at least a year. Respondents consider *the following factors as being of secondary importance for entrepreneurship development*: cooperation among entrepreneurs, encouragement of craft/entrepreneurship development, even under socialism, the availability of infrastructure facilities, and a favourable position along the state border.

Thirdly, the perception of the reasons that led to the current entrepreneurship development in Međimurje is based on the much deeper values of this region. Some of them are obvious in our respondents' answers (Table 12.6).

Table 12.6 Perception of fundamental values assessed by a scale from 1 to 5 (%).

Rank	*1*	*2*	*3*	*4*	*5*	*M*
1. children	1,4	0,0	1,4	8,0	87,8	4,8
2. honesty	0,0	0,0	2,3	8,0	87,3	4,9
3. work	0,0	0,5	0,9	23,9	72,8	4,7
4. marriage	1,4	0,9	8,0	15,5	72,3	4,6
5. freedom & independence	0,5	0,5	4,7	25,4	67,6	4,6
6. knowledge & education	0,0	0,0	4,2	27,7	66,2	4,6
7. friendship	0,0	0,0	8,9	31,0	58,2	4,5
8. love	0,5	0,0	8,0	33,3	55,9	4,9
9. environment protection	2,3	2,3	13,1	31,5	48,8	4,2
10. sexual life	0,9	4,2	14,6	32,4	46,0	4,2
11. leisure time	1,4	4,2	24,9	33,8	33,3	4,0
12. money	0,5	2,3	20,2	46,9	28,2	4,0
13. religion	18,3	18,3	31,0	17,4	13,1	2,9
nation	23,0	14,6	29,1	18,3	13,1	2,8
14. politics	28,2	22,5	32,9	8,9	5,2	2,4

Note: Presented values are evaluated by respondents on a scale of 1-5, where 1= not important at all, 5= very important; in this table value items are ranked by scale value '5= very important'-percentages; M= mean value.

Topping the list of desirable values are children, honesty, work, marriage, freedom and independence, knowledge and education. This is a mixture of traditional, individual and intellectual values which is in line with the hypotheses put forward by Jokić-Horvat as regards the specific mentality of the people of the region. This is the mentality of people raised with poor resources, focused only on their work and their experience; also, this set of values regards individual and business honesty as a prerequisite for deeper social communication.

Socio-Cultural and Economic Profile of Entrepreneurs and Their Perception of Međimurje

We must admit that our data suggest, as do some other studies of the development of Croatian entrepreneurship and the managerial elite, that a great many businesses were founded in Međimurje during the past decade (Sekulić and Šporer, 2000). As many as 67 per cent of the craft businesses/enterprises in our sample were founded between 1991 and 2001. *However, the specificity of Međimurje is that, relative to other Croatian counties, a third of the entrepreneurs had established their craft businesses/enterprises under socialism (before 1991).* This fact supports the thesis that there was relatively better-developed entrepreneurship in Međimurje even under Socialist Yugoslavia. The causes of such a situation are not to be sought in state policies aimed at the development of entrepreneurship, but in the diligence of local people, and the higher degree of political liberalism in Međimurje, where as far back as the eighties, craftsmen and 'private entrepreneurs' were regarded more positively than in other parts of Croatia (Jokić-Horvat, 1992).

The data showing that 28 per cent of the respondents stated that a family member (a parent, a sister or a brother) had their own craft business/enterprise also bears witness to the entrepreneurial tradition in the families of Međimurje – over at least two generations. Concerning the current ownership structure, relatively more of the analyzed craft businesses/enterprises are owned by individual owners (44.1 per cent), while a quarter of them are owned by a family (24.9 per cent) (Table 12.7).

Table 12.7 Present ownership structure of craft businesses/enterprises (%).

1. owned by the individual	44.1
2. owned by a few family members	24.9
3. other (co-ownership, managers)	31.0

In terms of the work force, entrepreneurship in Međimurje is dominated by family companies. In about 62.0 per cent of the enterprises analyzed, family members are employed, and in 38.0 per cent only the owner – manager is employed. In the 131 craft businesses/enterprises operated by a family work force, usually only one or two family members are employed (74.8 per cent), while in a quarter of enterprises three to five family members are employed (25.2 per cent out of 131 craft businesses/enterprises). In terms of schooling, most employees hold a secondary school diploma (70.0 per cent), or are highly skilled workers (11.4 per cent). Only 11.3 per cent of the work force hold a two-year college diploma or a university degree, which might be a limiting factor for future development. Very likely many of them are owners of enterprises.

Regarding the socio-demographic characteristics and professional origin of entrepreneurs among the respondents, there was a surprisingly high number of women: almost one third of the surveyed entrepreneurs were women (24.4 per cent). As expected, entrepreneurs are family persons (89.7 per cent of them are married), whose families have on the average four members.

Table 12.8 Respondent age structure (in %).

	%	*M*	*St.d.*	*Mode*	*Median*
1. up to 35 years of age	14.2	44,4	8,3	48,0	45.0
2. from 36 to 45 years of age	37.9				
3. from 46 to 63 years of age	47.9				

The age distribution shows that while the number of persons aged between 46 and 63 (47.9 per cent) is relatively high, most entrepreneurs are relatively young: 52.1 per cent are under 45 years of age. *While relatively young, this is a group of mature and experienced businessmen* (Table 12.8). This statement is supported by some data relating to the years of their 'entrepreneurial socialization'. In the years when they were between 15 and 25, almost a third of the respondents (30.8 per cent) were engaged in some type of entrepreneurship, mostly within a family craft business/enterprise. Similarly, over a half of the respondents (53.6 per cent, M = 29, Mode = 28.0, Median = 28.0) claim that they started some kind of business activities between 26 and 35 years of age. Therefore, the most intensive period of their 'entrepreneurial initiation' is actually the period around their thirtieth birthday, which, we believe, would hardly be possible without a substantial number of family businesses in the Međimurje region.

The degree of education is also relatively favorable. While the fathers of the present entrepreneurs mostly had a secondary school education, or some lower school education, a majority of present entrepreneurs hold a college diploma or a university degree (Table 12.9). Around 30.0 per cent of respondents completed university education, or some other form of higher education, while 26.3 per cent completed a two-year college course. However, a substantial number of entrepreneurs have completed only secondary school (44.1 per cent). In terms of their professional profile, most of them have a technical (44.6 per cent) or economic speciality (37.1 per cent). Compared with their parents, a great number of the respondents have made advances in their status, particularly as regards their education, since many of them hold a university degree.

Table 12.9 Respondents according to a school completed (in %).

	Respondent's completed school	Father's completed school
1. no schooling/incomplete elementary education	0,0	12.6
2. completed elementary education	0,0	20.2
3. secondary school (skilled, highly skilled, secondary school)	44.1	52.6
4. two-year college	26.3	8.0
5. university, MA, PhD degree	29.1	4.2

While it is reasonable to assume that in Međimurje some craftsmen and owners of small enterprises are also linked with the 'grey economy' (Table 12.12 – external barriers to growth), our data can hardly capture the extent of this phenomenon. However, it seems that the following *differentiates Međimurje from any other Croatian county: a) a relatively significant share of manufacturing/production companies in comparison with service enterprises* (Tables 12.2, 12.3 and 12.4) *and, b) a relatively large number of very successful small companies* – according to our respondents (Table 12.10).

Table 12.10 Perception of business operation during the past three years (in %).

Business operation with losses/without coverage of costs	34.4
Profit up to 5%	38.3
Profit of 5% or above	26.8
Other	0.5

About 65.0 per cent of craft businesses/enterprises have operated with some profit in the past three years, and among 34.4 per cent of those who have difficulties, the largest number 'can hardly cover operating costs'. In other words, this means that they are not typical 'losers' but companies which have been hindered in their business development by everyday problems. Financial data for 2000, from the local Chamber of Commerce, also confirm that the majority of Međimurje entrepreneuers are operating slowly but steadily, without significant losses (see: Međimurska županija, 2001).

Judging by the data at our disposal, we conclude that *among the entrepreneurs in Međimurje most are 'entrepreneurs with a tendency to growth'* (Table 12.11). The data relating to past and future investment also substantiates this thesis. For example, 69.0 per cent of entrepreneurs have made some investments in the past three years, and the average amount of investment was around USD 195.956,9. However, as the modal value of investment is closer to the amount of USD 58.823,5 we consider that a large number of entrepreneurs have made investments between USD 47.058,8 and 58.823,5.

Table 12.11 Perception of key business indicators in the coming year (in %).

	decrease	the same	increase	M
number of products/services in the market	4.7	34.3	60.1	2.5
investment in business	10.3	38.5	50.2	2.4
earnings/profit	16.0	40.4	42.7	2.3
number of employees	12.7	45.1	41.8	2.3

Note: Rank of items made by the values of 'increase'.

It is worth noting that *a relatively large number of entrepreneurs are planning to invest in their business next year* – as many as 55.9 per cent will make new investments. They will invest primarily in new machines, equipment and tools (45.1 per cent), infrastructures (28.6 per cent), and current assets (22.5 per cent), but less in research and development of new products (10.3 per cent) and land (8.9 per cent). The planned investments are similar to those in previous years (M = USD 192.582,1), although a relatively large number of entrepreneurs will invest around USD 117.647,0. *These data show that the technological modernization of production equipment is being undertaken by most of the entrepreneurs in Međimurje.* However, while 60.1 per cent of them are planning significantly to increase the number of their products in the market in the coming period (Table 12.11), there are not many [of them] who intend to invest in research and development for new products. Does this mean that they do not need this kind of investment, or are their development priorities wrong?

Perception of Barriers to Growth

According to recent research carried out in Slovenia in 2000 (Bartlet and Bukvič, 2001) *Slovenian* entrepreneurs consider the following as major barriers to the growth of their enterprises: 1) late payments for goods/services sold (49.1 per cent, M = 3.92 on a scale 1 to 5), 2) high severance payments to employees who received a notice of dismissal, 3) highly expensive credits/loans, 4) high costs of credit insurance, 5) slow bureaucracy, 6) high contributions for social insurance, 7) obligations to obtain numerous permits (licenses), 8) high profit tax, 9) rigid employment regulations, and 10) high bank fees for services (30.0 per cent, M = 3.41 on a scale from 1 to 5).

We will present the Međimurje entrepreneurs' evaluation of possible barriers to enterprise growth in terms of Bartlett's and Bukvič's classification of barriers (Table 12.12). As we can see, our data for Međimurje show that Croatian entrepreneurs consider *internal barriers* to growth to be: 1) high labor costs (brutto wages) – 38,5 per cent believe that this variable is 'a very high barrier' to the growth and business success of the enterprise (M=4.0 on a scale from 1 to 5), and 2) poor product selling/marketing – 23,0 per cent per cent of respondents consider this variable to be a very high barrier to the growth and business success of the enterprise (M= 3,3). It may be noted that the second barrier does not have as much weight as the first one.

Comparing to the Slovenian experience, Croatian entrepreneurs stress among the *internal barriers to growth* not only constraints imposed from outside the firm, but also the constraints which derive from their previous development and management skills. Actually, high labour costs according to our interviews with local experts and consultants score relatively high because of the 'high health security payments' and 'high pension payments'. At the same time, these variables are only part of the list of *external barriers* to growth. Looking at the structure of all the seven variables discussed here, we can say that Slovenian and Međimurje entrepereneurs perceive similar problems among external barriers (late payments, high social security payments, high profit tax, etc.). Yet, in Croatia, these problems are more widespread and intense than in Slovenia. This finding suggests that state institutions probably function better in Slovenia than in Croatia, especially when we are talking about policy against evident malpractice or the 'grey economy' (see also Tearney and Vitezić, 1999).

Financial barriers are the most numerous barriers we detected in this research. While Slovenian entrepreneurs ranked the cost of credits and high collateral requirements as 'very high barriers' to enterprise growth (44,2 per cent, 41,1 per cent), Međimurje entrepreneurs, in addition to these problems, also mentioned the lack of tax reliefs for investments (54,9 per cent), the banks' policy of ignoring small entrepreneurs (45,1 per cent), the lack of working capital (45,1 per cent), etc. We believe that this structure of financial barriers to enterprise growth in Međimurje can be explained by at least two broader factors.

Firstly, it is true that the majority of Croatian banks (of which almost 90 per cent are now in foreign ownership) are friendly, in their credit policies, to large enterprises and to individual citizens. They have begun to offer a certain amount of loans to small entrepereneurs only recently, and often with higher interest rates. There are still not many banks offering tailor-made credit for small and micro enterprises, with acceptable collateral requirements. Secondly, local entrepereneurs strongly believe that central and local governments do not offer equal support to foreign and domestic investments. The present laws offer foreign investors some tax reliefs which can not be used by domestic investors, and new (improved) laws are even intended to broaden the huge benefits for foreign entrepreneurs investing in Croatia. That is why the Međimurje entrepreneurs addressed all their complaints regarding the financial barriers to enterprise growth to the state and to the Croatian banks.

Generally speaking, if we compare the lists of barriers to enterprise growth facing *Slovenian entrepreneurs and the entrepreneurs from Međimurje, some important differences are noticeable* (Table 12.12). *Firstly*, in Croatia/Međimurje county, entrepreneurs face numerous barriers while running their businesses, and the barriers to enterprise and craft business growth are much more numerous than in Slovenia. Secondly, relative to Slovenia, the financial and external barriers to growth are much more pronounced in Međimurje county. *Thirdly*, among the institutional barriers in Međimurje, the inefficiency of justice, slow bureaucracy, and tough competition have all been recognized as great barriers to enterprise growth, unlike in Slovenia. *Finally*, while Slovenian entrepreneurs enjoy a certain amount of support at the national level, in Međimurje, the entrepreneurs are markedly critical of both the local environment and the national context. They are similarly dissatisfied with the lack of support from the local authorities, as well as with the absence of trust in society (strongly associated with irregular payments by business partners).

In his latest study of the barriers to SME development in Bosnia, Macedonia and Slovenia, Bartlett concluded that 'the results of the research indicate the key role of financial barriers in holding back growth and job creation in the transition economies of South-East Europe' (Bartlett, 2002). He thinks that these findings support the proponents of the 'finance-first' approach to SME development. Although our research does not cover the whole of Croatia, the Međimurje research data also lead to such a conclusion.

Market and Cooperation Among Entrepreneurs

While traditional economic sociology primarily studied the role of networks in the economy and in large organizations (Smelser and Swedberg, 1994), the more recent and very copious literature, dealing with small and medium-sized enterprises at the end of the nineties, focuses on the cooperation and networking of small and medium-sized enterprises, based on western experiences and models, as offering major development potential also for post-socialist entrepreneurs (Dubini, 1989; OECD, 1998; Bateman and Vehovec, 1999; Henley, 2000; Crnjak-Karanović, 2001). However, it is debatable whether foreign experiences can be successfully applied without taking into account the specific environment in which Croatian entrepreneurs and managers work.

Table 12.12 Perception of barriers to enterprise growth in Slovenia and Međimurje (Croatia).

Slovenia			Međimurje (Croatia)		
I. Internal barriers	*VHB %*	*M*	*Internal barriers*	*VHB %*	*M*
1. large severance pay	47,1	4.16	1. high labor costs (brutto wages)	38,5	4.0
2. high labor costs	22,7%	3.31	2. poor selling of goods/marketing	23,0	3.3
			3. poor quality of equipment	21,1	3.0
II. External barriers	*VHB %*	*M*	*External barriers*	*VHB%*	*M*
1. late payment	49,1	3.92	1. late payment	60,1	4.3
2. high social security payments	39,2	3.84	2. dump competition unofficial economy	50,7	4.1
3. high profits tax	36,8	3.60	3. high income tax	46,9	4.1
			4. high profits tax	43,2	4.0
			5. high health security payments	31,5	3.8
			6. access of raw materials	24,4	2.9
			7. high pension payments	23,9	3,5
III. Financial barriers	*VHB %*	*M*	*Financial barriers*	*VHB %*	*M*
1. cost of credit	44,2	3.87	1. lack of tax reliefs for investments	54,9	4.3
2. high collateral requirements	41,1	3.71	2. high collateral requirements	51,2	4,1
3. high bank charges	30,0	3.41	3. high bank charges	47,4	4,1
4. bank bureaucracy	26,4	3.16	4. banks ignore SMEs regarding loans	45,1	3,9
			5. lack of money for daily operations	45,1	4.0
			6. lack of investment/venture capital	43,7	3.9
			7. long time to get loan	36,2	3.7
			8. high costs of past loans	34,7	3.5
			9. bank bureaucracy	30,0	3.6
IV. Institutional barriers	*VHB %*	*M*	*Institutional barriers*	*VHB %*	*M*
1. bureaucracy	39,4	3.68	1. ineffective courts	53,5	4.0
2. too many licenses	37,3	3.64	2. slow bureaucracy	39,0	3.7
			3. strong competition	36,6	3.9
			4. slow process of getting licenses	23,9	3.2
			5. lack of support services/ centres for entrepreneurship	22,1	3.1
			6. lack of finance information	20,7	3.6
V. Social barriers	*VHB %*	*M*	*Social barriers*	*VHB %*	*M*
1. lack of state support	28,1	3.25	1. lack of support from LA	25,4	3.5
			2. lack of trust in society	21,6	3.5
			lack of support from Chamber and associations	21,6	3.4
			3. entrepreneurs do not wish to unite...	21,1	3.4

VHB: very high barrier M: mean

Cooperation and networking could be both beneficial and dangerous for post-socialist enterprises. Bartlett and Franičević (2001) point to potential advantages of networking: a) networks may promote the processes of innovation and learning, b) networks may increase efficiency and flexibility when firms have complementary areas of specialization, c) networks may facilitate risk-sharing between small firms, d) networks allow small firms to combine the advantages of the small scale with various large scale benefits. The same authors also warn policy makers of some dangers in the mere copying of foreign models, because: a) there is a complexity and diversity in SME networks, concerning their emergence, goals, behavior and duration, and b) the relative efficiency of various forms of industrial organization is contingent on a number of factors.

We believe that the willingness/unwillingness of both small and large enterprises to cooperate or use networking as a potential source of profit, income and/or market advantages is unmistakably of an evolutionary nature. Above all, it depends upon the previous development of the enterprise, the characteristics of the respective market, its earning potential, on the basis of known modus operandi, and its ownership structure. As for entrepreneurs in Međimurje, we have already shown that many of them are profit and development oriented. The question is whether such an orientation is the result of a turnover made in the domestic or the foreign market. And what market specifically?

Table 12.13 Primary markets for produce/services (in %).

1. local market (residence, county)	32.4
2. regional market (several counties)	28.6
3. the whole country	29.6
4. foreign countries	9.4

Table 12.13 shows that the primary markets for produce/service differ as far as entrepreneurs in Međimurje are concerned. Firstly, they are segmented into local, regional and national markets with almost equal shares (from 32.4 per cent to 29.6 per cent) and the participation of the foreign market amounting to only 9.4 per cent. Yet, out of the 68 enterprises which are also exporters, 19,2 per cent have made between 26 per cent and 50 per cent of their earnings in foreign markets in the overall turnover in the past year, and 28 per cent of them between 51 per cent and 100.0 per cent of the total turnover made in the past year. However, *the domestic market is more than dominant, so it is not surprising that craftsmen and entrepreneurs make most of their earnings in the domestic market.* Secondly, in the context of the domestic market, a major part is taken by local and regional markets, which definitely influences the possibilities of cooperation among entrepreneurs.

According to the views of 83.6 per cent of respondents, competition is tough. As to the number of competitors, almost one third of entrepreneurs (32.4 per cent) state that there are up to 5 competitors in their market, 30.7 per cent of them believe that there are between 6 and 10, and some have to deal with 11 or more competitors. While an average number of market competitors ranges around 70, the mode and median values show that most of entrepreneurs have around 10 competitors in the market. Among the major competitors are: 1) small and medium-sized craft businesses/enterprises (57.7 per cent), 2) large domestic companies (31.5 per cent), and 3) large international enterprises/international companies (30.5 per cent). In such highly competitive markets, a major source of earnings for our entrepreneurs comes from private companies. They account for 47.9 per cent of the enterprises' turnover, while the general population accounts for 40.8 per cent of the turnover of craft businesses and enterprises. It can be concluded that the market competitors of Međimurje entrepreneurs differ as to their market power, although large domestic and foreign companies definitely force domestic entrepreneurs to invest in technological development and to manage their current human and financial resources better.

As for *cooperation with foreign partners*, this is most often realized through export to: Germany (26 enterprises), Slovenia (19 enterprises), Austria (17 enterprises), Bosnia and Herzegovina (14 enterprises – the textile enterprise from Čakovec has succeeded in sub-contracting in this country), Italy (11 enterprises). Main foreign partners are mostly small and medium-sized enterprises (24,4 per cent), and, less frequently, large national companies (5.2 per cent) or large multinational companies in these countries (3.8 per cent). On the basis of interviews with entrepreneurs and managers, we conclude that *any form of export cooperation has a long prehistory and is based on knowing the owner* (in some cases from socialist times) and they do not want to terminate their cooperation in order to make other arrangements. Analyzing the main forms of cooperation with foreign companies (Table 12.14), we see *that the largest number of exporters export independently (23.5 per cent), through a certain form of manufacturing cooperation.* There are not many exporters who dislocate their production capacities by sub-contracting within the country – only 2.3 per cent of analyzed enterprises. Yet, there are several enterprises which – like the sub-contracting enterprises – export abroad through some other enterprises (4.7 per cent).

Table 12.14 Main forms of cooperation with foreign partners (in %).

Company – an independent exporter (a direct partner of a foreign company)	23.5
Company – sub-contractor in export business	4.7
Company – an independent exporter in agreement with sub-contracting companies in Croatia	2.6
Company – not exporter	57.7

We have not detected any strong cooperative business network either among the entrepreneurs in Međimurje or between them and their business partners. Cooperation with foreign business partners is based completely on the effort of an individual enterprise, without any support from inter-cooperation among domestic enterprises. How can one explain the relative unwillingness of entrepreneurs in Međimurje to network, despite such tough competition in both domestic and foreign markets, and the presence of various barriers to enterprise growth? There are several potential reasons.

Firstly, it is very likely that some of the entrepreneurs, among them many craftsmen and specialized manufacturing enterprises, have a monopolistic position in the market, which is not very conducive to cooperation and association. *Secondly*, the creation of business networks, in a country which does not offer any tangible benefits as regards inter-association of entrepreneurs, is a demanding process, in terms both of time invested and of work. Most entrepreneurs 'have no time for this'. *Thirdly*, the lack of trust between business partners, which is also obvious in the collection of outstanding debts, generates a 'chain reaction', so that entrepreneurs are very suspicious of any new form of business and/or industrial organization. *Fourthly*, at the level of values, it is worth noting that most of the entrepreneurs in Međimurje established their current enterprises primarily because they wanted to make use of their knowledge and skills (84.0 per cent, M= 4.2 on a scale from 1 to 5), realize their own business ideas (76.5 per cent, M= 4,1) and 'be their own master' (49.2 per cent, M= 3,3). Many of them view these potential forms of business cooperation as a threat to their own autonomy and personal independence. Such views also generate a latent but lasting suspicion towards any third party – whether in their own country or abroad.

Concluding Notes

A fundamental aim of this case study of the county of Međimurje in the Republic of Croatia is to identify key socio-cultural, value-related and economic aspects of the development of entrepreneurship to date, and the main factors in the future development of small and medium-sized enterprises in this part of Croatia. *Our starting hypothesis is that the development of entrepreneurship in Međimurje was generated from inside, during the socialist period, and is heavily dependent upon a long tradition of craftsmanship in this region, and that the potential willingness/ unwillingness for different forms of cooperation among entrepreneurs is conditioned by the previous development of a craft business/enterprise, the type of market, the business potential, and the ownership structure of a company.*

The available data showed that almost one third of surveyed crafts/enterprises have a long tradition – they were established before 1990, which means under the socialist regime in Croatia. Some of the enterprises were incorporated in the 19th century – in 1874. This does not mean that the socialist system deliberately helped the development of small entrepereneurs. All these small businesses survived under socialism in spite of the general system of state/social ownership, and mostly due to the hard work of the people involved, and periodic political and economic reform of the system itself. Unfortunately, we do not have any comparative data for other Croatian counties, regarding the age of their crafts and enterprises. However, according to the interviews with the Međimurje entrepreneurs, and with local experts and consultants, as well as the other data, we may say that Međimurje is, in an economic sense, recognizable by a high proportion of relatively old crafts and businesses.

Contrary to the thesis of some economists about the positive impact of a position close to the border on local entrepreneurship development, we do not find any direct impact of trans-border cooperation on the development of local businesses in Međimurje. The following factors in entrepreneurial development have been regarded as being of secondary importance: the inter-cooperation of entrepreneurs, the encouragement of craft business/entrepreneurship development under socialism, the availability of infrastructure facilities, a favorable position along the state border. Yet, there is evidence which suggests that huge social capital (new crafts and management skills, urban habits, etc.) has been imported into Međimurje by generations of workers employed abroad. After their return to Međimurje, they very often established their own small shops and crafts. This is the way that new knowledge and the modern entrepreneurial spirit has been imported and diffused in Međimurje.

Bearing in mind the typical picture of post-socialist small and micro enterprises in the literature, we can say that there are some characteristics that distinguish Međimurje from all the other Croatian counties. These are: a) a relatively large number of manufacturing/processing companies, compared with the service trade; and b) a relatively large number of successful small businesses. As one of our interviewees said: "Međimurje has the largest number of manufacturing trades in Croatia, relative to the size of population, and more export products that in the whole country". We found among the successful small businesses mostly the 'entrepreneurs with a tendency to growth', and the available data suggest that more than half our respondents fall into that category.

Such a good picture of the business prospects of the majority of the analyzed enterprises is somewhat disturbed by the fact that there are many barriers to future enterprise growth in their larger environment. The barriers to enterprise growth in Međimurje (Croatia) are stronger and more widespread than in Slovenia. Our data also supports the relevant findings of Bartlett, which claim that financial barriers have a crucial role in holding back growth and job creation in the transition economies of South-East Europe.

As regards our thesis about the possible evolution of cooperation among entrepreneurs, we draw attention to the real position of small and micro enterprises on the market. There are a large number of entrepreneurs in Međimurje still oriented towards the domestic market, and this partly explains why more complex forms of production cooperation with foreign partners are relatively weak. No significant entrepreneurial networking has been noticed, and the reasons are: poor competition and monopoly in the domestic market; the perception of networking as being both time-consuming and organizationally very demanding; lack of trust among business partners which generates additional suspicion towards new forms of industrial organization, while the desire of entrepreneurs to maintain their own independence and business autonomy as much as possible produces a similar effect.

One final remark. Međimurje, which is, from a business point of view, probably one of the most developed counties in Croatia, but which, due to its poor natural resources, has not to date attracted many foreign investors, poses numerous questions both to scholars and to local and national policy makers. We will mention a few: 1) will the advantages of business development to date, rooted in a long tradition and personal business autonomy, become handicaps to development in the completely new circumstances (globalization and technological development)?; 2) by what means and through what institutions can one raise the awareness of businessmen 'of the changed conditions relating to survival in the market'?; 3) how can the state respond to the requests of entrepreneurs for the elimination of growth barriers – by the consistent implementation of general measures to encourage competitiveness in the market, or by some specifically designed policies, adapted to particular types of entrepreneurs – tailor-made only for those who are growth-oriented (Smallbone and Welter, 2001)?; 4) which is the most desirable/productive function of a local political élite in advancing new entrepreneurship growth?

Note

1 Historically, during the times when a large part of Croatia was under Ottoman occupation, Međimurje was the centre of the most powerful aristocratic family of the time - the Zrinski. The Zrinski ruled over Međimurje from 1546, when Nikola Šubić Zrinski-Sigetski was assigned the area by king Ferdinand of the Habsburg monarchy, to the end of the 17th century. Međimurje was part of the Croatian national kingdom of the distant past, which is reflected by the fact that in 1857 it had 58.721 inhabitants, out of which there were only 612 Hungarians and 511 Germans (Jokić-Horvat, 1992; http://www.hgk.hr/komora/hrv/zupkom/Cakovec; HŽ, 2000).

References

Bartlett, W. (2002), 'Financial barriers to SME Growth in Bosnia, Macedonia and Slovenia', in *Conference on Economic Development and reconstruction Policies in South-East Europe: The Role of SMEs*, Dubrovnik, 25th-27th April, 2002, p. 22.

Bartlett, W. and Bukvić, V. (2001), 'Barriers to SME growth in Slovenia', in *Enterprise in Transition. Fourth International Conference on Enterprise in Transition*, The Faculty of Economics, University of Split, Split-Hvar, May 24-26, 2001, pp. 198-201.

Bartlett, W. and Franičević, V. (1999), 'Emerging policies towards enterprise promotion of small firms' in Croatia', *Enterprise in Transition. Third International Conference on Enterprise in Transition*, The Faculty of Economics, University of Split, Split-Šibenik, May 27-29, 1999, pp. 467-470.

Bartlett, W. and Franičević, V. (2001), 'Policy support for small firm networks in the economies in transition – issues and dilemmas', in *Enterprise in Transition. Fourth International Conference on Enterprise in Transition*, The Faculty of Economics, University of Split, Split-Hvar, May-24-26, 2001, pp. 423- 425.

Bartlett, W. and Prašnikar, J. (1995), 'Small firms and economic transformation in Slovenia', *Communist Economies & Economic Transformation*, vol 7, no. 1, pp. 83-103.

Bateman, M. (2000), 'Small enterprise development policy in the transition economies: progress with the wrong model?', *Zagreb International Review of Business and Economics*, vol. 2, no. 1, pp.1-36.

Bateman, M. (2001), 'Small enterprise development policy and the reconstruction of the Yugoslav successor states: a "local developmental state" policy model', *Enterprise in Transition. Fourth International Conference on Enterprise in Transition*, The Faculty of Economics, University of Split, Split-Hvar, May 24-26, 2001, pp. 1- 43.

Bateman, M. and Vehovec, M. (1999), 'The evolution of local supplier clusters: evidence of a bottom-up strategy for the shipbuilding industry in Croatia', in *Enterprise in Transition. Third International Conference on Enterprise in Transition*, The Faculty of Economics, University of Split, Split-Šibenik, May 27-29, 1999, pp. 471-474 + extended paper on CD ROM.

Brezinski, H. and Fritsch, M. (ed.) (1996), *The Economic Impact of New Firms in Post-Socialist Countries. Bottom-up Transformation in Eastern Europe*, Edward Elgar, Cheltenham, UK, Brookfield, USA.

Čengić, D. and Rogić, I. (ur.) (1999), *Privatizacija i Javnost (Privatization and the public)*, Institut Ivo Pilar, Zagreb.

Čengić, D., Rogić, I. (ur.) (2001), *Upravljačke Elite i Modernizacija* (Ruling elites and modernization), Institut Ivo Pilar, Zagreb.

Crnjak-Karanović, B. (2001), 'Get In or Get Lost: Is International networking essential for companies in small transitional countries?', in *Enterprise in Transition. Fourth International Conference on Enterprise in Transition*, The Faculty of Economics, University of Split, Split-Hvar, May 24-26, 2001, pp. 416- 417 + extended paper on CD ROM.

Dubini, P. (1989), 'The influence of motivation and environment on business start-ups: some hints for public policies', *Journal of Business Venturing*, vol. 4, no 1, pp. 11-26.

Franičević, V. (2001), 'Some considerations on post-socialist entrepreneurship', paper presented on *International Conference 'Post-Communist transition Ten Years Later. Challenges and Outcomes for Europe and the Role of CEI'*, Forle, 2-3 February 2001, vol. 26 pp. 1-26.

Franičević, V. and Bartlett, W. (2001), 'Small firm networking and economies in transition: an overview of theories', Issues and policies, Zagreb, *Zagreb International Review of Economics and Business*, vol. 4, no.1., pp. 63-89.

Henley, E. (2000), 'Self-employment in post-communist Eastern Europe: A refuge from poverty or road to riches?', *Communist and Post-Communist Studies*, vol. 33, no. 3, pp. 379-402.

HGK (2001), *Neki Aspekti Gospodarskih Gibanja po Županijama (Croatian Counties - Some Economic Indicators)*, Zagreb.

HGK-ŽGK (2001), *Pregled Gospodarskih Kretanja za Razdoblje I-XII/2000 (Review of Economic Results in 2000)*, Čakovec, svibanj 2001.

HŽ (2000), *EuroCity*, Zima/Winter 2000 (Special Issue: Međimurje County), Zagreb.

Jokić-Horvat, B. (1992), Analiza slučajeva poduzetništva u Međimurju (Analysis of Entrepreneurship Development in Međimurje –case studies), u: Čengić, D. (ur.) (1992), *Kako do uspješnog poduzeća? (How to Build a Successful Enterprise?)*, HGK, HUM-Croma, Zagreb, pp. 229-236.

Kovačević Z. and Obadić, A. (2001), 'The Importance of Small and Medium Enterprises for Croatian Development', in *Enterprise in Transition. Fourth International Conference on Enterprise in Transition*, The Faculty of Economics, University of Split, Split-Hvar, May-24-26, 2001, pp. 434-435.

Međimurska županija (2001), *Osnovni financijski rezultati poslovanja Međimurskih poduzetnika u 2000. godini (Basic Financial Results of Međimurje Entrepreneurs in 2000)*, Čakovec.

Meštrović, M. and Štulhofer, A. (ur.) (1998), *Sociokulturni Kapital i Tranzicija u Hrvatskoj (Sociocultural capital and transition in Croatia)*, Hrvatsko sociološko društvo, Zagreb.

Obrtnička komora Međimurske županije (2001), *Katalog obrtništva Međimurja (Međimurje Craftsmanship Register)*, Čakovec.

OECD (1998), *Fostering Entrepreneurship*, Paris, OECD.

Sekulić, D. and Šporer, Ž (2000), 'Formiranje poduzetničke elite u Hrvatskoj (Making of the Entrepreneurial Elite in Croatia)', Zagreb, *Revija za sociologiju*, vol. 31, no. 1-2, pp. 1-20.

Smallbone, D. and Welter, F. (2001), 'The role of government in sme development in the transition economies of Central and Eastern Europe and the Newly Independent States', in (2001), *Enterprise in Transition. Fourth International Conference on Enterprise in Transition*, The Faculty of Economics, University of Split, Split-Hvar, May 24-26, 2001, pp. 238-240

Smelser, N. J., Swedberg, R. (eds.) (1994), *The Handbook of Economic Sociology*, Princeton University Press, Princeton.

Tearney, G. M. and Vitezić, N. (1999), 'The Growth of Small Business: A Study of its Development in Croatia and Slovenia', in *Enterprise in Transition. Third International Conference on Enterprise in Transition*, The Faculty of Economics, University of Split, Split-Šibenik, May 27-29, 1999, pp. 538-541

ZAP (2001), *Informacija o Osnovnim Financijskim Rezultatima Poduzetnika RH u 2000 Godini (Basic financial results of Croatian entrepreneurs in 2000)*, Središnji ured Zagreb, srpanj 2001.

Županov, J. (2001), Industrializing and deindustrializing elite in Croatia in the second half of the 20th century, in Čengić, D., Rogić, I. (ur.) (2001), *Upravljačke Elite i Modernizacija (*Ruling elites and modernization), Institut Ivo Pilar, Zagreb, pp. 11-36.

Chapter 13

Small and Medium Enterprises and Their Role in the Innovative Environment of the Bratislava Region

Jana Gašparíková, Milan Buček and Štefan Rehák

Introduction

In this chapter we describe how decentralized innovation policy helps to develop innovation through its own instruments, contacts between SMEs and universities and research institutes. It is based on the preliminary results of research in the Bratislava region.

It is very important for a proper understanding of regional development in the Slovak Republic to investigate the real influence of regional and innovation policy on the industrial sector and in particular on SMEs. The question is, are these small and medium enterprises really innovative? The position of SMEs differs from that of large enterprises, and there is some support from studies that large enterprises are more innovative. We base our ideas on Lundvall's (1992) understanding that an innovation system is comprized of elements and relationships, which interact in the production, diffusion and the use of economically useful knowledge. It is considered a social system in the sense that innovation is the result of social interaction between economic factors. It is an open system interacting with its environment.

The paper concentrates on the problem of how decentralized economic and innovation policy helps to develop innovation institutions and human potential. It presents the results of the survey that was carried out by the Economic University's Department of Regional Development and Geography in Bratislava. The survey also intends to investigate the links between SMEs and research institutes.

The project carried by the Economic University concentrates on how innovation really can be promoted. In this way it is our wish that regional policy should be based on real recommendations resulting from our investigations. These investigations try to establish interesting causal links between innovation and the regional aspects of the economic activity of SMEs, taking into consideration also the unique position of Bratislava, which has many SMEs and research institutes.

In order to interpret innovation policy it is necessary to describe the changes in economic policy. In the following section the new economic conditions in the Slovak Republic and the industrial structure will be defined. The rest of the paper concentrates on Bratislava region in particular.

The Changing Economic Policy and Industrial Structure in Slovakia

Since 1989, the Central and Eastern European countries have undergone profound economic changes. Systems of central planning characterizing the Central and Eastern European economies have been dismantled, industry privatized, trade liberalized and economies generally stabilized. Slovakia is one of the countries, characteristic with rapid transition of its industry and increasing innovative activities in its core region, Bratislava.

The population of Slovakia is approximately 5.3 million, with about 2.9 million employed and just less than 0.34 million unemployed. The average nominal monthly wage of an employee is 290 EUR – being slightly higher in manufacturing (298 EUR) and lower in education and research (219 EUR). Measured in terms of purchasing power parity, GDP is approximately 1.35 billion EUR (55.5 billion SKK). The inflation rate is 8.4 per cent per annum, the general government domestic debt is 3.3 billion EUR and the general foreign government debt is 2.9 billion EUR (Statistical Office in Bratislava, 2000).

Economic life under the communist regime involved the concentration of industry in highly specialized industrial districts with priority given to heavy industry. Economic activity was centrally planned and vertically structured. A common feature was the absence of horizontal linkages between different economic activities.

Industry has an important (33 per cent) share of the total volume of Slovak production. In industrial organizations, there are 76,000 employees with an average monthly nominal wage of 15,378 SKK (375 EUR). Industry in Slovakia is mainly dominated by the chemical, machinery and food industries. Industrial enterprises fulfilled their production plans without any negative influences on employment. The presence of foreign capital (from 17 per cent to 100 per cent in most important enterprises) stabilized production programes, and the growth of the competitiveness of entrepreneurial activities form preconditions for development opportunities and the establishment of the Bratislava region in the economy of Slovak Republic. Figure 13.1 gives the SME share of industrial production in 1999.

The SME sector started from scratch after 1989. Before this period, practically no small and medium size enterprises existed but after the so-called 'Velvet Revolution', many small and medium size enterprises were set up in the wake of the social and economic changes that occurred either as new start-ups or spin-offs from large enterprises. Nevertheless, large enterprises remain the most important economically, creating the foundation for the economic well being of the country.

It is a fact that despite the new start-ups and spin-offs, large corporations create the economic potential of the country.

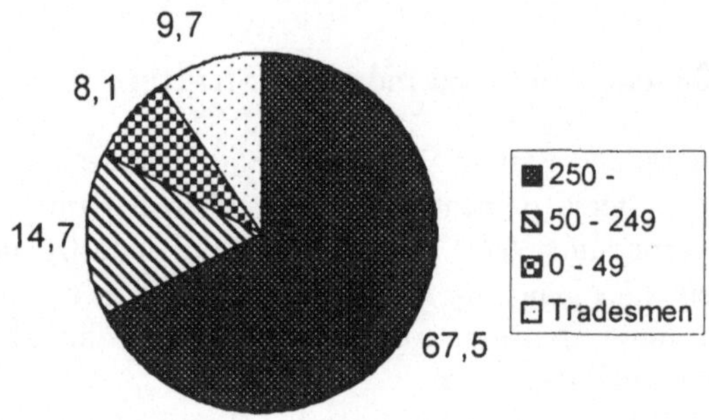

Figure 13.1 The share of SMEs in industrial production (1999).

The development of SMEs is influenced by state support (different state programs) but problems exist. The most urgent problem is investment policy – there is simply not enough investment in technology. Two other important processes also influence the situation in the SME sector. The privatization and revitalization processes help bankrupt enterprises to survive (especially in the machinery industry).

As of December 31, 2000, 60,920 legal entities were registered in Statistical Office. Out of these, 57,247 were small enterprises (49 employees) and 3,063 were medium size enterprises (50-249 enterprises). Concentrating on the ongoing trend, we witness an increasing tendency for the foundation of small enterprises and a decreasing tendency for the foundation of medium sized enterprises. However, while there are problems country-wide, Bratislava itself is in a relatively favoured position, as reflected by the fact that many new enterprises founded after 1989, are still in existence. Bratislava has very good location, because it lies on the borders of Austria and Hungary, with relatively good business contacts and logistics with both countries. These factors help to develop entrepreneurial attitudes and encourage SME formation.

What are the innovative abilities of enterprises in Slovakia? The results of a survey conducted by the Statistical Office are given in the report 'Innovation Activities in Manufacturing in the Slovak Republic' (2001). In this, 167 enterprises from the Bratislava region (148 small and medium size enterprises) were investigated. The report estimates that about 17 per cent of all manufacturing enterprises in the Slovak Republic are technological innovators, i.e. they have introduced technologically new or improved products or processes during the surveyed period (1987-1999). Innovative activity was the highest in large enterprises with more than 250 employees, of which 43 per cent were innovating, while only 17 per cent of medium size enterprises with 50-249 employees and 7.3 per cent of small enterprises with 20-49 employees were innovating. It means our sample does not show a high presence of innovation activities among small and medium size enterprises.

It was found that 31 per cent of the innovating enterprises have introduced a product innovation and 18 per cent introduced process innovation. The remaining innovators (51 per cent) have introduced both, i.e. product and process innovation. Approximately half of the innovating enterprises have carried out R&D on a systematic or occasional basis. The highest share of innovators with R&D activities was found among the large enterprises (61.9 per cent), followed by the small enterprises (54.3 per cent) and the medium size enterprises (45.3 per cent). Approximately one third of the innovators cooperate with other partners in developing innovation. Most of them (74.5 per cent) claimed to cooperate with private research institutes; out of them 56.3 per cent cooperated with universities and 40.2 per cent cooperated with research centers.

All the figures related to innovativeness indicate the increasing concern of firms for innovative activities. As one expects most of these innovative firms are concentrated in certain nodes, especially in Bratislava. That is why this region is one of the best places for the analysis of innovative relations between SMEs and the institutions in the wider Europe.

The Importance of Bratislava in the Slovak Republic

The evaluation of the level of regional development that meets the requirements and criteria of the European Union shows that the Bratislava region has a significantly higher GDP per capita (PPP in nominal value) than the other regions. Table 13.1 shows the regional variation together with the GDP per capita for the country as a whole, which is only 46 per cent of the EU average. More significant spatial variations differences are apparent at the county level (NUTS III).

The Bratislava region has a special position, not only in comparison with other Slovak regions, but also in comparison with the EU average. With the level equal to 97 per cent of the EU average and 265 per cent above the average of Central European countries, it can be classified as one of the most developed regions within Central Europe. The other regions in Slovakia range from 29 to 44 per cent of the EU average.

The Bratislava region covers an area of 2,053 kilometers. At the end of 1999, the population amounted to 617,000, which represents 11.4 per cent of the inhabitants of Slovak Republic. The number of economically active people was 335,800 in 1999. This number represents 82.9 per cent of people of working age and 16.5 per cent of economically active people of retirement age. 26 of the employees work in productive sectors and 20.7 per cent worked in industry, mainly in the food sector, transportation, electrical and optical instruments and publishing.

Table 13.1 Share of per capita GDP of the EU (in SKK).

Region/County	Per capita GDP in PPS		Per capita in % of the EU average		Per capita in % of the CEC average [1)]	
	1996	1997	1996	1997	1996	1997
Slovak Republic	8100	8800	45	46	116	119
Bratislava Region	17500	19900	97	105	250	269
Northwestern Region	6740	7200	37	38	97	97
County of Trenčín	6700	7600	37	40	95	103
County of Žilina	6800	6900	38	36	97	93
Southwestern Region	7330	7800	40	41	106	125
County of Trnava	8000	8400	44	44	114	113
County of Nitra	6900	7400	38	39	98	101
Eastern Region	6690	7200	37	38	97	97
County of Banská Bystrica	7300	7900	40	42	104	107
County of Prešov	5100	5500	28	29	73	74
County of Košice	7800	8300	43	44	112	113

1) Central European Countries (CEC).

Source: Regional GDP in CEC, The Statistical Office of the Slovak Republic, National Accounts 1999.

Generally speaking, the city of Bratislava holds the dominant position in the economy of its region, and its economic structure determines the economic profile and level of the entire region. Bratislava also has a very good position in the industrial sector.

Innovation Infrastructure of Bratislava

The Bratislava region, due to the city Bratislava, has the highest share of university educated people of Slovakia – 55 per cent of inhabitants have secondary education and 22 per cent are university educated.

Table 13.2 The distribution of firms by regions 1998.

Region	Total	Share in %	New enterprises (for 1000 persons)	Physical and legal entities (for 1000 persons)
Bratislava	**69 485**	**20.0**	**9.8**	**122.2**
Trnava	37 221	10.7	6.1	67.0
Trenčín	34 403	9.9	5.6	70.0
Nitra	43 617	12.6	5.4	72.1
Zilina	42 446	12.2	5.3	61.4
Banská Bystrica	38 598	11.1	5.0	65.0
Prešov	38 816	11.2	4.8	55.7
Košice	42 702	12.3	4.5	65.3
SR	**347 288**	**100.0**	**5.6**	**70.0**

Source: Regional comparisons in the Slovak Republic 1998, Statistical Office of the Slovak Republic, Bratislava, Calculating: Bucek et al.

Within the territory of Bratislava there are five universities with 24 faculties. The student population consists of 36,062 full time students (40 per cent) and 7,500 part time students. The Slovak Technical University is the largest educational establishment in the field of technology and has many faculties. In six faculties, more than 1,600 teachers pursue a wide range of teaching, research and professional interests. The increasing development of technology has been reflected by an increase in the size and diversity of research involvement and teaching at universities. The dominant position of Bratislava in the field of higher education is clearly demonstrated in following figures; 51 per cent of all professors and 52,3 per cent of students live in Bratislava.

Regional differences in the share of the labor force with completed university education in the economically active population are not so dramatically different, but still exist. The Bratislava region with a share of 11 per cent of the population has a 25 per cent share of the labor force with completed university education (Table 13.3).

Table 13.3 Regional differences in human potential.

Region	Share of employees with university education in the economically active population (%)	
	1997	**1998**
Bratislava Region	24.6	25.0
Northwestern Region	9.2	8.9
County of Trenčín	10.0	8.1
County of Žilina	8.5	9.8
Southwestern Region	8.0	7.7
County of Trnava	8.5	8.6
County of Nitra	7.6	6.9
Eastern Region	9.0	9.1
County of Banská Bystrica	10.3	9.6
County of Prešov	9.0	9.2
County of Košice	8.0	8.1
Slovak Republic	10.8	10.7

Source: Statistical Annual 1999, The Statistical Office of the Slovak Republic, Bratislava.

Bratislava as the Center of Research

The Bratislava region has been the centre of scientific research for a long time in Slovakia. Almost all of the government research centres and a large number of research centres in the higher education sector are situated here (Table 13.4).

In total there are 47 institutes of the Slovak Academy of Sciences located in the Bratislava region providing basic and applied research in the field of physical, life and social sciences. The Academy has undergone major changes in the past ten years, with many research institutes decreasing their employees.

Table 13.4 Number of R&D organizations by sector.

	Total no of organizations	Business enterprise sector	Government sector	Higher education sector
Bratislava Reg.	135	44	67	24
SR average	*39*	*21*	*11*	*8*
SR total	315	168	85	62

Source: Selected indicators of R&D Organizations in the Slovak Republic 2000, Statistical Office of the Slovak Republic, Bratislava.

Although the scientific potential in the Academy is large and the institutes are leading research institutes in the Slovak Republic, cooperation with SMEs still remains very weak. In reality, a small number of contacts, specialized for the business sector, resulted in the lack of demand from the private sector. Frequently mentioned shortcomings are associated with totally inadequate support from public administration both in the field of legislation and financing.

Financing R&D in the Bratislava Region

As opposed to the global trend of increasing expenditures on research and development, in Slovakia we observe decreasing expenditure relative to GDP, from 1.03 per cent GERD/GDP in 1996 to 0.68 per cent in 1999. This situation is similar in both the business and public sectors. The decline of expenditures on R&D is mainly caused by a 44 per cent fall in business sector spending between 1997-99. With the exception of general research activities, most expenditure is dedicated to the manufacture of chemical products, rubber, plastic products, machinery and basic metals.

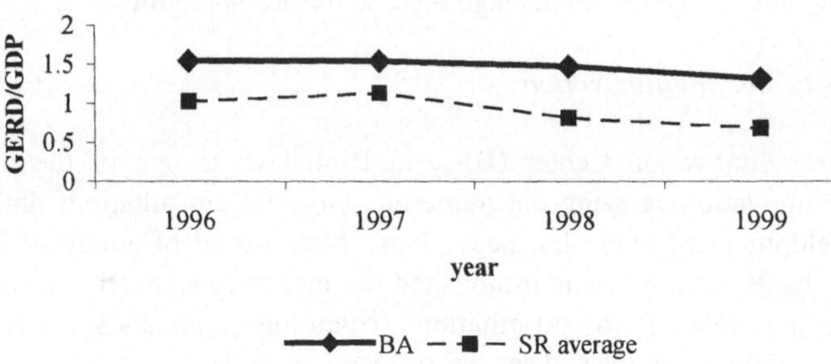

Figure 13.2 Trends in Gross Expenditures on R&D relative to GDP.

Source: M. Buček, calculations based on Yearbook of Research and Development 2000, Statistical Office of the Slovak Republic, Bratislava.

The uneven distribution of expenditures on R&D is a serious problem; most of the R&D capabilities are located in the capital city, Bratislava. Even though the share of expenditures on R&D is relatively high in the Bratislava region (1.32 per cent) compared to the Slovak average, it is still far below the EU average of 2 per cent. When we look at R&D expenditure in the Bratislava region we also see a downward trend in the public sector.

Financial Support for Research Institutes

Research institutes in Bratislava region are supported mostly from state funds; only 38 per cent of R&D expenditure comes from the business sector. Most R&D spending is focused on institutions such as the Slovak Academy of Sciences. A serious problem is caused by a very low share of capital expenditure in relation to current expenditure what means that investment in the future, new equipment, etc. is strongly neglected (only 17 per cent of the total GERD). It seems that a survival mentality is dominant. Commercial R&D in Bratislava tends to be carried out by large international firms, which operate independently. Government subsidies and employment programs have been established to encourage internal financial investment. Industrial R&D tends to be supply oriented and products are oriented towards low technology markets. It is clear that the financial situation in the different research institutes has a bad effect on technological and knowledge transfer.

A very low level of knowledge transfer can be seen to be a consequence of the limited growth of facilities such as scientific parks, technological areas or scientific centers, which are only at the early stage of their development, and the process of learning systematically how to manage these activities is ongoing.

Institutions Promoting Innovation

The Business Innovation Center (BIC) in Bratislava is one of the institutions promoting innovation carrying out numerous business consultations and assisting in the development of many business plans. Also a total of about 30 innovative companies have already been established in incubation centers most of these projects being related to information technology, logistics, environmental technology, heating systems and special services for industry.

In July 2000, FEMIRC Bratislava became a full member of the EU Innovation Relay Centre Network. The main mission of the IRC Slovakia is to support the development of innovation processes, especially for SMEs involved in national and transnational technology transfer, and the dissemination of information concerning the EU RTD programs.

The participation of Slovak RTD programs in EU programs is also a very important Technology transfer activity forms the substantial part of IRC work. The technology sectors, which IRC concentrates on, are tool processing for the automotive industry, wood processing, information technology, biotechnology, environment and non-nuclear energy and the agro food sector.

Awareness of the importance of public support for technology transfer and knowledge diffusion has increased and the need for effective exploitation of the results of scientific research and of human potential has been officially recognized as one of the top priorities for the Bratislava region's economic development. Also business research cooperation has been considered to be the necessary precondition for the process of the restructuring of the regional economy. In July 2001, the Slovak government approved a manual on industrial parks. This act helped individual projects to receive financial support for covering 70 per cent of all costs.

The Case Study: The Preconditions for Development of SMEs in the Bratislava Region

The main goal of the case study is the analysis of institutional, innovative and regional preconditions for the real development of small and medium enterprises in the Bratislava region. We have focused our attention on SMEs in the sectors mostly represented in the Bratislava electro-technical, machine and petrochemical industries. Our case study also concentrates more on the local and regional aspects stimulating or diminishing innovation potential in the SME sector in the Bratislava region. Our primary interest has not been to find out what kind of innovation resulted from cooperation, but how the innovation potential was used in the region, and this has motivated the construction of our questionnaire which has been designed to uncover the factors influencing technology and knowledge transfer in the region.

Our investigation also differs from the investigation conducted by the Statistical office, because it not only concentrates on partial findings concerning innovation from the perspective of SMEs, and how this knowledge and technology transfer is possible, but also from the perspective of research institutes.

The Bratislava region has many SMEs, research institutes and universities and as such, it has the excellent potential for possible contacts among firms and research institutes and for possible technology and knowledge transfers. Our interest is based on investigating the situation in three industrial sectors mentioned above: namely the chemical, electro-technical and machine industry, and on contacts with higher educational and research institutes.

We have concentrated on case studies involving 35 SMEs from the three industrial sectors and also involving 20 research institutes, looking at their potential for cooperation and collaboration. These firms and research institutes are examined for evidence of real positive or negative inputs of governmental and regional policy and their impact on SME innovative activities.

These investigations are based on two types of questionnaires – one is inspired by a questionnaire created in Austria (Vienna University of Economics and Business Administration) and has the following parts: a) institutional – where different institutions, governmental and private firms are investigated as potential partners assisting in new product development, and b) priorities concerning governmental policy. The other questionnaire investigated cooperation between research institutes and universities with different SMEs in order to discover the channels along which technological and knowledge transfers flow.

Table 13.5 Frequency of interactions with the following institutions in the innovation process.

Institutions in the Bratislava region that assist in the new product development process	Frequency of interactions (Number of firms)			
	Unknown	*Never*	*Sometimes*	*Frequently*
Universities				
University of Economics	0	28	1	0
Slovak Technical University	0	17	12	0
Comenius University	0	29	0	0
City University Bratislava	1	29	0	0
Private or public research organizations				
Slovak Academy of Sciences	0	25	5	0
Other research centers	0	19	9	1
Consultants				
BIC Bratislava	3	25	1	0
National Agency for the Development of SME's	1	25	3	0
European Information Center	0	30	0	0
House of Technology ZSVTS	1	24	5	0
Innovation Relay Center Slovakia	5	22	2	0
TIPS – Technology and Business Information	7	21	0	1
SARC – Center for the Advancement of Science and Technology	5	23	0	1
Venture Capital Firms				
Seed Capital Company	3	26	0	0
Innovate Fund	2	27	0	0
Slovak Guarantee and Development Bank	0	25	4	0
Slovak – American Business Fund	5	25	0	0
Chambers of Commerce				
Slovak Chamber of Commerce and Industry	0	15	9	3
Slovak Chamber of Entrepreneurs	0	27	1	1
Slovak Association of Entrepreneurs	1	26	1	1
Slovak Association of Cooperative Societies	2	25	2	0
Regional customers		5	12	10
Other firms in your region		4	18	7
Regional suppliers		10	6	11

The project intends to show ways of promoting the innovation potential in different SMEs and provide recommendations regarding changes that could be made to government policy in order to improve the situation.

The findings of the Stage I: Innovation and Business Environment of SMEs

During first period of the investigation, we concentrated our interest on the innovation and business environment of SME's in Bratislava.

a. The nature of technology and knowledge transfer. One of our findings was that the most frequent contacts were between different departments of the Slovak Technical University (13) and different research centers (9) and SMEs. Very occasionally there were also contacts between the institutes of the Slovak Academy of Sciences and SMEs, the House of Technology and the Slovak Chamber of Commerce which offered occasional information and help for the SME sector as well.

What was important was the discovery that there are very few contacts between industrial SME's and research institutes; but there is much more contact between the firms themselves (Table 13.5).

b. Appraisal of factors relevant for innovation potential. The appraisal of factors relevant for innovation development concentrated on different kinds of questions designed to reveal the approval that exists for research within the SME sector. In general, it can be said that there is appreciation of R&D in the SME sector. The importance of skilled workers in the region and the presence of basic research institutes and universities was generally acknowledged. It appears that one of the basic preconditions for regional economic development is fulfilled. The other conditions are not highly developed. For instance it is very difficult to access risk capital. Even more important is the finding that there are not sufficient measures to promote innovation, which results in inefficient technology and knowledge transfers. One of the most important reasons for the lack of efficient measures is local and regional taxes. These taxes are very high and hold back business expenditures on research and development and limit access to venture capital (Table 13.6).

Table 13.6 also shows responses to some of our survey questions that provide further insight into the conditions underpinning future innovative development in the region as they are perceived by the SMEs, and highlights the lack of fiscal incentives for R&D in the region.

c. *Priorities for government policy.* The other very important questions that were asked were related to the priorities given to different aspects of government policy, one of the crucial findings being that business is negatively influenced by insufficient logistics and transport.

Table 13.6 Conditions underpinning innovative development of firms/questionnaire.

Questions	Possibilities	Scores (1-7)	Answers
Basic research facilities are	many	4.37	few
Basic research facilities are	ineffective	3.35	effective
The institutions in your region that perform basic research	rarely transfer knowledge to your industry	2.21	frequently transfer knowledge to your industry
Qualified scientists and engineers in your region are in	scarce supply	3.79	sufficient supply
The size of the available pool of skilled workers in your region	is too small or inflexible, which hinders your growth	4.11	is sufficiently large and flexible to permit growth
Access to risk capital in your region is	difficult	2.83	easy
Business expenditures on research and development are	not encouraged by provincial and regional taxes and incentives	1.95	encouraged by provincial and regional taxes and incentives
Public support of the private investments in research and technology is	insufficient	2.22	sufficient

The other finding is the importance attributed to a lack of information and communication infrastructure. Regarding the nature of the environment, we may say that it is pro innovative. The sufficiently large and flexible pool of skilled workers is a likely indicator that the adoption rate, meaning the rate of adoption of new technologies and work techniques, is very high. The most frequent barrier to wider exploitation of new technologies in the SME sector is considered to be the lack of financial resources, which includes firms' own lack of resources, high interest and bank guarantee rates and taxes. The pro innovative character of many SMEs is also indicated by a survey carried out by the Statistical Office in 2000 (Innovation and Manufacturing in the Slovak Republic 2000) which finds that innovation in SMEs is oriented towards improving working conditions in order to increase labor productivity. While it appears that the cooperation between SMEs, private research institutes, universities and public sector research institutes has had a stimulating effect for business, the regional tax system and system of incentives has not.

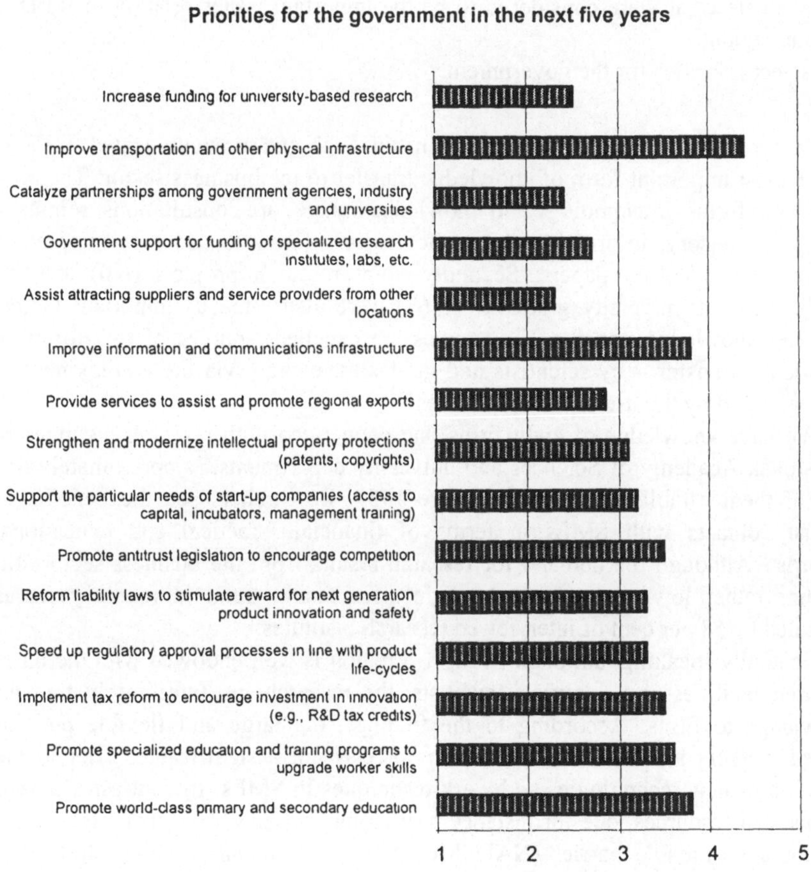

1 - not at all important 2 - not important 3 - slightly important 4 - important 5 - very important.

Figure 13.3 Priorities for the government in the next five years.

Part II: The Role of Academic Institutions in Innovative Activiities

The second part of the investigations was focused on the university departments of the Slovak Technical University and selected institutes of the Slovak Academy of Sciences in chemistry, engineering and electronics. We asked researchers to:

- rate the importance of different forms of technology transfer;
- evaluate cooperation with the business sector and the recent changes in demand for their research results;
- evaluate what were considered to be the important issues relating to R&D in the region;
- select priorities for the government.

Researchers consider informal relationships with entrepreneurs (rated 6.17) to be the most important form of knowledge transfer to the business sector. The most often used forms of technology and knowledge transfer are consultations, seminars, analyses, advisory, informal relations, access to information sources in research centers and scientific papers. Secondly, joint research projects (6.0) and the employment of university graduates (5.67) were also rated as important factors enabling knowledge transfer. Universities are excellent sources of two forms of knowledge transfer – by scientists and graduates, namely via the employment of graduates and by the use of library sources.

We have knowledge of eight firms that cooperated with research institutes of the Slovak Academy of Sciences and university departments. Approximately one half of them established contacts before 1989. Researchers see the benefits of mutual contacts with SMEs in terms of financial, practical and educational rewards. Although the demand for research results from the business sector still remains rather low, we can see a slightly increasing trend in recent years as indicated by 58 per cent of interviewed research institutes.

Generally speaking, although Bratislava region is well endowed with the basic research facilities and qualified scientists, the research institutes rarely transfer knowledge to firms. According to the findings, the large and flexible pool of skilled workers indicates that the labour force is not a significant barrier to the adoption of new technologies and work techniques in SMEs. In contrast, the lack of financial resources, due for instance to high interest and bank guarantees rates, present a formidable barrier (NADSME, 2000). Also our research shows the difficulty in accessing risk capital in the region, and highlights the inhibiting role of the regional tax and incentives system for business expenditures on research and development.

Conclusive Remarks and Policy Recommendations

We observed how both business and research evaluated and prioritized the different strands of government policy. Figure 13.4 shows the overall results of the study. The vertical axis is the scores given by research and business sectors, and it shows that the top priority for the research sector was to increase the funding for basic university research and the increase of governmental support for the funding of specialized research institutes. Research at universities and research institutes is currently crippled by financial problems so that researchers are forced to find resources outside the centers. However increasing funds for the research activities in these institutes could lead to a decline in cooperative efforts with the business sector. Increasing funding in the research sector was evaluated as only being slightly important by the business sector.

Table 13.7 Analysis of knowledge transfer.

1.	Consultation	Not Important		Very Important
2.	Seminars and conferences	Not Important		Very Important
3.	Required analyses	Not Important		Very Important
4.	Advisory meetings	Not Important		Very Important
5.	Joint research projects	Not Important	6,0	Very Important
6.	Informal relations among scientists and employees of private firms	Not Important	6,17	Very Important
7.	Associations	Not Important	na	Very Important
8.	Patents	Not Important	na	Very Important
9.	Licenses	Not Important	na	Very Important
10.	University facilities utilized by private firms	Not Important	na	Very Important
11.	Establishment of private firms by researchers	Not Important	na	Very Important
12.	Employment of research workers in private firms	Not Important	na	Very Important
13.	Establishment of incubator centers by university or research centers	Not Important	na	Very Important
14.	Employment of students in private firms	Not Important	na	Very Important
15.	Employment of university graduates	Not Important	5,67	Very Important
16.	Use of library	Not Important	na	Very Important
17.	Use of information sources in research institutes	Not Important	na	Very Important
18.	Presentations at fairs	Not Important	na	Very Important
19.	Professional journals	Not Important	na	Very Important

For business, the improvement of the information and communication infrastructure was the top priority, and was also considered to be highly important by the research sector. The second priority for the research sector was to implement tax reforms to encourage investment in innovation (R&D tax credits); this in line with our earlier remark that both sectors thought that the regional tax and incentives system did not encourage business expenditure on research and development. The business sector very much preferred the raising of educational standards such as the promotion of world class primary and secondary education and specialized education and training programs to upgrade worker skills, which they considered to be very important for their innovative activities.

Our investigations have showed there is a huge potential for recognizing the importance of innovation, but on the other hand, increased innovation is not closely linked to elaborated cooperation with research institutes. Knowledge transfer tends to be focused on internal problems, such as firm management and informal contact with other firms.

This situation is influenced by insufficient knowledge transfer between research institutes and firms and by firms concentrating on their own activities which absorb all their interests. Many firms struggle for survival, and for them, the innovative approach represents new management or new contacts with other firms. The institutions promoting knowledge transfer exist, but there is no agency that can help to promote knowledge transfer directly. One of the possible ways this might have been achieved was by the foundation of an agency within the Slovak Academy of Sciences in Bratislava where direct contact between research institutes and firms could be organized. However, this strategy failed because of insufficient financial support and a lack of balance between the research orientation of the institutes and the imprecise directives embodied in official legislation.

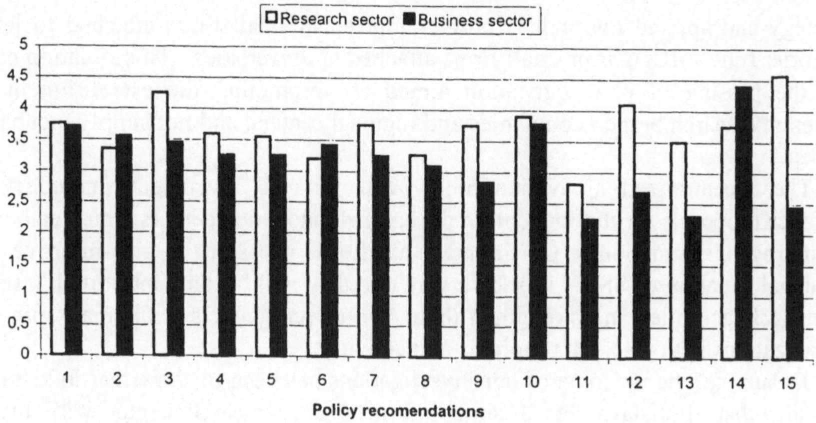

1. Promote world-class primary and secondary education
2. Promote specialized education and training programs to upgrade workers skills
3. Implement tax reform to encourage investment in innovation (e g , R&D tax credits)
4. Speed up regulatory approval processes in line with product life-cycles
5. Stimulate production of innovation
6. Promote antitrust legislation to encourage competition
7. Support the particular needs of start-up companies (access to capital, incubators, management training)
8. Strengthen and modernize intellectual property protections (patents, copyrights) at home and abroad
9. Provide services to assist and promote regional exports
10. Improve information and communications infrastructure
11. Assist in attracting suppliers and service providers from other locations
12. Government support for funding of specialized research institutes, labs, etc
13. Catalyze partnerships among government agencies, industry and universities
14. Improve transportation and other physical infrastructure
15. Increase funding for university-based research

Figure 13.4 Priorities for the economic policy of the government in the next five years.

The issue of poor legislation is very important, because its imprecision prohibits different research institutes from becoming involved. A lack of capital investment funds means that there is no possibility of establishing small companies as a way to produce practical outcomes from research activities initiated by research institutes. Researchers who want to continue in these activities could perhaps establish their own branch company and put up a share of the capital. The remaining share would come from research institutes or universities and from industrial companies. The new company, a so-called spin off company, would be a separate entity detached from the university. However, the legislation necessary to make this possible still does not exist. This lack of supporting legislation also has a negative influence on basic research and its orientation, which is not focused on practical application and lacks financial support.

The manner in which applied research is conducted in different applied research institutes has changed completely. This situation is because of two reasons. One of these is that applied research institutes attached to enterprises and factories were dissolved during the privatization process and have not been re-established – so the tremendous potential for technological transfer which was very much exploited during the previous era, has ceased to exist. Secondly, research strategy and applied research is now conducted in small firms attached to large factories (not SMEs), or in small firms attached to universities. This situation calls for the passing of new legislation aimed at promoting the establishment of different research branch companies and regional centers, and not simply incubator parks.

The decentralized innovation policy with its own instruments includes for instance proposals for the foundation of regional innovation centers which can help to improve this situation. On the other hand, it is necessary to also improve the financial situation of SMEs in such a way that they will become interested in their own R&D activities and strengthen their own direct contacts with small spin-off organizations with research programs and activities.

To sum up, the outcome of our investigations has been to show that in spite of the fact that Bratislava has a large industrial and research center with many possibilities for mutual contact between firms and research institutes and universities, it does not, in reality, make full use of the opportunities that exist. Some of the reasons mentioned above include ineffective contact between research institutes and SMEs, ineffective legislation and lack of finance, which have negative effects on the incidence of mutual contact among firms, their internal management, etc. One of the possible ways out of this conundrum is through regional tax reform.

References

Lundvall, B.A. (ed) *National System of Innovation: Towards a Theory of Innovation and Interactive Learning*, London: Pinter Publishers (1992).

NADSME Annual Report 2000, Bratislava 2001.

Statistical Office of the Slovak Republic (2001), *Innovation Activity in Manufacturing of the SR 1997-1999*, Bratislava.

Chapter 14

Spatial Industrial Dynamics in the Uddevalla Local Labour Market Region: An Application of the Lead-Lag Model

Charlie Karlsson and Martin Andersson

Introduction

One fundamental hypothesis within the field of spatial industrial dynamics is the idea that in most countries it is possible to identify a limited number of leading urban regions. They keep their lead by continuously initiating, imitating and developing activities that over time to a substantial degree tend to diffuse to other locations in a hierarchy of functional urban regions. There are a number of forces that might propel diffusion processes of this kind. One force often mentioned in the literature is the maturing of products and industries that makes them less dependent upon the external economies offered by the large urban regions. Another force is the change in the type and the organization of production taking place over time in the non-leading regions, which, for example, produce an increased demand for producer services. A third force worth mentioning is the secular rise in the real incomes in non-leading regions which give rise to an increased demand for various consumer services due to an income elasticity of demand greater than one.

Given the above hypothesis a number of questions may be formulated: Is it possible to document these kinds of decentralization processes? If so, what are their characteristics? How rapid are they? What differences are there between different products, different industries, different technologies, and so on? Are the follower regions catching up over time? These questions have been studied in a number of studies in Sweden using data for the period 1980 to the early 1990s (Forslund, & Johansson, 1995; Karlsson, 1997; Karlsson, 1999).

In the above studies it was for the actual period shown that the Stockholm region is the leading region in Sweden (and in the whole Nordic region). It introduces continuously new products and industries. These products and industries are mainly lacking in other regions in Sweden. When such products and industries are imitated and developed in other regions the Swedish economy is renewed. Industries that have a high specialization in the Stockholm region have a statistically significant tendency to grow in other parts of the country. More than

80 per cent of all industries that in 1980 had a high specialization in the Stockholm region grow in the rest of the country during the following decade. Industries that had a high specialization in the Stockholm region during the whole period 1980-93 increased their employment in the rest of the country with more than 40 per cent. More than 80 per cent of all industries that 1980 had a low specialization in the Stockholm region experienced a decrease in their employment in the rest of the country during the following decade. In another paper, Karlsson & Andersson (2001) we have shown that similar patterns have prevailed during the period 1990-99, even though Sweden in the early 1990s went through a major economic crisis which, for example, resulted in a loss of 20 per cent of the employment in the manufacturing industry. After the crisis the Swedish economy has experienced a rapid growth and in particular it seems as if it is industries related to the so-called 'new economy' that grow.

Having established that the patterns predicted by the leader-follower model have prevailed at an aggregated level we might also ask questions as regards the application of this model to the development in individual regions. What light can the leader-follower model through upon the development patterns in individual regions? It is a basic hypothesis of the leader-follower model that the model can function as a guide line for evaluating the development in individual regions and also give valuable hints about which industries that might provide the new jobs in a region when increased productivity in existing industries and increased competition from regions with lower costs reduces jobs in many existing industries.

The purpose of this paper is to apply the leader-follower model to analyse the general developments of the private sector in the Uddevalla local labour market region[1] (ULLM Region) during the period 1990-99 and to investigate what guidelines as regards the future development of the private sector in the region that can be deduced from this analysis.

The paper is organized as follows: The next section introduces important aspects of the leader-follower model within a spatial industrial dynamics framework. In the following section, the model to be used to analyse spatial industrial dynamics is presented. This model is then used in to analyse the general developments of the private sector in the Uddevalla local labour market region during the period 1990-99. In the last section the main results of the analysis are summarized, and some suggestions made for future research.

The Leader-Follower model

Forslund & Johansson (1995) have introduced a model of spatial industrial dynamics in the time and space hierarchy of functional urban regions. Their model combine elements of the spatial product life cycle, the 'filtering-down' and the regional life cycle theories. It is characterized by the idea that a leading urban region in a country keeps its lead by initiating, imitating, and developing activities that have a high tendency to successively diffuse to other locations in a hierarchy of functional urban regions. They see the large urban regions as the fundamental nodes in the innovation, production and distribution networks in every country. Many of the large urban regions are also key nodes in the international exchange and diffusion networks, which contain a large number of interaction functions. In particular, they are import nodes, with dense import networks that provide rich information about new products, new techniques, and so on from the world market. To a large extent, it is in these nodal locations that new technologies, new activities, new occupations, and new consumption patterns are created and introduced. Hence, large urban regions in the industrialized countries are looked upon as the key forces behind both the national and the international economic evolution.

As in all product cycle models, the dynamics of standardized and non-standardized activities are at the focus of their analysis. Standardized activities are characterized by their standardized products, and by the routinized methods that are used to produce these products. As products and production techniques become standardized, activities tend to migrate and a region can only 'survive' with a proper inflow of new activities. The Forslund-Johansson leader-follower-model here differs from the standard version of the spatial product cycle model in one important aspect. It does not assume that non-standardized activities generally develop to standardized activities. Non-standardized activities here include customized deliveries of goods and services for which each delivery has new and unique individual characteristics. In these cases the authors maintain one can not observe any spatial product cycles at all, and, hence, these functions tends to remain in the larger urban areas where their locational advantage is the greatest (Barkley, 1988). However, at an aggregated level, they claim, it is possible to observe how parts of clusters of such activities expand or contract. Hence, in that respect it is still possible to make references to Schumpeterian waves of varying length and amplitude.

According to the new perspective presented by Forslund & Johansson, the system of functional urban regions in a country forms a time and space hierarchy for which the largest functional urban region is leading by more or less continuously introducing new products (goods or services), new activities, and so on. Hence, it is assumed that most new products and industries have their early growth in the largest region, even if the activity has been initiated somewhere else. There exists a natural explanation to why new industries take off in the largest market in this way. The reason is that the regional home market is larger than in any other region in the country. A further reason is that the largest region has a larger share of R&D resources and a larger supply of highly educated labour than any other region.

What happens then when an industry has got a foothold in the largest region? For many products, as remarked above, a certain standardization and a routinization of production and deliveries are achieved over time. As products are standardized they also gradually become well known and demanded in larger and growing regional markets. With standardization and routinization follow a reduction of the set up costs for new production, and, thus more and more regional markets become large enough to make it possible to exploit economies of scale. This means that it will be possible for this type of production to find a profitable location in other regions than the largest region. For products that develop according to this pattern a gradual diffusion to other regions often takes place. This growth is often first observed in other large urban regions. For certain products the diffusion can stop here if the products need the external economies offered by large urban regions. However, in many cases the diffusion continues to medium-sized and small regions. In some cases continues until almost all regions have taken up the actual activity. Large, medium-sized and small functional urban regions are followers in such a way that they adopt the new products, new activities, and so on, some time after they have been introduced in the largest region.

Of course, leaders and followers can not be classified in a complete and strict sense. However, in frequency terms it is possible to order the functional urban regions in a hierarchy that remains invariant during long time periods (Forslund & Johansson, 1995). However, to keep their position in the hierarchy, the functional urban regions must adapt to smaller and larger external shocks. Such an adaptation may demand new location patterns: some ‘old’ activities must go and some ‘new’ activities must come. The speed of such an adaptation process is assumed to depend upon how general (non-production specific) and how polyvalent the actual urban infrastructure is. For functional regions with a non-general (production-specific) infrastructure, such adaptation processes can be very slow or even non-existing (Johansson & Karlsson, 1990). However, leading functional urban regions are expected to have a rich endowment with general urban infrastructure.

A Method for Analysing Spatial Industrial Dynamics

It is a more or less daily phenomenon in most industrialized countries to come across descriptions and analyses of industrial structure and structural change at the national level. In almost all cases these descriptions and analyses suffer from the basic weakness that they are strongly aggregated and that often much valuable information is hidden in the aggregated numbers. To solve this problem at least partly, a new analysis model and presentation format that can be used for disaggregated analyses of spatial industrial dynamics is presented here. This method was first introduced by Forslund and Johansson (1995).

This new approach, like previous methods, gives a general overview, but it also elucidates how the transformation of the structure of industries has taken place for half a decade[2]. Furthermore, this method can be used to make qualified statements about how the transformation of the structure of industries can be expected to continue for the next decade or so. The basic motive to develop a new prognosis method is that traditional linear prognosis methods do not give a good picture of the future industrial structure in different regions. The focus of the new method is to provide a qualitative picture of the composition and the development of the industrial structure in each region. At the same time the ambition is to draw the picture in such a way that it can be used as a basis to express the direction of the development in different regions more precisely.

To illustrate the method, regionalized employment data for the years 1990 and 1999 are used[3]. As a general point of departure, the total employment in the private sector[4] in Sweden distributed over 616 industries is classified into three groups:

- rapid employment growth – if the employment in the industry outside the Stockholm local labour market region[5] (SLLM Region) increased by 48 per cent or more during the period 1990-99;
- slow employment growth – if the employment in the industry outside the Stockholm local labour market region increased by less than 48 per cent during the period 1990-99;
- slow employment decline – if the employment in the industry outside the Stockholm local labour market region decreased by less than 29 per cent during the period 1990-99;
- rapid employment decline – if the employment in the industry outside the Stockholm local labour market region decreased by 29 per cent or more during the period 1990-99.

However, this division of industries based upon the development of employment between 1990 and 1999 produces a weak basis to make prognoses for enduring dynamic development traits for the future development of the industrial structure in different regions. To get a firmer point of departure, this division of the 616 industries is complemented by a second division of the same industries based upon whether they have an high, a medium, a low or a very low specialization in the year 1990 in the Stockholm local labour market region. As the measure of specialization, the location quotient[6] in the Stockholm local labour market region for all the 616 industries is used. Table 14.1 shows how it is possible, based upon these two divisions, to create an analysis scheme with 16 cells.

The Stockholm local labour market region is used as the norm for comparisons, as it is the most advanced, i.e. the leading region in the Nordic countries. It has come furthest in (i) developing new consumption goods and new consumption patterns, (ii) acting as an intermediary in new technologies, and (iii) crystalling new growth industries. The region also has a lead when it comes to automatization and rationalization of established production. Industries that have expanded and reached a strong over-representation in the Stockholm local labour market region can generally be expected to be industries that will have a strong growth potential in other regions in Sweden in the future. Industries that on the other hand have gone backwards and become strongly underrepresented in the Stockholm local labour market region are industries that with a high probability will also lose employment in other regions.

Table 14.1 An analysis scheme based upon a classification of industries given their regional specialization in the SLLM Region in 1990 and their employment growth and decline in the rest of the country during the period 1990-99.

	Employment growth and decline in the rest of Sweden 1990-99			
Regional specialization in the SLLM Region in 1990	Rapid growth	Slow growth	Slow decline	Rapid decline
High	H++	H+	H-	H--
Medium	M++	M+	M-	M--
Low	L++	L+	L-	L--
Very low	VL++	VL+	VL-	VL--

If one follows this method mechanically, one postulates that the industrial structure of the Stockholm local labour market region is a future picture of the industrial structure of an average region. However, the purpose is not to make precise forecasts for each individual region based upon the developments in the Stockholm region. Instead the point of using the Stockholm region as a reference region is that it gives a relevant basis for comparisons. In this way this method can give an appropriate starting point for studying the specific development tracks and development patterns in different regions. This could, for example, entail services produced for consumption within a region. Furthermore, this method provides an opportunity to make explicit how each functional region's specialization pattern diverges from a general development pattern.

To evaluate the potential of this method it could be worthwhile to discuss its limitations. In analyses within regional economics, one often starts from the idea of an export base. Expressed in simple words this means that the economic growth in a small open economy is dependent upon the income creation in firms that produce for markets outside the region. These firms create the export base of the region. Other production that is directed towards the internal market of the region is classified as derived production. For many regions in Sweden, part of the export base consists of production based upon natural resources such as food and paper production. Such production is relatively region-specific. In these cases the Stockholm local labour market region is not very well suited as a reference region. However, the main question is reality what additions to the export-directed production in the natural resources-based regions that can be expected when their traditional export base contracts. When trying to forecast such a structural change process, a well-chosen reference region can give important support. However, there are good reasons to stress that the export-oriented production in smaller regions always will be more specialized and less comprehensively structured than in a large region such as the Stockholm region.

Hence, even if there are important areas where one should use and interpret the general comparison model cautiously, there are other areas where the model has a very strong position. In particular, it will for most industries give a precise guide about ongoing labour saving rationalization. It also highlights the emergence of new activities in the following two areas:

- regionally-directed production of goods and services tied to private and public consumption;
- the production of producer services.

In the first case the argument is the following. In a long-term perspective, consumption patterns in Sweden show the same development tracks in all regions. What produces lags in time and hence causes the different time patterns in the different regions are mainly differences in the access and diffusion of information and the development of the average income level and the income distribution. The same observations can be made for the purchases of producer services by firms. Whether the new (increased) demand will give rise to new production within a specific region or not depends among other things upon

- whether the demand concerns production where the region can have special comparative advantages or disadvantages (e.g. spare time, recreational or cultural activities) or not;
- if the demand is directed towards sheltered service production (e.g. municipal services);
- if import substitution takes place (i.e. if a region gradually covers more and more of its own demand by increased intra-regional production and hence decreased imports).

It is in this connection possible to argue that a strongly urbanized region like the Stockholm region gives strong indications of the upper limit for a region's self-sufficiency, when it comes to production of the kind of goods and services discussed here.

The growth of specialized producer services is dependent upon the size of the market and the availability of the competence that the production of such services demands. The growth and the degree of differentiation of producer services such as consultancy services, R&D services, banking and financial services, insurance services, and real estate agents and managers, mirrors the growth and differentiation of other production activities in the region. The growth and differentiation of producer services in a region is also influenced by the status of the interregional infrastructure and its development and what possibilities that gives to export producer services to other regions. These are conditions, which indicate that a rapidly growing and strongly developed region with a well-developed infrastructure can be looked upon as a region that has an advantage over other regions or as being a forerunner to other regions. At the same time, it almost always holds that the more specialized a service is, the more dependent is the location of that kind of service production on high-accessibility in the system of regions.

The Method of Analysis Applied

In this section the method of analysis presented in last section is used to describe and analyse the overall industrial dynamics in the Uddevalla local labour market region.

Industrial Diversification in the Uddevalla region

As a first step we analyse the diversification of the region in terms of the number of private sector industries represented in 1990 and 1999. We know that there is a quite strong relationship between the number of industries represented in a region and its size in terms of population. This is also confirmed by the two regressions reported in Table 14.2 From the residual we see that the Uddevalla region is somewhat less diversified within the private sector than what is normal in Sweden among regions of this size.

Table 14.2 Regression results for the relationship between the number of private sector industries represented and population in local labour market regions in Sweden (logarithmic values).

	1990	1999
Constant	1.802	1.894
	(15.5)	(16.9)
Population	0.351	0.345
	(32.7)	(33.3)
Adj R2	0.93	0.93
Number of regions	81	81
Residual for the Uddevalla region	-22.3	-19.8
	(-5.1 %)	(-4.4 %)

Note: (t-values in parentheses).

In Table 14.3 it is shown how the 416 private sector industries represented in the Uddevalla region in 1990 and the 428 private sector industries represented in 1999 are distributed over the cells of the model of analysis. In the table we can for example see how there has been an increase in the number of industries among both categories of growing industries while there has been a loss of rapidly declining industries.

Table 14.3 Private sector industries in the ULLM Region in 1999 (1990) classified according to regional specialization in the SLLM Region in 1990 and employment growth and decline in the rest of Sweden 1990-99.

	Employment growth and decline in the rest of Sweden 1990-99				
Regional specialization in the SLLM Region in 1990	Rapid growth	Slow growth	Slow decline	Rapid decline	Sum
High	39 (32)	40 (39)	19 (17)	18 (20)	116 (108)
Medium	14 (15)	33 (31)	62 (60)	23 (25)	132 (131)
Low	16 (16)	19 (19)	42 (48)	39 (36)	116 (119)
Very low	9 (5)	8 (3)	23 (20)	24 (30)	64 (58)
Sum	78 (68)	100 (92)	146 (145)	104 (111)	428 (416)

Table 14.4 Share of private sector industries in the different industry groups represented in the ULLM Region in 1999 (%).

	Employment growth and decline in the rest of Sweden 1990-99				
Regional specialization in the SLLM Region in 1990	Rapid growth	Slow growth	Slow decline	Rapid decline	Average
High	72	82	79	67	75
Medium	70	94	97	66	86
Low	62	73	79	76	74
Very low	30	40	62	37	42
Average	60	77	82	58	69

In Table 14.4 we illustrate how the distribution of industries over the cells of the analysis scheme in the Uddevalla region differs from the overall distribution of all private sector industries in Sweden in 1999. We see that the region in relative terms has an underrepresentation of both rapidly growing and rapidly declining industries, while slowly growing and in particular slowly declining industries are overrepresented.

Private Sector Employment in the Uddevalla region

It is natural that the employment in the private sector in a region is closely related to its population size. This is also confirmed by the regressions presented in Table 14.5. However, for the Uddevalla region we see that in 1990 the employment in the private sector was substantially lower than what could be expected given the population size of the region. Interestingly enough this "employment deficit" had almost disappeared in 1999.

Table 14.5 Regression results for the relationship between total employment in private sector industries and population in local labour market regions in Sweden (logarithmic values).

	1990	1999
Constant	-1.907	-2.197
	(-13.2)	(-14.7)
Population	1.064	1.073
	(79.1)	(77.4)
Adj R2	0.99	0.99
Number of regions	81	81
Residual for the Uddevalla region	-2201	-206
	(-3.5 %)	(-0.4 %)

Note: (t-values in parentheses).

Table 14.6 shows the distribution of the employment in the Uddevalla region in 1990 and 1999 over the 16 cells in the analysis table used in this paper[7]. What we should observe in the table is the very high employment share for declining industries in general in 1999 – they account for more than 71 per cent of the employment in the region – and for slowly growing industries in particular – they account for more than half of the employment in the region. For Sweden as a whole the corresponding figure is 57.8 per cent. Rapidly growing industries have more than doubled their employment share between 1990 and 1999 but in 1999 they still account for less than 8 per cent of all private sector employment in the region (See Table 14.1a in the Appendix).

In Table 14.7 we analyse the specialization of the different industrial aggregates in the Uddevalla region by means of location quotients. In this table we observe in particular the low and declining specialization for growth industries in general and explicitly for rapidly growing industries. We also note the very high and increasing specialization for slowly growing industries. According to the logic of the underlying model this region shows cumbersome signs of a potential, substantial employment loss in the near future. A competing hypothesis is of course that this region offers the industries in the cell L- very special location advantages in the form of external economies of scale that give than a superior competitive power also in the medium and long term.

Table 14.6 The total employment in private sector industries in the ULLM Region in the year 1999 distributed over the cells of the model of analysis. The figures for Sweden as a whole are given in parentheses (%).

	Employment growth and decline in the rest of Sweden 1990-99				
Regional specialization in the SLLM Region in 1990	Rapid growth	Slow growth	Slow decline	Rapid decline	Sum
High	3.0 (10.1)	7.4 (13.0)	1.5 (2.5)	1.6 (3.9)	13.5 (29.5)
Medium	0.9 (1.8)	7.3 (8.7)	19.4 (19.1)	6.5 (8.1)	34.0 (37.7)
Low	3.1 (2.5)	2.7 (3.0)	31.1 (13.1)	4.0 (4.5)	40.9 (23.0)
Very low	0.8 (0.8)	3.2 (2.4)	4.6 (3.8)	2.9 (2.9)	11.5 (9.8)
Sum	7.8 (15.2)	20.6 (27.1)	56.5 (38.5)	15.0 (19.3)	100 (100)

Table 14.7 Specialization in the ULLM Region in the year 1999 (1990) in the different private sector groups measured by the location quotient (%).

	Employment growth and decline in the rest of Sweden 1990-99				
Regional specialization in the SLLM Region in 1990	Rapid growth	Slow growth	Slow decline	Rapid decline	Average
High	30 (21)	57 (62)	61 (57)	41 (47)	46 (51)
Medium	50 (82)	84 (84)	101 (90)	81 (79)	90 (85)
Low	126 (139)	90 (127)	240 (230)	90 (104)	180 (179)
Very low	99 (304)	136 (56)	121 (80)	101 (104)	117 (92)
Average	51 (57)	74 (75)	147 (134)	78 (83)	100 (100)

In Table 14.8 the employment changes in the private sector industries in the Uddevalla region during the period 1990-99 is analysed. Total private sector employment declined in the region with 10.7 per cent during the period (equal to a loss of 6585 jobs). This figure is very close to the national average that was -11.4 per cent, i.e. the region did a little better than Sweden as a whole. The most substantial differences between the developments in the region and those in Sweden as a whole are that slowly declining industries declined less in the region than in Sweden as a whole (-15.5 per cent), while rapidly growing industries grew slower in the region than in Sweden as a whole (119.6 per cent). The structural change process that is illustrated by Table 14.8 is a typical process in all dynamic economies[8]. The relevant policy response is obviously not to try to check the structural change to keep up the employment level but instead to concentrate on measures that can secure that the growth of new job opportunities keeps up with the losses of job opportunities.

Table 14.8 Relative changes in employment in the different industry groups in the ULLM Region during the period 1990-99. The figures for Sweden as a whole are given in parentheses (%).

	Employment growth and decline in the rest of Sweden 1990-99				
Regional specialization in the SLLM Region in 1990	Rapid growth	Slow growth	Slow decline	Rapid decline	Average
High	205.5 (112.2)	-2.8 (5.0)	-9.6 (-11.4)	-45.9 (-39.6)	2.0 (11.8)
Medium	74.5 (164.2)	16.3 (16.3)	-6.0 (-16.9)	-50.8 (-51.5)	-16.1 (-21.2)
Low	87.5 (102.5)	-10.9 (19.9)	-9.7 (-13.1)	-49.7 (-42.4)	-13.1 (-13.2)
Very low	6.7 (218.2)	201.0 (28.3)	25.7 (-18.6)	-48.0 (-47.2)	3.9 (-19.3)
Average	100.0 (119.6)	14.4 (11.8)	-6.3 (-15.5)	-49.5 (-46.8)	-10.7 (-11.4)

In Table 14.9 we illustrate the results from a simple shift-share analysis for the changes in employment in the Uddevalla region during the period 1990-99[9]. We see that the competitive shift component is positive indicating that the region did better during the period than the situation in 1990 gave us reason to expect. We see that most of this positive contribution did come from slowly declining industries. However, the rapidly growing industries in the region did under-perform during the actual period.

Table 14.9 The competitive share component of the employment change in the different industry groups in the ULLM Region during the period 1990-99.

	Employment growth and decline in the rest of Sweden 1990-99				
Regional specialization in the SLLM Region in 1990	Rapid growth	Slow growth	Slow decline	Rapid decline	Sum
High	506	-323	16	-105	94
Medium	-246	-1	1238	52	1043
Low	-138	-519	644	-321	-334
Very low	-884	1000	895	-27	984
Sum	-762	157	2793	-401	1787

Private Sector Entrepreneurship in the Uddevalla region

The number of plants in the private sector is closely related to the size of regions in terms of population. This is clearly confirmed by the regressions reported in Table 14.10. For the Uddevalla region we see that the region in 1990 had a slight deficit in the number of plants given the size of the region. In 1999 this deficit had grown and become quite substantial. The actual number of plants in the region in 1999 is 6.2 per cent below the estimated number.

Table 14.10 Regression results for the relationship between total number of plants in private sector industries and population in local labour market regions in Sweden (logarithmic values).

	1990	1999
Constant	-2.692	-2.934
	(-19.3)	(-22.3)
Population	0.943	0.963
	(73.4)	(79.1)
Adj R2	0.99	0.99
Number of regions	81	81
Residual for the Uddevalla region	-107	-425
	(-1.6 %)	(-6.2 %)

Note: (t-values in parentheses).

Much interest has in recent decades been focused on the role of small and medium sized enterprises for the creation of new job opportunities. In Table 14.11

we compare the average size of plants in the different cells in the Uddevalla region in 1999 with those in Sweden as a whole[10]. Industries that have a very low specialization in the Stockholm region have on average a plant size that is much larger than the other industries. This indicates that internal economies of scale are essential for these industries. This is what one could expect since these industries mainly are located in peripheral regions. On average the average plant size is somewhat larger in the Uddevalla region than in Sweden as a whole. However, industries with a high or a medium specialization in the Stockholm region on average has an average plant size in the region that is smaller than in Sweden as a whole. The opposite holds for industries with a low or a very specialization in the Stockholm region. A general pattern is that the average plant size has declined between 1990 and 1999 (See Table 14.4a in the Appendix).

Table 14.11 Average plant size in the different industrial aggregates in the ULLM Region in 1999. (Average plant size for Sweden as a whole is given within parentheses.)

	Employment growth and decline in the rest of Sweden 1990-99				
Regional specialization in the SLLM Region in 1990	Rapid growth	Slow growth	Slow decline	Rapid decline	Average
High	4.4 (7.4)	6.2 (7.8)	3.3 (4.3)	7.9 (14.2)	5.4 (7.6)
Medium	3.2 (4.0)	4.5 (5.1)	6.8 (6.4)	6.7 (7.8)	5.9 (6.1)
Low	10.5 (8.2)	5.1 (6.7)	18.9 (9.5)	7.2 (8.5)	13.5 (8.7)
Very low	21.2 (19.6)	62.3 (57.5)	27.6 (25.1)	32.6 (28.5)	33.3 (29.4)
Average	6.0 (7.0)	6.1 (7.0)	11.1 (7.5)	8.2 (10.0)	8.6 (7.7)

The changes in the average size of plants illustrated in Table 14.11[11] are of course the result of varying entrepreneurial behaviour in the various industry groups. In Table 14.12 we see how the relative number of plants in the different cells has changed during the period 1990-99 in the Uddevalla region and in Sweden as a whole. We see that the number of plants in the private sector as a whole only increased with 3.7 per cent in the whole of Sweden during the period 1990-99. However, in the rapidly growing industries the number of plants more than doubled. In the Uddevalla region the number of plants declined by 4.3 per cent. Interesting to observe is that in the growing industries the number of plants grow less in the Uddevalla region and in the declining industries the number of plants declined more than in Sweden as a whole. There seems to be something missing as regards entrepreneurial spirit in the Uddevalla region.

Table 14.12 Relative changes in the number of plants in the different industry groups in the ULLM Region during the period 1990-99. The figures for Sweden as a whole are given in parentheses (%).

	Employment growth and decline in the rest of Sweden 1990-99				
Regional specialization in the SLLM Region in 1990	Rapid growth	Slow growth	Slow decline	Rapid decline	Average
High	149.3 (119.6)	9.8 (13.6)	-12.7 (4.8)	-33.3 (-26.7)	16.1 (29.0)
Medium	71.3 (157.0)	19.2 (21.8)	-10.7 (-7.3)	-31.4 (-25.3)	-6.7 (0.0)
Low	26.2 (46.3)	16.3 (10.2)	-20.4 (-19.2)	-25.3 (-28.0)	-13.5 (-13.0)
Very low	110.0 (196.3)	100.0 (29.5)	-4.2 (-13.4)	-25.8 (-20.7)	2.2 (-3.7)
Average	88.1 (112.4)	16.0 (16.3)	-14.0 (-9.9)	-29.7 (-26.0)	-4.2 (3.7)

To complement the picture in Table 14.12 we show the competive shift component of the change of the number of plants in the different industry groups in the Uddevalla local labour market region[12]. In the table we see that the region under-performs in most of the industrial aggregates. The total under-performance is estimated to 247 plants. This figure can be compared with the total loss of plants in the region during the period 1990-99 that was equal to 289 plants. If we acknowledge that the average plant size in the region is 8.6 this under-performance is equal to a loss of more than 2,100 jobs in the region or equal to 35 per cent of the job loss in the region during the period 1990-99.

Table 14.13 The competitive share component of the change in the number of plants in the different industry groups in the ULLM Region during the period 1990-99.

	Employment growth and decline in the rest of Sweden 1990-99				
Regional specialization in the SLLM Region in 1990	Rapid growth	Slow growth	Slow decline	Rapid decline	Sum
High	45	-23	-48	-12	-38
Medium	-75	-20	-60	-48	-203
Low	-26	15	-13	11	-13
Very low	-9	10	9	-3	7
Sum	-65	-18	-112	-52	-247

Knowledge Intensity in the Private Sector in the Uddevalla region

One factor that varies significantly between different regions and that in different studies have been shown to be connected with variations in development, renewal and transformation in different regions is the supply of labour with a post senior high school education. In Table 14.14 we illustrate the results from two regressions, one for 1990 and one for 1999, for the relationship between the number of employees in the private with a long university education and the total number of employees in the private sector in the different local labour market regions in Sweden. We see that there is a strong relationship and that the elasticity is significantly higher than one, i.e. the number of employees with a long university education increases more rapidly than the number of private sector employees when the number of private sector employees increases. For the Uddevalla region we see that the residual is negative indicating a substantial deficit of employees with a long university education in the private sector in the Uddevalla region. Expressed with other words we can say that the knowledge intensity in the private sector in the Uddevalla region is lower than what is normal for regions of this size in Sweden. Interesting to observe is that the deficit has increased during the 1990s.

Table 14.14 Regression results for the relationship between the number of employees with a long university education and the number of employees in private sector industries in local labour market regions in Sweden (logarithmic values).

	1990	1999
Constant	-6.512	-5.580
	(-22.7)	(-23.7)
Private sector employment	1.305	1.260
	(43.8)	(50.4)
Adj R2	0.96	0.97
Number of regions	81	81
Residual for the Uddevalla region	-273	-536
	(-10.5 %)	(-14.9 %)

Note: (t-values in parentheses).

In Table 14.15 we repeat the regression in Table 14.14 but now for all types of post-senior high school education. Also in this case the Uddevalla exhibits a deficit and a worsening deficit even if the deficit is somewhat lower in percentage terms than was the case for long university education.

Table 14.15 Regression results for the relationship between the number of employees with any type and any length of post senior high school education and the number of employees in private sector industries in local labour market regions in Sweden (logarithmic values).

	1990	1999
Constant	-4.473	-3.838
	(-22.0)	(-23.4)
Private sector employment	1.213	1.193
	(57.3)	(68.5)
Adj R2	0.98	0.98
Number of regions	81	81
Residual for the Uddevalla region	-355	-1,218
	(-4.9 %)	(-12.3 %)

Note: (t-values in parentheses).

In Table 14.16 we compare the share of employees with long university education (three years or more) in the different cells in the Uddevalla region with those in Sweden as a whole and in Table 14.16 we measure the educational intensity in the region using an index. We see that the educational intensity in the region is substantially lower in the region than in Sweden as a whole. For the region as a whole the educational intensity is 42 per cent lower than in the country as a whole. Only in very few cases does the region out-perform the country as a whole.

Table 14.16 Share of the employees with a long university education (three years or more, including a Ph.D. training) in the different industrial aggregates in the ULLM Region in 1999. The figures for Sweden as a whole are given in parentheses (%).

	Employment growth and decline in the rest of Sweden 1990-99				
Regional specialization in the SLLM Region in 1990	Rapid growth	Slow growth	Slow decline	Rapid decline	Average
High	16.7	7.9	4.0	10.6	9.8
	(25.4)	(13.0)	(10.7)	(16.8)	(17.6)
Medium	4.5	8.5	3.3	1.8	4.2
	(15.7)	(13.2)	(5.4)	(4.8)	(7.6)
Low	2.6	2.2	6.5	6.5	5.9
	(5.6)	(3.6)	(4.6)	(6.1)	(4.9)
Very low	2.4	2.1	4.1	2.9	3.1
	(5.9)	(8.4)	(4.6)	(5.1)	(5.8)
Average	8.3	6.4	5.2	4.2	5.6
	(20.2)	(11.6)	(5.4)	(7.5)	(9.7)

Table 14.17 Educational intensity in the different industrial aggregates in the ULLM Region in 1999 measured in terms of employees with a long (three years or more) university education (Sweden as a whole = 100).

	Employment growth and decline in the rest of Sweden 1990-99				
Regional specialization in the SLLM Region in 1990	Rapid growth	Slow growth	Slow decline	Rapid decline	Average
High	66	61	37	63	56
Medium	29	64	61	38	55
Low	46	61	141	107	120
Very low	41	25	89	57	53
Average	41	55	96	56	58

Table 14.18 and Table 14.19 illustrate how the share of employees with any form of post senior high school education[13] (including Ph.D. training) varies between the different cells. The situation for the Uddevalla region is in this case similar to the situation reported for long university education in Table 14.16 and Table 14.17 but with a somewhat smaller difference between the Uddevalla region and the rest of Sweden.

Table 14.18 Share of the employees with any kind and any length of post senior high school education (including a Ph.D. training) in the different industrial aggregates in the ULLM Region in 1999. The figures for Sweden as a whole are given in parentheses (%).

	Employment growth and decline in the rest of Sweden 1990-99				
Regional specialization in the SLLM Region in 1990	Rapid growth	Slow growth	Slow decline	Rapid decline	Average
High	40.9 (48.4)	19.0 (28.8)	12.5 (23.7)	24.0 (32.8)	23.9 (35.7)
Medium	10.3 (28.5)	23.0 (28.4)	12.1 (15.4)	8.2 (14.4)	13.7 (18.8)
Low	10.1 (16.1)	8.6 (11.8)	18.1 (12.9)	15.8 (16.1)	16.5 (13.7)
Very low	10.8 (15.3)	7.8 (17.2)	11.4 (12.9)	8.4 (13.9)	9.6 (14.4)
Average	22.2 (39.3)	17.2 (25.7)	15.5 (14.8)	11.9 (18.3)	15.8 (22.2)

Table 14.19 Educational intensity in the different industrial aggregates in the ULLM Region in 1999 measured in terms of employees with all types of post senior high school education (Sweden as a whole = 100).

	Employment growth and decline in the rest of Sweden 1990-99				
Regional specialization in the SLLM Region in 1990	Rapid growth	Slow growth	Slow decline	Rapid decline	Average
High	85	66	53	73	67
Medium	36	81	79	57	73
Low	63	73	140	98	120
Very low	71	45	88	60	67
Average	56	67	105	65	71

Summary and Conclusions

In this chapter we apply the lead-lag model to the situation in the Uddevalla local labour market region and analyse the structure and the development of the private sector in the region during the period 1990-99. The results may be summarized as follows: The region is less diversified than what is normal for regions of similar size. In particular, we noticed a lack of rapidly growing industries and an overrepresentation of slowly declining industries. The private sector employs fewer people than is normal for regions of this size but the situation has improved considerably during the 1990s. What is worrying from a long-term perspective is the low employment rate in rapidly growing industries in general and in rapidly growing knowledge intensive industries in particular. The total private sector employment has decreased somewhat less than in the country as a whole. However, rapidly growing industries have not grown as fast in the region as in Sweden as a whole. A simple shift-share analysis shows that the region as a whole has performed somewhat better than expected but that was not the case for rapidly growing industries.

The Uddevalla region has fewer plants in the private sector than is normal for regions of similar size and the situation has detoriated during the 1990s. The total number of plants has increased during the 1990s but given the initial situation in 1990 the region has underperformed.

The most striking characteristic of the Uddevalla region is that its private sector has a much lower educational intensity than is normal for regions in this size category and furthermore that the situation has become worse during the 1990s. One reason for this situation is that it was only a little more than 10 years ago that this region got its own institution of higher education – a university college. 10 years is of course too short a period for this institution to significantly influence the situation in the region. This is particularly true since the university college was very small during its first years.

Turning now to policy conclusions at least two conclusions can be drawn from the analysis. The first conclusion is that the region must do more to encourage entrepreneurship in the region and not least to lower the fixed costs associated with the start-up and running of firms. The second conclusion is that the university college in the region must be expanded substantially. In particular, there is a need to offer a larger variety of high quality programs at the masters' level. To do this the number of qualified teachers, i.e. teachers with a Ph.D., must be expanded substantially. And to be able to recruit more qualified teachers the university college must expand and upgrade its research programs. However, any substantial expansion of the university college will demand much lobbying at the national level since decisions about higher education and university R&D are taken by the national government.

Notes

1 The Uddevalla local labour market region consists of the ten municipalities Färgelanda, Grästorp, Lilla Edet, Lysekil, Mellerud, Munkedal, Sotenäs, Trollhättan, Uddevalla and Vänersborg. The region is located 70-120 kilometers north of Gothenburg in Western Sweden. The region has a population just over 200,000 inhabitants.

2 Changes in the system of industrial classification currently limit the time period. As time goes by it will be possible to extend the time period.

3 Due to changes in statistical definitions data for earlier years can not be used.

4 This means all employment except the public sector and the agriculture, forestry and fishing sector.

5 Local labour market regions are aggregates of municipalities connected by labour force commuting. Local labour market regions could be looked upon as functional urban regions.

6 Location quotient = region i's share of the total employment in the actual industry in the country divided by region i's share of all employment in the country.

7 The total employment in the different industrial aggregates can be found in Table A2 in the Appendix.

8 The disappearance of a job among the industries in the cell VL-- (or any other cell) does not necessarily mean that the tasks disappear. What is typical for the period studied here is that great changes in the division of labour between different industries took place and that new patterns of specialisation between industries developed. Many of the tasks that disappeared within manufacturing industry showed up as new jobs within the rapidly growing service industries.

9 The absolute changes in employment are illustrated in Table A3 in the Appendix.

10 The total number of plants in the Uddevalla region in 1990 and 1999 can be found in Table A5 in the Appendix.

11 See the Appendix.

12 The absolute changes in the number of plants in the Uddevalla local labour market region during the period 1990-99 are illustrated in Table A6.

13 Swedish statistics do not make any distinction between university education and different types of vocational education.

References

Barkley, D.L. (1988), 'The Decentralisation of High Technology Manufacturing to Nonmetropolitan Areas', Growth and Change 19, 13-30.

Cheshire, P. & I. Gordon (1995), *Territorial Competition in an Integrating Europe*, Aldershot; Avebury.

Forslund, U.M. & B. Johansson (1995), 'The Mälardalen: A Leading Region in Scandinavia', in Cheshire & Gordon (1995) (eds.), 3-27.

Johansson, B. & C. Karlsson (1990), 'Stadsregioner i Europa', SOU 1990: 34, Stockholm; Allmänna Förlaget.

Karlsson, C. (1997), 'Spatial Industrial Dynamics – An Aggregated Study of Urban Growth Industries', Paper presented at the Regional Science Association 37th European Congress, Rome, Italy, 26-29 August.

Karlsson, C. (1999), 'Spatial Industrial Dynamics in Sweden: A Disaggregated Analysis of Urban Growth Industries', Growth and Change 30, 184-212.

Karlsson, C. and M. Andersson (2001), 'Spatial Industrial Dynamics in Sweden – An Empirical Test of the Lead-Lag Model', Paper to be presented at the 41st congress of the European Regional Science Association, 29 August-1 September 2001 in Zagreb, Croatia.

Appendix

Table 14.1a The total employment in private sector industries in the ULLM Region in the year 1999 (1990) distributed over the cells of the model of analysis (%).

	Employment growth and decline in the rest of Sweden 1990-99				
Regional specialization in the SLLM Region in 1990	Rapid growth	Slow growth	Slow decline	Rapid decline	Sum
High	3.0 (0.9)	7.4 (6.8)	1.5 (1.4)	1.6 (2.7)	13.5 (11.9)
Medium	0.9 (0.5)	7.3 (5.6)	19.4 (18.4)	6.5 (11.7)	34.0 (36.2)
Low	3.1 (1.5)	2.7 (2.8)	31.1 (30.7)	4.0 (7.1)	40.9 (42.0)
Very low	0.8 (0.7)	3.2 (0,9)	4.6 (3.3)	2.9 (5.0)	11.5 (9.9)
Sum	7.8 (3.5)	20.6 (16.1)	56.5 (53.9)	15.0 (26.5)	100 (100)

Table 14.2a Employment in the different private sector groups in the ULLM Region in the year 1999 (1990).

	Employment growth and decline in the rest of Sweden 1990-99				
Regional specialization in the SLLM Region in 1990	Rapid growth	Slow growth	Slow decline	Rapid decline	Sum
High	1662 (544)	4066 (4181)	801 (886)	911 (1683)	7440 (7294)
Medium	478 (274)	4009 (34479	10661 (11344)	3543 (7204)	18691 (22269)
Low	1721 (918)	1499 (1683)	17.059 (18.897)	2194 (4363)	22473 (25861)
Very low	446 (418)	1743 (579)	2541 (2021)	1599 (3076)	6329 (6094)
Sum	4307 (2154)	11317 (9890)	31062 (33148)	8247 (16326)	54933 (61518)

Table 14.3a Absolute changes in employment in the different industry groups in the ULLM Region during the period 1990-99.

	Employment growth and decline in the rest of Sweden 1990-99				
Regional specialization in the SLLM Region in 1990	Rapid growth	Slow growth	Slow decline	Rapid decline	Sum
High	1118	-115	-85	-772	910
Medium	204	562	-683	-3661	-3578
Low	803	-184	-1838	-2169	-3388
Very low	28	1164	520	-1477	235
Sum	2153	1427	-2086	-8079	-6031

Table 14.4a Average plant size in the different industrial aggregates in the ULLM Region in 1999 (1990).

	Employment growth and decline in the rest of Sweden 1990-99				
Regional specialization in the SLLM Region in 1990	Rapid growth	Slow growth	Slow decline	Rapid decline	Average
High	4.4 (3.6)	6.2 (7.0)	3.3 (3.2)	7.9 (9.7)	5.4 (6.1)
Medium	3.2 (3.2)	4.5 (4.6)	6.8 (6.4)	6.7 (9.3)	5.9 (6.6)
Low	10.5 (7.1)	5.1 (6.7)	18.9 (16.7)	7.2 (10.7)	13.5 (13.4)
Very low	21.2 (41.8)	62.3 (41.4)	27.6 (21.1)	32.6 (46.6)	33.3 (32.8)
Average	6.0 (5.7)	6.1 (6.1)	11.1 (10.1)	8.2 (11.5)	8.6 (9.2)

Table 14.5a Number of plants in the different industrial aggregates in the ULLM Region in 1999 (1990).

	Employment growth and decline in the rest of Sweden 1990-99				
Regional specialization in the SLLM Region in 1990	Rapid growth	Slow growth	Slow decline	Rapid decline	Sum
High	379 (152)	652 (594)	240 (275)	116 (174)	1387 (1195)
Medium	149 (87)	894 (750)	1573 (1761)	532 (776)	3148 (3374)
Low	164 (130)	293 (252)	904 (1135)	304 (407)	1665 (1924)
Very low	21 (10)	28 (14)	92 (96)	49 (66)	190 (186)
Sum	713 (379)	1867 (1610)	2809 (3267)	1001 (1423)	6390 (6679)

Table 14.6a Absolute changes in the number of plants in the different industry groups in the ULLM Region during the period 1990-99.

	Employment growth and decline in the rest of Sweden 1990-99				
Regional specialization in the SLLM Region in 1990	Rapid growth	Slow growth	Slow decline	Rapid decline	Sum
High	227	58	-35	-58	192
Medium	62	144	-188	-244	-226
Low	34	41	-231	-103	-259
Very low	11	14	-4	-17	4
Sum	334	257	-458	-422	-289

Index

accounting principles, 132, 144
acculturation, 253
agents of economic growth, 107, 229
agglomeration, 14, 24, 44, 47, 48, 50, 52, 64, 65, 68, 70, 84, 104, 105, 106, 122, 188, 192, 193, 194, 196, 245
agriculture, 3, 24, 66, 75, 81-86, 88-90, 92-98, 109, 146, 152, 166, 197, 221, 224, 249, 308
average plant size, 302, 303

Babadağ, 233, 234, 236
backward linkages, 53, 138, 139, 147
basic research facilities, 284
Baumol model, 85, 87, 95
Bratislava, 9, 270- 281, 284, 286, 288

catch-up, 19, 32, 43
chaos, 15, 30, 41, 42, 46
circular cauzation, 15, 25
CIS countries, 197, 199
city regions, 153, 159, 160
collective learning, 104, 106, 108, 122
communication infrastructure, 282, 286
competitive power, 6, 241, 299
complex systems, 3, 14, 41
convergence, 1, 3, 6, 13-18, 20, 22, 29, 41-60, 63, 64, 70- 78, 80-82, 84-88, 90, 92-100, 101, 104. 112-114, 116, 120, 166, 169, 208
cooperation, 8, 9, 105, 106, 198, 236, 245, 248, 254, 255, 261, 263, 264-266, 277-279, 282, 284, 286
cooperative relations, 8
core-periphery, 7, 40, 45, 159, 160
corporate hierarchies, 240
craft businesses, 256, 258, 264
craft-guilds, 253
cumulative causation, 3, 14, 15, 25, 27. 32

decentralization processes, 289
decentralized innovation policy, 270, 288
definition of SMEs, 108
Denizli, vi, 8, 229- 245
density function, 55, 56, 60, 61, 62, 66, 74
de-population, 149, 151-152, 155, 158, 159
diffusion networks, 291
diminishing returns, 14, 16, 21, 43, 104, 161
distribution dynamics, 3, 54, 56, 71, 74
divergence, 4, 6, 7, 21, 46, 52, 55, 58, 104, 113, 114, 161, 163, 164, 166-167, 169, 188, 192, 193, 194
divergence theories, 193
dual economy, 81, 82, 97
dualism, 80, 88, 90, 93, 100
Dublin, 163-167, 180-191

educational attainment, 32, 34, 40, 45, 113, 115
educational intensity, 9, 305, 307
employment, 6, 9, 33, 58-60, 66, 76, 77, 78, 84-90, 92-101, 107- 110, 112, 114, 117, 119, 134, 145, 152, 154, 156, 164-189, 197, 203, 209, 210, 211, 213, 221, 229, 238, 239, 240, 242, 250, 260, 268, 271, 278, 284, 290, 293, 294, 297-301, 304, 305, 307-310
employment growth, 97, 108, 165, 169, 171-181, 184, 186-188, 293- 294, 297
endogenous growth, 2, 3, 13, 21, 22, 33, 45, 47, 48, 51, 52, 114, 122, 123, 161, 189-190, 229
endogenous growth models, 45, 51
enterprise, 6, 108, 116, 167, 198, 217, 222, 247, 252-257, 260-268, 276
enterprise development, 247, 268
entrepreneurial spirit, 107, 215, 232, 266, 302

entrepreneurship, 52, 68, 225, 247-248, 251-257, 262, 265-267, 301, 308
EU Innovation Relay Centre Network, 278
European regions, 2, 21, 43, 72, 75-79, 81-82, 84, 87-100, 102-103, 108-109, 114, 119
export-oriented policies, 230, 235
external barriers, 258, 260, 261
external economies of scale, 299
externalities, 4, 5, 14, 31, 37, 43, 45, 51, 70-71, 84, 104, 105, 114, 120, 129, 131, 139, 143, 147, 162

filtering-down, 290
financial barriers, 247, 260- 261, 266
firm demography, 134
firm size, 146, 150, 156, 162-163, 238
following successful examples, 235
foreign investment, 188, 196, 205, 247
foreign-owned firms, 169, 186, 188
forward linkages, 131, 139, 192
functional urban regions, 9, 33, 289, 290, 291, 292, 308

general equilibrium model, 13, 131, 135, 136
geographical economics, 3, 13, 46
global conditions, 229
global production networks, 231, 236, 239
Greater Dublin Region, 190
gross domestic product (GDP), viii, 200, 201
gross value added (GVA), 163, 166

high technology industrial clusters, 105, 108
human capital, 4, 21, 32, 34, 37, 54, 103-116, 119-120, 213

incentives to growth, 225
increasing returns, 4, 5, 13, 14, 15, 21, 24, 26, 29, 32, 37, 43, 52, 70, 104, 105, 123, 162
incubator centers, 222, 285
industrial district literature, 104, 108
industrial mix, 50, 64, 68, 70
industrial policy, 169, 170, 176, 210, 247
industrial restructuring, 5, 7, 213
information, 33, 54, 66, 74, 87, 98, 105, 106, 109, 114, 120, 130, 135, 144, 163, 199, 205, 206, 219, 221-222, 236, 262, 278, 281-282, 284-286, 291-292, 295
innovating enterprises, 273
innovation, 2, 7, 9, 32, 34, 47, 103-107, 111, 112, 114-115, 117, 119, 121-123, 129, 157, 162, 189, 221-222, 224-225, 245, 263, 270-271, 273, 278-282, 286, 288, 291
innovation institutions, 270
innovation policy, 9, 270, 271
innovation system, 7, 105, 108, 121, 122, 270
innovative abilities, 272
innovative environment, 117
innovative milieux, 4, 104, 105, 107
institution, 307
institutional split, 241
institutional thickness, 106
interregional general equilibrium models, 147
interregional SAM, 131, 139, 140, 141
intersectoral migration, 84, 95, 100
Ireland, 1, 4, 5, 6, 7, 59, 102, 161, 163, 165, 167, 168-172, 174, 176, 179-180, 186, 188-190
Irish indigenous industry, 167, 168, 172, 174, 175, 177, 179, 190
Irish planning regions, 164

job centralization, 152
Jokić-Horvat, 253, 256, 267, 269

knowledge, 4, 9, 21, 22, 31, 32, 33, 34, 50, 98, 100, 104-108, 112, 114-115, 121, 129, 143, 144, 161, 229, 241, 254-266, 270, 278-282, 284, 286, 304, 307
knowledge intensity, 304
knowledge spillovers, 104, 143
knowledge transfer, 9, 33, 105, 108, 278, 279, 281, 284, 286

labour productivity convergence, 99
lagging regions, 1, 7, 13, 87, 211, 233
latent unemployment, 210
leader-follower model, 9, 290
leading firms, 8, 235, 236, 239
leading urban regions, 9, 289

lead-lag model, 9, 307
learning, 2, 4, 21, 33, 45, 71, 103, 104, 105-107, 113-115, 122, 129, 163, 244, 263, 278
Lithuania, 4, 5, 7, 192-208
local clustering, 232
local entrepreneurship, 234, 266
localized externalities, 4, 105
locally embedded relations, 106

market potential, 59, 60, 64-66, 68, 197
Markov chain, 30, 31, 32, 46, 72
Međimurje, 8, 246-267, 269
modelling SME, 130
multinational enterprises (MNEs), 6, 167
multi-partner workers' enterprises, 234
multiple equilibria, 25, 43
mutual aid, 236
mutual contact, 284, 288

neighborhood effects, 65, 68
neoclassical growth model, 3, 13, 24, 43
network relations, 230, 239, 240
new economic geography, 3, 13, 14, 15, 24-25, 43, 47, 48, 52
new economy, 64, 68, 290
new growth theory, 103
new industrial growth nodes, 229
Norway, 1, 4, 5, 149- 156, 158, 231
Norwegian regional development, 158
NUTS II, 163, 211, 212, 273
NUTS III, 163, 211, 212, 273

obstacles for entrepreneurship, 209
old crafts and businesses, 266
old-fashioned distribution mechanisms, 155
one-region SAM, 132, 133, 139, 141, 142

patents, 90, 114, 202
path-dependent characteristics, 242
pecuniary externalities, 14, 45, 143-144
place of production, 134, 136, 141-142
place of residence, 134, 136, 143, 220
post-socialist countries, 247
post-socialist entrepreneurship, 253, 268
Prague, 212- 213, 224, 226
production, 4-5, 8-9, 15, 22, 24-25, 32, 33, 48-49, 51, 76, 104, 106-107, 114, 116, 121, 122, 129-136, 139, 141-149, 152, 154-155, 157-158, 161, 169, 179, 192-193, 198-199, 203, 208, 209, 215, 217-220, 222, 224-226, 229-236, 239-246, 251-252, 258, 259, 264, 266, 270-272, 289, 291-295
production account, 131, 132, 134-135, 141, 144
production networks, 106, 122, 242, 244, 245
protection, 170, 186, 255
proximity dynamics, 106, 123
public sector, 151-158, 277, 282, 308
public social services, 225

R&D, 47, 51, 105, 113, 115, 117, 119-120, 161-162, 221, 273, 276-278, 281, 284, 286, 288, 291, 295, 308
R&D activities, 115, 120, 221, 273, 288
R&D expenditures, 113, 115, 117
R&D personnel, 113, 115, 117
regional convergence, 13, 72, 76, 78, 81, 84, 99, 101, 163, 169, 196
regional development, 1, 2, 4, 5, 6, 7, 13, 21, 25, 103, 122, 123, 149, 150-151, 154-158, 161, 163, 165, 192-196, 200, 205, 207-210, 225, 270, 273
regional differences, 16, 27, 32, 59, 193-196, 205, 207
regional differentials, 96
regional growth, 2, 3, 4, 5, 6, 24, 46, 48, 73, 90, 100, 103, 107-110, 113, 114, 115, 117, 120-121, 123, 150, 151, 156, 158, 163, 170, 180, 183-184, 186-188
regional innovation systems, 105
reproduction, 105, 115, 152
risk-sharing, 263
role of SMEs, 2, 4, 108, 129-131, 135, 147, 163, 170, 209, 215, 224, 229, 231, 236, 241-242
Russia, 197-199, 204, 240

Scandinavian countries, 149
sectoral distribution of SMEs, 209
sectoral dynamics, 75-76, 80-82, 85, 95-97
sheltered service production, 295
shift-share analysis, 300, 307
size class, 6, 169-186, 188-189
size distribution fallacy, 172
size of enterprises, 251

Slovak Academy of Sciences, 276, 278, 280-281, 283-284, 286
Slovenian entrepreneurs, 259-261
small entrepreneurs, 8, 225, 260
small entrepreneurship, 225
SME clusters, 4, 112, 119
social accounting matrix (SAM), 135
social barriers, 247
social cohesion, 7, 211, 225, 234
social environment, 254
spatial econometrics, 46, 99
spatial industrial dynamics, 9, 289, 290, 292
spatial interaction, 29, 31, 33, 46
spatial product life cycle, 290
specialization, 27, 85, 93, 123, 229, 235, 238, 242, 263
spin off company, 287
start-ups, 170, 172-176, 178-179, 182, 185-186, 188-189, 205, 268, 271
state-owned heavy industry, 210
stochastic equilibrium, 3, 14, 32, 38, 42
stochastic kernel, 3, 31, 56-57, 62-63, 66, 71, 74
Stockholm local labour market region, 293-294
Stockholm region, 289, 294-295, 302
structural change, 9, 76, 80-81, 86, 90, 93-95, 98-99, 149, 154, 192, 213, 292, 294, 300
structurally-deficient regions, 211
subcontracting relationships, 236
Sümerbank, 232-234, 242-243
survival enterprises, 247

taxes, 133, 135-136, 203, 281, 282
technical progress, 15-16, 21-23, 32-35, 43- 44, 51, 161, 225
technological capacity, 76, 90, 92-93
technological externalities, 14, 32, 104, 131, 144
technological spillovers, 68
technology, 9, 16, 19, 21-22, 32-34, 37, 41-42, 49, 51-53, 65, 68, 78, 80, 84, 87, 95, 98, 104-106, 114, 116, 122-123, 162, 188, 221, 224, 235, 238, 243, 272, 275, 278-279, 281-282, 284
technology gap, 32, 34, 37, 41, 42
technology transfer, 105, 278, 279, 284
territorial models, 4, 103, 104, 107, 112, 115, 117
textile, 8, 197, 230-239, 241-245, 264
traditional sectors of production, 232
trans-border cooperation, 8, 221, 266
transfer of technical know-how, 234

Uddevalla local labour market region, 290, 296, 303, 307-308
unemployment rates, 58, 90, 94, 116-117, 149, 151, 210
unintentional structural change, 154
universities, 9, 105, 115, 221, 241, 270, 273, 275, 279, 281-282, 284, 287-288
unwanted centralization, 155

Verdoorn coefficient, 26
virtual distribution, 65-67, 69

wood, 197, 278